Corporate Governance after the
Financial Crisis

CORPORATE GOVERNANCE AFTER THE FINANCIAL CRISIS

Stephen M. Bainbridge

OXFORD
UNIVERSITY PRESS

Oxford University Press is a department of the University of Oxford.
It furthers the University's objective of excellence in research, scholarship,
and education by publishing worldwide.

Oxford   New York
Auckland   Cape Town   Dar es Salaam   Hong Kong   Karachi
Kuala Lumpur   Madrid   Melbourne   Mexico City   Nairobi
New Delhi   Shanghai   Taipei   Toronto

With offices in
Argentina   Austria   Brazil   Chile   Czech Republic   France   Greece
Guatemala   Hungary   Italy   Japan   Poland   Portugal   Singapore
South Korea   Switzerland   Thailand   Turkey   Ukraine   Vietnam

First issued as an Oxford University Press paperback, 2016.
ISBN 978-0-19-049667-8

Library of Congress Cataloging-in-Publication Data

Bainbridge, Stephen M.
  Corporate governance after the financial crisis / Stephen M. Bainbridge.
    p. cm.
  Includes bibliographical references and index.
  ISBN 978-0-19-977242-1 (hardback : alk. paper)
  1. Corporate governance—Law and legislation—United States.
  2. Global Financial Crisis, 2008–2009. I. Title.
  KF1422.B319 2011
  346.73'0664—dc23   2011020328

Note to Readers
This publication is designed to provide accurate and authoritative information in regard to the subject
matter covered. It is based upon sources believed to be accurate and reliable and is intended to be current
as of the time it was written. It is sold with the understanding that the publisher is not engaged in rendering
legal, accounting, or other professional services. If legal advice or other expert assistance is required, the
services of a competent professional person should be sought. Also, to confirm that the information has
not been affected or changed by recent developments, traditional legal research techniques should be used,
including checking primary sources where appropriate.

*(Based on the Declaration of Principles jointly adopted by a Committee of the
American Bar Association and a Committee of Publishers and Associations.)*

CONTENTS

ACKNOWLEDGMENTS

I thank Helen Bainbridge and William Klein for their very helpful comments and editorial suggestions. I also thank UCLA School of Law Deans Michael Schill and Rachel Moran for granting me the research leave during which this book was written.

ABOUT THE AUTHOR

Stephen Bainbridge is the William D. Warren Distinguished Professor of Law at UCLA, where he currently teaches Business Associations, Advanced Corporation Law, and a seminar on corporate governance. In past years, he has also taught Corporate Finance, Securities Regulation, Mergers and Acquisitions, and Unincorporated Business Associations. Professor Bainbridge previously taught at the University of Illinois Law School (1988–1996). He has also taught at Harvard Law School as the Joseph Flom Visiting Professor of Law and Business (2000–2001), La Trobe University in Melbourne (2005 and 2007), and Aoyama Gakuin University in Tokyo (1999).

In 2008, Bainbridge received the UCLA School of Law's Rutter Award for Excellence in Teaching. In 1990, the graduating class of the University of Illinois College of Law voted him "Professor of the Year."

Professor Bainbridge is a prolific scholar, whose work covers a variety of subjects, but with a strong emphasis on the law and economics of public corporations. He has written over 75 law review articles, which have appeared in such leading journals as the Harvard Law Review, the Virginia Law Review, the Northwestern University Law Review, the Cornell Law Review, the Stanford Law Review, and the Vanderbilt Law Review. Bainbridge's recent books include: The New Corporate Governance in Theory and Practice (2008); Securities Law-Insider Trading (2nd ed. 2007); Business Associations: Cases and Materials on Agency, Partnerships, and Corporations (6th ed. 2006) (with Klein and Ramseyer); Agency, Partnerships, and Limited Liability Entities: Cases and Materials on Unincorporated Business Associations (2nd ed. 2007) (with Klein and Ramseyer); Agency, Partnerships & LLCs (2004); Corporation Law and Economics (2002).

Professor Bainbridge has served as a Salvatori Fellow with the Heritage Foundation (1994–1996), a member of the American Bar Association's Committee on Corporate Laws (2008–2011), a member of the Editorial Advisory Board of the Journal of Markets and Morality (2006–2011), and as

Chair of the Executive Committee of the Federalist Society's Corporations, Securities & Antitrust Practice Group (2007–2011).

In 2008 and 2011, Professor Bainbridge was named by Directorship magazine to its list of the 100 most influential people in the field of corporate governance.

Introduction

"People get religion of sorts about ethics and corporate governance in down markets. When things are going well, they tend to forget about it."[1] Given the savage economic downturns that bookended the last decade, it is hardly surprising that legislators, regulators, business people, and investors have gotten the corporate governance religion. But have they found true religion or are they worshiping false idols?

The economic crises of the last decade prompted two sweeping federal statutes affecting corporate governance. In response to the scandals that followed in the wake of the dotcom bubble, Congress passed the Public Company Accounting Reform and Investor Protection Act of 2002 (Sarbanes-Oxley or SOX), which President Bush praised at its signing for having made "the most far-reaching reforms of American business practices since the time of Franklin Delano Roosevelt."[2] At the end of the decade, when the economy suffered through an even worse downturn following the bursting of the housing bubble and the subprime mortgage crisis, populist outrage motivated Congress to pass the Wall Street Reform and Consumer Protection Act of 2010 (Dodd-Frank).[3]

Sarbanes-Oxley and Dodd-Frank are the latest iterations of the recurring pattern of federal intervention in corporate governance. In the United States, regulation of corporate governance traditionally was the states' job rather than that of the federal government. Since the New Deal, however, the federal

1. Kathyrn Jones, Who Moved My Bonus? Executive Pay Makes a U-Turn, N.Y. Times, April 5, 2009 (quoting James A. Allen).
2. The Public Company Accounting Reform and Investor Protection Act, Pub. L. No. 107–204, 2002 U.S.C.C.A.N. (116 Stat.) 745 (codified in scattered sections of 15 and 18 U.S.C.) [hereinafter cited as SOX].
3. The Wall Street Reform and Consumer Protection Act of 2010, Pub. L. No. 111–203, 124 Stat. 1376 (2010) (hereinafter cited as The Dodd-Frank Act).

government repeatedly has responded to major economic crises by significantly expanding its role in corporate governance regulation.

This pattern of boom, followed by bust, followed by federal regulatory intervention poses a number of interesting questions. To be sure, the whys and wherefores of booms and busts are high on that list, but we shall leave them to the practitioners of the dismal science. Instead, the focus herein is on the legal fallout of a bust.

The task before us, thus, is to assess the state of corporate governance after the crises. Have the changes wrought by SOX and Dodd-Frank improved corporate governance? Will "say on pay," for example, lead to executive compensation being better aligned with corporate performance? Each of the major corporate governance changes worked by those Acts will be taken up in turn.

In addition to assessing the post-crises changes on their own merits, we will use them as case studies of the relative merits of the federal government and the states as sources of corporate governance regulation. Cumulatively, the case studies will allow us to draw some conclusions about the desirability of future federal post-crisis regulatory interventions.

WHAT IS CORPORATE GOVERNANCE?

Corporate governance, broadly defined, consists of the institutional structures, legal rules, and best practices that determine which body within the corporation is empowered to make particular decisions, how the members of that body are chosen, and the norms that should guide decision making. As that definition suggests, corporate governance principles derive from many sources and take many forms. Some are mere rules of best practice, which are solely aspirational in character. Others derive from social norms, enforced privately through reputational sanctions and market forces. Still others derive from the hard law of corporation statutes and judicial opinions, enforced by legal sanctions. Taken together, these sources collectively specify the ends the corporation is established to pursue and the means by which it does so. They thus specify such matters as the rules and procedures for making decisions on corporate affairs, how rights and duties are distributed among different constituencies, and how the performance of those constituencies is monitored.

Our focus herein, however, is on a narrower conception in which corporate governance consists of the legal rules that both create and seek to constrain the principal-agent problem inherent in the public corporation's structure. Although shareholders nominally "own" the corporation, they have virtually no decision-making powers. They are entitled only to elect the firm's directors and to vote on an exceedingly limited—albeit not unimportant—number of corporate actions. Rather, management of the firm is vested in the hands of the board of directors, who in turn delegate the day-to-day running of the firm to its officers, who in turn delegate some responsibilities to the company's employees.

Separation of ownership and control is a feature of corporate design, not a bug. Most shareholders prefer to be passive investors. Vesting decision-making power in the corporation's board of directors and managers allows shareholders to remain passive, while also preventing the chaos that would result from tens of thousands of shareholders seeking to be involved in day-to-day decision making.[4]

At the same time, however, this separation creates the potential for shareholder and managerial interests to diverge. As the residual claimants on the corporation's assets and earnings, the shareholders are entitled to the corporation's profits. But it is the firm's management, not the shareholders, which decides how the firm's earnings are to be spent. A principal-agent problem thus arises out of the substantial risk that management will expend firm earnings on projects that benefit management, rather than shareholders.

This conflict of interest results in so-called agency costs. Principals expend resources to monitor their agents so as to detect and punish shirking. Agents promise not to shirk and provide bonds making that promise more credible. Even so, of course, there will still be some residual losses from undeterred shirking by agents.[5] A well-designed system of corporate governance seeks to reduce these costs by providing rules that make monitoring cheaper, bonds more credible, or deterrence more effective.

THE CRISES AND THE FEDERAL RESPONSES

The opening decade of the new century was a tumultuous one in many spheres, not the least of which was finance and corporate governance. As the decade opened, the tech stock bubble of the late 1990s burst. The dotcom crash was compounded by a sharp decline in consumer spending, rising energy prices, and the economic fallout of the September 11, 2001, terrorist attacks. Taken together, these economic reverses generated an extended bear market and a lengthy recession. Unemployment rose from 3.9 percent in December 2000 to 4.9 percent in August 2001 and eventually peaked at 6.3 percent in June 2003.[6] As for the stock market, it generated negative returns every year from

---

4. See generally Stephen M. Bainbridge, The Case for Limited Shareholder Voting Rights, 53 UCLA L. Rev. 601 (2006).

5. See Michael Jensen & William Meckling, Theory of the Firm: Managerial Behavior, Agency Costs, and Ownership Structure, 3 J. Fin. Econ. 305 (1976).

6. N. Gregory Mankiw, Essentials of Economics 535 (5th ed. 2008).

2000 to 2002, which was the first three-year consecutive decline since the Great Depression of the 1930s.

As the economic fallout continued, a string of high-profile financial scandals further rocked investor confidence. The now infamous scandal at Enron turned out not to be an isolated case, as news of corporate shenanigans at companies like WorldCom, Global Crossing, Tyco, Adelphia, and others soon followed. An investigation of stock market analysts by then-New York Attorney General Eliot Spitzer uncovered massive conflicts of interest. Another Spitzer investigation discovered that some large mutual funds had allowed selected clients to engage in questionable or even illegal trading.

In the meantime, a new asset bubble was growing, but this time in the housing rather than the stock market. The story of this second crisis is far more complex than that of the crisis that opened the decade. Indeed, as of this writing, the story still remains unfinished in some respects.

The basics, however, are well known. Low interest rates and seemingly ever-rising housing prices encouraged massive investment in housing. At the same time, there was rapid growth in securitization of the resulting mortgages. As the decade progressed, moreover, simple asset-backed securities (ABSs) evolved into ever more complex instruments, such as collateralized debt obligations (CDOs) and the like.

With the flood of new money pouring into the housing market and the supposed reduction of risk allowed by securitization, banks became willing to lend heavily to subprime mortgage borrowers with weak credit ratings. In 2006 and 2007, however, mortgage defaults increased significantly. Interest rates were rising, which meant that the adjustable rate mortgages so many subprime borrowers had taken out at low rates in the 2003–2004 period began to adjust upward. At the same time, housing price appreciation slowed and even began to reverse. As a result, many borrowers found themselves unable to afford their new, higher monthly payments and became saddled with homes that in many cases were now worth less than what the borrower owed on the mortgage. The resulting deterioration in mortgage performance adversely affected mortgage backed securities and their more complicated variants.

In July 2007, two Bear Stearns hedge funds that had invested heavily in CDOs failed. Over the next several months, doubts about Bear Stearns' viability grew, and by March 2008 its clients began moving substantial amounts of their business to other banks. An ad hoc government rescue was hurriedly put in place, culminating in JP Morgan's acquisition of Bear Stearns.

The crisis did not end with the rescue of Bear Stearns. Continued trauma in the housing and credit markets lead to the nationalization of Fannie Mae and Freddie Mac in September 2008. Shortly thereafter, the outgoing Bush administration allowed Lehman Brothers to fail, but bailed out AIG. In the face of the economic turmoil, banks were unable or unwilling to lend, credit dried up, and economic activity sputtered. The stock market again suffered massive losses. The economy sank into the deepest recession in decades.[7]

Because key legislators and regulators believed that corporate governance failures were at the heart of both the scandals of 2000–2002 and the more recent financial crisis of 2008, the last decade has seen more rapid change in the corporate governance legal regime than any period since the New Deal. The claim has some merit with respect to the fallout of the dotcom bubble and the Enron-era scandals. As for the subprime mortgage crisis and its fallout, however, the claim is much weaker.

The Sarbanes-Oxley Act: The Federal Response to Enron et al.

Although Sarbanes-Oxley was drafted in a period of economic unrest, it was primarily intended to address securities fraud. History teaches that market bubbles are fertile ground for fraud. Cheats abounded during the Dutch tulip bulb mania of the 1630s. The South Sea Company, which was at the center of the English stock market bubble in the early 1700s, was a pyramid scheme. Fraud was rampant before the Great Crash of 1929. Hence, it was hardly a shock that regulators found fraudsters and cheats when they started turning over the rocks in the rubble left behind when the stock market bubble burst in 2000.[8]

The chief villain in the Sarbanes-Oxley story, of course, is Enron. On October 16, 2001, Enron announced that it was taking a $544 million after-tax charge against earnings and reducing shareholders' equity by $1.2 billion in connection with transactions with a so-called special purpose entity (SPE) Enron had created to move debt off its balance sheet. A few weeks later, Enron announced a major restatement of its earnings for the four years 1997–2000 to account properly for transactions with two other SPEs. Enron's stock price collapsed, dropping from over $90 per share to less than $1. Shareholders and creditors filed numerous lawsuits. Criminal and civil fraud investigations ensued. In December 2001, Enron declared bankruptcy.

The Enron scandal produced a flurry of activity in Congress. Numerous reform bills were introduced. Most of these were mere publicity stunts, however, and meaningful legislative action seemed highly unlikely. But then the other shoes began to drop.

In January 2002, telecommunications giant Global Crossing filed bankruptcy. It soon came out that the company had been misrepresenting its

---

7. For useful overviews of the economic crisis, see John Lanchester, I.O.U.: Why Everyone Owes Everyone and No One Can Pay (2010); Richard A. Posner, A Failure of Capitalism: The Crisis of '08 and the Descent Into Depression (2009).

8. See generally Stephen M. Bainbridge, The Complete Guide to Sarbanes-Oxley 11–20 (2010), on which the discussion that follows draws.

financial situation and manipulating its recognition of revenues. A few months later, the Securities and Exchange Commission (SEC) announced an investigation of accounting fraud at WorldCom. It turned out that WorldCom management had inflated the company's assets by over $11 billion, capitalized expenses that should have been incorporated into the earnings statement, and reported phony revenues. WorldCom's own internal audit process uncovered the fraud, which it reported to the company's new outside auditor (KPMG), which notified the board of directors. In this case, unlike Enron, the company's internal controls thus eventually worked, a point that likely strongly influenced Congress's focus on such controls in drafting Sarbanes-Oxley.

Enron, Global Crossing, and WorldCom were not isolated cases. The SEC's Division of Enforcement, for example, announced that in the first two months of 2002 alone it brought an unprecedented number of new financial reporting cases (almost triple the number of the comparable period in the prior year, which itself had been a record). Allegations of improper revenue recognition, failure to properly recognize expenses, and cooking the books in a host of other ways were brought against numerous companies. In addition, unlike most prior periods, in which the SEC had focused mainly on small fry, the cases brought in 2001–2002 involved a record number of Fortune 500 companies. Between 2000 and 2002, moreover, hundreds of other companies restated earnings to adjust for prior flawed accounting practices. But why did so many managers go bad during this period? In short, greed.

As discussed in chapter 5, the 1990s saw a dramatic shift in the form of executive compensation to an emphasis on stock options and, to a lesser extent, other forms of equity-based compensation. In theory, options align the interests of managers and shareholders. In practice, however, the shift put tremendous pressure on managers to keep the stock price headed up no matter how the company actually was doing. Under the resulting compulsion to make the number (that is, the consensus forecast by analysts of the company's quarterly earnings), many managers succumbed to the temptation to cook the books.

The problem was confounded by the failures of key gatekeepers. The typical corporation relies on numerous such gatekeepers: auditors, rating agencies, securities analysts, investment bankers, and lawyers. They function as reputational intermediaries between investors and their corporate clients. Although the corporate client generally pays these service providers, investors trust information from such providers because the gatekeepers put their own reputations at stake. Because the value of a gatekeeper's services depends on its reputation, the market believes that a gatekeeper is not willing to risk its accumulated goodwill for a single client.

In the 1990s, however, the incentives for gatekeepers to police corporate conduct substantially weakened. Accounting firms typically provided a whole host of services to companies whose books they audited, such as tax preparation and software consulting. Because these other lines of business were more profitable than auditing, the accountants feared to anger management by vigorously pushing audits and challenging management's aggressive accounting treatments.

During that decade, a number of legal changes also reduced gatekeeper liability risk. The Supreme Court's 1994 Central Bank of Denver decision, for example, eliminated aiding and abetting liability in private securities fraud cases.[9] The 1995 Private Securities Litigation Reform Act (PSLRA) imposed significant restrictions on private securities fraud litigation. The 1998 Securities Litigation Uniform Standards Act abolished state court securities fraud class actions. Taken together, Columbia University securities law professor John Coffee argues, these changes "greatly reduced the incentives of plaintiffs in securities class actions to sue secondary participants such as auditors, analysts, and attorneys," which in turn reduced the incentive for gatekeepers to protect investor interests in a vigorous manner.[10]

The importance of a particular category of gatekeepers was highlighted by a striking commonality between the scandals at Enron, Global Crossing, WorldCom, and most of the other companies investigated by the SEC during this period. Although they differed in their details, all involved some form of accounting fraud. This commonality was further underlined by the coincidence that Enron, Global Crossing, and WorldCom had used the same accounting firm as their outside auditor, namely, Arthur Andersen. Indeed, Arthur Andersen's name figured prominently in many other cases of accounting fraud in the 1990s and early 2000s, including the scandals at Sunbeam, Waste Management, Qwest, and the Baptist Foundation of Arizona.

By mid-2002, the accounting firm had been indicted, subjected to SEC civil actions, and sued by many companies and their shareholders. In 2002, Arthur Andersen was convicted of obstruction of justice charges arising out of destruction of Enron documents. Although the U.S. Supreme Court later overturned the conviction on technical grounds relating to the jury instructions, the verdict sounded Arthur Andersen's death knell. The storied accounting firm effectively became defunct, with all of its clients and virtually all of its employees gone.

Accountants were not the only gatekeepers who fell down on the job, of course. Given the centrality of accounting fraud and auditor failures to the pre-SOX story, however, it is not surprising that accounting firms were

9. Central Bank of Denver, N.A. v. First Investment Bank of Denver, N.A., 511 U.S. 164 (1994).
10. John C. Coffee, Jr., Gatekeeper Failure and Reform: The Challenge of Fashioning Relevant Reforms, 84 B.U. L. Rev. 301, 320 (2004).

Sarbanes-Oxley's principal target. Ironically, we will see that accountants also proved to be Sarbanes-Oxley's principal beneficiaries.

In the wake of these developments, then-SEC chairman Harvey Pitt declared that restoring investor "confidence is the No. 1 goal on our agenda." As a first step, the SEC ordered over 900 of the country's largest corporations to certify under oath the accuracy and completeness of their corporate disclosures. This requirement triggered a new wave of high-profile earnings restatements. With the 2002 elections looming, pressure thus grew within Congress for legislative action.

In a remarkably brief period, with minimal legislative processing, Congress slapped together a number of reform proposals that had been kicking around Washington for a long time and sent the mix to President Bush for signing. In response to Enron and WorldCom, Congress included provisions intended to increase the penalties for securities fraud by corporate executives and require corporations to adopt more effective systems of internal control. In response to Arthur Andersen, Congress included provisions intended to reform oversight of the accounting profession and to improve the audit process.

In an influential law review article, which slammed the Sarbanes-Oxley Act as "quack corporate governance,"[11] Yale law professor Roberta Romano singled out five of Sarbanes-Oxley's corporate governance provisions for detailed criticism. First, she criticized Sarbanes-Oxley § 301's mandate that all public corporations must have an audit committee comprised exclusively of independent directors. Romano contended that the empirical evidence on the efficacy of director independence in general and audit committee composition in specific was, at best, mixed. Second, she pointed out that § 201 prohibited accounting firms from providing a wide range of non-audit services to public corporations they audit, even though the weight of the evidence was that provision of such services did not degrade audit quality. Third, she argued that § 402(a)'s prohibition of most loans by corporations to their executives was unjustified because such "loans in many cases appear to serve their purpose of increasing managerial stock ownership, thereby aligning managers' and shareholders' interests. . . ." Fourth, she argued that §§ 302's and 906's CEO and CFO certification rules imposed significant costs even though the evidence as to whether such certifications provide useful information to investors was ambiguous. Finally, she correctly predicted that § 404's requirement that management and the firm's outside auditor certify the effectiveness of the company's internal controls over financial reporting would prove hugely burdensome.

When § 404 was adopted, neither Congress nor the SEC appreciated just how costly it would prove. The SEC estimated that the average cost of

---

11. Roberta Romano, The Sarbanes-Oxley Act and the Making of Quack Corporate Governance, 114 Yale L.J. 1521 (2005).

complying with § 404 would be approximately $91,000. In fact, however, a 2005 survey put the direct cost of complying with § 404 in its first year at $7.3 million for large accelerated filers and $1.5 million for accelerated filers. "First-year implementation costs for larger companies were thus eighty times greater than the SEC had estimated, and sixteen times greater than estimated for smaller companies."[12] Although § 404 compliance costs have come down in subsequent years, a core set of costs have proven to be recurring. In addition, compliance costs have proven resistant to scaling and therefore to be disproportionately heavy for small firms.

Dodd-Frank: The Federal Response to the Financial Crisis

By the middle of the decade, experience with the high compliance costs imposed by the Sarbanes-Oxley Act, especially § 404, generated significant push back from the business community. The SEC and the Public Company Accounting Oversight Board (PCAOB) offered several iterations of regulatory relief. There was even talk of a legislative fix for § 404. The financial crisis of 2007–2008, however, brought talk of deregulation to an abrupt end. Instead, Congress began looking at a so-called "New New Deal," which would undertake massive new regulation of the financial markets.

The new economic crisis was far larger and infinitely more complex than the one that had motivated passage of the Sarbanes-Oxley Act. Because Sarbanes-Oxley was a response to a series of securities frauds rather than systemic market failures, the Act's focus was on various forms of fraud prevention. In contrast, the financial crisis that produced Dodd-Frank revealed massive systemic problems throughout the financial services industry and triggered such far-flung responses as the federal bailout of GM and Chrysler.

In short order, a nearly universal consensus formed among legislators, regulators, and opinion makers that corporate governance was again at fault. The Organization for Economic Cooperation and Development (OECD) commissioned a fact-finding study premised on concern "that the financial crisis can be to an important extent attributed to failures and weaknesses in corporate governance arrangements."[13] The Shareholder Bill of Rights Act of 2009 introduced in the U.S. Senate contained an express Congressional finding that a "central cause" of the economic crisis was a "widespread failure of

---

12. Joseph A. Grundfest & Steven E. Bochner, Fixing 404, 105 Mich. L Rev. 1643 (2007).

13. Grant Kirkpatrick, The Corporate Governance Lessons from the Financial Crisis, Fin. Market Trends, July 2009, at 2.

corporate governance."[14] In Europe, the High-Level Group on Financial Supervision in the EU concluded that financial institution corporate governance was "one of the most important failures" in the crisis.[15] In the U.K., a government-commissioned review by Sir David Walker concluded that the "need is now to bring corporate governance issues to center stage."[16]

In fact, however, systemic flaws in the corporate governance of Main Street corporations were not a causal factor in the housing bubble, the bursting of that bubble, or the subsequent credit crunch. In the wake of the earlier dotcom bubble, Bengt Holmstrom and Steven Kaplan published a comprehensive review of U.S. corporate governance concluding that the U.S. corporate governance regime was "well above average" in the global picture.[17] Indeed, the trend throughout the last decade with respect to major corporate governance practices was toward enhanced management efficiency and accountability. Pay for performance compensation schemes, takeovers, restructurings, increased reliance on independent directors, and improved board of director processes all tended to more effectively align management and shareholder interests.

These improvements had demonstrable results. Holmstrom and Kaplan showed that even when the fallout from the bubble was taken into account, returns on the U.S. stock market equaled or exceeded those of its global competitors during five time periods going back as far as 1982. Likewise, U.S. productivity exceeded that of its major Western competitors.

According to a more recent survey by U.K. legal expert Brian Cheffins, "[a] striking aspect of the stock market meltdown of 2008 is that it occurred despite the strengthening of U.S. corporate governance over the past few decades and a reorientation toward the promotion of shareholder value."[18] A 2010 report commissioned by the NYSE reached the same conclusion, finding that "the current corporate governance system generally works well."[19]

As a test to validate this claim, Cheffins conducted a study that identified 37 firms that were removed from the S&P 500 index in 2008. Companies are removed from the index when they go bankrupt or, among other things, have their market capitalization fall below $4 billion. Accordingly, companies removed from the index often are in financial distress. Cheffins then

---

14. Sean Bosak & Daniel J. Blinka, Fallout from a Crisis: Boards of Directors, In-House Counsel, and Corporate Risk Management in a New Era 5 (2010).

15 Peter O. Mulbert, Corporate Governance of Banks After the Financial Crisis: Theory, Evidence, Reforms 9 (ECGI Law Working Paper No. 130/2009, Apr. 2010).

16. Id.

17. Bengt R. Holmstrom & Steven N. Kaplan, The State of U.S. Corporate Governance: What's Right and What's Wrong?, 15 J. App. Corp. Fin. 8 (2003).

18. Brian R. Cheffins, Did Corporate Governance "Fail" During the 2008 Stock Market Meltdown? The Case of the S&P 500, 65 Bus. Law. 1, 2 (2009).

19. Report of the NYSE Commission on Corporate Governance 2 (Sept. 23, 2010).

conducted a detailed examination of the corporate governance practices at the 37 companies in question.

In general, Cheffins found little evidence of corporate governance problems among the sample firms, except for those in the financial sector. Businesses in that sector dominated the list of firms removed from the index due to falling market capitalization, being acquired in a "rescue merger" required prevent a likely bankruptcy, or outright bankruptcy.

That banks and related financial institutions should have proved uniquely at risk is hardly surprising. The crisis arose out of problems in the subprime mortgage market, after all. Banks have a number of characteristics, moreover, that make their corporate governance problems radically different than those of nonfinancial firms.

A bank borrows short-term by taking in deposits and then lends long-term. This system of fractional reserves, pursuant to which banks retain only a modest fraction of their deposits as liquid assets, makes banks vulnerable to runs. Deposit insurance was developed to help prevent runs by assuring depositors that they would be able to get their money back even if the bank failed, but it created a moral hazard. The presence of deposit insurance reduces the incentives of depositors to monitor the riskiness of the decisions bankers make. If the bank takes on risky trading for its own account, the depositors won't care, because the taxpayer will step in via the FDIC and make them whole (up to a very generous cap). Shareholders will not care because the corporate law rule of limited liability protects their personal assets from claims by the firm's creditors. If the deal is profitable, they reap the benefits; if the deal fails, the taxpayer steps in to clean up the mess. The trouble, of course, is that when decision makers face only the consequences of a risk paying off and not those of the risk going south, they take on socially undesirable amounts of risk.

Even financial institutions not part of the deposit insurance regulatory scheme often have artificially low costs of capital that allow them to take risks that are socially unacceptable. Fannie Mae and Freddie Mac infamously benefited from an implicit guarantee. Although they were nominally private entities, investors and creditors believed that the government would not let them fail. The same was true of truly private financial institutions that had become "too big to fail." Their creditors and investors believed that the government would bail out the financial system. Hence, they were willing to accept discounted investment returns because they believed the government would make them whole regardless of whether the bank's risks paid off or not.

Increasing problems faced by regulators and others in monitoring banks and other financial institutions compounded the bad incentives problem. During the run up to the crisis, securitization of bank loans helped make bank financial statements less transparent. It also allowed banks to rapidly shift their risk profiles. Hence, securitization made it harder for outsiders to monitor banks.

But was excess risk taking by financial institutions the result of corporate governance failures? To be sure, Cheffins found that financial sector boards of directors were subjected to greater media criticism than boards in other sectors and that executive pay controversies were far more common in the financial sector than elsewhere. Almost from the outset of the financial crisis, moreover, regulators identified executive compensation schemes that focused bank managers on short-term returns to shareholders as a contributing factor to the emergency.[20]

Yet, on close examination, the evidence turns up some very curious findings. First, the U.K.'s corporate governance regime is generally regarded as more shareholder empowering than the U.S. regime, which in the minds of many governance activists makes it superior. If governance failures were a key factor in the crisis, one thus would expect the U.K. to have been less susceptible to a financial crisis than the United States. Instead, the U.K. went through essentially the same financial crisis as the United States at about the same time. Accordingly, while governance practices "such as independent board chairs and 'say on pay' votes have been available to U.K. shareholders for years," they apparently "did little to prevent the crisis or mitigate its effects on the U.K. financial system."[21] "Indeed, stock prices fell faster in Britain during 2008 than they did in the United States, underpinned by a banking crisis every bit as serious as America's."[22]

Second, and even more surprising, there is some evidence that corporate governance standards widely regarded as best practice were actually associated with poorer performance during the crisis. A study by U.S.C business school professors Erkens, Hung, and Matos of 296 financial institutions in 30 countries found that board independence and high institutional investor ownership, which we'll see in the chapters that follow are usually assumed to be good practices, were associated with poor stock performance during the crisis.[23] They further found that financial institutions with more independent boards were more likely to raise equity capital during the crisis, which ultimately resulted in a wealth transfer from shareholders to creditors. As for institutional ownership, higher levels thereof were associated with greater risk taking, which ultimately resulted in greater losses.

20. Mulbert, supra note 15, at 8.

21. Christopher M. Bruner, Corporate Governance in a Time of Crisis 25 (2010), http://ssrn.com/abstract=1617890.

22. Cheffins, supra note 18, at 4.

23. David Erkens et al., Corporate Governance in the 2007–2008 Financial Crisis: Evidence from Financial Institutions Worldwide (Sept. 2010), http://ssrn.com/abstract=1397685.

A study by Beltratti and Stulz found no evidence that banks with higher scores on the Institutional Shareholder Services' Corporate Governance Quotient performed better than lower-scoring firms.[24] Beltratti and Stulz attributed the crisis to flawed bank capital structures, instead of corporate governance failures. Banks that relied on long-term sources of capital fared better than those that relied on short-term funding.

We can draw a couple of important conclusions from this evidence. First, what constitutes good corporate governance depends on which constituency's interests one is seeking to advance. Governance regimes that advantage shareholders may not be good for taxpayers. As we will see, however, virtually all of the reforms mandated after the crisis were designed to empower shareholders. The risk thus is that the reforms may make the next crisis more likely and potentially more severe.

Second, one size does not fit all in corporate governance. The problems of Wall Street and Main Street are quite different and may require quite different solutions. As we will see, however, the response to the crisis consisted almost without exception of one-size-fits-all mandates, from which derogation by private ordering is not allowed.

Why did corporate governance veer in untoward directions after the crisis? The crisis shifted the corporate governance game onto a new playing field and created an environment in which a new set of players took prominence. Specifically, it reengaged the federal government as a regulator, bringing with it powerful interest groups like unions, pension funds, activist investors, trial lawyers, and their academic allies.

The preliminary federal legislative response to the financial crisis was the Emergency Economic Stabilization Act of 2008,[25] which authorized the Treasury Department to establish a Troubled Asset Relief Program (TARP) to buy distressed assets from financial institutions. The goal was to ease the credit freeze by improving bank balance sheets and thereby encouraging them to lend.

The program required firms receiving TARP funds to comply with a number of corporate governance rules that went far beyond the mandates of existing state or federal law. Most of these provisions related to executive compensation. TARP firms were obliged to obtain an advisory shareholder vote on the firm's executive compensation program. They were further required to set up compensation committees comprised exclusively of independent members of the board of directors. If the company used a compensation consultant to

24. Andrea Beltratti & Rene M. Stulz, Why Did Some Banks Perform Better During the Credit Crisis? A Cross-Country Study of the Impact of Governance and Regulation (ECGI Finance Working Paper No. 254/2009), http://www.nber.org/papers/w15180.
25. Pub. L. No. 110–343, 122 Stat. 3765 (2008).

advise the committee, disclosure was required of the identity of the consultant and all services provided by his firm during a three-year period. The firm's senior executive officers and the next 20 highest compensated employees were subject to compensation clawbacks of bonuses paid on the basis of materially inaccurate performance metrics. Disclosure was required of executive perquisites and so-called luxury expenditures, such as lavish office renovations or entertainment. The CEO and CFO were required to provide an annual certification that the company was compliant with all TARP governance and compensation requirements.

The cap on senior executive pay, however, was TARP's most innovative and controversial governance mandate. As reinforced by the Obama administration's stimulus legislation, the American Recovery and Reinvestment Act of 2009,[26] pay caps were imposed on firms receiving TARP funds so long as any of the firm's TARP obligations remained outstanding. The rules were highly complex, and will be examined in detail in chapter 4. Suffice it for now to note that TARP firms were prohibited from taking a tax deduction exceeding $500,000 for senior management compensation and from paying bonuses to top managers.

Dodd-Frank was far more ambitious than the TARP program. It sweepingly revised virtually the entire scheme of financial regulation. Most of the Act thus lies far outside the scope of this project. Six provisions of the Act, however, do impose important new corporate governance regulations. Unlike TARP, moreover, Dodd-Frank's governance rules apply not just to Wall Street banks but to all Main Street public corporations.

1. Section 951 creates a so-called "say on pay" mandate, requiring periodic shareholder advisory votes on executive compensation.
2. Section 952 mandates that the compensation committees of reporting companies must be fully independent and that those committees be given certain specified oversight responsibilities.
3. Section 953 directs that the SEC require companies to provide additional disclosures with respect to executive compensation.
4. Section 954 expands Sarbanes-Oxley Act's rules regarding clawbacks of executive compensation.
5. Section 971 affirms that the SEC has authority to promulgate a so-called "proxy access" rule pursuant to which shareholders would be allowed to use the company's proxy statement to nominate candidates to the board of directors.
6. Section 972 requires that companies disclose whether the same person holds both the CEO and Chairman of the Board positions and why they either do or do not do so.

26. Pub. L. No. 111–5, 123 Stat. 115 (2009).

A seventh provision, Section 989G, is one of the few deregulatory moves made by Dodd-Frank. It affords small issuers an exemption from the internal controls auditor attestation requirement of Section 404(b) of the Sarbanes-Oxley Act.

Compared to some of the proposals floated in Congress following the 2007–2008 financial crisis, Dodd-Frank's corporate governance provisions are relatively modest. Senators Maria Cantwell's and Charles Schumer's Shareholder Bill of Rights, for example, would have mandated the use of majority voting in the election of directors.[27] It also would have banned the use of staggered boards of directors and required creation of board-level risk management committees.[28] None of these provisions made it into the final Dodd-Frank Act. Other provisions of the Cantwell-Schumer bill made it into Dodd-Frank only in a much-weakened form. Instead of instructing the SEC to adopt a proxy access rule, Dodd-Frank merely affirms that the SEC has authority to do so. Instead of requiring that companies separate the positions of CEO and Chairman of the Board, with the latter being an independent director, Dodd-Frank merely requires companies to disclose their policy with respect to filling those positions. Even so, however, the remaining provisions impose important new duties and expand the federal regulatory role in corporate governance.

What do these provisions have to do with the causes and consequences of the financial crisis? In short, not much. As we shall see in the chapters that follow, a powerful interest group coalition centered on activist institutional investors hijacked the legislative process so as to achieve long-standing policy goals essentially unrelated to the crisis.

Are Dodd-Frank's governance provisions quackery, as were Sarbanes-Oxley's? In short, yes. Without exception, the proposals lack strong empirical or theoretical justification. To the contrary, there are theoretical and empirical reasons to believe that each will be at best bootless and most will be affirmatively bad public policy. Finally, each of Dodd-Frank's governance provisions erodes the system of competitive federalism that is the unique genius of American corporate law by displacing state regulation with federal law. Dodd-Frank is thus shaping up to be round two of federal quack corporate governance regulation.

---

27. Press release, Sen. Charles E. Schumer, Schumer, Cantwell Announce "Shareholder Bill of Rights" to Impose Greater Accountability on Corporate America (May 19, 2009). Specifically, they proposed that nominees to the board of directors would have "board directors to receive at least 50% of the vote in uncontested elections in order remain on the board." Id.

28. Id. Dodd-Frank § 165 does mandate risk management committees, but only for non-bank financial services companies supervised by the Federal Reserve and bank holding companies.

The basic thesis of this work is that the federal government—especially Congress—normally pays little attention to corporate governance. Only in response to major economic crises does corporate governance become a matter of national political concern. This recurrent pattern inherently tends to result in flawed legislation. This is so because, in the first instance, federal corporate governance regulation tends to be enacted in a post-crisis climate of intense political pressure, which discourages taking the time necessary to conduct careful analysis of costs and benefits. Second, federal corporate governance regulation tends to be driven by populist anti-corporate emotions. Finally, the content of federal corporate governance regulation is often derived from pre-packaged proposals advocated by policy entrepreneurs skeptical of corporations and markets. Their agenda therefore is often at odds with the interests of Main Street corporations and their retail investors.

Chapter 1 therefore takes up the foundational question of who sets the rules of the game. Virtually all U.S. corporations are formed ("incorporated") under the laws of a single state by filing articles of incorporation with the appropriate state official. Selecting a state of incorporation has important consequences, because of the so-called "internal affairs doctrine," which is a conflicts of law rule holding that corporate governance matters are controlled by the law of the state of incorporation. Virtually all U.S. jurisdictions follow the internal affairs doctrine, even if the corporation in question has virtually no ties to the state of incorporation other than the mere fact of incorporation.

Because it is state law that historically has provided the rules of the corporate governance game, the state with the most—or, perhaps more accurately, the most important—incorporations wins. As it has been for a century, Delaware is the runaway winner of the competition among the states to grant corporate charters. More than half of the corporations listed for trading on the NYSE and nearly 60 percent of the Fortune 500 corporations are incorporated in Delaware. The vast bulk of economically significant corporate governance disputes thus are resolved under Delaware law.

The passage of Sarbanes-Oxley and Dodd-Frank, along with various other developments to be discussed below, however, demonstrates that Delaware has new competition as the standard setter for corporate governance. The new competitor is not, however, another state. Instead, it is the federal government. When a corporate governance issue has national ramifications, the federal government is increasingly willing to nationalize the relevant legal regime.

The condition of corporate governance after the crises of the last decade thus provides an opportunity to examine the extent to which the vertical competition between Delaware and the federal government in fact has displaced the horizontal competition between Delaware and other states. As we will see, there is no doubt that the vertical competition between Delaware and Washington has become at least as important as the horizontal competition between Delaware and its sister states. Accordingly, evaluating the status of post-crisis corporate governance also provides an opportunity to assess whether federal competition promotes efficiency. The chapters that follow serve as a series of case studies by which to evaluate these claims.

Chapters 2 through 5 focus on the board of directors. Chapter 2 explores the changing role of the board. The literature traditionally identified three functions performed by boards of public corporations. First, the board monitors and disciplines top management. Second, while boards rarely involve themselves in day-to-day operational decision making, most boards perform at least some managerial functions. Broad policy making, for example, is commonly a board prerogative. Even more commonly, however, individual board members provide advice and guidance to top managers with respect to operational and policy decisions. Finally, the board provides the corporation access to a network of contacts that may be useful in gathering resources and/or obtaining business. Outside directors affiliated with financial institutions, for example, facilitate the firm's access to capital.

The last decade, however, has seen a series of changes that collectively narrowed the board's role to that of monitoring. Many of the changes driving this development will be examined in detail in the chapters that follow. In chapter 2, I explain the origins in the 1970s of the reconceptualization of the board's role and structure, as the advising and managing board models were replaced by the monitoring board model. I then identify the changes wrought in the last decade that carved the monitoring model into stone. Chapter 3 concludes that the changes have gone too far in narrowing the scope of the board's role.

One of the key changes giving rise to the monitoring board has been the ever-increasing emphasis on director independence. In the wake of the Enron scandal, the NYSE convened a blue ribbon panel to consider changes to the NYSE's corporate governance listing standards designed to prevent future Enron-type failures. Like many corporate governance reformers in the past, the panel focused on independent directors as the solution to corporate governance's ills. Among other recommendations, the NYSE Corporate Accountability and Listing Standards Committee's report proposed new stock exchange listing standards requiring that independent directors comprise a majority of any listed corporation's board of directors.

The Sarbanes-Oxley Act subsequently mandated that all the self-regulatory organizations (SROs) adopt such rules. With few exceptions, all public corporations in the United States now must have a majority of independent directors. The logic of this requirement is that independent directors will do a better job of monitoring management than would insiders and others who are dependent on the goodwill of the CEO and top management.

Chapter 3 argues that independence has become a fetish—i.e., an idea eliciting unquestioning reverence, respect, and devotion. Director independence is not a panacea for the ills of corporate governance and, at least in some settings, is undesirable. Chapter 4 therefore argues that the one-size-fits-all approach mandated by the Sarbanes-Oxley Act and the new SRO listing standards is seriously flawed.

The ascendancy of the monitoring model raises the question: What exactly do we want directors to monitor? The traditional answer, of course, is management performance. Over the last decade, boards have become more active in disciplining management, as evidenced by the increased rate of CEO terminations. CEO firings remain rare, however. Instead, the board's principal carrot and stick is CEO compensation. Many critics argue that boards fail properly to align pay with CEO performance.

Chapter 4 therefore focuses on executive compensation, which for at least the last decade has been the most controversial issue in corporate governance. Chapter 5 begins with the question of whether executive compensation practices contributed to the crises. It then provides a review of state law developments regarding the fiduciary duties of the board of directors and federal law regarding disclosure of executive compensation. Next, the chapter discusses the executive compensation restrictions imposed on financial institutions as part of the TARP bailout. Finally, the chapter discusses Dodd-Frank's executive compensation provisions, paying special attention to "say on pay," pursuant to which shareholders would be entitled to a non-binding advisory vote on executive compensation.

Furthermore, chapter 5 explains that, in passing the Sarbanes-Oxley Act, Congress was concerned principally with the process by which disclosures are prepared and the information within them is gathered and verified. Much of the Act thus was concerned with accounting and auditing. Have these rules improved such corporate governance goals as honest corporate disclosures, the effectiveness of the board as a monitor of management, and so on? It turns out that the benefits of these rules are hard to identify. In contrast, their costs are easy to identify and have proven to be quite high. It is not clear that the game is worth the candle, especially when one considers the possibility that boards may have become so preoccupied with these issues that they failed to devote adequate time to managing the sort of financial risks that came to a head in the crisis of 2007–2008.

Chapter 6 focuses on two key corporate governance gatekeepers: namely, the auditors and the lawyers. Sarbanes-Oxley intended to rework their relationship with the board and management with two goals in mind. First, Congress wanted the gatekeepers to better serve as a source of independent information for the board. Second, Congress wanted them to be more effective monitors of the top management team.

Chapter 7 takes up the ongoing debate over the proper role of shareholders in corporate governance. Recent years have seen several developments empowering shareholders. The major stock exchanges, for example, adopted new listing standards expanding shareholder approval requirements with respect to corporate compensation plans. Many states have amended their corporation laws to allow firms to use a majority vote—rather than the current plurality— to elect directors. Institutional investors are using the SEC shareholder proposal rule (14a-8) to propose amendments to corporate bylaws requiring such a majority vote. Finally, and most significantly, the SEC adopted the new proxy access rule, under which shareholders will be able to nominate directors and have their nominees listed in the company's proxy statement and on its proxy card. Although the D.C. Circuit struck down the rule in July 2011, proxy access remains a hot button issue.

Chapter 7 cautions that active investor involvement in corporate decision making seems likely to disrupt the very mechanism that makes the public corporation practicable: namely, the centralization of essentially non-reviewable decision-making authority in the board of directors. The chief economic virtue of the public corporation is not that it permits the aggregation of large capital pools, as some have suggested, but rather that it provides a hierarchical decision-making structure well-suited to the problem of operating a large business enterprise with numerous employees, managers, shareholders, creditors, and other inputs. The board-centric governance model in which shareholders have but limited powers thus has significant advantages, which are being steadily eroded by each new shareholder empowerment measure.

With the various case studies provided by the preceding chapters in hand, the Conclusion returns to a more global focus to consider the impact the post-crisis reforms collectively have had on the effectiveness of the corporate governance system. It looks at a wide variety of evidence, ranging from cost-benefit analyses, studies of delisting decisions by former public corporations, decisions to go public or not by start-ups, and the competitive standing of U.S. capital markets in the global economy. On balance, the evidence strongly suggests that the creeping federalization of corporate governance is producing costs well in excess of the benefits.

A NOTE ON OMISSIONS

The informed reader will have noted a number of important corporate governance topics omitted from the plan of the present work. In particular, neither the market for corporate control nor securities litigation appear at length herein. This is not because those subjects are unimportant. It is simply that Congress left them alone. Neither Sarbanes-Oxley nor Dodd-Frank changed the rules of the game in those areas. Because this is a book about the way the federal response to the crises of the last decade has affected corporate governance, such topics simply lie outside its ken.

CHAPTER 1
Who Makes the Rules?

Although states are not the sole regulators of corporate governance, since both the federal government and the stock exchanges play important parts, as do nonlegal sources such as best practice guidelines, state corporate law remains the predominant source of corporate governance rules. It is the law of the state of incorporation that determines the rights of shareholders, for example, "including . . . the voting rights of shareholders."[1] Likewise, "the first place one must look to determine the powers of corporate directors is in the relevant State's corporation law. 'Corporations are creatures of state law' and it is state law which is the font of corporate directors' powers."[2]

The crises of the last decade, however, brought to the fore the question of whether we should prefer the federal government to the states as the principal regulator of corporate governance. If so, we should criticize Sarbanes-Oxley and Dodd-Frank for not having gone far enough in displacing state law. If not, of course, we should criticize them for representing the latest moves in a creeping federalization of corporate governance law.

DOES DELAWARE COMPETE HORIZONTALLY?

The basic case for federalizing corporate law rests on the so-called "race to the bottom" hypothesis. As the theory goes, states compete in granting corporate charters. This competition is possible due to the intersection of the internal affairs choice of law doctrine, under which corporate governance matters are controlled by the law of the state of incorporation, and the constitutional restrictions on a state's ability to exclude foreign corporations from doing

1. CTS Corp. v. Dynamics Corp., 481 U.S. 69, 89 (1987).
2. Burks v. Lasker, 441 U.S. 471, 478 (1979) (citations omitted).

business within their borders.[3] In 1839, for example, the U.S. Supreme Court held that federal courts should presume a state would recognize foreign corporations in the absence of an express statement to the contrary by the legislature.[4] A subsequent Supreme Court decision implied that states could not exclude foreign corporations from doing business within the state, provided that the business constituted interstate commerce under the Commerce Clause of the U.S. Constitution.[5] These decisions made it possible for states to treat their corporate law as a product sold in a national market. If New Jersey adopts a restrictive corporation law, as it did early in the twentieth century, New Jersey–based businesses are free to incorporate in a less restrictive state, such as Delaware, as many did, while continuing to conduct business within New Jersey.

Providing an attractive corporate law product is potentially a source of considerable income for states. The state collects franchise taxes from their corporations annually simply for the privilege of being incorporated. As a result, the more charters the state grants, the more franchise and other taxes it collects. According to race to the bottom theorists, because it is corporate managers who decide on the state of incorporation, states compete by adopting statutes favoring the interests of corporate managers vis-à-vis other corporate stakeholders. As the clear winner in this state competition, Delaware is usually presented as the poster child for bad corporate governance law.[6]

A competing story accepts that states compete for corporate charters, but argues that this competition leads to a race to the top.[7] As the theory goes, investors will not purchase, or at least not pay as much for, securities of firms incorporated in states that cater too excessively to management. Lenders will not lend to such firms without compensation for the risks posed by

---

3. A foreign corporation is one incorporated either by a state or nation other than the state in question. A pseudo-foreign corporation is one that has most of its ties to the state in question rather than to the state of incorporation. Many Delaware corporations are pseudo-foreign corporations. They are incorporated in Delaware, but most of their operations are located in one or more other states. In most states, there is no significant legal difference between a foreign and a pseudo-foreign corporation, and the internal affairs doctrine will be applied to invoke the law of the state of the incorporation. California and New York are the principal exceptions to this rule. Both states purport to apply parts of their corporate laws to pseudo-foreign corporations formed in other states but having substantial contacts with California or New York. See, e.g., Cal. Corp. Code § 2115; N.Y. Bus. Corp. L. §§ 1317–20.

4. Bank of Augusta v. Earle, 38 U.S. 519, 597 (1839).

5. Paul v. Virginia, 75 U.S. 168 (1869).

6. See generally William Cary, Federalism and Corporate Law: Reflections Upon Delaware, 83 Yale L.J. 663 (1974).

7. See generally Ralph K. Winter, State Law, Shareholder Protection, and the Theory of the Corporation, 6 J. Legal Stud. 251 (1977). Judge Winter later moderated the strength of his claim in Ralph K. Winter, The "Race for the Top" Revisited: A Comment on Eisenberg, 89 Colum. L. Rev. 1526 (1989).

management's lack of accountability. As a result, those firms' cost of capital will rise, while their earnings will fall. Among other things, such firms thereby become more vulnerable to a hostile takeover and subsequent management purges. Corporate managers therefore have strong incentives to incorporate the business in a state offering rules preferred by investors. Competition for corporate charters thus should deter states from adopting excessively pro management statutes.

Some recent evidence, however, suggests that the basic premise of both stories—i.e., the states compete actively for corporate charters—is wrong.[8] Lucian Bebchuk and Alma Cohen, for example, argue that:

> [The] conventional view regards incorporation choices as a "pure" choice of a legal regime, based only on a comparison of states' corporate law systems and a judgment on which of those systems would be best for the firm. . . . On this view, all states are viewed as "selling" their corporate law system to all publicly traded firms, and not especially to the firms located in them.[9]

They then assert that their study disproves that conventional view, arguing that their findings "cast substantial doubt on the proposition that there is a vigorous competition among states over corporate charters."

Bebchuk and Cohen's chosen foil, however, is a caricature of the race hypothesis. No one ever claimed that, say, a Los Angeles–based lawyer sits down and thumbs through all 50 state corporation statutes before deciding where to incorporate a client. Instead, a fairer picture of the conventional view is that each state views itself as competing with Delaware, not with the other 48. The claim that states compete not to attract incorporations but rather to retain local businesses finds support in the evidence that 97 percent of all U.S. public corporations are incorporated either in their home state or Delaware.[10]

A theory of home state versus Delaware competition also finds support from a behavioral economic analysis of the role lawyers play in choosing the state of incorporations. Lawyers are subject to the same bounded rationality constraints everyone else is, as well as the familiar incentives of agency cost economics. Under such conditions, lawyers naturally will adopt

8. E.g., Lucian A. Bebchuk & Assaf Hamdani, Vigorous Race or Leisurely Walk: Reconsidering the Competition over Corporate Charters, 112 Yale L.J. 553 (2002); Marcel Kahan & Ehud Kamar, The Myth of State Competition in Corporate Law, 55 Stan. L. Rev. 679 (2002).

9. Lucian Bebchuk & Alma Cohen, Firms' Decisions Where to Incorporate, 46 J. L. & Econ. 383 (2003).

10. David M. Wilson, Climate Change: The Real Threat to Delaware Corporate Law, Why Delaware Must Keep a Watchful Eye on the Content of Political Change in the Air, 5 Entrepreneurial Bus. L. J. 477, 481 (2010).

a decision-making heuristic, with home state versus Delaware being far and away the most logical heuristic for them to choose.

In other words, even if state competition is more of a brisk walk than a race, Delaware still competes.[11] Because of its small population and economy, Delaware is uniquely able to rely on franchise fees to fund a considerable portion of its government. In fact, Delaware generates $740–800 million per year in franchise taxes, which amounts to a quarter of the state's budget.[12] This income flow is of great benefit to Delaware, but it also puts Delaware at risk. If Delaware were to make disadvantageous changes in its law, some firms incorporated there would leave and other firms would not migrate into Delaware. If Delaware law became sufficiently unattractive to decision makers, another state might well decide to begin competing directly and vigorously with Delaware.[13] Pennsylvania and Nevada, for example, have long been lurking in the wings as potential competitors.[14] The potential for such deleterious effects on its budget thus forces Delaware to constantly update and improve its law.

Although the empirical evidence is hardly uncontested, there is substantial evidence that however much state competition actually occurs tends to lead to efficient results. Roberta Romano's event study of corporations changing their domicile by reincorporating in Delaware, for example, found that such firms experienced statistically significant positive cumulative abnormal returns.[15] In other words, reincorporating in Delaware increased shareholder wealth. This finding strongly supports the race to the top hypothesis. If shareholders thought that Delaware was winning a race to the bottom, shareholders should dump the stock of firms that reincorporate in Delaware, driving down the stock price of such firms. As Romano found, however, and all of the other major event studies confirm, there is a positive stock price effect upon reincorporation in Delaware.[16]

The event study findings are buttressed by a Robert Daines study in which he compared the Tobin's Q of Delaware and non-Delaware corporations. Daines found that Delaware corporations in the period 1981–1996 had a higher Tobin's Q than those of non-Delaware corporations, suggesting that Delaware law increases shareholder wealth.[17]

---

11. Mark J. Roe, Delaware's Shrinking Half-Life, 62 Stan. L. Rev. 125, 129 (arguing it is "indisputable" that Delaware competes, "albeit possibly weakly").

12. Wilson, supra note 10, at 485.

13. Roe, supra note 11, at 129.

14. See Kahan & Kamar, supra note 8, at 693 (noting efforts of Nevada and Pennsylvania, as well as Maryland, to compete with Delaware).

15. Roberta Romano, Law as a Product: Some Pieces of the Incorporation Puzzle, 1 J.L. Econ. & Org. 225, 265–73 (1985).

16. See Roberta Romano, The Advantage of Competitive Federalism for Securities Regulation 64–73 (2002) (discussing the relevant studies and criticisms thereof).

17. Robert Daines, Does Delaware Law Improve Firm Value?, 62 J. Fin. Econ. 525 (2001). Tobin's Q is named for economist James Tobin. It is the ratio between the

Additional support for the event study findings is provided by takeover regulation. Compared to most states, which have adopted multiple anti-takeover statutes of ever-increasing ferocity, Delaware's single takeover statute is relatively friendly to hostile bidders.[18] Given the clear evidence that hostile takeovers increase shareholder wealth,[19] this finding is especially striking. The supposed poster child of bad corporate governance, Delaware, turns out to be quite takeover-friendly and, by implication, shareholder-friendly.

The takeover regulation evidence is especially important, because state anti-takeover laws are the principal arrow in the quiver of modern race to the bottom theorists. Lucian Bebchuk and Allen Ferrell point out that state takeover regulation demonstrably reduces shareholder wealth but that most states have nevertheless adopted anti-takeover statutes.[20] Even many advocates of the race to the top hypothesis concede that state regulation of corporate takeovers appears to be an exception to the rule that efficient solutions tend to win out.[21] But so what? Nobody claims that state competition is perfect. The question is only whether some competition is better than none. Delaware's relatively hospitable environment for takeovers suggests an affirmative answer to that question.

THE EMERGENCE OF THE NORTH DAKOTA ALTERNATIVE

In 2007, North Dakota threw down the gauntlet to Delaware by adopting the Publicly Traded Corporations Act, which "is designed to strengthen corporate

market value of an asset and the asset's replacement value. As applied to corporate valuation, Tobin's Q is calculated by dividing the corporation's market value by its book value. A Tobin's Q greater than 1 thus indicates that the firm is worth more as a going concern than the sum of the replacement value of its assets. See James Tobin, A General Equilibrium Approach to Monetary Theory, 1 J. Money, Credit & Banking 15 (1969).

Although subsequent research suggests that this effect may not hold for all periods, see Guhan Subramanian, The Disappearing Delaware Effect, 20 J.L. Econ. & Org. 32 (2004) (presenting evidence that the Delaware effect disappears when examined over a longer time frame), Daines' study remains an important confirmation of the event study data.

18. See Jonathan M. Karpoff & Paul H. Malatesta, The Wealth Effects of Second Generation Takeover Legislation, 25 J. Fin. Econ. 291 (1989) (explaining that Delaware has a weak statute whose adoption did not adversely affect stock prices of Delaware corporations).

19. See generally Stephen M. Bainbridge, Corporation Law and Economics 612–14 (2002) (reviewing studies).

20. Lucian Ayre Bebchuk & Allen Ferrell, Federalism and Corporate Law: The Race to Protect Managers from Takeovers, 99 Colum. L. Rev. 1168 (1999).

21. See, e.g., Roberta Romano, Competition for Corporate Charters and the Lesson of Takeover Statutes, 61 Fordham L. Rev. 843 (1993).

democracy and improve the performance of publicly traded corporations."[22] It is specifically designed to give shareholders greater rights and to reflect "the best thinking of institutional investors and governance experts."[23] The idea, presumably, is that North Dakota will attract incorporations away from Delaware by being more shareholder-friendly than Delaware.

I am confident in predicting that the North Dakota experiment will fail. First, the Act does nothing to address Delaware's other advantages. There is a considerable body of case law interpreting the Delaware corporate statute (DGCL), which allows legal questions to be answered with confidence. Delaware has a separate court, the Court of Chancery, devoted largely to corporate law cases. The Chancellors have great expertise in corporate law matters, making their court a highly sophisticated forum for resolving disputes. They also tend to render decisions quite quickly; facilitating transactions that are often time sensitive.[24] At least in the near term, North Dakota cannot replicate these advantages.

Second, turning to the statutes, North Dakota inevitably loses whether state competition is a race to the top or to the bottom. If state competition is a race to the bottom, which Delaware wins by catering to management interests at the expense of shareholders, the managers who control the incorporation decision will continue to choose Delaware. Incorporation in North Dakota would limit managers' ability to extract private rents, so they have no incentive to do so.

If state competition is a race to the top, the position I believe both theory and the empirical evidence supports, North Dakota will still lose. Corporate law in almost all states places sharp limits on shareholder involvement in corporate decision making.[25] Taken together, these myriad rules form a regime I have called "director primacy."[26]

We will examine the director primacy theory of corporate governance in detail in chapter 7 in connection with our analysis of the shareholder empowerment debate. Suffice it to say for now that the director primacy account begins with the observation that the size and complexity of the public corporation ensures that stakeholders face significant collective action problems in making decisions, suffer from intractable information asymmetries, and have

---

22. North Dakota Corporate Governance Council, Explanation of the North Dakota Publicly Traded Corporations Act 1 (April 5, 2007), http://ndcgc.org/Reference/Explain405.pdf. The Act also offers a franchise tax rate 50 percent of that imposed on public corporations by Delaware.

23. North Dakota Corporate Governance Council, available at http://ndcgc.org/.

24. Jill E. Fisch, The Peculiar Role of the Delaware Courts in the Competition for Corporate Charters, 68 U. Cin. L. Rev. 1061 (2000).

25. See chapter 7.A infra.

26. See, e.g., Stephen M. Bainbridge, Director Primacy: The Means and Ends of Corporate Governance, 97 Nw. U. L. Rev. 547 (2003).

differing interests. Under such conditions, consensus-based decision-making structures are likely to fail. Instead, it is cheaper and more convenient to assign the decision-making function to a central decision maker wielding the power to rewrite intra-corporate contracts by fiat.

The analysis to this point, of course, suggests only that the decision-making structure should be one based on authority rather than participatory democracy. Yet, it turns out that corporate law also was wise to assign ultimate decision-making authority to a group—i.e., the board of directors—rather than a single individual. As we will discuss in chapter 2, groups turn out to have significant advantages vis-à-vis individuals at exercising critical evaluative judgment, which is precisely the skill set principally needed at the top of the corporate hierarchy. In addition, groups solve the problem of "who watches the watchers" by placing a self-monitoring body at the apex of the corporate hierarchy. Thus the chief economic virtue of the public corporation is that it provides a hierarchical decision-making structure well suited to the problem of operating a large business enterprise with numerous employees, managers, shareholders, creditors, and other inputs. In turn, it is the separation of ownership and control that makes this structure viable.

While it is true that "'Delaware has not explicitly embraced director primacy,' the relevant statutory provisions and the [case law] have largely intimated that directors retain authority and need not passively allow either exogenous events or shareholder action to determine corporate decision-making."[27] In contrast, North Dakota's statute displaces this efficient and long-established system of director primacy in favor of shareholder primacy. Yet, if the race to the top account is to be believed, shareholders prefer director primacy to shareholder primacy, and North Dakota will therefore fail to displace Delaware.

DELAWARE'S VERTICAL COMPETITION

No one seriously doubts that Congress has the power under the Commerce Clause to preempt the field of corporation governance law. Although it has never opted to do so, Congress has long been in the business of piecemeal federalization of corporate governance.

> Washington makes corporate law. From 1933 to 2002, that is, from the passage
> of the securities laws to the passage of Sarbanes-Oxley, Washington has made

---

27. Harry G. Hutchison, Director Primacy and Corporate Governance: Shareholder Voting Rights Captured by the Accountability/Authority Paradigm, 36 Loy. U. Chi. L.J. 1111, 1195 (2005).

rules governing the voting of stock and the solicitation of proxies to elect directors. It has made the main rules governing insider trading, stock buybacks, how institutional investors can interact in corporate governance, the structure of key board committees, board composition (how independent some board members must be), how far states could go in making merger law, how attentive institutional investors must be in voting their proxies, what business issues and transactional information public firms must disclose (which often affect the structure and duties of insiders and managers to shareholders in a myriad of transactions), the rules on dual class common stock recapitalizations, the duties and liabilities of gatekeepers like accountants and lawyers, and more.[28]

In this sense, both Sarbanes-Oxley and Dodd-Frank simply represent additional milestones in a process of gradual federalization. In another sense, however, they represent a significant departure. Unlike past federal corporate governance regulations, many of those in the two post-crisis laws cross the traditional boundary between state and federal law.

The Boundary Between State Corporate and Federal Securities Law

Until Sarbanes-Oxley and Dodd-Frank, the key federal statute affecting corporate governance was the Securities Exchange Act of 1934. The Exchange Act on its face says little about regulation of corporate governance. Instead, the Act's basic focus is trading of securities and securities pricing. Virtually all of its provisions are thus addressed to such matters as the production and distribution of information about issuers and their securities, the flow of funds in the market, and the basic structure of the market.

This approach resulted from Congress's interpretation of the Great Crash and the subsequent Depression. Rightly or wrongly, many people believed that excessive stock market speculation and the collapse of the stock market had caused the Great Depression. The drafters of the Exchange Act were thus primarily concerned with preventing a recurrence of the speculative excesses that they believed had caused the market's collapse.

Disclosure was the chief vehicle by which the Act's drafters intended to regulate the markets. Indeed, it was widely acknowledged that allocating primary responsibility over corporate disclosure to the federal government was essential. Brandeis's famous dictum—"Sunlight is . . . the best of disinfectants; electric light the most efficient policeman"[29]—was well accepted by the 1930s;

---

28. Mark J. Roe, Washington and Delaware as Corporate Lawmakers, 34 Del. J. Corp. L. 1, 10 (2009).
29. Louis D. Brandeis, Other People's Money 92 (1914).

indeed, it was the basic concept around which the federal securities laws were ultimately drafted.[30] However, the states faced serious obstacles in attempting to regulate corporate disclosure. Although the Supreme Court had upheld state blue sky laws against constitutional challenge,[31] the Commerce Clause limited the states' ability to apply those laws extraterritorially. As a result, most blue sky laws did not regulate out-of-state transactions. The problem was exacerbated by the difficulty of attaining uniformity and coordination among the states. Promoters could evade restrictive state laws simply by limiting their activities to more permissive jurisdictions. Because state securities laws thus could not effectively assure full disclosure, federal intervention was accepted as essential to maintaining the national capital markets.

Opponents of the legislation, however, quickly claimed that it went far beyond its stated purposes. According to Richard Whitney, President of the NYSE and a leading opponent of the bill, a number of provisions, including the predecessor to Section 19(c), collectively gave the Commission "powers . . . so extensive that they might be used to control the management of all listed companies,"[32] a charge repeated by Congressional opponents of the bill.[33] Others acknowledged that early drafts of the legislation had justifiably raised such concerns, but argued the legislation had been redrafted so as to eliminate any legitimate fears on this score.[34]

The bill's supporters strenuously denied that they intended to regulate corporate management. The Senate Banking and Currency Committee went to the length of adding a proposed Section 13(d) to the bill, which provided: "[n]othing in this Act shall be construed as authorizing the Commission to interfere with the management of the affairs of an issuer."[35] The Conference Committee deleted the provision because it was seen "as unnecessary, since it is not believed that the bill is open to misconstruction in this respect."[36]

Admittedly, this debate need not be read as going to preemption of state corporate law. After all, interference with management might mean a variety of things. Perhaps the debate was really about charges of creeping socialism. Opposition to New Deal legislation typically included charges of radicalism

---

30. Ernst & Ernst v. Hochfelder, 425 U.S. 185, 195 (1976); SEC v. Capital Gains Research Bureau, Inc., 375 U.S. 180, 186 (1963).

31. Hall v. Geiger-Jones Co., 242 U.S. 539 (1917); Caldwell v. Sioux Falls Stock Yards Co., 242 U.S. 559 (1917); Merrick v. N.W. Halsey & Co., 242 U.S. 568 (1917).

32. Letter from Richard Whitney to all NYSE members (Feb. 14, 1934), reprinted in 78 Cong. Rec. 2827 (Feb. 20, 1934).

33. E.g., 78 Cong. Rec. 8271 (1934) (Sen. Steiwer); id. at 8012 (Rep. McGugin); id. at 7937 (Rep. Bakewell); id. at 7710 (Rep. Britten); id. at 7691 (Rep. Crowther); id. at 7690 (Rep. Cooper).

34. E.g., 78 Cong. Rec. 7863 (1934) (Rep. Wolverton); id. at 7716–17 (Rep. Ford); id. at 7713 (Rep. Wadsworth).

35. S. 3420, 73d Cong., 2d Sess. § 13(d) (1934).

36. H.R. Conf. Rep. No. 1838, 73d Cong., 2d Sess. 35 (1934).

and collectivism. The Exchange Act was no different. Even with this gloss, however, the legislative history still suggests that Congress's focus was mainly on regulating the securities industry, not listed companies. Moreover, Congress not only insisted it was not trying to regiment industry but also rejected explicit proposals for establishing a federal law of corporations.

During the New Deal era there were a number of efforts to grant the SEC authority over corporate governance. While the Exchange Act was being drafted, the Roosevelt administration considered developing a comprehensive federal corporation law. The Senate Banking and Currency Committee's report on stock exchange practices also suggested that the cure for the nation's "corporate ailments . . . may lie in a national incorporation act."[37] In the late 1930s, then-SEC Chairman William O. Douglas orchestrated yet another effort to replace state corporate law with a set of federal rules administered by the SEC. In this, he was anticipated and assisted by Senators Borah and O'Mahoney, who introduced a series of bills designed to regulate corporate internal affairs.[38]

Proposals for a federal corporation statute did not stop when the New Deal ended.[39] In the 1970s, the SEC considered imposing a variety of corporate governance reforms, as a matter of federal law.[40] After vigorous objections that the Commission had exceeded its statutory authority, the rules were substantially modified before adoption.[41]

Consequently, none of these proposals ever came to fruition. Legislative inaction is inherently ambiguous, even when that inaction takes the form of rejecting a specific proposal. All that can be said with certainty is that Congress chose not to act. However, while the evidence admittedly is not conclusive, there is considerable reason to believe that the Seventy-Third Congress did not intend for the SEC's power over listing standards to extend to matters of corporate governance. Granted Congress did not expressly state any such limitation. But Congress apparently did not believe it was necessary to do so. True, arguments based on rejections of proposed amendments must be taken with a grain of salt, especially those made after enactment of the original legislation. But surely the Congress that repeatedly denied any intent to redesign corporate management, and later repeatedly rejected proposals to federalize

37. S. Rep. No. 1455, 73d Cong., 2d Sess. 391 (1934).

38. Joseph C. O'Mahoney, Federal Charters to Save Free Enterprise, 1949 Wis. L. Rev. 407.

39. E.g., Protection of Shareholders' Rights Act of 1980: Hearing before the Subcomm. on Securities of the Sen. Comm. on Banking, Housing, and Urban Affairs, 96th Cong., 2d Sess. (1980); The Role of the Shareholder in the Corporate World: Hearings before the Subcomm. on Citizens and Shareholders Rights and Remedies of the Sen. Comm. on the Judiciary, 95th Cong., 1st Sess. (1977).

40. Exchange Act Rel. No. 14,970 (July 18, 1978).

41. Exchange Act Rel. No. 15,384 (Dec. 6, 1978).

corporate law, did not intend to sneak those powers back into the bill through the back door by authorizing the SEC to adopt corporate governance rules.

Where then is the line between federal and state law? The clearest answer to that question came when the SEC attempted to regulate dual class stock. Although the corporate norm is one vote per share, state law permits deviations from the norm, authorizing corporations to adopt various forms of dual class voting schemes. A corporation thus might have two classes of common stock, for example, with one class of stock carrying the traditional one vote per share but the other carrying ten votes per share. If the holders of the super-voting stock form a cohesive group, such as a family, trust, or top management team, they can often exercise voting control while owning a rather modest percentage of the equity. In the late 1980s, dual class stock became controversial as it became an increasingly common form of takeover defense.

The NYSE long refused to list issuers having either a class of nonvoting common outstanding or multiple classes of common stock with disparate voting rights. The AMEX likewise refused to list nonvoting common stock, but its policy with respect to disparate voting rights plans was more flexible. Issuers adopting such plans would be listed as long as the plan satisfied certain guidelines designed to create a minimum level of participation to which the lesser voting rights class was entitled. In contrast, the NASD imposed no voting rights listing standards in either the over-the-counter market or the NASDAQ system.

With the renewal of corporate interest in dual class stock during the 1980s, however, issuers began pressuring the NYSE to adopt a more flexible listing standard. In 1988, the NYSE asked the SEC for permission to amend its listing standards to allow certain forms of dual class stock. In response, the SEC adopted Rule 19c-4, which effectively amended the rules of all the exchanges (and the NASD) to prohibit them from listing an issuer's equity securities if the company issued securities or took other corporate action nullifying, restricting, or disparately reducing the voting rights of existing shareholders.[42] As such, Rule 19c-4 was the SEC's first direct attempt to regulate substantively a matter of corporate governance applicable to all public corporations. The Business Roundtable challenged the Rule, arguing that corporate governance regulation is primarily a matter for state law and that the SEC therefore had no authority to adopt rules affecting substantive aspects of corporate voting rights. The D.C. Circuit agreed, striking down the rule as beyond the Commission's regulatory authority.[43]

---

42. For a detailed treatment of Rule 19c-4 and the surrounding legal issues, see Stephen M. Bainbridge, The Short Life and Resurrection of SEC Rule 19c-4, 69 Wash. U. L.Q. 565 (1991).

43. Bus. Roundtable v. SEC, 905 F.2d 406 (D.C. 1990).

The Commission based its authority to adopt Rule 19c-4 on its powers under Securities Exchange Act § 19(c), which permits it to amend exchange rules provided that the Commission's action furthers the Act's purposes. Rule 19c-4 fell because the D.C. Circuit determined that its attempt to regulate corporate voting rights furthered none of the Exchange Act's purposes. In defending Rule 19c-4, the SEC trotted out its long-standing view that § 14(a) was intended to promote corporate democracy. In striking down the Rule, the D.C. Circuit adopted a much narrower view of § 14(a)'s purposes. According to the court, federal proxy regulation has two principal goals. First, and foremost, it regulates the disclosures shareholders receive when they are asked to vote. Second, it regulates the procedures by which proxy solicitations are conducted. Section 14(a)'s purposes thus do not include regulating substantive aspects of shareholder voting.

Although § 14(a)'s legislative history is relatively sparse, it tends to support the D.C. Circuit's interpretation. In defending Rule 19c-4, the SEC placed great weight on a House Committee Report statement that "[f]air corporate suffrage is an important right that should attach to every equity security bought on a public exchange."[44] While it is indisputable that Congress intended § 14(a) to give the SEC broad powers over corporate proxy solicitations, there is reason to believe that Congress had in mind an entirely different set of issues than those raised by nonvoting stock when it referred to fair corporate suffrage.

The controversy over federal proxy regulation was resolved early in the legislative process. As originally introduced, the proxy provision mandated substantial disclosures and gave the SEC authority to adopt additional

44. H.R. Rep. No. 1383, 73d Cong., 2d Sess. 13 (1934). In addition to arguing from the legislative history and prior administrative practices, the SEC pointed to some loose language in a few cases suggesting a broad reading of the Congressional intent for § 14(a). Of course, prior to the D.C. Circuit's decision to invalidate Rule 19c-4 there were no judicial interpretations of the Act squarely on point. Moreover, when the cases upon which the SEC relied are read in context, they too support the conclusion that § 14(a) was narrowly drawn to deal with disclosure and procedural abuses. The Commission, for example, placed great emphasis on a prior DC Circuit decision describing the principal purpose of § 14 as assuring "to corporate shareholders the ability to exercise their right—some would say their duty—to control the important decisions which affect them in their capacity as stockholders and owners of the corporation." Medical Committee for Human Rights v. SEC, 432 F.2d 659, 680–81 (D.C. Cir. 1970) (citations omitted), vacated as moot, 404 U.S. 403 (1972). This comment, however, was made in the rather different context of applying the shareholder proposal rule. Notice, moreover, the court's emphasis on the ability to exercise voting rights, which seems consistent with the interpretation that § 14 was intended solely to assure that shareholders could make effective use of whatever voting rights state law provides. As the Supreme Court once put it: "The purpose of § 14(a) is to prevent management or others from obtaining authorization for corporate action by means of deceptive or inadequate disclosure in proxy solicitation." J. I. Case Co. v. Borak, 377 U.S. 426, 431 (1964).

disclosure requirements. The proposal met with substantial criticism. For example, AT&T pointed out that the bill required the proxy statement to include a list of all shareholders being solicited, which would force AT&T to prepare three large volumes, at a total cost of $950,000, every time proxies were solicited. Section 14(a) was redrafted in response to these criticisms. In doing so, Congress did what it often does when it has a tough problem to solve: it told somebody else to solve it. In effect, the Act simply made it unlawful to solicit proxies "in contravention of such rules and regulations as the Commission may prescribe as necessary or appropriate in the public interest or for the protection of investors."[45]

In implementing § 14(a), the SEC has affected corporate governance to a greater extent than under any other provision of the Exchange Act. Rule 14a-4 restricts management's use of discretionary power to cast votes obtained by a proxy solicitation. Rule 14a-7 requires management cooperation in transmitting an insurgent's proxy materials to shareholders. Rule 14a-8 requires management to include qualified shareholder proposals in the corporation's proxy statement at the firm's expense. Although some opponents of the legislation anticipated these sorts of intrusions into internal corporate affairs, § 14(a)'s impact on corporate governance in fact is rather narrow. Most of the SEC's proxy rules relate to disclosure. Full disclosure of matters to come before a shareholder meeting, for example, was the original justification for the shareholder proposal rule.[46] While the Commission's authority under § 14(a) is not limited to disclosure issues, its other proxy rules relate to the procedures by which the proxies are to be prepared, solicited, and used.

The limited scope of proxy regulation is consistent with a proper interpretation of the phrase "fair corporate suffrage." In using that term, Congress did not mean to address the substantive question of how many votes per share to which a stockholder is entitled. Instead, as the D.C. Circuit recognized in *Business Roundtable*, Congress was talking about an entirely different concern: the need for full disclosure and fair solicitation procedures. The House Committee, for example, contended that management should not be able to perpetuate itself in office through "misuse" of corporate proxies.[47] It noted that insiders were using the proxy system to retain control "without adequate disclosure." It protested that insiders were soliciting proxies "without fairly informing" shareholders of the purpose of the solicitation. The passage concludes by stating that in light of these abuses § 14(a) gives the "Commission power to control the conditions under which proxies may be solicited. . . ."

45. Securities Exchange Act, Pub. L. No. 73–291, § 14(a), 48 Stat. 881, 895 (1934).
46. Med. Comm. for Human Rights v. SEC, 432 F.2d 659, 677 (D.C. Cir. 1970), vacated as moot, 404 U.S. 403 (1972).
47. H.R. Rep. No. 1383, 73d Cong., 2d Sess. 13 (1934).

In sum, the passage says nothing about the substance of the shareholders' voting rights. Instead, the focus is solely on enabling shareholders to make effective use of whatever voting rights they possess. Other references to proxy solicitations elsewhere in the legislative history likewise focus on disclosure concerns.[48]

In sum, the D.C. Circuit correctly confirmed that the SEC has extensive authority to adopt rules assuring full disclosure and fair solicitation procedures. However, the court also drew a critical distinction between substantive and procedural regulation of shareholder voting. As to the former, the SEC has little, if any, authority.

Where then do we draw the line between the state and federal regulatory regimes? As a general rule of thumb, federal law appropriately is concerned mainly with disclosure obligations, as well as procedural and antifraud rules designed to make disclosure more effective. In contrast, regulating the substance of corporate governance standards was appropriately left to the states. But then Sarbanes-Oxley and Dodd-Frank upended the traditional balance by directly regulating the substance of corporate governance in important, albeit so far limited, areas.

The Problem of Therapeutic Disclosure

Although the SEC largely respected the boundary drawn by *Business Roundtable*, it has long used so-called therapeutic disclosure to affect substantive corporate behavior. Unlike most disclosure requirements, which are directed at aiding investors in valuing securities or make informed voting decisions, therapeutic disclosure is intended to deter targeted conduct by corporations and their managers. It seeks to do so by forcing corporations and their managers to disclose purported misconduct, thereby exposing to litigation or, at least, social shaming. As famed securities lawyer A.A. Sommer explained, by way of analogy, "if every instance of adultery had to be disclosed, there would probably be less adultery."[49]

Therapeutic disclosure requirements undoubtedly affect corporate behavior, but it is troubling on at least two levels. First, seeking to effect substantive goals through disclosure requirements is inconsistent with the original Congressional intent behind the federal securities laws. When the New Deal era Congresses adopted the Securities Act and the Securities Exchange Act,

---

48. For detailed treatment of § 14(a)'s legislative history, and relevant subsequent legislative nonevents, see Stephen M. Bainbridge, Redirecting State Takeover Laws at Proxy Contests, 1992 Wis. L. Rev. 1071; Stephen M. Bainbridge, The Short Life and Resurrection of SEC Rule 19c-4, 69 Was. U. L.Q. 565 (1991).

49. A.A. Sommer, Jr., Therapeutic Disclosure, 4 Sec. Reg. L.J. 263, 266–67 (1976).

there were three possible statutory approaches under consideration: (1) the fraud model, which would simply prohibit fraud in the sale of securities; (2) the disclosure model, which would allow issuers to sell very risky or even unsound securities, provided they gave buyers enough information to make an informed investment decision; and (3) the blue sky model, pursuant to which the SEC would engage in merit review of a security and its issuer. The federal securities laws adopted a mixture of the first two approaches, but explicitly rejected federal merit review. As such, the substantive behavior of corporate issuers is not within the traditional federal regulatory scheme.

Second, therapeutic disclosure blurs the boundaries between the federal and state regulatory spheres. Indeed, it can amount to a de facto preemption of state law. The Commission has frequently justified its rules requiring disclosure of such matters as executive compensation or related party transactions as bringing shareholders into the compensation committee or board meeting room and thereby enabling them to see specific decisions through the eyes of the directors. This goal, however, flies in the face of the separation of ownership and control created by state corporate law. Under state law, shareholders have no right to approve most board decisions, let alone to initiate corporate action. In other words, they have no right to be brought within the meeting room.

In addition to the substantive invasions of substantive corporate governance described in the chapters that follow, both Sarbanes-Oxley and Dodd-Frank included therapeutic disclosure requirements. For example, Sarbanes-Oxley § 506 requires companies to disclose whether the audit committee of their board of directors includes at least one financial expert and, if not, why not. Likewise, Sarbanes-Oxley § 406 requires companies to disclose whether they have adopted a code of ethics for their senior financial managers and, if not, why not. In order for the company to claim it has adopted the requisite code of ethics, the code must establish standards "reasonably necessary to deter wrongdoing and to promote honest and ethical conduct, including the ethical handling of actual or apparent conflicts of interest between personal and professional relationships." The code must provide for avoidance of conflicts of interest by identifying an appropriate person to whom the covered officers must disclose any material transaction or relationship that reasonably could give rise to a conflict between the officer's personal interest and business duties. The code must obligate the officers covered to ensure "full, fair, accurate, timely, and understandable disclosure" in reports and documents filed by the company with the SEC. The code must mandate personal and corporate compliance with applicable governmental laws, rules, and regulations. It should provide for prompt internal reporting of code violations to an appropriate person or persons, whom the code should identify. The code should be filed with the SEC as an exhibit to the company's annual report and posted to the company's website.

In both cases, Congress doubtless didn't care about the content of these disclosures. Instead, Congress expected companies would adopt the requisite code of ethics and appoint the requisite financial expert rather than risk the public embarrassment, negative media reports, and shareholder complaints likely to follow such a refusal.

Dodd-Frank § 953 instructs the SEC to adopt rules requiring corporations to include in their annual proxy statements disclosures showing the relationship between executive compensation and the company's financial performance. It further requires new SEC rules mandating disclosure in the proxy statement of the median annual compensation of all employees of the company other than the CEO, the total annual compensation of the company's CEO, and the ratio of the two amounts. The rules are unlikely to provide investors with meaningful information. Instead, they are intended to shame corporations by highlighting the disparity between CEO and shop floor employee pay.

Section 973 directs the SEC to adopt a new rule requiring reporting companies to disclose whether the same person or different persons holds the positions of CEO and Chairman of the Board. In either case, the company must disclose its reasons for doing so. Separation of the two positions has been a long-standing goal of many in the activist shareholder community and their academic allies. Congress opted not to mandate such a separation, opting instead for requiring disclosure. As we will see below, however, some policy entrepreneurs hope that the provision will shame companies into separating the two positions.

Sections 953 and 973 both impinge on state corporate law. It is state law that regulates board of director decisions relating to executive pay. In doing so, state law has never opted to evaluate the ratio between CEO and employee pay, let alone to give shareholders a say in setting that ratio. Likewise, state law regulates board structure. The states have never required firms to separate the CEO and Chairman positions. While neither §§ 953 not 973 directly preempts the relevant state laws, as a practical matter the former supersede state law. What corporations decide with respect to these issues now will be driven mainly by the implications of §§ 953 and 973, not solely by state law.

The Role of Policy Entrepreneurs and Bubbles in the Federalization of Corporate Governance

Federal interventions in corporate governance differ in a number of important respects from the ongoing process of adaptive regulation by states. First, the players are different. There are many interest groups with skin in the corporate governance game, such as corporate managers, shareholders, unions, consumers, NGOs, and anti-corporate populists. In Delaware, however, most of these groups are relatively powerless. Instead, the dominant interest group in Delaware is the bar:

> The bar is small, discrete, and highly organized. Its members tend to have a large personal stake in the subject matter of the regulation. They also tend to be more wealthy than other groups and to have good political connections. Indeed, many members of the Delaware legislature are themselves members of the bar. Such legislators tend to be represented disproportionately on legislative committees that draft the provisions of the Delaware Corporation Code.[50]

In addition, Delaware tends to be highly sensitive to the interests of managers and investors. Other interest groups are generally powerless in Delaware.[51]

In contrast, at the federal level, while managers and the Delaware bar have some influence, the other interest groups with a stake in corporate governance also have considerable influence. In particular, Washington is subject to swings in national public opinion from which Delaware is largely insulated.[52]

Second, federal interventions tend to be episodic. The most important almost always follow some major economic crisis. In ordinary times, Washington typically has more important issues on its plate than corporate governance. In a bubble period, such as those that preceded the crises of the last decade, moreover, federal regulatory action becomes even less likely because interest groups such as shareholders and consumers are lulled into inaction by the seemingly ever-rising value of their portfolios.[53] At the same time, however, the stage is being set for a post-bubble burst of regulation.

In the euphoria associated with a bubble, regulators and private gatekeepers tend to let their guard down, potential fraudsters see an explosion of opportunities, and investors become both more greedy and trusting. The net effect is a boom in fraud during bubbles, especially toward the end, when everybody is trying to keep the music going. When the bubble inevitably

---

50. Jonathan R. Macey & Geoffrey P. Miller, Toward an Interest-Group Theory of Delaware Corporate Law, 65 Tex. L. Rev. 469, 506 (1987). This analysis suggests another reason to think Delaware law tends to race to the top. As the principal interest group affecting Delaware law, the local bar has a strong interest in maintaining Delaware's dominance. Unlike New York, Washington, or Los Angeles, to cite but a few examples, Delaware lacks the population, economic size, and financial centers necessary to sustain a large and prosperous corporate bar. The bar thus has an active interest in maintaining the efficiency and attractiveness of Delaware corporate law.

51. Id. at 490 ("Because the physical assets of most large Delaware corporations are located in other states, Delaware lawmakers ordinarily are not subject to pressures from unions, environmental groups, local communities, or other special interests associated with the corporation's physical plant or assets.").

52. Roe, supra note 28, at 17.

53. Larry E. Ribstein, Bubble Laws, 40 Hou. L. Rev. 77, 79 (2003).

bursts, investigators reviewing the rubble begin to turn up evidence of speculative excess and even outright rampant fraud. Investors burnt by losses
from the breaking of the bubble and outraged by evidence of misconduct
by corporate insiders and financial bigwigs create populist pressure for new
regulation.

It is in the post-bubble environment, "when scandals and economic rever-
sals occur" and "when corporate transactions grab the attention of the American
public and the U.S. Congress," that Congress often acts.[54] Because the venue for
post-bubble regulatory action shifts from Delaware to Washington, interest
groups frozen out of the Delaware process to participate meaningfully in the
legislative or rule-making processes. Because such periods typically involve
an upswing in populist anger and accompanying intense public pressure for
action, they offer "windows of opportunity to well-positioned policy entrepreneurs to market their preferred, ready-made solutions when there is little
time for reflective deliberation."[55] This pattern is a reoccurring phenomenon
in American law, going back even before the New Deal.[56]

> [The pattern recurs because] deep-seated popular suspicion of speculation
> comes in bad financial times to dominate otherwise popular support for mar-
> kets, resulting in the expansion of regulation. That is to say, financial exigencies
> embolden critics of markets to push their regulatory agenda. They are able to
> play on the strand of popular opinion that is hostile to speculation and markets
> because the general public is more amenable to regulation after experiencing
> financial losses.[57]

Sarbanes-Oxley and Dodd-Frank are the latest iterations of this process.

Because of the political context in which they occur, federal corporate governance interventions tend to be adopted quickly under emergency conditions. Time pressure gives advantages to those interest groups and other
policy entrepreneurs who have prepackaged purported solutions that can be
readily adapted into legislative form. Many of the Sarbanes-Oxley Act's provisions were "recycled ideas" that had been "advocated for quite some time by
corporate governance entrepreneurs," for example.[58] Unfortunately, because
the policy entrepreneurs tend to be critics of markets and corporations, bubble
laws often "impose regulation that penalizes or outlaws potentially useful
devices and practices and more generally discourages risk-taking by punishing

54. Roe, supra note 28, at 7.
55. Roberta Romano, The Sarbanes-Oxley Act and the Making of Quack Corporate
Governance, 114 Yale L.J. 1521, 1590 (2005).
56. Ribstein, supra note 53, at 83–94; Romano, supra note 55, at 1590–94.
57. Romano, supra note 55, at 1593.
58. Romano, supra note 55, at 1523.

negative results and reducing the rewards for success."[59] The chapters that follow will offer numerous case studies of just such regulations.

WHERE WAS DELAWARE DURING THE CRISES?

Delaware sat out both the Enron era and the subprime mortgage crisis. Indeed, Delaware affirmatively avoided opportunities to address the crises. When the Treasury Department and the Federal Reserve engineered J.P. Morgan's acquisition of Bear Stearns in March 2008, for example, the agreement contained a number of deal protection devices of dubious validity under Delaware law. When Bear Stearns shareholders challenged the deal, the Delaware Chancery court stayed the case brought before it and allowed a case filed in New York to proceed. Although Delaware courts usually are eager to seize the leading role in cases involving their law, in this instance the Delaware court seemingly wanted no part of a case in which its law might require it to enjoin "a transaction that was supported, indeed, arguably driven and financed by the Federal Reserve with the full support of the Treasury—a transaction that may have been necessary to prevent the collapse of the international financial system."[60]

Delaware's reticence in the face of the crises is not surprising. First, state legislation tends to be adaptive and iterative. Unlike the federal government, which typically acts on in times of crisis, both Delaware and the drafters of the Model Business Corporation Act revise their statutes at least annually. Changes in state law tend to be small and incremental.

Second, courts rather than legislators make much state corporate law. Unlike a legislature or an administrative body such as the SEC, courts are ill suited to make sweeping systemic changes in response to a crisis. Courts cannot reach out to make new law; they can only decide the cases brought before them. The adjudicatory process is inherently incremental, as courts build on existing precedents. The adversarial process does not lend itself to neutral and unbiased investigations; nor does it lend itself to wide-ranging inquiries into root causes of major social upheavals. The court lacks the staffing and other resources that legislatures and administrative bodies can use to conduct extensive fact finding hearings. In sum, the court is simply not the appropriate forum for developing the sort of systematic legal change that the crises of the last decade supposedly demanded.

59. Ribstein, supra note 53, at 83.
60. Edward Rock & Marcel Kahan, How to Prevent Hard Cases from Making Bad Law: Bear Stearns, Delaware and the Strategic Use of Comity, 58 Emory L.J. 713, 744 (2009).

Finally, and most importantly, Delaware decision makers know that their state's dominant position exists at Congressional suffrage. As Delaware Vice Chancellor Leo Strine observes, "the capacious constitutional authority of Congress over interstate commerce is something that Delaware and other state corporate lawmakers have constantly had to take into account. . . ."[61] Writing before Dodd-Frank became law, Strine further observed that: "The proxy access and 'say on pay' initiatives are only the most recent examples of this dynamic and come close on the heels of the Sarbanes-Oxley Act, crisis-inspired legislation that made clear that if investor outrage was widespread enough, even a Republican-controlled Congress was prepared to enact federal laws affecting corporate governance without anguish about intruding into territory traditionally reserved to state law."[62]

Professor Mark Roe implicitly invokes the old joke about where an 800-pound gorilla sits to expound the threat identified by Strine:

> The big gorilla of American economic lawmaking is the Congress which, when it wants to, can dwarf the Delaware Court of Chancery, the Delaware General Assembly, and the Delaware Corporate Law Council, which drafts Delaware's corporate law. They all have considerable freedom to act, but not on a corporate governance issue about which Washington has acted, and not if they upset those who can influence Washington. . . . Washington is not just a potential big player in corporate lawmaking, but an actual big player, always considering, and often acting, on the most important corporate governance issues of nearly every decade. And Washington could always do more. . . . If Washington wanted to, it could take over all corporate law-making from the states, obliterating Delaware as a producer of state-made corporate law.

As Strine makes clear, Delaware is fully aware of this risk. Delaware will abstain from intervening in a crisis, and tolerate or even anticipate minor federal crisis responses that infringe on Delaware's regulatory sphere, when necessary, to avoid triggering a backlash that would result in federalizing corporate law, just as it did in both 2002 and 2008.

61. Leo E. Strine Jr, Breaking the Corporate Governance Logjam In Washington: Some Constructive Thoughts on A Responsible Path Forward, 63 Bus. Law. 1079, 1081 (2008).
62. Id.

QUACK FEDERAL CORPORATE GOVERNANCE REGULATION

Quack corporate governance regulation will have most, if not all, of the following features:

1. It is effected by a bubble law, enacted in response to a major negative economic event.
2. It is enacted in a crisis environment.
3. It is a response to a populist backlash against corporations and/or markets.
4. It is adopted at the federal rather than state level.
5. It transfers power from the states to the federal government.
6. It is supported by interest groups that are strong at the federal level but weak at the Delaware level.
7. Typically, it is not a novel proposal, but rather a long-standing agenda item of some powerful interest group.
8. The empirical evidence cited in support of the proposal is, at best, mixed and often shows the proposal to be unwise.

The corporate governance provisions of both Sarbanes-Oxley and Dodd-Frank demonstrably satisfy the first four criteria. The remainder of this book demonstrates that most of the provisions also meet all or substantially all of the final four. They thus almost uniformly qualify for the sobriquet "quack corporate governance."

CHAPTER 2
The Board's Role

Both Dodd-Frank and Sarbanes-Oxley worked many specific changes in corporate governance. None of those changes are so fundamental, however, as the impetus these statutes gave to the ongoing process by which the very purpose and role of the board of directors is being reshaped.

The most basic principle of corporate governance is, as the Delaware General Corporation Law puts it, that the corporation's business and affairs "shall be managed by or under the direction of a board of directors."[1] To be sure, while the corporation statute envisions a board-centered governance structure, the statutory theory long failed to translate into real world practice. Accordingly, informed observers long have believed that corporations are run neither by the board nor, for that matter, the shareholders, but rather by imperial CEOs or, at best, top management teams. Adolf Berle compared corporate managers to "princes and ministers."[2] Ralph Nader went so far as to compare directors to "cuckolds" who are "often the last to know when [their] dominant partner—management—has done something illicit."[3]

Starting in the 1970s, however, the ground began to shift under management's feet. A combination of new legal requirements and enhanced market expectations empowered both boards and shareholders vis-à-vis management. For example, the rise of the hostile takeover bid as a viable market transaction meant that managers who let their company's stock price fall became vulnerable to displacement by an acquirer. In turn, as managers sought to resist tender offers and proxy contests, judicial review of such takeover defenses came to hinge in large part on whether independent and

---

1. DGCL § 141(a).
2. A.A. Berle, Jr., For Whom Corporate Managers Are Trustees, 45 Harv. L. Rev. 1365, 1366 (1932).
3. Ralph Nader et al., Taming the Giant Corporation 64 (1976).

disinterested directors made the relevant decisions.[4] Other judicial decisions emphasized that a rational decision-making process in which the board gathered all material information reasonably available to it was a prerequisite to applying the business judgment rule to protect board decisions from substantive review.[5]

Sarbanes-Oxley and Dodd-Frank both came down solidly on the side of the board vis-à-vis management. Numerous provisions of both acts are intended to empower boards and to make them more independent of management. In addition, however, both acts also contribute to a major change in the board's basic functions. As we will see, both acts prioritize the board's role of monitoring management at the expense of the board's other roles.

As a result of all these changes, modern boards of directors typically are smaller than their antecedents, meet more often, are more independent from management, own more stock, and have better access to information. They are evolving from being "managerial rubber-stamps to active and independent monitors."[6] Granted, the transformation remains incomplete. There are still some Imperial CEOs to be found. As a growing body of empirical data confirms, however, "boards with new backbone are dumping imperial CEOs."[7] The trend of corporate governance is bringing the statutory framework and real world practice increasingly into line.

THE BOARD'S TRADITIONAL FUNCTIONS

The board of directors has many functions, but they fall into three basic categories. These are management, oversight, and service. The balance between

4. See, e.g., Moran v. Household Int'l, Inc., 409 A.2d 1059, 1074–1075 (Del. Ch. 1985) (holding that a corporation's justification for takeover defenses "is materially enhanced . . . where, as here, a majority of the board favoring the proposal consisted of outside independent directors who have acted in accordance with the foregoing standards"); see also Weinberger v. UOP, Inc., 457 A.2d 701, 709 n.7 (Del. 1983) (holding that "the result [in a freeze-out merger] could have been entirely different if [the board] had appointed an independent negotiating committee of its outside directors to deal with [the majority shareholder] at arm's length," because doing so would have been "strong evidence that the transaction meets the test of fairness").

5. See, e.g., Brehm v. Eisner, 746 A.2d 244, 264 n.66 (Del. 2000) (holding that "directors' decisions will be respected by courts unless the directors are interested or lack independence relative to the decision, do not act in good faith, act in a manner that cannot be attributed to a rational business purpose or reach their decision by a grossly negligent process that includes the failure to consider all material facts reasonably available.")

6. Paul W. MacAvoy & Ira M. Millstein, The Active Board of Directors and Its Effect on the Performance of the Large Publicly Traded Corporation, 11 J. App. Corp. Fin. 8 (1999).

7. Matthew Benjamin, Giving the Boot, U.S. News & World Rep., March 28, 2005, at 48.

them has varied over time and from firm to firm. In recent decades, however, the trend has been to elevate the importance of monitoring at the expense of the others. Sarbanes-Oxley and Dodd-Frank did much to further that trend.

Management

If one looked solely to corporation statutes for guidance, one would assume that the board of directors plays a very active role in the corporation's management. Besides the general allocation of the conduct of the corporation's business and affairs to the board, corporation statutes include many specific mandates that only the board can fulfill. Approval by the board of directors is a statutory prerequisite, for example, to mergers and related transactions such as sales of all or substantially all corporate assets, the issuance of stock, distribution of dividends, and amendments to the articles of incorporation. Approval by the board of directors of related party transactions involving top managers or board members is a statutory option for substantially insulating such transactions from judicial review for fairness. The board typically has non-exclusive power to amend bylaws. And so on.

In fact, of course, the typical modern public corporation is too big for the board to manage on anything resembling a day-to-day basis. As we'll discuss in the next chapter, moreover, these days most board members are outsiders who have full-time jobs elsewhere and therefore can devote relatively little time to the running of the business for which they act as directors. As early as 1922, the Delaware Chancery Court therefore held that the directors' principal role was one of supervision and control, with the detailed conduct of the business being a matter that could properly be delegated to subordinate employees.[8]

The formulation of typical modern corporation statutes reflects this shift. Section 8.01(b) of the Model Business Corporation Act (MBCA) reflects these basic truisms in two respects. First, the statute provides that the "business and affairs of the corporation" shall be "managed under the direction of" the board. This formulation is intended to make clear that the board's role is to formulate broad policy and oversee the subordinates who actually conduct the business day-to-day.[9] Second, the statute also provides that corporate powers may be exercised "under the [board's] authority." This formulation allows the board to delegate virtually all management functions to senior corporate officers, who in turn of course will delegate most decisions to subordinate employees.

---

8. Cahall v. Lofland, 114 A. 224, 229 (1921), aff'd, 118 A. 1 (1922).
9. Model Bus. Corp. Act Ann. § 8.01 cmt. [hereinafter cited as MBCA].

Even so, modern boards typically retain some managerial functions. Indeed, courts have held that some decisions are so important that the board of directors must make them.[10] In some states, such basic matters as filing a lawsuit[11] or executing a guarantee of another corporation's debts are extraordinary matters reserved to the board.[12] In recent years, courts also have imposed substantial managerial responsibilities on the board of directors—especially its independent members—in connection with shareholder derivative litigation, conflict of interest transactions, and mergers and acquisitions.

Best practice also assigns important managerial roles to the board. Broad policy making or, at least, review and approval of major policies, for example, are board prerogatives. Boards are also responsible for hiring the top management team, especially the CEO, and setting their compensation.

Monitoring Managers

Although it is a "fundamental precept of Delaware corporation law" that the board "has ultimate responsibility for the management of the enterprise," that law also recognizes that "modern multi-function business corporations" are "large, complex organizations" and that modern boards are comprised mainly "of persons dedicating less than all of their attention to that role."[13] As we just saw, boards are not obliged to run the corporation on a day-to-day basis. Instead, directors "satisfy their obligations by thoughtfully appointing officers, establishing or approving goals and plans and monitoring performance."[14] Accordingly, most board of director activity "does not consist of taking affirmative action on individual matters; it is instead a continuing flow of supervisory process, punctuated only occasionally by a discrete transactional decision."[15]

10. See Lee v. Sentina Bros., 268 F.2d 357, 365–66 (2d Cir. 1959) (officers have no apparent authority with respect to extraordinary matters, which are reserved to the board).

11. Compare Custer Channel Wing Corp. v. Frazer, 181 F. Supp. 197 (S.D.N.Y. 1959) (president had authority to do so) with Lloydona Peters Enter., Inc. v. Dorius, 658 P.2d 1209 (Utah 1983) (no authority to do so); Ney v. Eastern Iowa Tel. Co., 144 N.W. 383 (Iowa 1913) (no authority to do so with respect to the corporation's largest shareholder).

12. Compare Sperti Products, Inc. v. Container Corp. of Am., 481 S.W.2d 43 (Ken. App. 1972) (president had authority) with First Nat'l Bank v. Cement Products Co., 227 N.W. 908 (Iowa 1929) (no authority to do so); Burlington Indus., Inc. v. Foil, 202 S.E.2d 591 (N.C. 1974) (president lacked authority, inter alia, because making such guarantees was not part of the corporations' ordinary business).

13. Chapin v. Benwood Foundation, 402 A.2d 1205, 1211 (Del. Ch. 1979).

14. Id.

15. Bayless Manning, The Business Judgment Rule and the Director's Duty of Attention: Time for Reality, 39 Bus. Law. 1477, 1494 (1984).

In carrying out this function, the board of directors serves as one of the chief constraints on the problem financial economists refer to as agency costs. As we saw in the introduction, corporate law separates ownership and control. New Deal era corporate governance scholars Adolf Berle and Gardiner Means famously explained that this separation "produces a condition where the interests of owner and of ultimate manager may, and often do, diverge and where many of the checks which formerly operated to limit the use of power disappear."[16] Economists Michael Jensen and William Meckling later formalized this concern by developing the concept of agency costs,[17] which several generations of scholars have come to believe is "the fundamental concern of corporate law" and governance.[18]

Jensen and Meckling defined agency costs as the sum of the monitoring and bonding costs incurred to prevent shirking by agents, plus any residual loss from undeterred shirking. In turn, shirking is defined to include any action by a member of a production team that diverges from the interests of the team as a whole. As such, shirking includes not only culpable cheating, but also negligence, oversight, incapacity, and even honest mistakes. In other words, shirking is simply the inevitable consequence of bounded rationality and opportunism within agency relationships.

A simple example of the agency cost problem is provided by the bail upon which alleged criminals are released from jail while they await trial. The defendant promises to appear for trial. But that promise is not very credible: The defendant will be tempted to flee the country. The court could keep track of the defendant—monitor him—by keeping him in jail or perhaps by means of some electronic device permanently attached to the defendant's person. Yet, such monitoring efforts are not free—indeed, keeping someone in jail is quite expensive (food, guards, building the jail, etc.). Alternatively, the defendant could give his promise credibility by bonding it, which is exactly what bail does. The defendant puts up a sum of money that he will forfeit if he fails to appear for trial. (Notice that the common use of bail bonds and the employment of bounty hunters to track fugitives further enhances the credibility of bail as a deterrent against flight.) Of course, despite these precautions, some defendants will escape jail and/or jump bail. Hence, there will always be some residual loss in the form of defendants who escape punishment.

A sole proprietorship with no agents will internalize all costs of shirking, because the proprietor's optimal trade-off between labor and leisure is,

---

16. Adolf A. Berle & Gardiner C. Means, The Modern Corporation and Private Property 6 (1932).

17. Michael C. Jensen & William H. Meckling, Theory of the Firm: Managerial Behavior, Agency Costs, and Ownership Structure, 3 J. Fin. Econ. 305 (1976).

18. Kent Greenfield, The Place of Workers in Corporate Law, 39 B.C.L. Rev. 283, 295 (1998).

by definition, the same as the firm's optimal trade-off. Agents of a firm, however, will not internalize all of the costs of shirking: the principal reaps part of the value of hard work by the agent, but the agent receives all of the value of shirking. In a classic article, economists Armen Alchian and Harold Demsetz offered the useful example of two workers who jointly lift heavy boxes into a truck.[19] The marginal productivity of each worker is difficult to measure and their joint output cannot be separated easily into individual components. In such situations, obtaining information about a team member's productivity and appropriately rewarding each team member are very difficult and costly. In the absence of such information, however, the disutility of labor gives each team member an incentive to shirk because the individual's reward is unlikely to be closely related to conscientiousness.

Although agents ex post have strong incentives to shirk, ex ante they have equally strong incentives to agree to a corporate contract containing terms designed to prevent shirking. Bounded rationality, however, precludes firms and agents from entering into the complete contract necessary to prevent shirking by the latter. Instead, there must be some system of ex post governance: some mechanism for detecting and punishing shirking. Accordingly, an essential economic function of management is monitoring the various inputs into the team effort: management meters the marginal productivity of each team member and then takes steps to reduce shirking.

The process just described, of course, raises a new question: who will monitor the monitors? In any organization, one must have some ultimate monitor who has sufficient incentives to ensure firm productivity without himself having to be monitored. Otherwise, one ends up with a never ending series of monitors monitoring lower level monitors. Alchian and Demsetz solved this dilemma by consolidating the roles of ultimate monitor and residual claimant. According to Alchian and Demsetz, if the constituent entitled to the firm's residual income is given final monitoring authority, he is encouraged to detect and punish shirking by the firm's other inputs because his reward will vary exactly with his success as a monitor.

Unfortunately, this elegant theory breaks down precisely where it would be most useful. Because of the separation of ownership and control, it simply does not describe the modern publicly held corporation. As the corporation's residual claimants, the shareholders should act as the firm's ultimate monitors. But while the law provides shareholders with some enforcement and electoral rights, these are reserved for fairly extraordinary situations. In general, shareholders of public corporations lack the legal right, the practical

19. Armen A. Alchian & Harold Demsetz, Production, Information Costs, and Economic Organization, 62 Am. Econ. Rev. 777 (1972).

ability, and the desire to exercise the kind of control necessary for meaningful monitoring of the corporation's agents.

The apparent lack of managerial accountability inherent in the modern corporate structure has long troubled legal commentators. To be sure, agency costs are an important component of any viable theory of the firm. A narrow focus on agency costs, however, easily can distort one's understanding of the firm. Corporate managers operate within a pervasive web of accountability mechanisms that substitute for monitoring by residual claimants. Important constraints are provided by a variety of market forces. The capital and product markets, the internal and external employment markets, and the market for corporate control all constrain shirking by firm agents. In addition, the legal system evolved various adaptive responses to the ineffectiveness of shareholder monitoring, establishing alternative accountability structures to punish and deter wrongdoing by firm agents, most notably the board of directors.

Service

A diverse board that includes outsiders can provide a number of services to the top management team. Outsiders can provide access to networks to which insiders do not belong, thereby assisting the firm in gathering resources and obtaining business. Outside directors affiliated with financial institutions, for example, facilitate the firm's access to capital. In addition to simply providing a contact between the firm and the lender, the financial institution's representative can use his board membership to protect the lender's interests by more closely monitoring the firm than would be possible for an outsider. In turn, that reduction of risk should result in the lender accepting a lower return on its loans, thereby reducing the firm's cost of capital.

Another example is the politically connected board member, whose access to legislators and regulators may aid the firm in dealing with the government. Such board members not only assist with obtaining government contracts, but also with clearing red tape and providing the firm with political cover in times of trouble.

A core service provided by boards of directors, especially its outside members, is providing advice and counsel to the CEO. By virtue of being outsiders, the board members can offer the CEO alternative points of view. In particular, the board can serve as a source of outside expertise. Complex business decisions require knowledge in such areas as accounting, finance, management, and law. Members who possess expertise themselves or have access to credible external experts play an important role in the board's service function.

The relative balance between these functions has shifted over time. Survey data and other forms of fieldwork in the 1970s suggested that boards had a mainly advisory role. Survey data from the 1990s, by contrast, shows an emphasis on managerial functions in the sense of broad policy making and setting strategy. By the end of the 1990s, survey data showed that boards were becoming active and independent monitors of the top management team.[20] What drove this shift?

THE RISE OF THE MONITORING BOARD

Boards historically have had bad press. In the eighteenth century, Adam Smith famously complained that one could not expect the directors of a joint stock company, "being the managers rather of other people's money than of their own, . . . should watch over it with the same anxious vigilance with which the partners in a private copartnery frequently watch over their own."[21] Almost two centuries later, William O. Douglas complained that there were too many boards whose members did "not direct"[22] and dismissed directors as "business colonels of the honorary type—honorary colonels who are ornamental in parade but fairly useless in battle."[23]

Much of the criticism was merited. A well-known British judicial opinion from the early twentieth century, describing the selection of a rubber corporation's board, provides an amusing illustration of the basic problem:

> The directors of the company, Sir Arthur Aylmer Bart, Henry William Tugwell, Edward Barber and Edward Henry Hancock were all induced to become directors by Harboard or persons acting with him in the promotion of the company. Sir Arthur Aylmer was absolutely ignorant of business. He only consented to act because he was told the office would give him a little pleasant employment without his incurring any responsibility. H.W. Tugwell was partner in a firm of bankers in a good position in Bath; he was seventy-five years of age and very deaf; he was induced to join the board by representations made to him in January, 1906. Barber was a rubber broker and was told that all he would have to do would be to

20. Renee B. Adams et al., The Role of Boards of Directors in Corporate Governance: A Conceptual Framework and Survey, 48 J. Econ. Lit. 58, 64–65 (2010).

21. 2 Adam Smith, An Inquiry into the Nature and Causes of the Wealth of Nations 264–65 (Edwin Cannan ed., Univ. of Chicago Press 1976) (1776).

22. William O. Douglas, Directors Who Do Not Direct, 47 Harv. L. Rev. 1305 (1934).

23. William O. Douglas, Democracy and Finance 46 (1940).

give an opinion as to the value of rubber when it arrived in England. Hancock was a man of business who said he was induced to join by seeing the names of Tugwell and Barber, whom he considered good men.[24]

Unfortunately, such practices were the norm rather than the exception.

In the 1970s, however, a crisis of confidence threatened not just the comfortable world of the board of directors but the very foundations of corporate capitalism. The triggering event was the collapse of Penn Central "in 1970 amidst personality clashes, mismanagement, and lax board oversight."[25] Subsequent investigations revealed that Penn Central's board had been mere figureheads who were wholly unaware of the company's deteriorating financial condition and passively rubberstamped such transactions as paying over $100 million in dividends to shareholders even as the company was going down the tubes.[26]

The collapse of Penn Central was followed in short order by the widespread corrupt payments scandal in which hundreds of prominent public corporations were implicated. The scandal was an offshoot of the Watergate investigations. The probes brought to light numerous illegal corporate contributions to the Nixon campaign. Investigation of those violations then revealed an even broader pattern of both domestic and foreign corporations making illegal campaign contributions, bribes to government officials, kickbacks on contracts, and the like. Eventually the government targeted some 50 corporations for criminal prosecution or SEC civil litigation. Another 400 voluntarily disclosed having made improper payments.[27] By the end, it was clear that senior management at many of these companies had been well aware of the corrupt payments, but their boards had been too far out of the loop to prevent them.[28]

The scandals swept the legitimacy of the corporate form itself into the tumultuous political battles of the day. The period was one in which multiple progressive movements—including the anti-war movement, civil rights, feminism, gay rights, consumer protection, and environmentalism—intertwined in a constantly shifting flux of activism. A number of these groups came to see the institution of the corporation as being a root cause of social problems.

This view found a classic expression in Ralph Nader's philippic *Taming the Giant Corporation*. Nader and his co-authors claimed that public confidence in

---

24. In re Brazilian Rubber Plantations & Estates Ltd., [1911] 1 Ch. 425.

25. Brian R. Cheffins, Did Corporate Governance "Fail" During the 2008 Stock Market Meltdown? The Case of the S&P 500, 65 Bus. Law. 1, 7 (2009).

26. Jeffrey N. Gordon, The Rise of Independent Directors in the United States, 1950–2005: Of Shareholder Value and Stock Market Prices, 59 Stan. L. Rev. 1465, 1515 (2007).

27. Id. at 1516.

28. Cheffins, supra note 25, at 7.

American corporations was declining precipitously in the face of antisocial corporate behavior.[29] They blamed a myriad of social ills—pollution, workplace hazards, discrimination, unsafe products, and corporate crime—on corporate managers accountable to neither boards, shareholders, nor society.[30]

Consistent with the generally accepted diagnosis of the Penn Central collapse and the questionable payments scandal, Nader and his coauthors laid much of the blame at the feet of boards of directors. In turn, they blamed the board's impotence in large part on state corporate law, which purportedly had been "reduced to reflecting the preferences of the managers of the largest corporations."[31] Accordingly, Nader called for a federal corporation law, displacing state law, whose precepts would ensure greater management accountability both to shareholders and to society.

Among other things, Nader's proposed federal statute would create a cadre of full-time professional directors. Only cadre members would be allowed to serve on boards. Incumbent managers would be prohibited from sitting on their corporation's boards as well as nominating or selecting candidates for the board. Once elected, by way of cumulative voting, the board members would serve on a full-time basis, with no outside employment, and for no more than four two-year terms. Board members would be provided with staffs and full access to corporate information. Each board member would be responsible for some specified aspect of the business, such as employee welfare or law compliance.[32]

Although Nader was an outlier, at least in terms of the ferocity of his attacks and the radical nature of his proposals, many mainstream regulators and scholars of the period likewise concluded that state corporate law was moving away from, not toward, greater managerial accountability. Former SEC Chairman William Cary famously argued, for example, that competition among states for incorporations produced a "race to the bottom" in which shareholder interests were sacrificed.[33]

Leading mainstream figures like Cary believed that the race to the bottom, combined with the wave of scandals in the 1970s and the New Left's critique of corporate capitalism, as exemplified by Nader, had eroded public confidence in the modern business corporation and, as a result, had brought into question the very legitimacy of the economic system in which the corporation was the dominant actor. In order to arrest those trends, Cary urged adoption of a federal statute designed to promote greater management accountability to

29. Ralph Nader et al., Taming the Giant Corporation 17–32 (1976).
30. Id. at 62–65.
31. Id. at 60.
32. See generally id. at 118–31.
33. William L. Cary, Federalism and Corporate Law: Reflections Upon Delaware, 83 Yale L.J. 663 (1974).

shareholders, although not going so far as to require federal incorporation.[34] Like Nader's more ambitious scheme, Cary's proposal for partially federalizing corporation law ultimately went nowhere. Along with other similar proposals, however, they contributed to a shift in best practices and ultimately laid the groundwork for the creeping federalization of corporate law exemplified by Sarbanes-Oxley and Dodd-Frank.

Eisenberg's Influence

Although the modern understanding of the board's role and function has no single parent, if one were to insist on finding someone to whom to give the bulk of the credit—or blame—the leading candidate probably would be Professor Melvin Eisenberg. In *The Structure of the Corporation*, "perhaps the most important work on corporate law since Berle and Means's *The Modern Corporation and Private Property*,"[35] Eisenberg argued that boards were essentially passive, with most of their functions captured by senior executives.[36] According to Eisenberg, the board's principal remaining function was selection and supervision of the firm's chief executive, but most boards failed adequately to perform even that residual task.[37]

As a solution, Eisenberg articulated a corporate governance model that explicitly separated the task of managing large publicly held corporations from that of monitoring those who do the managing. In this monitoring model, directors did not undertake decision making or policy making, which were assigned to senior management. Instead, the board's principal function was to monitor the performance of the company's senior executives. Other functions such as advising the CEO, authorizing major corporate actions, and exercising control over decision making were of minor importance or were merely pro forma.[38]

The American Law Institute Principles

Eisenberg perhaps came closest to enshrining the monitoring model in corporate law in the First Tentative Draft of what ultimately became the American Law Institute (ALI)'s *Principles of Corporate Governance: Analysis*

34. Id. at 696–703.
35. Dalia Tsuk Mitchell, Status Bound: The Twentieth-Century Evolution of Directors' Liability, 5 N.Y.U. J.L. & Bus. 63 (2009).
36. Melvin Aron Eisenberg, The Structure of the Corporation 139–41 (1976).
37. Id. at 162–72.
38. Id. at 157–62.

and Recommendations. Eisenberg served as Reporter for Parts I through III of the *Principles*, which gave him chief drafting responsibility for the board composition and role standards. In 1984, moreover, Eisenberg succeeded Stanley Kaplan as Chief Reporter for the entire project.

In monitoring management, the board was to do more than just look at results. Rather, the board was to establish elaborate mechanisms by which it could closely oversee management performance.[39] At the heart of these mechanisms were three oversight committees of the board: audit, nomination, and compensation.

Because financial data is the basic metric for management performance, Eisenberg had long argued that the board should have an audit committee comprised of independent directors. The committee was to select the corporation's independent auditor and, among other things, review the corporation's financial results in consultation with the auditor. Shifting responsibility for selecting the auditor from management to an independent board committee would reduce management's ability to influence the presentation of financial data to its benefit. Shifting responsibility for interacting with the auditor from management to the audit committee would address the information asymmetry between management and the board by giving the latter access to an independent source of key information.[40]

Tentative Draft No. 1 of the *Principles* also envisioned a nominating committee to be comprised exclusively of outside directors, including at least a majority of independent directors, and was charged with, among other things, recommending candidates for director positions.[41] The exclusion of officers or

39. American Law Institute, Principles of Corporate Governance: Analysis and Recommendations 65 (Tent. Draft No. 1 1982) [hereinafter "TD No. 1"] ("the concept of monitoring requires the employment of sophisticated and independent systems designed to gather and disseminate information concerning management performance, and independent directors who are sophisticated in interpreting both financial and nonfinancial data."). The Principles divide corporations into three categories. The "large publicly held corporation" has two thousand or more record stockholders and $100 million in total assets. "Publicly held corporation" has five hundred or more record stockholders and $5 million in total assets. "Small publicly held corporation" are those companies that fall within the definition of publicly held corporation, but do not qualify as a large publicly held corporation. In general, the board composition and function provisions of Tentative Draft No. 1 applied only to large publicly held corporations. For small publicly held corporations, these provisions generally were recommended as rules of good corporate practice. See, e.g., TD No.1 at 89 (audit committees).

40. Eisenberg, supra note 36, at 210–11.

41. TD No.1 at § 3.06(a). Not all outside directors qualified as independent under the Principles, because the Principles set out an elaborate standard for determining whether a director is independent, which looked to whether the director has a significant relationship with the corporation's senior executives. Tentative Draft No. 1 defined significant relationship very broadly. It included employment, prior employment within the two preceding years, family relationships, and various economic

employees from membership on the nominating committee was intended to ensure that senior executives did not play a significant role in the selection of board members. In addition, it seems likely that the drafters expected that a nominating committee comprised of independent directors would screen out individuals who in fact are biased toward the incumbent senior executives even though those individuals might otherwise meet the *Principles'* definition of an independent director. The same concern is further reflected in the rule allowing the nominating committee to consider candidates proposed by the senior executives, but giving only the committee the power to recommend such candidates to the board or shareholders. Again, the same concern presumably motivated the Reporter's proposed standard of good corporate practice pursuant to which the committee "should have the power (but not the obligation) to list [candidates recommended by the committee but rejected by the board of directors] in the corporation's proxy materials, appropriately designated, in addition to the board's nominees."[42]

The recommended compensation committee, like the nominating committee, was to be comprised solely of outside directors, including at least a majority of independent directors.[43] As the name suggests, it was to review and approve (or recommend to the full board) the compensation of senior executives and generally oversee the corporation's compensation policies. A separate compensation committee was recommended because of concerns that inside directors, even if recused from considering their own compensation, would not be able to objectively evaluate the compensation of other senior executives in light of the close relationship between one executive's compensation and that of another.

The Principles Are Downgraded

The board of directors' function and composition provisions quickly were caught up in larger debate over the direction of the entire ALI corporate governance project. Critics charged that the *Principles'* early drafts were more concerned with ensuring management accountability than with allowing flexibility in structuring corporate decision-making systems, a charge which some of the project's proponents defiantly conceded.[44] In addition, critics

relationships. The final Principles define "significant relationship" to include the same basic types of relationships as did Tentative Draft No. 1, although some of the details differ in minor ways.

42. TD No. 1 at 103–04.

43. Id. at § 3.07(a).

44. See, e.g., Donald E. Schwartz, Genesis: Panel Response, 8 Cardozo L. Rev. 687, 688–89 (1987).

complained that the early drafts were not restating existing law, but rather were advocating significant legal changes, many of which would increase the scope and frequency of judicial review of board actions and, concomitantly, the risk of liability for directors and officers.

As they became increasingly aware of this risk, many prominent corporate executives came out in strong opposition to the early drafts of the *Principles*. They did not hesitate to make the corporate bar aware of their views. Indeed, it has been alleged "that corporations were hiring members of the ALI to represent their interests in that body's deliberations and that they were removing their legal business from law firms with partners who were sympathetic to the ALI's pro-litigation outlook."[45]

If the crisis atmosphere of the 1970s had persisted, perhaps neither the business community nor the corporate bar would have resisted sweeping reforms. By the time the ALI began drafting the *Principles*, however, the atmosphere of crisis had essentially dissipated. The reformers had moved on to other issues or had settled into comfortable partnerships and professorships. Absent their prompting, federal intervention no longer seemed likely. Indeed, several events seemed almost to foreclose any chance of near-term federal intervention. The *Santa Fe* decision more or less eliminated the threat that courts would create a de facto federal law of corporations under Rule 10b-5.[46] The Republican Party controlled both the White House and the Senate, ending the threat of federal legislative intervention.

With the *Principles'* political rationale having disappeared, the business community was free to evaluate the drafts on their own terms. This was the turning point at which opposition began gathering strength. Unlike most ALI projects, the corporate governance project directly affected the prerogatives and pocketbooks of senior corporate managers. Opposition from the corporate bar thus followed as a matter of course.

Opposition from the business community and the corporate bar received academic respectability and political cover from the emergent body of law and economics scholars. In general, law and economics academics opposed

45. Jonathan R. Macey, Naderite Mossbacks Lose Control Over Corporate Law, Wall Street Journal, June 24, 1992, at A19.

46. In the early 1970s, SEC Rule 10b-5 was being given an increasingly expansive reading that in time might have led to a federal common law of corporations. See Stephen M. Bainbridge, The Short Life and Resurrection of SEC Rule 19c-4, 69 Wash. U.L.Q. 565, 613 (1991). The Supreme Court applied the brakes in a series of cases, most notably Santa Fe Industries, Inc. v. Green, 430 U.S. 462 (1977). The Supreme Court held that the federal securities laws were fundamentally intended to assure full disclosure. Id. at 477–78. Once complete disclosure is made, the transaction's fairness and terms are essentially non-issues under federal law, instead being a matter for state corporate law. Id. at 478–80. The Court made clear that it was rejecting the use of Rule 10b-5 as a means of federalizing corporate law. See id. at 478–79.

mandatory rules, were skeptical of the utility of independent directors, and resisted attempts to expand the scope of judicial review of management actions. Between the steady barrage of critical academic commentary they directed at the project and their growing strength within the ALI, coupled with voting support from the corporate bar, the influence of these scholars gradually began to be felt. For example, while Tentative Draft No. 2 strongly rejected the notion that market forces alone will result in the creation of effective monitoring systems, the final version of the *Principles* significantly softened and scaled back the discussion of market forces.

The Final Principles

In response to the sharp criticism to which Tentative Draft No. 1 was subjected, subsequent drafts were revised in a number of respects. Some of the changes were merely cosmetic. For example, while the word monitoring no long appears in the *Principles'* description of the board's function, the basic division between monitoring and management functions was retained under new terminology. The *Principles* thus still urge that the company be managed by its principal senior executives, and assert that the selection and oversight of those executives is the board's basic function.

A more meaningful change was the conversion of virtually all of the proposed mandatory board composition and function rules into mere recommendations of corporate practice. Where Tentative Draft No. 1 prohibited the board of a large publicly held corporation from managing the firm on a regular basis, for example, the *Principles* restore the board's traditional power to do so. Where Tentative Draft No. 1 required that independent directors make up a majority of a large publicly held corporation's board, the *Principles* merely recommend such a composition as a matter of corporate practice. The ALI further explicitly made clear that such recommendations concerning corporate practice were "not intended as legal rules, noncompliance with which would impose liability."[47]

The Monitoring Model Becomes Best Practice

The ALI's famous Restatements of the Law have proven immensely influential. Courts routinely rely on them as authoritative statements of black letter law. The unique role of Delaware in corporate law probably would have tempered the impact the ALI project would have in this field relative to others that had

47. See TD No. 2 at 83.

been restated, but the original mandatory provisions of Tentative Draft No. 1 nevertheless likely would have had some law reform effect if they had remained intact. The changes effected over the decade-long process by which the final *Principles* came into being, however, ensured that the final board function and composition provisions would be mere guides as to one organization's view of best practice. The *Principles* therefore had to compete with other influential sources of best practice guidance.

As it turned out, however, the monitoring model quickly "became conventional wisdom, endorsed by the Chairman of the SEC, the corporate bar, and even the Business Roundtable."[48] Several key sources of best practice embraced the model. In 1978, for example, the American Bar Association's Section of Business Law promulgated a Corporate Director's Guidebook that embraced an Eisenberg-like model in which the management and monitoring of management roles were separated with the latter task being assigned to a board comprised mainly of outside directors.[49] A formal statement by the Business Roundtable likewise adopted the monitoring model.[50]

The absorption of the monitoring model into generally accepted best practice continued throughout the 1990s.[51] By 1997, Eisenberg thus was able to declare that "key structural elements of the monitoring model—including a board that has at least a majority of independent directors, and audit, nominating, and compensation committees—[were] already well-established."[52] A board of directors' failure to comply with best practices is not a violation of corporate law, however, a point the Delaware Supreme Court has taken pains to drive home.[53]

CODIFYING THE MONITORING MODEL

The first steps toward transforming the monitoring model into law came in 1977 when the NYSE amended its listing standards to require the board of

---

48. Gordon, supra note 26, at 1518.

49. ABA Section of Corporation, Banking and Business Law, Corporate Director's Guidebook, 33 Bus. Law. 1591, 1619–28 (1978).

50. Statement of the Business Roundtable: The Role and Composition of the Board of Directors of the Large Publicly Owned Corporation, 33 Bus. Law. 2083 (1978).

51. See Ira M. Millstein & Paul W. MacAvoy, The Active Board of Directors and Performance of the Large Publicly Traded Corporation, 98 Colum. L. Rev. 1283, 1288–89 (1998) (reviewing best practice guidelines).

52. Melvin A. Eisenberg, The Board of Directors and Internal Control, 19 Cardozo L. Rev. 237, 239 (1997).

53. See, e.g., Brehm v. Eisner, 746 A.2d 244, 256 (Del. 2000) ("Aspirational ideals of good corporate governance practices . . . are highly desirable, [and] often tend to benefit stockholders. . . . But they are not required by the corporation law and do not define standards of liability.").

directors of a domestic listed company to have an audit committee comprised solely of directors independent of management. This requirement grew directly out of the same ferment that prompted the ALI to begin work on the *Principles*. As the SEC noted in approving the NYSE rule change, "support for audit committees independent of management" had grown "in the wake of recent revelations of questionable and illegal corporate payments."[54]

Finding the Monitoring Model in the Sarbanes-Oxley Act

After the Enron scandal broke, its board of directors appointed a special investigative committee whose report concluded that senior managers "were enriched, in the aggregate, by tens of millions of dollars they should never have received."[55] The report laid much of the blame at the feet of Enron's board of directors, which "failed . . . in its oversight duties" with "serious consequences for Enron, its employees, and its shareholders."[56] Unfortunately, Enron was not alone. As a NYSE report opined, the post-dotcom bubble period had seen a "'meltdown' of significant companies due to failures of diligence, ethics, and controls" on the part of directors and senior managers.[57]

The Sarbanes-Oxley Act's legislative history makes clear that Congress shared these concerns. Pre-SOX Congressional investigations regarding Enron and WorldCom, for example, "found that directors had extensive social and professional ties with corporate officers and their fellow directors that compromised their ability to be impartial and undermined their ability to provide an adequate check on directors' and officers' conduct."[58] Even the most cursory glance at the text of the statute, moreover, reveals a slew of new federal rules relating to corporate governance, including director and officer duties, responsibilities of auditors, and obligations for corporate lawyers, many of which were expressly intended to empower the board of directors—especially independent directors—vis-à-vis management.[59] Many of these provisions "seem designed to reduce conflicts of interest or interpersonal pressures in

54. In re NYSE, Exchange Act Release No. 13,346, 11 SEC Docket 1945 (Mar. 9, 1977).
55. William C. Powers, Jr., et al., Report of Investigation by the Special Investigative Committee of the Board of Directors of Enron Corp. 3 (Feb. 1, 2002).
56. Id. at 22.
57. NYSE, Corporate Governance Rule Proposals Reflecting Recommendations from the NYSE Corporate Accountability and Listing Standards Committee, as Approved by the NYSE Board of Directors (August 1, 2002).
58. Lisa M. Fairfax, The Uneasy Case for the Inside Director, 96 Iowa L. Rev. 127, 149 (2010).
59. See Larry E. Ribstein, Market vs. Regulatory Responses to Corporate Fraud: A Critique of the Sarbanes-Oxley Act of 2002, 28 J. Corp. L. 1, 26 (2002) (explaining that "corporate reformers have emphasized independent directors as a way to curb insider abuse").

order to make it more likely that the directors will act as judgmental monitors of management rather than as reciprocating colleagues."[60] Still others "require directors to engage in processes that may increase their self-awareness and diligence, or because they increase the ability and incentives to directors to act diligently on behalf of public shareholders."[61]

Among the former are such mandates as a majority of independent directors on the board, an audit committee comprised solely of independent directors, new ethics codes and committee charters, and financial literacy requirements. Among the latter are provisions intended to redress the information asymmetry between management and the board, such as the new rules on the auditor-board and legal counsel-board relationships, and the board's new obligations with respect to internal controls. Viewed collectively, these provisions leave little doubt that Congress intended that the Sarbanes-Oxley Act change the dynamics that allegedly allowed independent board members to be mere management cuckolds. The monitoring model thus lies at the heart of the Sarbanes-Oxley Act.

Finding the Monitoring Model in Dodd-Frank

Unlike Sarbanes-Oxley, the Dodd-Frank backstory is not one in which failures by Main Street boards of directors figure prominently. As we saw in the preceding chapter, however, special interests centered around shareholder activists successfully hijacked the legislative process to pursue goals unrelated to the housing bubble or the credit crisis. Most of these were intended to empower shareholders at the expense of both boards and managers.

The requirement for independent compensation committees, for example, mandates long-standing best practices that emerged directly from Eisenberg's work on the monitoring model. The separation of the CEO and board chairman positions likewise is an outgrowth of that work. Perhaps most notably, Eisenberg's *The Structure of the Corporation* advocated as long ago as 1976 that shareholder access to the corporation's proxy machinery was a necessary corollary of the shareholders' undoubted right to nominate directors.[62] Dodd-Frank's proxy access provision provides the statutory framework for implementing that part of Eisenberg's model.

---

60. Robert Charles Clark, Corporate Governance Changes in the Wake of the Sarbanes-Oxley Act: A Morality Tale for the Policymakers Too, 22 Ga. St. U. L. Rev. 251, 267 (2005).

61. Id.

62. Eisenberg, supra note 36, at 114.

We will examine most of the relevant Sarbanes-Oxley and Dodd-Frank provisions in detail in subsequent chapters. Before turning to their individual merits, however, it seems appropriate to assess the changes to the board of directors' role and functions for which they serve as the capstone. Because they all rest on the intellectual foundation provided by the monitoring model, an assessment of that model is essential to evaluating the state of corporate governance after the crises.

Recall that we identified three roles for the board: monitoring, advising, and networking. There is an inherent conflict among these roles. Suppose the CEO comes to the board for advice on a proposed project. The board advises the CEO to go forward with the proposal, but the project thereafter fails miserably. The board's role in the original decision inevitably compromises its ability to evaluate and, if necessary, discipline the CEO. The monitoring model seeks to avoid this problem by giving primacy to the board's oversight role.

Yet, in doing so, the monitoring model raises its own set of problems. Do we really want to block boards from playing advisory and service roles? Can we really disentangle those roles from monitoring? Does a focus on monitoring bring its own costs?

Can Monitoring and Management Be Separated?

Eisenberg's somewhat unique theory of corporate law treats it as a species of constitutional law.[63] If we pursue the analogy, his monitoring model can be understood as a separation of powers doctrine. The board and management are individual branches of the corporate government, with clearly delineated duties, which must be kept strictly separate in order to maintain the system of checks and balances on which organizational accountability and thus organizational legitimacy depend.

In practice, however, the line between management and monitoring is fuzzy at best. This is so because while monitoring the performance of senior executives is the board's major function, that task necessarily involves activities best described as managing the corporation.

If the board terminates the CEO due to lagging corporate performance, we might call that a pure example of the monitoring function. If the board terminates the CEO because it believes the lagging performance resulted from bad policy decisions by the CEO, that action still fairly could be called monitoring but it also begins to take on managerial aspects. If finding a new CEO whose

---

63. Eisenberg, supra note 36, at 1.

policy preferences are aligned with those of the board drives the recruitment process, that action takes on an even greater managerial aspect. Providing leadership and guidance to an interim CEO during the interregnum before a new permanent CEO is found also is a common board role, but again is more a managerial than an oversight function.

Not all disciplinary actions rise to the level of termination, of course. In fact, it seems certain that most do not. This is critical because, as we have seen, the power to review is the power to decide. Accordingly, lesser punishments can become almost impossible to distinguish from management. If the board instructs the CEO to change from one policy to another, that order is just as much a management decision as when the CEO instructs a subordinate to do so.

Not only are the two roles almost impossible to untangle, but it also seems clear that performing a management role improves the board's oversight function. On the one hand, the very presence of independent directors who must give their approval to major corporate decisions should go a long way toward encouraging managers to make better and more faithful decisions.

> The mere fact that the top executives know they have to make formal presentations about key issues on a regular basis to an audience that may probe and criticize, and that has the power to remove them, elicits a great deal of valuable behavior. Executives gather facts more carefully and completely, make ideas and judgments more explicit, anticipate and deal with competing considerations, and find modes of articulation that can withstand scrutiny outside the inner circle. The consequence of all these efforts to better "explain and sell" the executive viewpoint may well be to clarify strategic thinking and improve decision making. . . . Similarly, the fact the top executives know they have to present a proposed major financing, business acquisition, or compensation plan to a board that will ask questions and has power to say "yes" or "no" will tend to limit the range of proposals that the executives dare propose and push them somewhat closer and more reliably toward plans that benefit shareholders. The impact is valuable, even if clearly imperfect.[64]

On the other, managing also makes directors better informed. When the board engages in policy and business strategy decisions, the information the board must gather to make an informed choice inevitably also is relevant to the board's overall evaluation of management's performance.

In the real world, management and monitoring thus are inextricably intertwined. As we have seen, both corporation statutes and case law assign a multitude of managerial functions to the board, with best practice assigning even more.

64. Clark, supra note 60, at 280–81.

Boards are thus involved in a host of basic corporate decisions, including entering and exiting major lines of business, approving securities offerings or major borrowing, mergers and acquisitions, payment of dividends, risk management, disclosure, auditing, and so on. In many of these cases, of course, the board is reviewing proposals made by management. Once again, however, recall that the power to review is the power to decide. The board is deciding whether the proposal has enough merit to go forward. The board's role in these decisions is thus an executive and managerial one, rather than one of mere oversight. At the end of the day, even Eisenberg concedes "the board also has important decision-making functions."[65]

The Monitoring Model Is Too Formalized

Because the monitoring model contemplates a sort of juridical role for the board, the model implies a more formal relationship between the board and management than should or does take place in the real world. Rather than focusing on hiring and firing the CEO, boards typically have a much more richly textured role. Individual directors pass concerns onto the CEO, for example, who in turn bounces ideas off board members. Indeed, even when it comes to discipline, real-world practice likely differs from the formality of the monitoring model. Rather than struggling to overcome the collective action problems that impede firing a CEO, for example, an individual director may try to obtain better performance through a private reprimand. Such seemingly mild sanctions often can be effective without the shaming aspects associated with more formalized disciplinary actions.

Monitoring Risks Morphing into Adversarial Oversight

Information is the coin of the realm in the world of corporate boards. The more information boards have, the better they are able to carry out their quasi-managerial functions such as advising senior managers, making major policy decisions, and providing networking services. More and higher quality information, of course, also empowers directors to be more effective in their oversight capacity.

The trouble is that the increasing use of independent directors—as documented in the next chapter—means that outsiders dominate modern boards. Because these outsiders lack the sort of informal information networks that employment by or routine business dealing with the firm would provide, there

---

65. Eisenberg, supra note 52, at 239.

is an inherent information asymmetry between modern boards and the top management team. As we will see, outsiders increasingly can rely on external sources of information for some of what they need, but they still remain dependent on management for much key information.

Because information can be used to management's detriment in the board's oversight capacity, however, management has an incentive to strategically use its position as an informational chokepoint. This inherent incentive for managers to withhold information from the board may force the latter to make the difficult decision of whether their firm's unique circumstances counsel weaker oversight and better managerial services by board members or stronger oversight and a less effective managerial role on the board's part. By demanding a strong monitoring role by the outside directors, however, the monitoring model impedes boards from making such tradeoffs. Instead, it pushes the board toward an adversarial relationship with management, which further incentivizes the latter to exercise discretion with respect to the information allowed to reach the board. Obviously, managers will be loath to pass on bad news. Even good news, however, will be massaged, phrased, and packaged not so as to aid the board in making decisions but to cast management in the best possible light. Ironically, the adversarial relations potentially arising from adherence to the monitoring model thus not only make it more difficult for the board to carry out its managerial functions, they also make it harder for the board to serve as an effective monitor.

The aggressive oversight contemplated by the monitoring model may have even more deleterious effects on the management-board relationship than just the perpetuation of information asymmetries. A certain amount of cognitive tension in the relationship between the board and top management is beneficial to the extent that it promotes the exercise of critical evaluative judgment by the board. Groups that are too collegial run the risk of submitting to groupthink and various other decision-making errors.[66] If aggressive monitoring fosters an adversarial relation between directors and managers, however, this beneficial form of conflict may transform into more harmful forms. At best, rigid adherence to the monitoring model may transform a collaborative and collegial relationship into one that is cold and distant. At worst, it can promote adversarial relations that result in destructive interpersonal conflict. Adversarial relations between two groups tend to encourage each group to circle the wagons and become defensive vis-à-vis the other. They encourage zero sum gamesmanship rather than collaboration. They divert energies into unproductive areas.

66. See generally Stephen M. Bainbridge, Why a Board? Group Decision Making in Corporate Governance, 55 Vand. L. Rev. 1 (2002).

The preceding assessment does not deny that the monitoring is a key board function. It does not even deny that monitoring is first among equals. Instead, it simply shows that one size does not fit all.

Firms differ. Every firm has a unique culture, traditions, and competitive environment. A start-up with inexperienced entrepreneurs needs an advisory board more than a monitoring one. A company in crisis needs board leadership more than oversight. A well-run, mature corporation staffed by managers with a penchant for hard, faithful work benefits most from a board that provides benevolent oversight and a sympathetic sounding board.

Likewise, different firms have differing arrays of accountability mechanisms. The monitoring board, after all, is not the only mechanism by which management's performance is assessed and rewarded or punished. The capital and product markets within which the firm functions, the internal and external markets for managerial services, the market for corporate control, incentive compensation systems, and auditing by outside accountants, are just some of the ways in which management is held accountable for its performance. The importance of the board's monitoring role in a given firm depends in large measure on the extent to which these other forces are allowed to function. For example, managers of a firm with strong takeover defenses are less subject to the constraining influence of the market for corporate control than are those of a firm with no takeover defenses. The former needs a strong monitoring board more than does the latter.

Accordingly, purported reforms that "reduce the board's role to monitoring and constrain a corporation's ability to choose a managing board threaten to deprive corporations of the full opportunity to utilize the board of directors as a resource."[67] Yet, that is precisely what Sarbanes-Oxley and Dodd-Frank do. None of the board provisions of either act contemplate any opportunity for private ordering. Neither contemplates allowing corporations to tweak the extent to which its unique board in its unique circumstances will allocate resources to oversight versus other functions. As a result, they qualify as quack corporate governance.

BOARDS AFTER THE CRISES

There seems little doubt that the monitoring model has influenced board behavior. In 1995, only one in eight CEOs was fired or resigned under board pressure. By 2006, however, almost a third of CEOs were terminated

---

67. Jill E. Fisch, Taking Boards Seriously, 19 Cardozo L. Rev. 265, 268 (1997).

involuntarily.[68] Over the last several decades, the average CEO tenure has decreased, which also has been attributed to more active board oversight.[69] In sum, boards of directors, "which once served largely as rubber stamps for powerful CEOs, have become more independent, more powerful, and under more pressure to dump leaders who perform poorly."[70]

At the same time, however, directors themselves recognize that one size does not fit all. Instead, they understand their role to be much broader than mere monitoring. According to a survey by the National Association of Corporate Directors (NACD), for example, boards believe their key roles include such issues as planning for CEO succession, strategic business planning, and risk management.[71]

Whatever boards do, they are spending more time doing it. The average number of board meetings per year increased from seven in 1998 to nine in 2008.[72] The average number of board committee meetings likewise increased significantly after Sarbanes-Oxley became law in 2002.[73] More meetings, of course, meant more time and, presumably, effort. A 2005 survey found that directors spent an average of more than 200 hours per year on firm business, which was a significant increase from the 100 to 150 hours per year typical of boards prior to the passage of Sarbanes-Oxley.[74] A closer look at the data is even more informative. A 2006 survey found that prior to Sarbanes-Oxley, 66 percent of board members reported they worked less than 200 hours per year on firm business. After Sarbanes-Oxley became law, 65 percent of board members reported working more than 200 hours per year and 30 percent claimed to work more than 300 hours per year on firm business.[75] At the same time, the average number of boards on which directors serve has declined post-SOX.[76]

While the data do not establish a causal relationship, they do suggest at least a correlation between the passage of Sarbanes-Oxley and the time

68. Chuck Lucier et al., The Era of the Inclusive Leader, Strategy & Bus., Summer 2007, at 3.

69. Denis B.K. Lyons, CEO Casualties: A Battlefront Report, Directors & Boards, Summer 1999, at 43.

70. Lauren Etter, Why Corporate Boardrooms Are in Turmoil, Wall St. J., Sept. 16, 2006, at A7.

71. Nat'l Ass'n Corp. Directors, Public Company Governance Survey (2008).

72. Report of the Task Force of the ABA Section of Business Law Corporate Governance Committee on Delineation of Governance Roles and Responsibilities, 65 Bus. Law. 107, 130–31 (2009) (footnotes omitted).

73. James S. Linck et al., Effects and Unintended Consequences of the Sarbanes-Oxley Act on Corporate Boards (May 16, 2006).

74. Ed Speidel & Rob Surdel, High Technology Board Compensation, Boardroom Briefing, Spring 2008, at 25.

75. Peter D. Hart Research Associates, A Survey of Corporate Directors (Feb. 2006).

76. Linck et al., supra note 73, at 16–17.

commitment required of board members. Much of the additional time appears to be devoted to oversight activities, which is consistent with the assumption that the Sarbanes-Oxley Act reinforced the monitoring model's influence. If so, the additional time and effort being expended by directors may have important costs. Recall the risk that monitoring can morph into unproductive adversarial conflict between boards and management. As Peter Wallison observes, the "congressional imprimatur" Sarbanes-Oxley put on the monitoring model therefore "may have set up an adversarial relationship between managements and boards that will, over time, impair corporate risk-taking and thus economic growth."[77]

Even if a firm's board and management maintain an appropriately balanced relationship, the additional time and effort elicited by the Sarbanes-Oxley Act may not be directed productively. Wallison argues that boards today "are more focused on compliance with standards and regulations than they are on obtaining a competitive advantage."[78] If directors in fact are spending much of their time complying with their obligations under the Sarbanes-Oxley Act and much of the rest overseeing the corporation's compliance with Sarbanes-Oxley, there is comparatively less time available for the board to spend on its traditional functions.

It thus may not be unreasonable to speculate that the unrelenting need to focus on compliance post-SOX may have contributed in some small measure to the financial crisis at the end of the decade. Financial institution directors distracted by the emphasis on internal controls and disclosure may have let slide tasks like risk management oversight. If so, the law of unintended consequences will truly have claimed an epic victim.

WHY A BOARD?

Boards of directors have long had—and still have, in many quarters—bad press, as we have seen throughout this chapter. In 2009, the SEC complained that the financial crisis had "led many to raise serious concerns about the accountability and responsiveness of some companies and boards of directors . . ."[79] Prominent Canadian corporate governance commentator Stephen Jarislowsky argues that corporate boards "have enormous responsibility for" the financial crisis of 2007–2008.[80]

77. Peter J. Wallison, Capital Punishment, Wall St. J., Nov. 4–5, 2006, at A7.
78. Id.
79. Facilitating Shareholder Director Nominations, Exchange Act Rel. No. 60,089 (June 10, 2009).
80. Janet McFarland, Jarislowsky Blames Financial Mess on Lax Governance Rules, The Globe & Mail (Toronto), Oct. 24, 2008, at B12.

Given the perception that boards too often prove passive, supine, co-opted, or otherwise in the pocket of an imperial CEO, one wonders why Congress did not consider even more drastic reforms. Professor Lawrence Mitchell, for example, proposed the direct election of CEOs by shareholders, creditors, and employees, each voting as a class.[81] Mitchell contends that the model of a "monitoring board doesn't work. . . . While there have been numerous scholarly and popular calls for board reform in the post-Enron era, most suggestions tinker around the edges of a dysfunctional institution."[82] Believing that the board cannot be reformed, Mitchell argues for giving de jure recognition to the reality that "the real seat of corporate power remains in the CEO."[83]

It's not terribly surprising that such a radical proposal did not gain traction despite the perception of widespread board failures during both of the last decade's crises. Such a major restructuring of a foundational corporate governance principle, not to mention such a major preemption of state law, doubtless would have been too big a bite for Congress to chew even in the context of the multi-thousand-page Dodd-Frank project. Yet, perhaps Congressional efforts to preserve and strengthen the institution of the board—however flawed they may be in detail—also were sound in principle.

The board of directors' utility arises out of the very fact that it places a collective body rather than a single individual at the head of the corporate hierarchy. It is striking how much emphasis the legal rules governing the board of directors put on the need for collective rather than individual action.[84] As the Restatement (Second) of Agency puts it, for example, a director "has no power of his own to act on the corporation's behalf, but only as one of a body of directors acting as a board."[85] The commentary to the MBCA's provisions on board meetings further explains:

> A well-established principle of corporate common law accepted by implication in the Model Act is that directors may act only at a meeting unless otherwise expressly authorized by statute. The underlying theory is that the consultation and exchange of views is an integral part of the functioning of the board.[86]

81. Lawrence E. Mitchell, On the Direct Election of CEOs, 32 Ohio N.U. L. Rev. 261 (2006).

82. Id. at 261.

83. Id. at 262.

84. At one time, many states in fact required that the board have at least three members, although most have eliminated that requirement. MBCA § 8.03(a) cmt.

85. Agency Restatement § 14 C cmt.

86. MBCA § 8.20 cmt. An alternative explanation is suggested by Jeffrey Gordon's persuasive demonstration that voting within a corporation is subject to Arrow's impossibility theorem, in the sense that voting on most matters of day-to-day policy would result in cyclical majorities. Although we will rely more heavily on information- and incentive-based arguments for the board's authority than does Gordon, he does present a convincing argument that corporate law's authority-based board of directors

This emphasis on collective action runs afoul of the old joke that a camel is a horse designed by a committee, yet the Model Act's "underlying theory" is pervasively reflected in the statutory rules governing corporate boards.[87] The drafters seem to have intuited that a collective is better able to carry out the board's functions than could a single autocrat.

The Board as Critical Evaluator

Research in behavioral economics has identified a number of pervasive cognitive errors that bias decision making. Several of the identified decision-making biases seem especially pertinent to managerial decision making, especially the so-called overconfidence bias. The old camel joke captures the valid empirical observation that individuals are often superior to groups when it comes to matters requiring creativity. Research on brainstorming as a decision-making process, for example, confirms that individuals working alone generate a greater number of ideas than do groups, especially when the assigned task is "fanciful" rather than "realistic."[88] Individuals often become wedded to their ideas, however, and fail to recognize flaws that others might identify. In contrast, there is a widely shared view that groups are superior at evaluative tasks. Group decision making presumably checks individual overconfidence by providing critical assessment and alternative viewpoints.

This learning confirms that a collective hierarch is preferable to an individual. Recall that the board has three basic functions: managing, monitoring, and service. At the core of the board's service role is providing advice and

system is explicable in very large measure as a device for avoiding the cycling problem by restricting owner voice. Jeffrey Gordon, Shareholder Initiative and Delegation: A Social Choice and Game Theoretic Approach to Corporate Law, 60 U. Cin. L. Rev. 347 (1991).

87. Many of these housekeeping rules doubtless seem formalistic or even a little silly, but the requirement that the board act only after meeting as a collective body actually has a sound economic basis. Work by experimental psychologists has found that group decision making, under certain circumstances, can be superior to decision making by individuals. Where evaluation of complex problems requiring the exercise of critical judgment is concerned, the evidence is clear that the performance of a group will be superior to that of the group's average member. This result has been confirmed by experiments requiring performance of a wide variety of tasks. See, e.g., Larry K. Michaelsen et al., A Realistic Test of Individual Versus Group Consensus Decision Making, 74 J. App. Psych. 834 (1989) (test taking in team learning settings); Marjorie E. Shaw, A Comparison of Individuals and Small Groups in the Rational Solution of Complex Problems, 44 Am. J. Psych. 491 (1932) (puzzle solving); see generally Gayle W. Hill, Group Versus Individual Performance: Are N + 1 Heads Better than One?, 91 Psych. Bull. 517 (1982).

88. Gayle W. Hill, Group Versus Individual Performance: Are N + 1 Heads Better than One?, 91 Psych. Bull. 517, 527 (1982).

counsel to the senior management team, especially the CEO. At the intersection of the board's service and monitoring roles is the provision of alternative points of view. The board's policy-making role typically consists of evaluating and selecting among a range of options presented by subordinates, rather than developing such plans in the first instance. Accordingly, all of the board's basic functions emphasize the exercise of critical evaluative judgment, which is precisely where groups are stronger than individuals.

The Board as an Adaptive Response to Bounded Rationality

Vesting decision-making authority in a group rather than a single individual is a high value-added adaptive response to the problem of bounded rationality. Decision making requires the use of scarce resources for four purposes: (1) observation, or the gathering of information; (2) memory, or the storage of information; (3) computation, or the manipulation of information; and (4) communication, or the transmission of information.[89] How do groups minimize these transaction costs vis-à-vis individual decision makers? Multiple sources of information may make it less costly to gather information, but it seems unlikely that directors qua directors do much to facilitate the observation process. Any such savings, moreover, likely are offset by increased communication costs. By decentralizing both access to information and decision-making power, group decision making requires additional resources and imposes additional delays on the decision-making process.

The relevant advantages of group decision making therefore likely arise with respect to either memory and/or computation. As to the former, groups develop a sort of collective memory that consists not only of the sum of individual memories, but also an awareness of who knows what. Consequently, institutional memory is superior when the organization is structured as a set of teams rather than as a mere aggregate of individuals. There is some laboratory evidence, moreover, that the collective memory of groups leads to higher quality output.[90] Group members, for example, seem to specialize in memorizing specific aspects of complex repetitive tasks.

As to the relationship between group decision making and computation-based costs, an actor can economize limited cognitive resources in two ways. First, by adopting institutional governance structures designed to promote more efficient decision making. Second, by invoking shortcuts; i.e., heuristic

89. Roy Radner, Bounded Rationality, Indeterminacy, and the Theory of the Firm, 106 Econ. J. 1360, 1363 (1996).

90. Susan G. Cohen & Diane E. Bailey, What Makes Teams Work: Group Effectiveness Research from the Shop Floor to the Executive Suite, 23 J. Mgmt. 239, 259 (1997).

problem-solving, decision-making processes. Here we focus on the former approach, positing that group decision making provides a mechanism for aggregating the inputs of multiple individuals with differing knowledge, interests, and skills. Numerous studies suggest that groups benefit from both by pooling of information and from providing opportunities for one member to correct another's errors.[91] In the corporate context, the board of directors thus emerged as an institutional governance mechanism to constrain the deleterious effect of bounded rationality on the organizational decision-making process.

The Board as a Constraint on Agency Costs

Individuals are subject to the temptations to shirk or self-deal. The internal dynamics of group governance, however, constrain self-dealing and shirking by individual team members. In this regard, group decision making has a bi-directional structure. In the vertical dimension, a group may be superior to an individual autocrat as a monitor of subordinates in the corporate hierarchy. In the horizontal dimension, intra-group governance structures help constrain shirking and self-dealing at the apex of the hierarchy.

Vertical monitoring. Suppose an individual autocrat rather than a board of directors capped the corporate hierarchy. Under such circumstances, a bilateral vertical monitoring problem arises. On the one hand, the autocrat must monitor his/her subordinates. On the other hand, someone must monitor the autocrat. In theory, if corporate law vested ultimate decision-making authority in individual autocrats, their subordinates could monitor chief executives. Economist Eugene Fama contends, for example, that lower-level managers monitor more senior managers.[92]

It seems unlikely, however, that such upstream monitoring happens often or in a sufficiently systematic way to provide a meaningful constraint on upper management. In any case, this monitoring mechanism does not take full advantage of specialization. Fama and Jensen elsewhere point out that one response to agency costs is to separate "decision management"—initiating and implementing decisions—from "decision control"—ratifying and monitoring decisions.[93] Such separation is a defining characteristic of the central

---

91. See Gayle W. Hill, Group Versus Individual Performance: Are N + 1 Heads Better than One?, 91 Psych. Bull. 517, 533 (1982).

92. See, e.g., Eugene F. Fama, Agency Problems and the Theory of the Firm, 88 J. Pol. Econ. 288, 293 (1980).

93. Eugene F. Fama & Michael C. Jensen, Separation of Ownership and Control, 26 J. L. & Econ. 301, 315 (1983).

office typical of M-form corporations.[94] The monitoring mechanisms described herein could be accomplished through a simple pyramidal hierarchy of the sort found in U-form corporations. The M-form corporation adds to this structure a rationalization of decision-making authority in which the central office has certain tasks and the operating units have others, which allows for more effective monitoring through specialization, sharper definition of purpose, and savings in informational costs.[95] In particular, the central office's key decision makers—the board of directors and top management—specialize in decision control. Because low- and mid-level managers specialize in decision management, expecting them to monitor more senior managers thus requires them to perform a task for which they are poorly suited.

A different critique of Fama's hypothesis is suggested by evidence with respect to meeting behavior. In mixed status groups, higher status persons talk more than lower status members. Managers, for example, talk more than subordinates in business meetings.[96] Such disparities result in higher status group members being more inclined to propound initiatives and wielding greater influence over the group's ultimate decision. Consequently, a core board function is providing a set of status equals for top managers.[97] As such, corporate law's insistence on the formal superiority of the board to management begins to make sense. To the extent law shapes social norms, admittedly a contested proposition, corporate law empowers the board to more effectively constrain top management by creating a de jure status relationship favoring the board.

94. The term "M-form corporation" refers to the so-called multidivisional method of organizing a business enterprise. The enterprise typically consists of multiple businesses in related areas operating within a larger organizational framework and often results from a strategy of acquiring diversified but related businesses. Within M-form corporations, operating activities tend to be decentralized down to the divisional level, while supervisory and service operations are centralized at the corporate level. An M-form corporation may be organized either as a formal holding structure with a parent and multiple subsidiary corporations or as an integrated enterprise contained within a single corporation in which subordinate operating units are organized as divisions rather than as separate subsidiary corporations. Most economists believe that M-form organizations tend to outperform the older U-form system of organization. See, e.g., Oliver E. Williamson, Markets and Hierarchies: Analysis and Antitrust Implications 135–38 (1975). In contrast, the term "U-form corporation" is a shorthand form of the term "unitary corporation." Such firms are organized into functional, rather than operational, departments. Id. at 133. Hence, for example, all of the enterprise's sales functions are concentrated into a single division. Id.

95. Oliver E. Williamson, The Economic Institutions of Capitalism 320 (1985).

96. Sara Kiesler & Lee Sproull, Group Decision Making and Communication Technology, 52 Org. Behav. & Human Decision Processes 96, 109–110 (1992).

97. Robert J. Haft, The Effect of Insider Trading Rules on the Internal Efficiency of the Large Corporation, 80 Mich. L. Rev. 1051, 1061 (1982) (describing the board as "a peer group—a collegial body of equals, with the chief executive as the prima inter pares").

Horizontal monitoring. Who watches the watchers? Because all members of the corporate hierarchy—including our hypothetical autocrat—are themselves agents of the firm with incentives to shirk, a mechanism to monitor their productivity and reduce their incentive to shirk must also be created or one ends up with a never ending series of monitors monitoring lower level monitors. As we've seen, Alchian and Demsetz offered a model that solved this problem by vesting the ultimate monitor with the residual claim on the firm's assets. Unfortunately, although common stockholders are the corporation's residual claimants, they also are essentially powerless to meaningfully monitor management behavior.

Consequently, corporate law and governance must provide alternatives to monitoring by the residual claimants. A hierarchy of individuals whose governance structures contemplate only vertical monitoring, such as that hypothesized above, cannot resolve the problem of who watches the watchers. By adding the dimension of horizontal monitoring, however, placing a group at the apex of the hierarchy provides a solution to that problem. Where an individual autocrat would have substantial freedom to shirk or self-deal, the internal dynamics of group governance constrain self-dealing and shirking by individual team members and, perhaps, even by the group as a whole. Within a production team, for example, mutual monitoring and peer pressure provide a coercive backstop for a set of interpersonal relationships founded on trust and other noncontractual social norms.[98] Of particular relevance here are effort and cooperation norms.[99]

While the old adage opines "familiarity breeds contempt," personal proximity to others in fact deeply affects behavior. As people become closer, their behavior tends to improve: "something in us makes it all but impossible to justify our acts as mere self-interest whenever those acts are seen by others as

---

98. Production teams are defined conventionally as "a collection of individuals who are interdependent in their tasks, who share responsibility for outcomes, [and] who see themselves and who are seen by others as an intact social entity embedded in one or more larger social systems. . . ." Susan G. Cohen and Diane E. Bailey, What Makes Teams Work: Group Effectiveness Research from the Shop Floor to the Executive Suite, 23 J. Mgmt. 239, 241 (1997). See also Kenneth L. Bettenhausen, Five Years of Groups Research: What have we Learned and What Needs to be Addressed?, 17 J. Mgmt. 345, 346 (1991) (defining teams as "intact social systems that perform one or more tasks within an organizational context"). Williamson's industrial organization matrix identifies two forms such teams may take: primitive and relational. In both, team members perform nonseparable tasks. They are distinguished by the degree of firm-specific human capital possessed by such members. In primitive teams, workers have little such capital; in relational teams, they have substantial amounts. Most boards of directors probably qualify as relational teams.

99. Social norms are relevant to other aspects of decision making besides agency costs. Group norms of reciprocity, for example, facilitate the process of achieving consensus within groups.

violating a moral principle"; rather, "[w]e want our actions to be seen by others—and by ourselves—as arising out of appropriate motives."[100] Small groups strengthen this instinct in several ways. First, they provide a network of reputational and other social sanctions that shape incentives. Because membership in close-knit groups satisfies the human need for belongingness, the threat of expulsion gives the group a strong sanction by which to enforce compliance with group norms. Because close-knit groups involve a continuing relationship, the threat of punishment in future interactions deters the sort of cheating possible in one-time transactions.[101] Because people care about how they are perceived by those close to them, communal life provides a cloud of witnesses whose good opinion we value. We hesitate to disappoint those people and thus strive to comport ourselves in accordance with communal norms. Effort norms will thus tend to discourage board members from simply going through the motions, but instead to devote greater cognitive effort to their tasks. Finally, there is a transaction costs economics explanation for the importance of closeness in trust relationships. Close-knit groups know a lot about one another, which reduces monitoring costs and thus further encourages compliance with group norms. Members of close-knit groups therefore tend to internalize group norms.

Group decision making thus is a powerful constraint on agency costs. It creates a set of high-powered incentives to comply with both effort and cooperation norms. This analysis thus goes a long way toward explaining the formalistic rules of state corporate law governing board decision making.[102]

100. James Q. Wilson, What is Moral and How do we Know It?, Commentary, June 1993, at 37, 39. See also Kenneth L. Bettenhausen, Five Years of Groups Research: What have we Learned and What Needs to be Addressed?, 17 J. Mgmt. 345, 348 (1991).

101. See generally Oliver E. Williamson, The Economic Institutions of Capitalism 48 (1985) ("Informal peer group pressures can be mobilized to check malingering. . . . The most casual involves cajoling or ribbing. If this fails, rational appeals to persuade the deviant to conform are employed. The group then resorts to penalties by withdrawing the social benefits that affiliation affords. Finally, overt coercion and ostracism are resorted to.").

102. The case should not be overstated. Cohesive groups are subject to inherent cognitive biases that limit their effectiveness. A widely-cited example is the so-called risky shift phenomenon. There seems to be a polarizing effect in group decision making, so that post-discussion consensus is more extreme than the individual pre-test results. See Norbert L. Kerr, Group Decision Making at a Multialternative Task: Extremity, Interfaction Distance, Pluralities, and Issue Importance, 52 Org. Behav. and Human Decision Processes 64 (1992). The most significant group bias for our purposes, however, is the "group think" phenomenon. Highly cohesive groups with strong civility and cooperation norms value consensus more greatly than they do a realistic appraisal of alternatives. Irving Janis, Victims of Groupthink (1972). In such groups, groupthink is an adaptive response to the stresses generated by challenges to group solidarity. To avoid those stresses, groups may strive for unanimity even at the expense of quality decision making. To the extent groupthink promotes the development of social norms, it facilitates the board's monitoring function (see the next section).

Summary

Replacing the board of directors with a de jure Imperial CEO was never in the cards. To the contrary, both Sarbanes-Oxley and Dodd-Frank made efforts to strengthen the hand of the board vis-à-vis the CEO and the rest of the top management team. Given the superiority of group over individual decision makers with respect to the sorts of tasks assigned to boards, the goal is commendable. Unfortunately, the means by which both Sarbanes-Oxley and Dodd-Frank sought to do so often proved seriously flawed. The over-emphasis on the board's monitoring function is just the beginning, as subsequent chapters will detail.

It may also be relevant to other board functions, such as resource acquisition, to the extent that it promotes a sort of esprit de corps. Yet, the downside is an erosion in the quality of decision making. The desire to maintain group cohesion trumps the exercise of critical judgment. Adverse consequences of groupthink thus include not examining alternatives, being selective in gathering information, and failing to be either self-critical or evaluative of others. Studies of meeting behavior, for example, conclude that people tend to prefer options that have obvious popularity. Sara Kiesler & Lee Sproull, Group Decision Making and Communication Technology, 52 Org. Behav. & Human Decision Processes 96 (1992). In the corporate setting, board culture often encourages groupthink. Boards emphasize politeness and courtesy at the expense of oversight. CEOs can foster and channel groupthink through their power to control information flows, reward consensus, and discourage reelection of troublemakers. The groupthink phenomenon therefore demands close attention with respect to a variety of corporate governance issues, but is most directly relevant to the board composition debate discussed below.

CHAPTER 3
Director Independence

As the monitoring model came to dominate thinking about the board's role, the board's composition inevitably came to the fore. A board comprised of insiders is poorly positioned to monitor the CEO. Research on group decision making shows that in mixed status groups, higher status persons talk more than lower status members. Managers, for example, talk more than subordinates in business meetings. Such disparities result in higher status group members being more inclined to propound initiatives and having greater influence over the group's ultimate decision.[1] Group dynamics thus help ensure the CEO's dominance over inside directors. As a practical matter, moreover, the CEO typically served as the chairman or chairwoman of the board, giving him or her substantial control over both the selection of new directors and the board's agenda. Not surprisingly, director independence therefore is a long-standing goal of corporate reformers, especially those affiliated with the monitoring model school of thought.

Even before the Sarbanes-Oxley Act and the concomitant stock exchange listing standard changes mandated that most public companies have a majority independent board, the increasing emphasis on monitoring contributed to a long-term decline in the percentage of insiders on boards, as shown in Table 3.1.

In the wake of the crises of the last decade, the trend toward board independence accelerated as Congress and other regulators appointed independent directors as the capitalist cavalry and charged them with riding to the system's rescue:

> The percentage of independent directors has grown from 78 percent in 1998 to 82 percent in 2008. (These statistics understate the magnitude of this change, given enhanced rigor in the definition of "independence.")

1. Sara Kiesler & Lee Sproul, Group Decision Making and Communication Technology, 52 Org. Beh. & Human Decision Processes 96 (1992).

Table 3.1: RATIO OF INSIDE TO OUTSIDE
DIRECTORS 1950–2000

Year	Mean Percentage of Inside Directors	Decade to Decade % Change
1950	49%	n/a
1955	47%	
1960	43%	–12%
1965	42%	
1970	41%	–5%
1975	39%	
1980	33%	–20%
1985	30%	
1990	26%	–21%
1995	21%	
2000	16%	–38%

Source: Jeffrey N. Gordon, The Rise of Independent Directors in the United States, 1950–2005: Of Shareholder Value and Stock Market Prices, 59 Stanford Law Review 1465, 1473 n.9 (2007). Used by Permission.

Independent directors now run the nomination process (pursuant to exchange listing requirements), often with the assistance of a director search consultant, leading to increased reliance on external sources for recruiting directors. In 2008, 60 percent of new director nominations came through a search firm, 21 percent came from independent directors, and the CEO recommended 9 percent, down from 14 percent in 2005.

Fewer active CEOs and other similarly senior executives now serve on boards, with only 31 percent of new independent directors also holding positions as active CEOs, COOs, chairmen, presidents, or vice chairmen, down from 49 percent in 1998.[2]

Director independence is the corporate governance success story of the decade. Yet, while conventional wisdom regards director independence with near fetishistic devotion, close examination suggests that independence is no panacea for the ills of corporate governance. The increasingly one-size-fits-all nature of the law of director independence, moreover, is almost certainly less desirable than an enabling approach allowing firms to self-select optimal degrees of director independence.

2. Report of the Task Force of the ABA Section of Business Law Corporate Governance Committee on Delineation of Governance Roles and Responsibilities, 65 Bus. Law. 107, 130–31 (2009) (footnotes omitted).

State corporation statutes are silent on the issue of board composition. Issues such as board size, director qualifications, and independence are left to private ordering. If state statutory law were all that mattered, firms would thus be free to select the board structure and composition optimal to their unique circumstances.

The state common law of corporations does provide some incentives for corporations to include at least some independent directors on the board. It has long been the case, for example, that approval of related party and other conflicted interest transactions by vote of a majority of the disinterested and independent directors effectively immunizes such transactions from judicial review by invoking the defendant-friendly business judgment rule as the standard of review.[3] In connection with going private transactions initiated by a controlling shareholder, the Delaware Supreme Court called upon boards to create "an independent negotiating committee of its outside directors to deal with [the buyer] at arm's length."[4] Indeed, the Court went on to equate "fairness in this context" to the conduct that might be expected from "a theoretical, wholly independent, board of directors acting upon the matter before them." Similarly, with respect to antitakeover defenses, the Court has held that the validity of such defenses is "materially enhanced . . . where, as here, a majority of the board favoring the proposal consisted of outside independent directors."[5] Taken together with similar decisions in other areas of corporate law, these judicially created safe harbors provide substantial incentives for both boards and managers to favor director independence.

Having said that, however, state law typically is far more concerned with director disinterestedness than independence. Consider, for example, the Delaware law on excusal of demand in shareholder derivative litigation. In *Grimes v. Donald*,[6] the Delaware Supreme Court identified three reasons for excusing demand: "(1) a majority of the board has a material financial or familial interest; (2) a majority of the board is incapable of acting independently for some other reason such as domination or control; or (3) the underlying transaction is not the product of a valid exercise of business judgment."[7] As to the first prong, directors are interested if they have a personal financial stake in

3. Marciano v. Nakash, 535 A.2d 400, 405 n.3 (Del. 1987) (opining that "approval by fully-informed disinterested directors under section 144(a)(1) . . . permits invocation of the business judgment rule and limits judicial review to issues of gift or waste with the burden of proof upon the party attacking the transaction").
4. Weinberger v. UOP, Inc., 457 A.2d 701, 709 n.7 (Del. 1983).
5. Moran v. Household Intern., Inc., 500 A.2d 1346, 1356 (Del. 1985).
6. 673 A.2d 1207 (Del. 1996).
7. Id. at 1216.

the challenged transaction or otherwise would be materially affected by the board's actions. Consequently, for example, the Delaware Chancery Court excused demand on director interest grounds where five of nine directors approved a stock appreciation rights plan likely to benefit them.[8]

Although the second prong is framed in terms of independence, it is not concerned with whether a director is generically independent of management. While being employed by the corporation would preclude a director from being deemed independent for all purposes under Sarbanes-Oxley and Dodd-Frank, for example, it does not preclude a finding that the director is independent under state law. This is so, in part, because state law views independence from a transactional perspective rather than one of status. The other critical difference is that state law links independence to self-interest in the underlying transaction. Accordingly, demand is not excused simply because the plaintiff has named a majority of the board as defendants.[9] Indeed, it is not enough even to allege that a majority of the board approved of, acquiesced in, or participated in the challenged transaction.[10] In other words, merely being named as defendants or participants does not render the board incapable, as a matter of law, of objectively evaluating a pre-suit demand and, accordingly, does not excuse such a demand. Instead, demand typically is excused under this prong only if a majority of the board was dominated or controlled by someone with a personal financial stake in the transaction.[11]

State law thus fails to satisfy the more exacting standards of independence pursued by reformers like Ralph Nader or Melvin Eisenberg. Instead, the reformers want independence to be defined by status. In general, any material relationship between the director and the corporation or its top management team would be regarded as disabling the director from being deemed independent as they wished it to be defined.

8. Bergstein v. Texas Int'l Co., 453 A.2d 467, 471 (Del. Ch. 1982).

9. See Rales v. Blasband, 634 A.2d 927, 936 (Del. 1993) (holding that the "mere threat" of personal liability in connection with the litigation is not enough, although a "substantial likelihood" of personal liability in connection therewith will excuse demand).

10. Aronson v. Lewis, 473 A.2d 805, 817 (Del. 1984) ("In Delaware mere directorial approval of a transaction, absent particularized facts supporting a breach of fiduciary duty claim, or otherwise establishing the lack of independence or disinterestedness of a majority of the directors, is insufficient to excuse demand . . .").

11. See id. at 814 ("where officers and directors are under an influence which sterilizes their discretion, they cannot be considered proper persons to conduct litigation on behalf of the corporation").

DIRECTOR INDEPENDENCE IN THE STOCK EXCHANGE LISTING STANDARDS AND THE SARBANES-OXLEY ACT

The Sarbanes-Oxley Act did relatively little that was self-executing to reform boards of directors. Besides some minor tweaking of rules like those governing disclosure of stock transactions by directors and so on, the only substantive changes worked by the Act itself dealt with the audit committee of the board of directors.

Instead, Congress and the SEC left the heavy lifting on board reform to the stock exchanges. All three major exchanges—the NYSE, NASDAQ, and the American Stock Exchange (AMEX)—amended their corporate governance listing requirements to require that a majority of the members of the board of directors of most listed companies must be independent of management. All three also adopted new rules defining independence using very strict, bright-line rules. Finally, all three significantly expanded the duties and powers of independent directors.

The Importance of Exchange Listing Standards

Listing of a company's equity securities for trading on a prestigious stock market, such as the NYSE, confers significant benefits on the company and its management. The greater liquidity of listed securities relative to those sold in the over-the counter (OTC) market reduces listed issuers' cost of capital.[12] Listing also confers considerable prestige on the firm and its managers. Listed companies therefore desire to remain so, while many unlisted firms pursue eligibility for listing as their primary goal. By virtue of their power to set listing standards with which listed companies must comply, the exchanges thus wield considerable power over the governance of public corporations. Indeed, in many respects, many of the mandatory details of corporate governance now come from exchange listing standards rather than the more vague and enabling state law.

Listing standards are subject to approval by the SEC under § 19(b) of the Securities Exchange Act of 1934, as amended, 15 U.S.C. § 78s (2001). Per § 19(b)(2), however, the SEC's powers with respect to corporate governance-related listing standards are quite limited. The SEC "shall approve a proposed" listing standard if the standard "is consistent with the requirements" of the

---

12. See Gary C. Sanger & John J. McConnell, Stock Exchange Listings, Firm Value, and Security Market Efficiency: The Impact of NASDAQ, 21 J. Fin. & Quant. Anal. 1 (1986); Note, Stock Exchange Listing Agreements as a Vehicle for Corporate Governance, 129 U. Pa. L. Rev. 1427, 1437 n.48 (1981) (citing unpublished SEC study).

Exchange Act and the rules thereunder. As nothing in the Exchange Act prohibits an exchange from regulating corporate governance through its listing standards, proposals to do so are not inconsistent with the Act. Hence, because nothing in the statute contemplates any form of merit review, the SEC effectively must rubberstamp such proposals.[13] Having said that, however, by virtue of the unique relationship between the SEC and the exchanges, the Commission naturally exercises considerable informal influence over exchange rule making. The late Donald Schwartz aptly referred to this influence as the SEC's "raised eyebrow" power.[14]

The NYSE's Pre-SOX Listing Standards

The NYSE long required that that all listed companies have at least three independent directors.[15] A director was treated as independent unless, inter alia, (1) the director was employed by the corporation or its affiliates in the past three years, (2) the director had an immediate family member who, during the past three years, was employed by the corporation or its affiliates as an executive officer, (3) the director had a direct business relationship with the company, or (4) the director was a partner, controlling shareholder, or executive officer of an organization that had a business relationship with the corporation, unless the corporation's board determined in its business judgment that the relationship did not interfere with the director's exercise of independent judgment.

The NYSE's pre-SOX listing standards also required that listed companies have an audit committee comprised solely of independent directors. The committee had to have at least three members, all of whom must be "financially

13. See Stephen M. Bainbridge, Revisiting the One Share/One Vote Controversy: The Exchange's Uniform Voting Rights Policy, 22 Sec. Reg. L.J. 175, 183 (1994). For an argument that the exchanges' authority to adopt corporate governance listing standards is uncertain, at best, and may be limited to provisions that "substantively relate to the operation of securities markets so as to promote investor confidence and provide reliability," however, see American Bar Association Section of Business Law Committee on Federal Regulation of Securities, Special Study on Market Structure, Listing Standards and Corporate Governance 70–71 (May 17, 2002) available at http://www.abanet.org/buslaw/fedsec/nosearch/20020517.pdf [hereinafter cited as ABA Committee Report].
14. Donald E. Schwartz, Federalism and Corporate Governance, 45 Ohio St. L.J. 545, 571 (1984). In the mid-1990s, the SEC used that power to coerce the exchanges into adopting uniform voting rights listing standards. See Stephen M. Bainbridge, Revisiting the One-Share/One-Vote Controversy: The Exchanges' Uniform Voting Rights Policy, 22 Sec. Reg. L.J. 175, 183–86 (1994) (criticizing the role played by SEC Chairman Arthur Levitt in the exchanges' adoption of voting rights listing standards).
15. NYSE, Listed Company Manual § 303.01, http://nysemanual.nyse.com/lcm/

literate." At least one committee member had to have expertise in accounting or financial management.

As the Enron crisis was peaking, the NYSE appointed a blue ribbon panel of Wall Street Brahmins to evaluate whether the new environment called for changes in the exchange's corporate governance listing standards. The panel reported back with a number of proposed new governance standards, including a mandate that independent directors comprise a majority of any listed corporation's board of directors.[16] The exchange forwarded the proposals to the SEC for approval. At that point, however, the listing standards proposal was caught up in the larger legislative process surrounding Sarbanes-Oxley and final action on the proposal was deferred until that process was completed.

The Sarbanes-Oxley Act, Independent Directors, and the Exchanges

The Sarbanes-Oxley Act expressly addressed the question of board composition only in § 301, which required the SEC to require that the exchanges adopt new rules for audit committees. The specified duties and powers of that committee will be addressed in chapter 5. Suffice it for present purposes to note that § 301 requires each member of the audit committee to be independent, which was defined therein to mean that the director could not "(i) accept any consulting, advisory, or other compensatory fee from the issuer; or (ii) be an affiliated person of the issuer or any subsidiary thereof."

Section 301's focus on the audit committee is broadly consistent with the general thrust of the Sarbanes-Oxley Act, which as a whole is mainly concerned with accounting and auditing issues. Congress was well aware of the pending exchange rule-making proposals and presumably was content to leave the details to the SEC and the exchanges so long as the final listing standards met the specified minimum requirements regarding the audit committee. In November 2003, the process concluded when the SEC gave final approval to revised exchange listing standards on director independence.[17]

The Majority Independent Board

As approved by the SEC, the NYSE listing standards now require that all listed companies "must have a majority of independent directors.[18] In addition, as we will see below, the NYSE has mandated the use of several board committees

---

16. Report of the NYSE Corporate Accountability and Listing Standards Committee 6 (June 6, 2002) [hereinafter cited as NYSE Committee Report].

17. Exchange Act Rel. No. 48,745 (Nov. 4, 2003).

18. NYSE Listed Company Manual § 303A.01.

consisting of independent directors. Finally, the NYSE's Listed Company Manual provides that: "To empower non-management directors to serve as a more effective check on management, the non-management directors of each listed company must meet at regularly scheduled executive sessions without management."[19] The listed company's Form 10-K must disclose the identity of the independent director who chairs the mandatory executive sessions. Although the rule does not indicate how many times per year the outside directors must meet to satisfy this requirement, emerging best practice suggests that there should be such a meeting held in conjunction with every regularly scheduled meeting of the entire board of directors.

The NASDAQ and AMEX standards are substantially similar. One wrinkle is that NASDAQ expressly states an expectation that executive sessions of the outside directors will be held at least twice a year. Note that all three exchanges exempt controlled companies—those in which a shareholder or group of shareholders acting together control 50 percent or more of the voting power of the company's stock—from the obligation to have a majority independent board.

Who Is Independent?

As we saw, Delaware state corporate law asks a very simple question to determine whether a director is independent: to wit, whether "through personal or other relationships the directors are beholden to" management.[20] In contrast, the exchange listing standards use multi-part bright-line standards to determine whether a director is independent. The NYSE, for example, has five such standards looking at the relationships between the listed company and a director and his immediate family members. A director will not be independent, for example, if that director "is, or has been within the last three years, an employee of the listed company, or an immediate family member is, or has been within the last three years, an executive officer, of the listed company."[21] The NASDAQ and AMEX have substantially similar tests.

The trouble with economic tests is that they fail to capture the myriad of other ways in which individuals can be biased toward others. Many nominally independent directors have full-time jobs as executives at other firms or as partners in business service companies such as law firms or financial institutions. Directors tend to be white males, educated at top 20 schools, and share a host of other social ties. When their fellow directors get into trouble, the

19. Id., § 303A.03.
20. Aronson v. Lewis, 473 A.2d 805, 815 (Del. 1984).
21. NYSE Listed Company Manual § 302A.02(b)(i).

reaction of these nominally independent directors may be one of leniency, motivated by a "'there but for the grace of God go I' empathy."[22]

The problem is not just one of undue empathy, however. Social ties have a deterrent effect on director behavior that can be just as important, if not more so, than economic relationships. As Delaware Vice Chancellor Leo Strine observes:

> To be direct, corporate directors are generally the sort of people deeply enmeshed in social institutions. Such institutions have norms, expectations that, explicitly and implicitly, influence and channel the behavior of those who participate in their operation. Some things are "just not done," or only at a cost, which might not be so severe as a loss of position, but may involve a loss of standing in the institution. In being appropriately sensitive to this factor, our law also cannot assume—absent some proof of the point—that corporate directors are, as a general matter, persons of unusual social bravery, who operate heedless to the inhibitions that social norms generate for ordinary folk.[23]

Unfortunately, operationalizing this insight proves quite problematic.

The NYSE definition of independence perhaps seeks to address this problem of structural bias by providing that "[n]o director qualifies as "independent" unless the board of directors affirmatively determines that the director has no material relationship with the listed company. . . ."[24] The commentary to that section explains that:

> It is not possible to anticipate, or explicitly to provide for, all circumstances that might signal potential conflicts of interest, or that might bear on the materiality of a director's relationship to a listed company. . . . Accordingly, it is best that boards making "independence" determinations broadly consider all relevant facts and circumstances. In particular, when assessing the materiality of a director's relationship with the listed company, the board should consider the issue not merely from the standpoint of the director, but also from that of persons or organizations with which the director has an affiliation. Material relationships can include commercial, industrial, banking, consulting, legal, accounting, charitable and familial relationships, among others. . . .

The commentary thus contemplates an inquiry broad enough to encompass social ties as well as economic relationships ("broadly consider all relevant facts"). Yet, one suspects such inquiries tend to be superficial, at best,

---

22. Zapata Corp. v. Maldonado, 430 A.2d 779, 787 (Del. 1981).
23. In re Oracle Corp. Derivative Litigation, 824 A.2d 917, 938 (Del. Ch. 2003).
24. NYSE Listed Company Manual § 303A.02(a).

and mainly focused on objective factors rather than the sort of soft biases of social ties.

The key problem, of course, is that the board of directors rather than some outside impartial adjudicator is making the independence determination. These directors presumably have at least ties of class, and probably social relations, among themselves and with the candidate whose independence is to be determined. The finder of fact is thus structurally biased against making a finding of structural bias. No workable solution to this problem has been forthcoming.

Board Committees

The NYSE Listed Company Manual mandates the establishment of three committees of the board of directors: a Nominating and Corporate Governance Committee (§ 303A.04), a Compensation Committee (§ 303A.05), and an Audit Committee (§ 303A.06). All three must be comprised solely of independent directors. As such, they significantly extend the mandate for a board dominated by directors independent of management. We will examine the work of all three committees in the chapters that follow.

THE UNCERTAIN CASE FOR DIRECTOR INDEPENDENCE

As we have seen, the board of directors has three basic functions. First, while boards rarely are involved in day-to-day operational decision making, most boards have at least some managerial functions. Second, the board provides networking and other services. Finally, the board monitors and disciplines top management.

Independence is potentially relevant to all three board functions. As to the former two, outside directors provide both their own expertise and interlocks with diverse contact networks. As to the latter, at least according to conventional wisdom, board independence is an important device for constraining agency costs. On close examination, however, neither rationale for board independence justifies the sort of one size fits all mandate adopted by the exchanges at the behest of Congress and the SEC.

Independence, Interlocks, and Decision Making

Putting outside directors on the board can create valuable relationships with a variety of potential strategic partners. This is relevant not only to the board's resource gathering function, but also to its monitoring and service functions. Complex business decisions require knowledge in such areas as accounting, finance, management, and law. Providing access to such knowledge can be seen as part of the board's resource gathering function. Outside board members may either possess such specialized knowledge themselves or have access to credible external sources thereof.

Reliance on outside specialists is a rational response to bounded rationality. The expert in a field makes the most of his limited capacity to absorb and master information by limiting the amount of information that must be processed by limiting the breadth of the field in which the expert specializes. As applied to the corporate context, more diverse boards with strong outsider representation likely contain more specialists, and therefore should get greater benefits from specialization.[25]

Having said that, however, a full-time senior employee has other informational advantages over outsiders who devote but a small portion of their time and effort to the firm. At the minimum, the presence of outsiders on the board increases decision-making costs simply because the process takes longer. Outsiders by definition need more information and are likely to take longer to persuade than are insiders.[26] More subtly, and perhaps more importantly, long-term employees make significant investments in firm-specific human capital. Any employee who advances to senior management levels necessarily invests considerable time and effort in learning how to do his or her job more effectively. Much of this knowledge will be specific to the employee's firm, such as when other firms do not do comparable work or the employee's firm has a unique corporate culture. In either case, the longer the employee works for the firm, the more firm-specific the employee's human capital becomes. Such an employee is likely to make better decisions for the firm than an outsider, even assuming equal levels of information relating to the decision

---

25. Conversely, however, note that, because their decisions are publicly observable, board members have a strong incentive to defer to expert opinion. Because even a good decision maker is subject to the proverbial "act of God," the market for reputation evaluates decision makers by looking at both the outcome and the action before forming a judgment. If a bad outcome occurs, but the action was consistent with approved expert opinion, the hit to the decision maker's reputation is reduced. In effect, by deferring to specialists, a decision maker operating under conditions of bounded rationality is buying insurance against a bad outcome. In a collegial, multi-actor setting, the potential for log rolling further encourages deference. A specialist in a given field is far more likely to have strong feelings about the outcome of a particular case than a non-expert. By deferring to the specialist, the non-expert may win the specialist's vote in other cases as to which the non-expert has a stronger stake. Such log rolling need not be explicit, although it doubtless is at least sometimes, but rather can be a form of the tit-for-tat cooperative game. In board decision making, deference thus invokes a norm of reciprocation that allows the non-expert to count on the specialist's vote on other matters.

26. Michael P. Dooley & E. Norman Veasey, The Role of the Board in Derivative Litigation: Delaware Law and the Current ALI Proposals Compared, 44 Bus. Law. 503, 533 (1989).

at hand. The insider can put the decision in a broader context, seeing the relationships and connections it has to the firm as whole.

Insider access to information is particularly significant due to the nature of decision making within large corporations. Recall that the corporation is a classic example of an authority-based decision-making structure character-ized by the existence of a central agency to which all relevant information is transmitted and which is empowered to make decisions binding on the whole. Unlike many other organizations, the corporation's central agency is not a single autocrat, but rather a multi-member body—the board of directors—that usually functions by consensus. Put another way, the board of directors is best understood as a collegial body using consensus-based decision making. Because consensus works best where team members have equal information and comparable interests, insiders may find it easier to reach consensus than would a diverse body of outsiders. Insiders are more likely to have comparable access to information and similar interests than are outsiders. Insiders have many informal contacts within the organization, which both promote team formation and provide them with better access to information. Hence, insofar as efficient decision making is the goal of corporate governance, independence may not be desirable. To the contrary, these factors suggest that an all-insider board might be preferable.

Independence and Agency Costs

Corporate law provides a number of accountability mechanisms designed to constrain agency costs. Chief among them is the board of directors, especially the independent directors. To be sure, outsiders have neither the time nor the information necessary to be involved in the minutiae of day-to-day firm management. What outsiders can do, however, is monitor senior managers and replace those whose performance is sub-par. Accordingly, proponents of the monitoring model have always been among the strongest proponents of director independence.

It is not clear, however, why one would expect independent directors to be an effective constraint on shirking or self-dealing by management. Monitoring the performance of the firm's officers and employees is hard, time-consuming work. Moreover, most outside directors have full-time employment elsewhere, which commands the bulk of their attention and provides the bulk of their pecuniary and psychic income. Independent directors therefore may prefer leisure or working on their primary vocation to monitoring management. As Adam Smith observed three centuries ago:

> The directors of [joint stock] companies, however, being the managers rather of other people's money than of their own, it cannot well be expected, that they

should watch over it with the same anxious vigilance with which the partners in a private co-partnery frequently watch over their own. Like the stewards of a rich man, they are apt to consider attention to small matters as not for their master's honour, and very easily give themselves a dispensation from having it. Negligence and profusion, therefore, must always prevail, more or less, in the management of the affairs of such a company.[27]

Other factors impede an independent director from monitoring management, even if he wishes to do so. Although boards meet more often and longer now than they did pre-SOX, board meetings are still few and of short length, relative to the amount of time insiders spend with one another. Moreover, outside directors are generally dependent upon management for information.

Collective action problems also impede the board's ability to effectively monitor and discipline managers. Even though faithful monitoring may be in an individual director's interest, he or she may assume that other directors will do the hard work of identifying sub-par performances, permitting the free rider to shirk. As in any free-riding situation, this will tend to result in sub-optimal levels of monitoring. Even in cases of clearly sub-par management performance, moreover, other collective action problems may prevent the board from taking necessary remedial steps. Some director must step forward to begin building a majority in favor of replacing the incumbent managers, which again raises a free-rider problem. Furthermore, if an active director steps forward, he or she must not only overcome the forces of inertia and bias, but also must likely do so in the face of active opposition from the threatened managers who will try to cut off the flow of information to the board, co-opt key board members, and otherwise undermine the disciplinary process. Board members are likely to have developed warm personal relationships with the CEO and other managers, who will in turn have cultivated that type of sentiment. Those relationships make it hard for boards to fire senior managers, especially when personal friendships of long standing are in play. In addition, some board members will have been responsible for hiring the managers and will need to make the cognitively difficult admission of their error in order to fire the managers.

Finally, the insiders may effectively control nominally independent directors. As we've seen, it has long been common practice for a corporation's outside directors to include lawyers and bankers (of both the investment and commercial varieties) who are currently providing services to the corporation or may wish to provide services in the future. University faculty or administrators, to take another common example, may be beholden to insiders who

27. Adam Smith, The Wealth of Nations 700 (Modern Library ed. 1937).

control corporate donations to their home institutions. None of these outsiders are likely to bite the hand that feeds them.

Even if the independent directors are not actually biased in favor of the insiders, moreover, they often are predisposed to favor the latter. As noted above, outside directors tend to be corporate officers or retirees who share the same views and values as the insiders. Because outside directors are nominated by the incumbent board members and passively elected by the shareholders, structural bias remains one of the key insoluble riddles of corporate governance.

Pre-Crises Empirical Evidence

The logic of the Sarbanes-Oxley Act and the stock exchange board composition rules is that independent directors will be an effective constraint on the agency costs inherent in the corporate separation of ownership and control. As we have just seen, however, theory predicted that independent directors were unlikely to be effective in doing so. Before independent directors can become effective monitors of management, the system must incur costs to remedy the information asymmetry between outsiders and insiders. It also must incur costs to prevent outside board members from shirking. Put another way, hiring agents to watch other agents may compound instead of reduce agency costs.

The empirical evidence on the relationship between board composition and firm performance available when Sarbanes-Oxley was adopted was inconclusive, at best. If independent directors effectively constrain agency costs, one would have expected the evidence to show a correlation between the presence of independent outsiders on the board and firm performance. But it did not.

True, some early studies found positive correlations between independence and performance. Rosenstein and Wyatt, for example, found that shareholder wealth increased when management appointed independent directors.[28] Weisbach studied board decisions to remove a CEO, finding that boards comprised mainly of independent directors were more likely to base the removal decision on poor performance, as well as being more likely to remove an underperforming CEO, than were insider-dominated boards. He also found that CEO removals by outsider-dominated boards added to firm value, while CEO removals by insider-dominated boards did not.[29] Baysinger and Butler

---

28. Stuart Rosenstein & Jeffrey G. Wyatt, Outside Directors, Board Independence, and Shareholder Wealth, 26 J. Fin. Econ. 175 (1990).

29. Michael S. Weisbach, Outside Directors and CEO Turnover, 20 J. Fin Econ. 431 (1988).

found that corporate financial performance tends to increase (up to a point) as the percentage of independent directors increases.[30] Cotter found that boards dominated by outsiders generate higher shareholder gains from tender offers.[31]

Other studies, however, such as that by MacAvoy, found that board composition had no effect on profitability.[32] Klein likewise found little evidence of a general association between firm performance and board composition, but found a positive correlation between the presence of insiders on board finance and investment committees and firm performance.[33] Rosenstein and Wyatt found that the stock market experienced a significantly positive price reaction to announcements that insiders had been appointed to the board when insiders owned more than 5 percent of the firm's stock.[34]

A 1999 meta-analysis of numerous studies in this area concluded that there was no convincing evidence that firms with a majority of independent directors outperform other firms. It further concluded that there was some evidence that a "moderate number" of insiders correlates with higher performance.[35] A 1998 meta-analysis likewise found no evidence that board composition affects financial performance.[36]

A literature review by Wagner et al. further complicated the empirical landscape by effectively splitting the baby.[37] Their meta-analysis of 63 correlations found that, on average, increasing the number of outsiders on the board is

30. Barry D. Baysinger & Henry N. Butler, Revolution Versus Evolution in Corporation Law: The ALI's Project and the Independent Director, 52 Geo. Wash. L. Rev. 557, 572 (1984).

31. James F. Cotter et al., Do Independent Directors Enhance Target Shareholder Wealth During Tender Offers?, 43 J. Fin. Econ. 195 (1997).

32. Paul MacAvoy, et al., ALI Proposals for Increased Control of the Corporation by the Board of Directors, in Statement of the Business Roundtable on the American Law Institute's Proposed "Principles of Corporate Governance and Structure: Restatement and Recommendations" C-1 (Feb. 1983).

33. April Klein, Firm Performance and Board Committee Structure, 41 J. L. & Econ. 275 (1998).

34. Stuart Rosenstein & Jeffrey G. Wyatt, Outside Directors, Board Independence, and Shareholder Wealth, 26 J. Fin. Econ. 175 (1990).

35. Sanjai Bhagat & Bernard Black, The Uncertain Relationship Between Board Composition and Firm Performance, 54 Bus. Law. 921, 922 (1999).

36. Dan R. Dalton et al., Meta-Analytic Reviews of Board Composition, Leadership Structure, and Financial Performance, 19 Strategic Mgmt. J. 269 (1998). A more recent study of Australian firms found that corporate boards "chaired by non-executives and dominated by non-executive directors at the full board and compensation committee levels are no more adept at enforcing CEO pay-for-firm-performance than are executive-dominated boards." Alessandra Capezio et al., Too Good to be True: Board Structural Independence as a Moderator of CEO Pay-for-Firm-Performance, 48 J. Mgmt. Stud. 487 (2011).

37. John A. Wagner et al., Board Composition and Organizational Performance: Two Studies of Insider/Outsider Effects, 35 J. Mgmt. Stud. 655 (1998).

positively associated with higher firm performance. On the other hand, increasing the number of insiders on the board had the same effect. In other words, greater board homogeneity was positively associated with higher firm performance, which is not what the Sarbanes-Oxley Act's proponents would have predicted.

INCENTIVIZING THE INDEPENDENTS

A simple anecdote nicely captures the uncertainty of the case for board independence. The head of Enron's audit committee, Robert Jaedicke, was "a professor of accounting at Stanford University, who could hardly have been more qualified for the job."[38] And we all know what happened at Enron.

In addition to the post-crisis changes in the law, however, there have been a number of developments in recent years that may have provided independent directors with greater abilities to monitor management and stronger incentives to do so. The sections that follow tease out whether these changes have strengthened the case for the post-crisis fetish for independence.

Compensation Practices

The most basic way of incentivizing people to do a good job is to pay them for doing so. Oddly, however, it long was against the law for corporations to compensate directors at all.[39] Because boards at that time consisted mainly of people associated with the firm, such as founding entrepreneurs, insiders, or representatives of major shareholders, their stake in the company provided alternative incentives for good performance. As independent directors with no such stake in the company became more common, however, legislatures and courts recognized that compensation now was a necessary incentive and changed the law to allow it. By the mid-1970s, almost all public corporations paid their directors, and the amount of director compensation grew rapidly in the following years.

In the mid-1990s, prominent corporate governance expert Charles Elson began arguing that the prevailing norm of cash compensation failed adequately to incentivize directors. Indeed, he contended that the combination of growing cash compensation and management's control of the board nomination

---

38. Special Report, Corporate Governance—Designed by Committee, The Economist, June 15, 2002, at 69, 71.

39. See Charles M. Elson, Director Compensation and the Management-Captured Board—The History of a Symptom and a Cure, 50 SMU L. Rev. 127, 135–48 (1996).

process acted "to align the interests of the outside directors with current management rather than with the shareholders. . . . Directors whose remuneration is unrelated to corporate performance have little personal incentive to challenge their management benefactors."[40]

Whereas other reformers focused on the nomination process, as we will see below, Elson proposed a radical change in the form of director compensation:

> To ensure that directors will examine executive initiatives in the best interest of the business, the outside directors must become substantial shareholders. To facilitate this, directors' fees should be paid primarily in company stock that is restricted as to resale during their term in office. No other form of compensation, which serves to compromise their independence from management, should be permitted. The goal is to create within each director a personally based motivation to actively monitor management in the best interest of corporate productivity and to counteract the oversight-inhibiting environment that management appointment and cash-based/benefit-laden fees create.[41]

In 1996, a NACD blue ribbon panel adopted many of Elson's ideas, recommending the use of stock-based compensation and further opining that directors should personally invest an amount in company stock sufficiently large so as to decouple the director's financial interests from those of management.[42] The core idea rapidly caught on, although few firms went so far as to eliminate all cash compensation and benefits. According to a 2007 report by the Conference Board, 90 percent of surveyed companies made some form of stock-based compensation to directors, with 38 percent paying all or part of the basic retainer in stock.[43]

In theory, this change in board compensation practices should align director incentives with the interests of shareholders. Lucian Bebchuk and Jesse Fried, however, claim that the incentives thereby created are minimal:

> Consider, for example, a director who owns 0.005 percent of the company's shares. And suppose that the director is contemplating whether to approve a compensation arrangement requested by the CEO that would reduce shareholder value by $10 million. Given the director's fraction of total shares, the reduction in the value of the director's holdings that would result from approval of the CEO's request would be only $500. Such a cost, or even one several times

40. Id. at 162–64.
41. Id. at 165.
42. National Association of Corporate Directors, Report of the NACD Blue Ribbon Commission on Director Professionalism (1996).
43. The Conference Board, Directors' Compensation and Board Practices in 2006 6–8 (2007).

larger, is highly unlikely to overcome the various factors exerting pressure on the director to support the CEO's request.[44]

Bebchuk and Fried's critique is unpersuasive for several reasons. First, although Bebchuk and Fried elsewhere invoke the behavioral research on social and psychological factors in support of various arguments, here they fail to take into account the behavioral research suggesting that most individuals are loss averse. Because directors are loss averse, small losses to a director's stock portfolio will have greater psychological weight than small incentives provided by the CEO, all else being equal. Second, Bebchuk and Fried's hypothetical amount of stock ownership, while perhaps not an uncommon level, fails to take into account the possibility that for many directors the shares they own in the company on whose board they serve will constitute a substantial part of that director's net worth. In other words, what matters is not the percentage a director's holdings represent of the company's float but rather the percentage those holdings represent of the director's personal assets. A director with a portfolio of $1 million, $100,000 of which consists of stock of the company in question, has an incentive to keep the stock price up regardless of whether the company's float is $1 billion or $100 billion.

Jeffrey Gordon identifies a more serious concern with stock-based compensation. He argues that stock-based compensation may create the same sort of perverse incentives for directors that it famously did for the managers of Enron.[45] Importantly, however, much stock-based director compensation takes the form of restricted stock grants rather than stock options. Some economists argue that recipients of restricted stock are less likely to engage in earnings management and other forms of financial fraud than are recipients of stock options.[46] Whether that is true or not, stock options only reward their recipients in the event that the stock price goes up, but holders of restricted stock have the potential for both upside gains and downside losses. Because preventing downside risks from materializing is just as much a part of the monitoring job as promoting potential upside gains, restricted stock seems likely to strike the correct incentive balance.

Does stock-based compensation in fact provide incentives for independent directors not to shirk? A literature review published in 2000 identified five studies providing empirical support for the proposition that increased director

44. Lucian Bebchuk & Jesse Fried, Pay Without Performance: The Unfulfilled Promise of Executive Compensation 34 (2004).

45. Jeffrey N. Gordon, The Rise of Independent Directors in the United States, 1950–2005: Of Shareholder Value and Stock Market Prices, 59 Stan. L. Rev. 1465, 1488 (2007).

46. *See,* e.g., Natasha Burns & Simi Kedia, The Impact of Performance-Based Compensation on Misreporting, 79 J. Fin. Econ. 35 (2006).

stockownership leads to better decision making by directors.[47] Subsequently, a 2005 study found that banks paying a high percentage of compensation in stock exhibited higher performance and growth than competitors emphasizing cash compensation.[48] As such, it seems plausible to conclude that the trend toward paying directors in stock has tended to better align independent director incentives with shareholder interests.

Reputational Concerns

Shareholder activist Nell Minow claims that public corporation directors are "the most reputationally sensitive people in the world."[49] Certainly, a reputation as a poor corporate steward adversely affects the directors' self-esteem, his relationships with peers, and his employability with other corporations. Directors thus have strong incentives to care about their reputations. Indeed, directors whose performance is below par have never faced a greater risk of public obloquy than they do today.

David Skeel identifies a number of ways in which so-called shaming sanctions come into play in corporate governance, several of which apply in full measure to independent directors.[50] First, the "perp walk" beloved of prosecutors not only shames the individual defendants in a given case, but also chills others considering similar misconduct. Second, a criminal conviction subjects defendants to criticism from the bench. Finally, Skeel notes, activist shareholders publicly identify firms and/or individual managers and directors believed to be underperforming. CalPERS' annual focus list of firms alleged to have poor corporate governance is the most famous—and probably most successful—example of this phenomenon. According to Skeel, attention from CalPERS frequently "spurs the companies [on the list] to make immediate changes such as separating the CEO and board chair positions or adding independent directors."

To Skeel's list, we might add the 24/7 media environment. Today, there is "a bigger audience for business news than ever before, and a greater capacity to deliver it."[51] Cable TV networks, newspapers, websites, and blogs provide

---

47. R. Franklin Balotti et al., Equity Ownership and the Duty of Care: Convergence, Revolution, or Evolution?, 55 Bus. Law. 661, 672–77 (2000) (summarizing studies).

48. David A. Becher et al., Incentive Compensation for Bank Directors: The Impact of Deregulation, 78 J. Bus. 1753 (2005).

49. David A. Skeel, Jr., Shaming in Corporate Law, 149 U. Pa. L. Rev. 1811, 1812 n.3 (2001).

50. David A. Skeel, Jr., Corporate Shaming Revisited: An Essay for Bill Klein, 2 Berkeley Bus. L.J. 105 (2005).

51. Gregory J. Millman, No Longer Just Gray: Business Journalism Takes Off, Fin. Exec., Oct 1, 2006, at 18.

nonstop coverage. Although this coverage often amounts to cheerleading that creates celebrity CEOs, the post-Enron "drumbeat of revelations of excessive executive pay and perks and forgiven loans, with directors winking at each other or simply looking the other way, has provided sensational grist for the business press."[52] Reputations that took years to construct can now be unmade in moments.

Finally, as the leading center of corporation law in the United States, the Delaware courts play an important role in establishing behavioral norms by naming names. As Edward Rock explains:

> Delaware courts generate in the first instance the legal standards of conduct (which influence the development of the social norms of directors, officers, and lawyers) largely through what can best be thought of as "corporate law sermons." These richly detailed and judgmental factual recitations, combined with explicitly judgmental conclusions, sometimes impose legal sanctions but surprisingly often do not. Taken as a whole, the Delaware opinions can be understood as providing a set of parables—instructive tales—of good managers and bad managers, of good lawyers and bad lawyers, that, in combination, fill out the normative job description of these critical players. . . . [T]hese standards of conduct are communicated to managers by corporate counsel, and . . . play an important role in the evolution of (nonlegal) norms of conduct.[53]

A study by Suraj Srinivasan of the University of Chicago School of Business confirms the effectiveness of reputational sanctions. Srinivasan studied a sample of 409 companies that had restated earnings during the period 1997–2001 to determine whether there was any impact on outside directors. Srinivasan found that director turnover was higher for firms that restated earnings downward and that the likelihood of director turnover increased proportionately with the severity of the restatement. Srinivasan also found that directors of firms that restated their earnings downward tended to lose their board positions at other firms. Srinivasan concluded that the evidence showed outside directors, especially those who served on the audit committee, experienced significant labor market reputational costs for financial reporting failures.[54]

A study of uncontested board elections provides further evidence of reputational effects. The authors found that directors attending less than

---

52. Tom Horton, Integrity, Directors & Boards, Jan. 1, 2003, at 10.
53. Edward B. Rock, Saints and Sinners: How Does Delaware Corporate Law Work?, 44 UCLA L. Rev. 1009, 1016–17 (1997).
54. Suraj Srinivasan, Consequences of Financial Reporting Failure for Outside Directors: Evidence from Accounting Restatements and Audit Committee Members, 43 J. Accounting Research 291 (2005).

75 percent of board meetings and those receiving negative ISS recommendations receive 14 percent and 19 percent fewer votes, respectively, than their counterparts. Although the authors could not identify direct effects on the reputation of the directors received reduced votes, at the very least it seems likely that their self-esteem suffers. In any case, reduced votes had several positive indirect effects, including higher CEO turnover and reduced executive compensation.[55]

Judicial Insistence on Informed Decision Making

Independent board members who shirked their duties long had little need to fear legal consequences. As Yale law professor Joseph Bishop observed in a widely-cited 1968 law review article, "The search for cases in which directors of industrial corporations have been held liable in derivative suits for negligence uncomplicated by self-dealing is a search for a very small number of needles in a very large haystack."[56] In the 1980s, however, the Delaware Supreme and Chancery Courts began to emphasize the need for directors to avail themselves, "prior to making a business decision, of all material information reasonably available to them."[57] At least in theory, where the directors failed to so inform themselves, they now faced the prospect of personal monetary liability.

Although the cases dealing with this nascent duty aptly were described as "a long-overdue judicial affirmation of the need for better informed directors,"[58] they tended to arise in the context of specific transactions. Hence, for example, courts expect directors to gather all reasonably available material information about the company's value when selling the company in a merger or other acquisition. This line of cases thus opened the question of what standard applied to the board's more general oversight role, in which monitoring of management takes place outside the context of a particular transaction.

<hr />

55. Jie Cai et al., Electing Directors (May 2007), available at http://papers.ssrn.com/sol3/papers.cfm?abstract_id=910548.

56. Joseph W. Bishop Jr., Sitting Ducks and Decoy Ducks: New Trends in the Indemnification of Corporate Directors and Officers, 77 Yale L.J. 1078, 1099 (1968).

57. Aronson v. Lewis, 473 A.2d 805, 811 (Del. 1984); see also Smith v. Van Gorkom, 488 A.2d 858, 872 (Del. 1985). In addition to an informed decision, there are a number of other preconditions that must be satisfied in order for the business judgment to insulate a board's decisions or actions from judicial review. See generally Stephen M. Bainbridge, Corporation Law and Economics 270–83 (2002) (discussing preconditions).

58. Krishnan Chittur, The Corporate Director's Standard of Care: Past, Present, and Future, 10 Del. J. Corp. L. 505, 543 (1985).

In the seminal 1996 *Caremark* decision, Delaware Chancellor William Allen made clear that the board's duty to be informed extended to its general oversight duties. Specifically, Allen opined that the directors' duty of care includes an affirmative obligation to ensure "that appropriate information will come to its attention in a timely manner as a matter of ordinary operations."[59] In *Caremark*, the corporation had no program of internal controls to ensure that the corporation complied with key federal statutes governing its operations. When the corporation ran afoul of one of those statutes and was obliged to pay a substantial fine, a derivative suit was brought against the directors. In reviewing the merits of that claim for purposes of evaluating the settlement, Allen rejected the defendants' argument that "a corporate board has no responsibility to assure that appropriate information and reporting systems are established by management . . ."[60] Instead, he imposed an affirmative obligation for management and the board to implement systems of internal control. Although Allen's analysis was mere dicta given the procedural posture of the case, the Delaware Supreme Court subsequently affirmed that *Caremark* articulates the necessary conditions for assessing director oversight liability."[61]

In *Guttman v. Huang*, Delaware Vice Chancellor Leo Strine noted that *Caremark* "is rightly seen as a prod toward the greater exercise of care by directors in monitoring their corporations' compliance with legal standards."[62] In that case, Strine applied *Caremark* to allegations that the board of directors had failed adequately to exercise oversight over the company's internal accounting controls, holding that liability might be imposed where there was evidence that "the company lacked an audit committee, that the company had an audit committee that met only sporadically and devoted patently inadequate time to its work, or that the audit committee had clear notice of serious accounting irregularities and simply chose to ignore them or, even worse, to encourage their continuation."[63]

Granted, as a practical matter, the liability risk faced by independent directors probably remains low.[64] "Nevertheless the directors' perception of risk seems to have increased over the period, perhaps because of lawyers' exaggerations, perhaps because of scare-mongering by liability insurers, or perhaps because of the saliency of outlier cases like Enron and WorldCom, in which outside directors paid out-of-pocket to settle claims."[65] Accordingly, the fear of

---

59. In re Caremark Int'l Inc. Deriv. Litig., 698 A.2d 959, 970 (Del. Ch. 1996).
60. Id. at 969–70.
61. Stone v. Ritter, 911 A.2d 362, 365 (Del. 2006).
62. Guttman v. Huang, 823 A.2d 492, 506 (Del. Ch. 2003).
63. Id. at 507.
64. See Bernard Black et al., Outside Director Liability, 58 Stan. L. Rev. 1055 (2006).
65. Gordon, supra note 45, at 1484.

litigation encourages boards to establish a "tone at the top" that encourages honesty, integrity, and compliance with legal requirements. In particular, board members are cautioned not to rely passively on management and outside advisors. While board members are not private investigators charged with conducting corporate espionage to detect wrongdoing, they are obliged to make a candid inquiry before accepting the reports they receive from management and outside advisors. As the Delaware Supreme Court observed in *Smith v. Van Gorkom*, the board must "proceed with a critical eye in assessing information" provided by others.[66]

New Metrics

In a provocative article, Jeffrey Gordon argues that the last 50 years have seen the rise of "a new corporate governance paradigm that looks to the stock price as the measure of most things."[67] This paradigm emerged because stock prices have become more informative. Companies must disclose vastly increased amounts of information per evolving SEC rules. Financial disclosures have become more transparent due to improvements in accounting standards. The resulting improvements in the quantity and quality of information made available to markets that themselves have become more liquid and efficient has made market prices an increasingly accurate metric by which to measure management performance.

Gordon argues this development radically simplified the task of independent directors. Outsiders no longer needed to struggle with the information asymmetry inherent in their relationship with management, because "the increasing informativeness and value of stock market signals" allow them to rely on "stock price maximization as the measure of managerial success."[68]

Stock market performance, however, is an exclusively output-based metric. In at least some cases, input-based metrics may be more appropriate. This is so even if we think that monitoring is the board's sole proper function.

The board's supervisory function can be usefully subdivided into two broad categories. First, boards assess the abilities and effort of the top management team. Although this is a constant process, it is most salient in connection with hiring, promotion, and compensation decisions. In the latter contexts, the board can focus mainly on monitoring outputs. Specifically, the board will focus on corporate performance metrics. A purely output-based metric, however, is both inaccurate and unfair. Corporate performance may be skewed by

66. Smith v. Van Gorkom, 488 A.2d 858, 872 (Del. 1985).
67. Gordon, supra note 45, at 1472.
68. Id at 1470–72.

temporary conditions beyond the abilities of even the most competent and dedicated management team. Unfortunately, monitoring managerial abilities and efforts using inputs is notoriously difficult. Much management work entails forms of non-separable team production in which the contributions of individual team members cannot be separately metered.

Second, boards engage in oversight of management conduct. Here boards examine individual management decisions and actions for misfeasance and malfeasance. This form of monitoring inevitably focuses on inputs. If all the board knows is that the corporation is hugely profitable, without knowing whether massive law breaking is the foundation on which that profitability rests, the board is failing to be an effective monitor.

Stock price-based metrics thus may have made life easier for independent directors. It is not clear that they have made independent directors better monitors.

Is There Proof in the Pudding?

There is some evidence that the post-SOX regulatory changes and the new market forces affecting independent directors have had an impact. Robert Felton's review of studies of post-SOX boards of directors found that the average number of companies on whose board a director sits has gone down, presumably because boards and committees meet more often and have to process more information. The amount of time required for board service has especially gone up for members of audit committees, who have a host of new duties. Overall, "the average commitment of a director of a U.S. listed company increased from 13 hours a month in 2001 to 19 hours in 2003 (and then fell to 18 hours in 2004)."[69] Whether this strengthens the case for director independence is questionable, however, because many of the factors discussed in the preceding sections likely would have produced similar increases in effort by insider-dominated boards.

Somewhat stronger evidence that the fetish for independence has had at least some beneficial effects is provided by Michael Useem and Andy Zelleke's survey of governance practices. They found that boards of directors increasingly view delegation of authority to management as properly the subject of careful and self-conscious decision making. The surveyed board members acknowledged that they do not run the company on a day-by-day basis, but rather are seeking to provide stronger oversight and supervision. Increasingly, boards are establishing written protocols to allocate decision-making rights

---

69. Robert F. Felton, A New Era in Corporate Governance, McKinsey Q., 2004 No. 2, 28, 60.

between the board and management, although the protocols vary widely, ranging from detailed and comprehensive to skeletal and limited in scope. Useem and Zelleke conclude that executives still set much of the board's decision-making agenda. At the same time, they found that boards are increasingly asserting their sovereignty in recent years and that an emergent norm requires management to be mindful of what information boards want to hear and what decisions boards believe they should make.[70]

A critical issue, of course, has always been board access to information. Indirect evidence that independent directors now have good access to information is provided by a study by Enrichetta Ravina and Paola Sapienza of independent directors' trading results. The authors found that independent directors earn substantial positive abnormal returns when trading in their corporation's stock. Even more interestingly, the difference between their results and those of the same firm's executive officers is relatively small, although it widens in firms with weaker governance regimes.[71] It seems reasonable to infer from this evidence that outsiders now have good access to material information about firm performance; indeed, that their access to such information is comparable to that of executive officers.[72]

Does One Size Now Fit All?

The post-SOX regulatory environment rests on the conventional wisdom that board independence is an unalloyed good. As the preceding sections demonstrated, however, the empirical evidence on the merits of board independence is mixed. Accordingly, even though there is some reason to think independent board members are finally becoming properly incentivized and, as a result, more effective, the clearest take-home lesson from the preceding analysis is still that one size does not fit all.

This result should not be surprising. On one side of the equation, firms do not have uniform needs for managerial accountability mechanisms. The need for accountability is determined by the likelihood of shirking, which in turn is determined by management's tastes, which in turn is determined by each

70. Michael Useem & Andy Zelleke, Oversight and Delegation in Corporate Governance: Deciding What the Board Should Decide, 14 Corp. Gov.: An Int'l Rev. 2 (2006).

71. Enrichetta Ravina & Paola Sapienza, What do Independent Directors Know? Evidence from Their Trading (December 2006), available at http://ssrn.com/abstract=928246.

72. Note that this raises doubts about the extent to which independent directors are relying on stock price-based metrics. If independent directors are performing as well as insiders, it may be assumed that the former—like the latter—have access to material nonpublic information.

firm's unique culture, traditions, and competitive environment. We all know managers whose preferences include a penchant for hard, faithful work. Firms where that sort of manager dominates the corporate culture have less need for outside accountability mechanisms.

On the other side of the equation, firms have a wide range of accountability mechanisms from which to choose. Independent directors are not the sole mechanism by which management's performance is monitored. Rather, a variety of forces work together to constrain management's incentive to shirk: the capital and product markets within which the firm functions; the internal and external markets for managerial services; the market for corporate control; incentive compensation systems; auditing by outside accountants; and many others. The importance of the independent directors' monitoring role in a given firm depends in large measure on the extent to which these other forces are allowed to function. For example, managers of a firm with strong takeover defenses are less subject to the constraining influence of the market for corporate control than are those of a firm with no takeover defenses. The former needs a strong independent board more than the latter does.

The critical mass of independent directors needed to provide optimal levels of accountability also will vary depending upon the types of outsiders chosen. Strong, active independent directors with little tolerance for negligence or culpable conduct do exist. A board having a few such directors is more likely to act as a faithful monitor than is a board having many nominally independent directors who shirk their monitoring obligations.

The post-SOX standards, however, strap all listed companies into a single model of corporate governance. By establishing a highly restrictive definition of director independence and mandating that such directors dominate both the board and its required committees, the new rules fail to take into account the diversity and variance among firms. The new rules thus satisfy our definition of quack corporate governance. The one-size-fits-all model they mandate should be scrapped in favor of allowing each firm to develop the particular mix of monitoring and management that best suits its individual needs. Unfortunately, as we will see throughout our review of the post-crisis federal regulatory scheme, neither Congress nor the SEC has given any deference to the principle of private ordering.

WHAT HAVE WE LOST?

The fetish for board independence has costs. Two are already on the table; namely, those associated with the information asymmetry between outsiders and insiders and those occasioned by the need to incent outsiders to perform. A third is the lost value of insider representation.

Oliver Williamson suggests that one of the board's functions is to "safe-guard the contractual relation between the firm and its management."[73] Insider board representation may be necessary to carry out that function. Many adverse firm outcomes are beyond management's control. If the board is limited to monitoring management, and especially if it is limited to objective measures of performance, however, the board may be unable to differentiate between acts of god, bad luck, ineptitude, and self-dealing. As a result, risk-averse managers may demand a higher return to compensate them for the risk that the board will be unable to make such distinctions. Alternatively, managers may reduce the extent of their investments in firm-specific human capital, so as to minimize nondiversifiable employment risk. Insider representation on the board may avoid those problems by providing better information and insight into the causes of adverse outcomes.

Insider representation on the board also will encourage learned trust between insiders and outsiders. Insider representation on the board thus provides the board with a credible source of information necessary to accurate subjective assessment of managerial performance. In addition, however, it also serves as a bond between the firm and the top management team. Insider directors presumably will look out for their own interests and those of their fellow managers. Board representation thus offers some protection against dismissal for adverse outcomes outside management's control.

Such considerations likely explain the finding by Klein of a positive correlation between the presence of insiders on board committees and firm performance.[74] They also help explain the finding by Wagner et al. that increasing the number of insiders on the board is positively correlated with firm performance.[75]

The fetish for independence cost us these potential benefits from insider representation. Congress's refusal to permit private ordering means that those firms where those costs are highest are unable to opt out of the one size fits all straightjacket.

DID THE FETISH FOR INDEPENDENCE CONTRIBUTE TO THE FINANCIAL CRISIS?

In an important report for the OECD, Grant Kirkpatrick noted evidence that the fetish for independence may have contributed to the financial crisis

---

73. Oliver E. Williamson, The Economic Institutions of Capitalism 298 (1985).

74. See April Klein, Firm Performance and Board Committee Structure, 41 J. L. & Econ. 275 (1998).

75. See John A. Wagner et al., Board Composition and Organizational Performance: Two Studies of Insider/Outsider Effects, 35 J. Mgmt. Stud. 655 (1998).

of 2007–2008.[76] The strict conflict of interest rules embedded in the new definitions of independence made it difficult for financial institutions to find independent directors with expertise in their industry. A survey of eight U.S. major financial institutions, for example, found that two-thirds of directors had no banking experience. Given the inherent information asymmetries between insiders and outsiders, the lack of board expertise significantly compounded the inability of financial institution boards to effectively monitor their firms during the pre-crisis period. More expert boards could have done more with the information made available to them and, moreover, would have been better equipped to identify gaps therein that needed filling.

In addition, the need to find independent directors put an emphasis on avoiding conflicted interests at the expense of competence. In other words, the problem was not just that the new definition of independence excluded many candidates with industry expertise, it was also that the emphasis on objective indicia of conflicts dominated the selection process to the exclusion of indicia of basic competence and good judgment. The financial crisis thus appears, in part, to have been an unintended consequence of the Sarbanes-Oxley Act.

A NOTE ON CEO/CHAIRMAN DUALITY

The exchange listing standards require appointment of an independent lead director if the listed company's CEO serves as the chairman of the board of directors. The lead director presumably chairs the executive sessions of the independent board members. Because the lead director's identity and contact information must be disclosed, he also acts as a point person for shareholder relations. The lead director should have a voice in setting the board's agenda, as a check on the CEO/Chairman's control of board meetings. The lead director should serve as a rallying point for the other independent directors in times of crisis, especially those involving CEO termination or succession.

The lead director position was a compromise with those commentators who wanted the exchanges to mandate a non-executive chairman of the board of directors. The proponents of splitting the CEO and board chairman role, however, continued to press the idea and sought to use Dodd-Frank as a vehicle for doing so. In the end, however, Dodd-Frank Section 973 merely directed the SEC to adopt a new rule requiring reporting companies to disclose whether the same person or different persons hold the positions of CEO and

76. Grant Kirkpatrick, The Corporate Governance Lessons from the Financial Crisis, 2009 Fin. Mkt. Trends 1.

Chairman of the Board.[77] In either case, the company must disclose its reasons for doing so.

The legislative history expressly states that the Act "does not endorse or prohibit either method."[78] Even so, however, it seems likely that some policy entrepreneurs still hope that the provision will shame companies into separating the two positions:

> Mr. Joseph Dear, Chief Investment Officer of the California Public Employees' Retirement System, on behalf of the Council of Institutional Investors, wrote in testimony for the Senate Banking Committee that "Boards of directors should be encouraged to separate the role of chair and CEO, or explain why they have adopted another method to assure independent leadership of the board."[79]

If this is the effect Section 973 ends up having, it will be without compelling support in the empirical literature. To be sure, an independent chairman of the board is becoming more common:

> Approximately 16 percent of S&P 500 companies now have an independent chair; among S&P Mid and Small Cap companies the figure is higher (23 percent and 27 percent, respectively). In 2008, 95 percent of S&P 500 boards had an independent lead or presiding director, compared with only 36 percent in 2003.[80]

The latter figure represents the impact of exchange listing standards, of course, and thus should not be taken as evidence in favor of a non-executive chairman. The real question is whether the relatively modest number of companies with such an independent chair is due to market failure or reflects optimal board design.

A study by Olubunmi Faleye finds support for the hypothesis that firms actively weigh the costs and benefits of alternative leadership structures in their unique circumstances and concludes that requiring a one size fits all model separating the CEO and Chairman positions may be counterproductive.[81] A study by James Brickley, Jeffrey Coles, and Gregg A. Jarrell found little evidence that combining or separating the two titles affected corporate performance.[82] A subsequent study by the same authors found "preliminary

---

77. Dodd-Frank § 953.
78. S. Rep. No. 111–176, at 147 (2010).
79. Id.
80. ABA Section of Business Law Task Force Report, supra note 13, at 131
81. Olubunmi Faleye, Does One Hat fit All? The Case of Corporate Leadership Structure (January 2003).
82. James A. Brickey et al., Leadership Structure: Separating the CEO and Chairman of the Board, 3 J. Corp. Fin. 189 (1997).

support for the hypothesis that the costs of separation are larger than the benefits for most firms."[83]

As John Coates summarizes the field, the evidence is mixed, at best:

> At least 34 separate studies of the differences in the performance of companies with split vs. unified chair/CEO positions have been conducted over the last 20 years, including two "meta-studies." . . . The only clear lesson from these studies is that there has been no long-term trend or convergence on a split chair/CEO structure, and that variation in board leadership structure has persisted for decades, even in the UK, where a split chair/CEO structure is the norm.[84]

Although Coates concludes that splitting the CEO and Chairman positions by legislation "may well be a good idea for larger companies," he further concludes that mandating such a split "is not clearly a good idea for all public companies."[85]

Proponents of a mandatory non-executive Chairman of the Board have overstated the benefits of splitting the positions, while understating or even ignoring the costs of doing so. Michael Jensen identified the potential benefits in his 1993 Presidential Address to the American Finance Association, arguing that: "The function of the chairman is to run the board meetings and oversee the process of hiring, firing, evaluation, and compensating the CEO. . . . Therefore, for the board to be effective, it is important to separate the CEO and Chairman positions."[86] In fact, however, overseeing the "hiring, firing, evaluation, and compensating the CEO," is the job of the board of directors as a whole, not just the Chairman of the Board.

To be sure, in many corporations, the Chairman of the Board is given unique powers to call special meetings, set the board agenda, and the like.[87] In such companies, a dual CEO-Chairman does wield powers that may impede board oversight of his or her performance. Yet, in such companies, the problem is not that one person holds both posts; the problem is that the independent

83. James A. Brickley et al., Corporate Leadership Structure: On the Separation of the Positions of CEO and Chairman of the Board, Simon School of Business Working Paper FR 95–02 (Aug. 29, 2000), http://ssrn.com/abstract=6124.

84. John Coates, Protecting Shareholders and Enhancing Public Confidence through Corporate Governance (July 30, 2009), http://blogs.law.harvard.edu/corpgov/2009/07/30/protecting-shareholders-and-enhancing-public-confidence-through-corporate-governance/.

85. Id.

86. Michael C. Jensen, Presidential Address: The Modern Industrial Revolution, Exit and the Failure of Internal Control Systems, 48 J. of Fin. 831, 866 (1993).

87. James Verdonik and Kirby Happer, Role of the Chairman of the Board 2 (explaining that "one of the duties of the Chairman is to call meetings of the Board of Directors and the shareholders. . . . Chairmen often set the agenda for Board meetings"), http://www.directorsforum.com/role-of-the-chairman-verdonik-happer.pdf.

members of the board of directors have delegated too much power to the Chairman. The solution is to adopt bylaws that allow the independent board members to call special meetings, require them to meet periodically outside the presence of managers, and the like.

Indeed, the influence of an executive chairman may not even be a problem. Brickley, Coles, and Jarrell concluded that the separation and combination of titles is part of the natural succession process. A successful CEO receives a variety of rewards from the company, one of which may be a fancier title. If the power that comes with the combined title came as a reward for sustained high performance, that power may actually redound to the company's benefit.

Turning from the benefit side to the cost side of the equation, even if splitting the posts makes it easier for the board to monitor the CEO, the board now has the new problem of monitoring a powerful non-executive Chairman. The board now must expend effort to ensure that such a Chairman does not use the position to extract rents from the company and, moreover, that the Chairman expends the effort necessary to carry out the post's duties effectively. The board also must ensure that a dysfunctional rivalry does not arise between the Chairman and the CEO, both of whom presumably will be ambitious and highly capable individuals. In other words, if the problem is "who watches the watchers?," splitting the two posts simply creates a second watcher who also must be watched.

In addition, a non-executive Chairman inevitably will be less well informed than a CEO. Such a Chairman therefore will be less able to lead the board in performing its advisory and networking roles. Likewise, such a Chairman will be less effective in leading the board's in monitoring top managers below the CEO, because the Chairman will not know those managers as intimately as the CEO.

Section 973 meets all of the criteria of quack corporate governance. It advanced a long-standing agenda item of an important set of policy entrepreneurs, albeit not as far as they would have preferred. Those interest groups are powerful at the federal level but not in Delaware. It impinges on state corporate law, although opponents managed to fend off outright preemption. The empirical evidence provides no real justification for the disclosure, let alone actually splitting the two positions. It is quack corporate governance.

CHAPTER 4
Executive Compensation

Executive compensation emerged as a hot-button issue in the wake of both crises. Politicians, pundits, regulators, activist shareholders, and a host of other opinion makers and ordinary citizens alike complained about corporate fat cats getting ever richer while the economy struggled. During the 2008 Presidential campaign, for example, Senator John McCain "blasted what he called the 'outrageous' and 'unconscionable' rewards received by leaders of Bear Stearns Cos. and Countrywide Financial Corp. despite the credit crisis."[1] A political ad by then-Senator Barack Obama likewise attacked "chief executives 'who are making more in 10 minutes than ordinary workers are making in a year.'"[2]

It is thus not surprising that both Sarbanes-Oxley and Dodd-Frank included new executive compensation regulations. A key question is whether these provisions addressed actual corporate governance failures or were simply a sop to populist outrage. In either case, one must also ask whether the new restrictions are likely to be effective.

WHY DO WE CARE?

There is no dispute that most large public U.S. corporations handsomely remunerate their CEOs. A 2008 Congressional report observed that in fiscal year (FY) 2005 the median CEO among 1400 large companies "received $13.51 million in total compensation, up 16 percent over FY 2004."[3] But why is this

---

1. Joann S. Lublin, U.S. News: Candidates Target Executive Pay, Wall St. J., Apr. 12, 2008, at A4.
2. Id.
3. House Report 110–088, at 3 (2008).

a matter of legislative or regulatory concern? Several possible answers suggest themselves.

"No Man Can Be Worth $1,000,000 a Year"

Complaints during times of economic distress about supposedly excessive executive compensation are hardly new. In the 1930s, during the Great Depression, for example, a lawsuit challenging executive bonuses as corporate waste gave rise to the aphorism "no man can be worth $1,000,000 per year."[4] This complaint rested, at least in part, not on a belief that executives were being paid too much relative to their company's performance but on the belief that the amounts they were being paid were simply too high.

Similar populist themes abound in the rhetoric surrounding the crises of the last decade. A 2008 House of Representatives committee report, for example, noted that "in 1991, the average large-company CEO received approximately 140 times the pay of an average worker; in 2003, the ratio was about 500 to 1."[5] Delaware Vice Chancellor Leo Strine observed in a 2007 law review article that both workers and investors "feel that CEOs are selfish and taking outrageous pay at a time when other Americans are economically insecure."[6] William McDonough, the then-Chairman of the Public Company Accounting Oversight Board (PCAOB), complained that:

> We saw . . . an explosion in compensation that made those superstar CEOs actually believe that they were worth more than 400 times the pay of their average workers. Twenty years before, they had been paid an average of forty times the average worker, so the multiple went from forty to 400—an increase of ten times in twenty years. That was thoroughly unjustified by all economic reasoning, and in addition, in my view, it is grotesquely immoral.[7]

The rhetoric of class warfare makes a poor foundation for economic policy. As a justification for regulating executive compensation, however, it is particularly inapt. First, why single out public corporation executives? Many occupations today carry even larger rewards. The highest paid investment

4. Harwell Wells, "No Man Can Be Worth $1,000,000 a Year": The Fight Over Executive Compensation in 1930s America, 44 U. Rich. L. Rev. 689, 726 (2010).

5. House Report 110–088, at 3.

6. Leo E. Strine, Jr., Toward Common Sense and Common Ground? Reflections on the Shared Interests of Managers and Labor in a More Rational System of Corporate Governance, 33 J. Corp. L. 1, 10–11 (2007).

7. William J. McDonough, The Fourth Annual A.A. Sommer, Jr., Lecture on Corporate, Securities & Financial Law, 9 Fordham J. Corp. & Fin. L. 583, 590 (2004).

banker on Wall Street in 2006 was Lloyd Blankfein of Goldman Sachs, for example, who "earned $54.3 million in salary, cash, restricted stock and stock options,"[8] or about 4 times the median CEO salary from the year before. The pay of some private hedge fund managers dwarfed even that sum. Hedge fund manager James Simons earned $1.7 billion in 2006, for example, and two other hedge fund managers also cracked the billion-dollar level that year.[9] Not to mention, of course, the considerable sums earned by top athletes and entertainers.

Second, regulating executive compensation may scratch the public's populist itch, but it does little to address inequalities of income and wealth. To be sure, as Brett McDonnell observes, fat cat "CEOs have become poster boys for" the dramatic increase in "inequality in income and wealth in this country."[10] Even if one assumes that redressing such inequalities is appropriate social policy, however, capping or cutting CEO pay is not an effective means of doing so.

Steven Kaplan and Joshua Rauh determined that executives of nonfinancial corporations comprise just over 5 percent of the individuals in the top 0.01 percent of adjusted gross income. Hedge fund managers, investment bankers, lawyers, executives of privately-held companies, highly paid doctors, independently wealthy individuals, and celebrities make up the bulk of the income bracket. They further found that the representation of corporate executives in the top bracket has remained constant over time and that realized CEO pay is highly correlated to stock performance. Accordingly, they conclude that "poor corporate governance or managerial power over shareholders cannot be more than a small part of the picture of increasing income inequality, even at the very upper end of the distribution."[11]

McDonnell is critical of the Rauh and Kaplan paper on several grounds, but even he concedes that "it does seem quite plausible that investment bankers, the managers of hedge funds and private equity funds, and corporate lawyers are at least as large a part of the problem of rising inequality as are the top officers of public corporations."[12] If so, regulation that singles out public company executives is unfairly under-inclusive. Such regulation, moreover, will have important distortive effects. If public corporation CEO salaries lag relative to those paid in other fields, the best and brightest will shift career tracks to the higher-paying jobs.

8. Jenny Anderson & Julie Creswell, Top Hedge Fund Managers Earn Over $240 Million, N.Y. Times, Apr. 24, 2007.

9. Id.

10. Brett H. McDonnell, Two Goals for Executive Compensation Reform, 52 N.Y.L. Sch. L. Rev. 586, 587 (2008).

11. Steven N. Kaplan & Joshua Rauh, Wall Street and Main Street: What Contributes to the Rise in Highest Incomes, NBER Working Paper No. 13,270 (July 2007).

12. McDonnell, supra note 10, at 594.

In sum, we need not decide here whether wealth and income inequality in society deserves legislative attention. In either case, regulating executive compensation is an inapt and unfair approach to that broader social issue. The disparities between CEO and worker pay packets thus cannot justify what Sarbanes-Oxley and Dodd-Frank did to executive compensation.

Pay Without Performance

A more trenchant justification for regulating executive compensation rests on the claim that, as the Senate committee report on the bill that became Dodd-Frank put it, "[t]he economic crisis revealed instances in which corporate executives received very high compensation despite the very poor performance by their firms."[13] According to this view, the executive compensation scandal is not the rapid growth of management pay in recent years, but rather the failure of compensation schemes to award high pay only for top performance.

This line of argument rests on two premises. First, that top executive compensation is not set through arms-length negotiations. Instead, top managers have effectively captured the boards of directors who nominally set their pay.[14] Second, "managers have used their influence [over corporate boards of directors] to obtain higher compensation through arrangements that have substantially decoupled pay from performance."[15]

The Arm's-Length Bargaining Model of Executive Compensation

The literature identifies three particular ways in which the interests of shareholders and managers may diverge. First, and most obviously, managers may shirk—in the colloquial sense of the word—by substituting leisure for effort.[16] Second, managers who make significant non-diversifiable investments in firm-specific human capital and hold undiversified investment portfolios in which equity of their employer is substantially overrepresented will seek to minimize firm-specific risks that shareholders eliminate

---

13. S. Rep. No. 111–176, at 133 (2010).

14. Lucian Bebchuk & Jesse Fried, Pay Without Performance: The Unfulfilled Promise of Executive Compensation 5 (2004) (arguing that "directors have been influenced by management, sympathetic to executives, insufficiently motivated to bargain over compensation, or simply ineffectual in overseeing compensation").

15. Adolf A. Berle & Gardiner C. Means, The Modern Corporation and Private Property 6 (1932).

16. Michael C. Jensen, A Theory of the Firm: Governance, Residual Claims, and Organizational Forms 144 (2000).

through diversification.[17] As a result, managers generally are more risk averse than shareholders would prefer. Third, managers' claims on the corporation are limited to their tenure with the firm, while the shareholders' claim have an indefinite life. As a result, managers and shareholders will value cash flows using different time horizons; in particular, managers will place a low value on cash flows likely to be received after their tenure ends.[18] Finally, CEOs may be attracted by size—and thus by growth—for its own sake, because of the perquisites and power that come with sheer size, even though growth (especially in market share) may be at the expense of profit (return on investment).

In theory, executive compensation schemes that realign the interests of corporate managers with those of the shareholders ameliorate these divergences in interest. In fact, however, two of the three most common forms of executive compensation merely exacerbate the problem.

Executive compensation commonly is grouped into three basic categories: (1) salary and benefits that do not depend on the firm's performance; (2) options and other incentive compensation that is based on the performance of the firm's stock price; and (3) bonuses and other incentive compensation that is based on the firm's performance according to specified accounting metrics. Salary and other non-performance-based compensation schemes lack incentives that align manager and shareholder interests; in theory, moreover, they can cause those interests to further diverge. Managers compensated with fixed claims on the corporation's assets will want to reduce risk, because they will value preservation of assets more than creating new wealth. Likewise, they will favor retention of earnings within the firm, rather than disbursement to shareholders.

Because accounting metrics can be disaggregated to reflect the performance of particular divisions within a firm, bonuses and other accounting-based compensation schemes are an important tool for incentivizing mid-level managers, whose contributions are limited to a particular area of the firm. In contrast, bonuses paid to senior managers may actually induce counterproductive behavior. A number of empirical studies show that bonus-based compensation affects the choice of accounting techniques, with managers favoring those that shift income to current periods.[19] Other problems with bonuses include the undemanding performance targets set by many boards, the lowering of performance targets when it appears that management will not achieve the target necessary for bonuses to be paid, and the granting of gratuitous bonuses in connection with corporate acquisitions.[20]

17. Id. at 144–45. In general, equity holdings are commonly assumed thought to make managers less risk averse up to a point at which they hold "too much" equity.
18. Id. at 145.
19. Id. at 147 (summarizing studies).
20. Bebchuk & Fried, supra note 14, at 124–30.

Accordingly, the literature tends to focus on stock options and other forms of incentive compensation premised on the company's stock market performance. The economist most closely identified with the modern principal-agent theory, Michael Jensen, observes that such forms of compensation "are well suited to control the effort and horizon problems, since the market value of the stock reflects the present value of the entire future stream of expected cash flows."[21] The proposition is established sufficiently to have found its way out of the academic literature and into the case law.[22]

The logic of stock options and their ilk, of course, is that the firm only pays for performance. Ideally, for example, a firm with a current stock market price of $10 per share might grant its CEO one million options vesting in two years with a two-year exercise period and a strike price of $20 per share. In order for the CEO to reap any return from such options, the firm's stock price must double during the next four years, which would light a substantial fire under the CEO. Conversely, however, the firm might grant the CEO one million at-the-money options vested and exercisable immediately, which provide a financial windfall but minimal incentive effect. Whether effective pay for performance schemes of the former type or ineffective schemes of the latter type will prevail depends mainly on the process by which the board of directors sets compensation.

According to proponents of options, in particular, and the current system of executive compensation, in general, pay packages are "the product of arm's-length bargaining" between managers "attempting to get the best possible deal for themselves and boards seeking to get the best possible deal for shareholders."[23] As a result, financial economists loyal to the arm's-length bargaining model assume compensation schemes are generally efficient, while courts generally defer to board of director decisions.

According to proponents of the arm's-length bargaining model, the substantial size of executive paychecks is not inconsistent with the proposition that executive compensation schemes effectively address the principal-agent problem. To the contrary, the size of such paychecks is deemed to be evidence that the principal-agent problem is being addressed. As the theory goes, when a corporation asks its managers to accept variable performance-based compensation in lieu of fixed salary and benefits, the firm increases the manager's risk exposure. Because risk and return are positively correlated, managers will demand a higher return on their services in compensation for the additional risk. In other words, firms must pay managers a risk premium to induce them

21. Jensen, supra note 16, at 146.
22. See, e.g., Carlton Inv. v. TLC Beatrice Intern. Holdings, Inc., 1996 WL 189435 at *4 (Del. Ch. 1996) (stating that the "theory of stock option grants is premised on a belief in their beneficial employee incentive effect").
23. Bebchuk & Fried, supra note 14, at 2.

to accept variable performance-based compensation in lieu of a fixed salary. In turn, overall pay should rise as reliance on performance-based compensation increases, which is consistent with the pattern observed in the 1990s, during which both the absolute value of executive compensation and the percentage comprised of stock options increased.[24]

The Managerial Power Model

An alternative school of thought contends that executive compensation is not the product of arm's-length bargaining, but rather is tainted by the same set of agency costs it purportedly solves. According to this view, boards of directors—even those nominally independent of management—have strong incentives to acquiesce in executive compensation that pays managers rents (i.e., amounts in excess of the compensation management would receive if the board had bargained with them at arm's length).[25] Among these are: Directors often are chosen de facto by the CEO. Once a director is on the board, pay and other incentives give the director a strong interest in being reelected; in turn, due to the CEO's considerable influence over selection of the board slate, this gives directors an incentive to stay on the CEO's good side. Finally, directors who work closely with top management supposedly develop feelings of loyalty and affection for those managers, and are inculcated with norms of collegiality and team spirit, which induce directors to "go along" with bloated pay packages.[26]

Proponents of the managerial power model acknowledge that executive compensation is subject to a number of constraints, but contend that these are largely ineffectual. Stock ownership by directors only weakly aligns director and shareholder interests, leaving board members unwilling to incur the pecuniary and social costs of bucking when bloated pay packages come up for approval. "The markets for capital, corporate control, and managerial labor" purportedly apply constraints that are "hardly stringent" and "permit substantial deviations from arm's-length contracting."[27]

Instead, managerial power theorists argue that the principal constraint on executive compensation is the risk of incurring "outrage." When a board approves a compensation package under which the CEO or other top managers will receive rents, they will incur a cost for doing so only when the package

---

24. See John C. Coffee, What Caused Enron? A Capsule Social and Economic History of the 1990s, 89 Cornell L. Rev. 269, 297 (2004).

25. See Bebchuk & Fried, supra note 14, at 62 (defining the concept of "rents" for their purposes).

26. Id. at 31–34.

27. Id. at 4.

is perceived negatively "by outsiders whose views matter to the directors and executives."[28] To avoid this constraint, managers and directors devote considerable attention to camouflaging both the level and performance-insensitivity of executive compensation.

Which Side Is Right?

Leading managerial power theorists Lucian Bebchuk and Jesse Fried acknowledge that some of the compensation practices they criticize occur even in firms with stockholders holding large blocks. They spin these findings by arguing that managers retain significant power even in firms with large shareholders, but this is unpersuasive. Why would a controlling shareholder permit managers to extract rents at its expense? Does it not seem more plausible that large blockholders tolerate the challenged compensation practices because they are consistent with shareholder interests rather than representing management's ability to extract rents inconsistent with shareholder wealth maximization? Support for this explanation is provided by a study finding that "highly paid CEOs are more skilled when firms are small or when there are fewer environmental constraints on managerial discretion. This *link between pay and skill is especially strong if there is a blockholder* to monitor management. . . ." [29] As such, the observation that the allegedly questionable compensation practices occur both in companies with dispersed and those with concentrated ownership may suggest that those practices—in both types of firms—are attributable to phenomena other than managerial power.

Indeed, there is much evidence that executive compensation packages are bargained at arm's length and are well designed to align managerial and shareholder interests. Consider, for example, the much maligned practice of management perquisites. If managerial power has widespread traction as an explanation of compensation practices, one would assume that the evidence would show no correlation between the provision of perks and shareholder interests. In fact, however, an interesting study of executive perks found just the opposite:

> Raghuram Rajan, the IMF's chief economist, and Julie Wulf, of the Wharton School, looked at how more than 300 big companies dished out perks to their executives in 1986–99. It turns out that neither cash-rich, low-growth firms nor firms with weak governance shower their executives with unusually generous perks. The authors did, however, find evidence to support two competing explanations.

28. Id. at 5.
29. Robert Daines et al., The Good, the Bad and the Lucky: CEO Pay and Skill 5 (Nov. 2004) (emphasis supplied).

First, firms in the sample with more hierarchical organizations lavished more perks on their executives than firms with flatter structures. Why? Perks are a cheap way to demonstrate status. Just as the armed forces ration medals, firms ration the distribution of conspicuous symbols of corporate status.

Second, perks are a cheap way to boost executive productivity. Firms based in places where it takes a long time to commute are more likely to give the boss a chauffeured limousine. Firms located far from large airports are likelier to lay on a corporate jet.[30]

In other words, executive perks seem to be set with shareholder interests in mind, which is inconsistent with the possibility that managerial power offers a unified field theory of executive compensation.

Additional support for that proposition is provided by Todd Henderson and James Spindler's analysis of a number of compensation practices criticized by Bebchuk and Fried, including perquisites, corporate loans, and encouragement of conspicuous consumption by top management.[31] In brief, they hypothesize that firms seek to discourage top employees from saving so as to avoid the final period problem that arises when such employees accumulate sufficient wealth to fund a luxurious retirement. Reduced savings by such employees encourages them to seek continued employment, which vitiates the final period problem and provides ongoing incentives against shirking. By encouraging current consumption, the oft-decried practices of providing top employees with munificent perks and loans in fact maximize the joint welfare of managers and shareholders.

A number of exhaustive literature reviews have concluded that the evidence for the managerial power hypothesis is far less compelling than its proponents claim. Iman Anabtawi concludes, for example, that "there is limited evidence to suggest that managers exert influence over boards of directors to decouple their pay from their performance."[32] Kevin Murphy likewise offers "evidence inconsistent with the managerial power hypothesis."[33] Franklin Snyder concludes that "most of the results that [Bebchuk and Fried] see as requiring us to postulate managerial dominance turn out to be consistent with a less sinister explanation."[34] Holmstrom and Kaplan note that many observers complain

30. In Defence of the Indefensible, Is Showering the Boss With Perks Good For Shareholders?, The Economist, Dec. 2, 2004.

31. M. Todd Henderson & James C. Spindler, Corporate Heroin: A Defense of Perks, Executive Loans, and Conspicuous Consumption (2005).

32. Iman Anabtawi, Overlooked Alternatives in the Pay Without Performance Debate 39 (Dec. 21, 2004).

33. Kevin J. Murphy, Explaining Executive Compensation: Managerial Power versus the Perceived Cost of Stock Options, 69 U. Chi. L. Rev. 847, 868 (2002).

34. Franklin G. Snyder, More Pieces of the CEO Compensation Puzzle, 28 Del. J. Corp. L. 129, 165 (2003).

that executive compensation packages "represent unmerited transfers of shareholder wealth to top executives with limited if any beneficial incentive effects," but offer a review of the evidence providing "several reasons to be skeptical of these conclusions."[35] They report, for example, that the six-fold increase in CEO pay between 1980 and 2003 could be fully attributed to the six-fold increase in market capitalization of large U.S. companies over the same time period. In other words, CEOs got richer because their shareholders got richer. Indeed, "[t]he fact that shareholders of U.S. companies earned higher returns *even after* payments to management does not support the claim that the U.S. executive pay system is designed inefficiently; if anything, shareholders appear better off with the U.S. system of executive pay than with the systems that prevail in other countries."[36]

In sum, the managerial power claims on which Sarbanes-Oxley's and Dodd-Frank's executive compensation provisions rest on highly contestable evidence. As such, those provisions provide yet another example of how policy entrepreneurs used populist outrage to advance their agenda.

Did Executive Compensation Practices Cause the Crises?

The strongest case for federal regulation of executive compensation rests on claims that unwise compensation practices causally contributed to the economic crises of the last decade. In fact, there is some evidence that that was the case. On close examination, however, that evidence does not support federal regulation in the form it took.

Executive Compensation and Dotcom Fraud in the Late 1990s

In 1994, widespread public complaints about rapid growth in executive compensation prompted a burst of financial populism by President Bill Clinton and Congress, who changed the tax laws to cap at $1 million the deduction corporations may take for executive compensation. Performance or incentive-based forms of compensation, most notably stock options, however, were exempt from this cap (as they still are). The result was a dramatic shift in executive compensation away from cash and toward stock options. The stock market bubble of the late 1990s didn't help matters, as constantly rising stock prices made stock options seem like a sure thing.

---

35. Bengt R. Holmstrom & Steven N. Kaplan, The State of U.S. Corporate Governance: What's Right and What's Wrong?, 15 J. App. Corp. Fin. 8, 12 (2003).
36. Id.

Compensatory stock options normally issue with a strike price equal to the company's stock market price on the options' issue date. If the company's stock price subsequently rises, the executive can exercise the options and sell the shares at the higher market price. In theory, the resulting potential for profit aligns shareholder and manager interests and thus incentivizes executives to maximize the company's stock price.

In practice, however, stock options put tremendous pressure on managers to keep the stock price headed up no matter how the company actually is doing. CEOs insisted that the company beat—or, at least, make—the "number" (that is, the consensus forecast by analysts of the company's quarterly earnings). A company that failed to do so could see its stock price fall drastically as analysts complained and investors jumped off the bandwagon, with resulting catastrophic consequences for the value of the firm's executives' stock options. Under this compulsion to make the number, the temptation to resort to accounting trickery proved too much for many managers to bear.

Did Compensation Practices Encourage Excess Risk Taking?

In the wake of the 2008 credit crunch, much attention was devoted to the role executive compensation played in the housing bubble and its aftermath. As the story goes, executives faced little downside risk. Limited liability means that corporate officers and directors, like shareholders, are not liable for the firm's debts or other obligations. In addition, many executives have golden parachutes or other lucrative severance packages.[37]

At the same time, options and other forms of incentive-based pay offered executives potentially enormous upside gains. As long as the stock price kept going up, the value of their options kept going up. Keeping the stock price headed up required ever-increasing returns. Because risk and return are positively correlated, however, this meant taking on ever-increasing risks. At least in part, this explains why banks were so eager to lend to risky subprime borrowers. It also explains why banks kept lending even after the housing bubble burst. Because interest rates initially remained low, borrowers continued to demand loans, which in turned meant that banks could continue to originate mortgage-backed securities (MBSs), and thus keep profits high.

The relatively short vesting period for compensatory stock options relative to the long maturity of mortgage loans meant that banks were rewarding executives for short-term returns while not holding them responsible for long-term risks. A risky mortgage will carry a high interest rate to compensate the lender for bearing the risk of default. Because defaults will be spread out

37. Richard A. Posner, A Failure of Capitalism 93 (2009).

over the 30-year life of the mortgage rather than front-loaded, the loan is likely to be profitable in the early years. This will certainly be the case for a portfolio of many loans.

Because shareholders have a long-term investment horizon, they prefer risk-return policies that produce sustainable share price appreciation. They therefore would be skeptical of such lending practices. Stock options, however, give management a short-term investment horizon creating incentives "to push the share price up, but not necessarily in a sustainable way."[38] A case study of executives of gold mining companies paid in stock options, for example, found that they took fewer measures to hedge obvious risks than did executives of firms with less volatile compensation.[39] Likewise, a senior bank executive with a few years left before retirement and options with short vesting periods has an incentive to take risks that an investor with a long-term horizon would deem unwise.[40]

Scholars are divided as to whether this incentive structure causally contributed to either the housing or credit crunch. Grant Kirkpatrick contends that incentive pay encouraged high levels of risk taking.[41] Richard Posner argues that the structure of executive compensation practices encouraged management to cling to the housing bubble and "hope for the best."[42] In contrast, Peter Mulbert contends that the empirical evidence does not support treating compensation as a major causal factor.[43] What seems clear, however, is that the problem was localized to the financial sector. Whether or not financial institution executive compensation practices contributed to the crisis, there is no evidence that executive compensation at Main Street corporations did so.

EXECUTIVE COMPENSATION UNDER STATE CORPORATE LAW

A compensation contract between the corporation and one of its officers does not differ in kind from any other conflicted interest transaction covered by the statutes considered in this section. If the disinterested directors, following full

38. Michel Crouhy et al., The Essentials of Risk Management 87 (2006).

39. Danielle Blanchard & Georges Dionne, Risk Management and Corporate Governments 5–6 (September 2003).

40. This divergence between managerial and investor interests is why some argue that managerial power theories of executive compensation are consistent with the belief that compensation contributed to the crisis. They contend that compensation packages negotiated at arm's length would do more to expose managers to long-term risks.

41. Grant Kirkpatrick, The Corporate Governance Lessons from the Financial Crisis, 2009 Fin. Mkt. Trends 1, 2.

42. Posner, supra note 36, at 93.

43. Peter O. Mulbert, Corporate Governance of Banks After the Financial Crisis: Theory, Evidence, Reforms (ECGI Law Working Paper No. 130/2009, Apr. 2010).

disclosure, approve the contract in good faith, the transaction will receive the protection of the business judgment rule.[44] As a result, successful shareholder challenges to executive compensation typically involve close corporations in which disinterested director approval was not obtained.

The difficulty shareholders have in holding either executives or directors liable for allegedly excessive executive compensation is forcefully illustrated by the long-running litigation over Michael Ovitz's pay for the brief period he was President of the Walt Disney Company. Disney CEO and Chairman of the Board Michael Eisner recruited Ovitz to join Disney as Eisner's second-in-command and possible successor. Before joining Disney, Ovitz headed the powerful CAA Hollywood talent agency.

Ovitz was given a five-year employment contract, with a combination of salary, stock options, and severance benefits that the Delaware Supreme Court called "extraordinarily lucrative." After only 14 months, it was obvious—at least to Eisner—that hiring Ovitz had been a mistake. Ovitz had engaged in conduct that might have characterized as grounds for termination with cause. Eisner, however, with the advice of Executive Vice President and General Counsel Sanford Litvack, who said it was a "no brainer," decided not to pursue that option. Instead, Eisner terminated Ovitz without cause. Disney's board was informed of the decision beforehand, but did not formally vote to fire Ovitz or to determine whether cause existed.

Ovitz's severance package was valued at approximately $130 million. If Ovitz had been terminated for cause or had resigned, it would have been much smaller. Shareholders sued derivatively, arguing that the Disney board had breached its fiduciary duties in both hiring and firing Ovitz and that Ovitz had breached his duties as an officer with respect to his conduct in office.

In a lengthy and highly fact-driven opinion, the Delaware Supreme Court held that Disney directors had not violated their duty of care nor acted in bad faith in connection with their handling of the hiring and subsequent no fault termination of Ovitz.[45] It further held that Ovitz had not violated his duties.

The court emphasized that business judgment rule protects director decisions even when the "information and decision-making process" "was not so tidy" as would have been the case had the directors "followed a 'best practices' (or 'best case') scenario" or falls "short of what best practices would have

44. See, e.g., Zupnick v. Goizueta, 698 A.2d 384 (Del.Ch.1997) (after holding that approval of a stock option based compensation plan by the disinterested directors shifted the burden of proof to plaintiff to show waste, the court further held: "To state a cognizable claim for waste where there is no contention that the directors were interested or that shareholder ratification was improperly obtained, the well pleaded allegations of the complaint must support the conclusion that 'no person of ordinary, sound business judgment would say that the consideration received for the options was a fair exchange for the options granted.'").
45. In re The Walt Disney Co. Derivative Litigation, 906 A.2d 27 (Del. 2006).

counseled."[46] Additionally, the court found that the board's compensation committee had the power to approve Ovitz's pay package, without referring the matter to the full board, and exercised due care in doing so. The full board was entitled to rely on Eisner and the compensation committee. Finally, the court rejected the shareholders' argument that Ovitz's compensation package gave him an incentive to get fired and therefore was inherently wasteful.[47] The deal had a rational business purpose—i.e., to induce Ovitz to leave his highly lucrative position at CAA. There was no evidence that the deal "irrationally incentivized Ovitz to get himself fired."[48]

The *Disney* case makes clear that, absent evidence of self-dealing, Delaware corporate law will focus almost exclusively on the process by which executive compensation is set rather than the amount or form of such compensation. As the court explained in an earlier decision in the lengthy litigation:

> Courts do not measure, weigh or quantify directors' judgments. We do not even decide if they are reasonable in this context. Due care in the decisionmaking context is process due care only. . . .
>
> . . . Thus, directors' decisions will be respected by courts unless the directors are interested or lack independence relative to the decision, do not act in good faith, act in a manner that cannot be attributed to a rational business purpose or reach their decision by a grossly negligent process that includes the failure to consider all material facts reasonably available.[49]

In effect, boards thus can insulate themselves from liability exposure in this area by hiring competent legal counsel to advise them on the appropriate decision-making process and hiring an expert compensation consultant to advise them with respect to setting an appropriate form and level of compensation. Of course, the board will not pay those experts; instead, they are paid out of the corporate treasury. In effect, the board can use the shareholders' money to buy themselves litigation insurance.

EXECUTIVE COMPENSATION REGULATION UNDER SARBANES-OXLEY AND DODD-FRANK

The Sarbanes-Oxley Act contained several executive compensation provisions, to which the concomitant stock exchange listing standard amendments added

46. Id. at 56.
47. Id. at 75.
48. Id.
49. Brehm v. Eisner, 746 A.2d 244, 264 (Del. 2000).

still more. Dodd-Frank's executive compensation provisions revisited several of the Sarbanes-Oxley rules. Accordingly, this section looks at the post-crisis federal compensation regime functionally rather than statute by statute.

Capping Compensation

President Obama observed of the bank bailouts that "I did not run for office to be helping out a bunch of fat cat bankers on Wall Street."[50] His criticism reflected genuine and widespread populist outrage directed at TARP fund recipient financial institutions that had paid multimillion dollar bonuses to executives despite being indebted to the federal Treasury. As President Obama argued, if TARP recipients could "afford massive bonuses," they should also be able to pay "back every penny to taxpayers."[51]

The final TARP regime contained a number of executive compensation restrictions, including a de facto cap on the size of pay packages. TARP recipients whose aggregate distressed assets acquired by the program exceeded $300 million could not deduct more than $500,000 in compensation paid to senior executive officers (SEOs). SEOs were defined to include the firm's CEO, CFO, and top three other most highly compensated executives. The $500,000 per SEO deduction limit included all forms of compensation, including options, bonuses, and other performance-based pay.

In addition, TARP recipients were banned from paying bonuses, retention awards, or incentive compensation to covered employees. The number of employees to whom the prohibition applied depended on the amount of TARP funds the firm had received. If the firm had received less than $25 million in TARP assistance, for example, only the most highly compensated employee was subject to the prohibition. If the firm had received $500 million or more in TARP funds, however, the firm's SEOs and the 20 other most highly compensated employees were covered. A sliding scale applied to firms falling in between those extremes.

The final rules also banned golden parachute payments to SEOs and five other most highly compensated employees of TARP recipients. Golden parachute was defined very broadly to encompass essentially all severance arrangements.

TARP's de facto pay cap was problematic for several reasons. First, our analysis of the role executive compensation played in the crisis of 2007–2008,

---

50. Derrick Henry, Obama Decries "Fat Cat Bankers," N.Y. Times, Dec. 14, 2009.
51. Jesse Lee, The President to Wall Street: "We Want Our Money Back, and We're Going to Get It," White House Blog, Jan. 14, 2010, http://www.whitehouse.gov/blog/2010/01/14/president-wall-street-we-want-our-money-back-and-were-going-get-it.

if any, suggests it was the form compensation took rather than the dollar amount that was the problem. Accordingly, one could make a case for restrictions on performance-based plans, at least if the restrictions addressed the way such pay plans incentivized managers to maximize short-term returns without regard to long-term risks. There was no justification for the one-size-fits-all cap on the amount of compensation, the sweeping ban on all performance-based pay regardless of structure, or the prohibition of severance packages. Instead, these restrictions played to the crowd. They were motivated by the political storm created by the perception that taxpayer funds were being used to finance big paydays for the Wall Street "fat cats" who supposedly had driven the economy into the ditch.

Second, the executive pay restrictions skewed decision making by potential TARP recipients. A study of large financial institutions found a clear link between compensation practices and the decision to accept TARP funds. In general, firms whose executives were more likely to be affected by the TARP pay restrictions were less likely to accept those funds.[52] Some banks that did accept TARP funds reportedly repaid them more quickly than expected so as to get out from under the compensation rules.[53]

Third, the compensation rules skewed decision making by individuals in the financial services industry. There is both anecdotal and survey evidence that financial institutions not subject to the TARP restrictions were able to hire top executives away from TARP recipients.[54] At a time when the banking industry desperately needed to retain its best and brightest, the ban on retention awards thus seemed especially unwise.

Finally, our analysis suggests that it was not SEO compensation that was the problem but rather the compensation packages of the traders and other relatively junior employees who actually made day-to-day decisions on issues ranging from whether to make a loan to whether to trade in some fancy derivative. It was their incentive to take excess risk for short-term gain that brought many financial institutions to their knees. Yet, TARP focused exclusively on the very highest paid managerial echelons.

Ban on Loans to Directors and Executive Officers

Sarbanes-Oxley § 402 prohibits a corporation from directly or indirectly making loans to its directors and executive officers. Contrary to conventional wisdom, § 402 does not prohibit all loans to insiders. Important classes of

---

52. Brian Cadman et al., Executive Pay Restrictions: Do They Restrict Firms' Willingness to Participate in TARP? (Aug. 2010).
53. Id. at 2.
54. Id.

exempt transactions include corporate credit cards issued to employees, borrowing by employees against a 401(k) account, margin loans by a brokerage house to its employees, and loans by financial institutions to their employees. On the other hand, § 402 prohibits not only loans made by the corporation to its insiders, but also prohibits the corporation from arranging "for the extension of credit." As a result, an employer can no longer arrange for a bank to lend money to one of its insiders. Even such innocuous transactions as the home mortgage assistance programs formerly run by many employers in high-cost locations (like Silicon Valley) thus are no longer permitted.

When Sarbanes-Oxley first came into force there were a great many ambiguities associated with § 402. In particular, Sarbanes-Oxley failed to define the two key operative terms: "personal loans" and "extensions of credit." Under state corporate law indemnification statutes, for example, corporations frequently do (and in some cases must) advance legal expenses to covered officers and directors. Given the sweeping language of the prohibition on "extensions of credit," some observers believed that § 402 effectively prohibited any such advancement of funds. In support of such an interpretation, they cited Delaware case law holding that advancement of expenses "is essentially simply a decision to advance credit."[55] Sensibly, however, a federal court held in *Envirokare Tech, Inc. v. Pappas*,[56] that § 402 does not prevent a corporation from advancing expenses to officers or directors pursuant to state indemnification statutes:

> Section 402(a) . . . added a new Section 13(k) to the Securities and Exchange Act of 1934 which makes it "unlawful" for a reporting company, directly or indirectly, "to extend or maintain credit, to arrange for the extension of credit, or to renew an extension of credit, in the form of a personal loan to or for any director or executive officer . . . of that issuer. Envirokare claims that this provision forecloses the advancement of expenses to officers and directors by reporting companies because these advances, though authorized by their by-laws and state law are forbidden extensions of credit. Envirokare earns full points for creativity, but the argument is unpersuasive. . . .
>
> Sarbanes-Oxley was enacted in the wake of the corporate scandals of a few years ago, which included the making of huge loans by certain companies to their executives, perhaps most notably a $400 million loan by WorldCom to its now-convicted former chief executive officer, Bernard Ebbers. Envirokare has not called the Court's attention to even a hint that Congress was concerned with stopping the advancement of defense costs to corporate officials pursuant to by-laws and state corporation statutes, and the Court is aware of none. Moreover,

55. Advanced Min. Systems, Inc. v. Fricke, 623 A.2d 82, 84 (Del. Ch. 1992).
56. 420 F.Supp.2d 291 (S.D.N.Y. 2006).

Congress, had it intended such a radical step as prohibiting such advances, surely would have made its purpose evident in explicit terms.

This conclusion is reinforced by the absurd consequences that would flow from the adoption of the position taken by Envirokare. As Professor Coffee has pointed out, such an interpretation of the statute "would on its face bar a $2,000 travel advance to a Vice President who is about to fly to London to close a deal for his corporation." It would render it equally unlawful for a corporate officer to take a few dollars from petty cash to buy postage stamps for the purpose of mailing a company's tax return to the Internal Revenue Service.[57]

Common sense thus prevailed. Unfortunately, even though Sarbanes-Oxley has been on the books for a decade, many questions remain open. Whether § 402 prohibits certain forms of cashless option exercises, for example, remains widely debated.

Whether the ban on executive loans itself was necessary likewise remains debatable. As the *Pappas* court noted, Congress was concerned with large loans made to executives. Such loans can be used to hide executive compensation. From a tax perspective, salary and dividends are taxable to the recipient, but the proceeds of a loan are not taxable income. From an accounting perspective, loans are corporate assets, so the money in a sense stays on the books, while the company must deduct salary and dividends from assets.

Yet, it is not clear that a flat prohibition—rather than just enhanced disclosure of insider loans—was appropriate. Section 402 directly preempts the interested party transaction provisions of state corporate law, which currently permit the making of loans to directors and officers provided the loans are approved by a majority of the disinterested directors or the shareholders. While that requirement may not have prevented every instance of abuse, preemption of state law ought to be undertaken only when states have clearly failed and the federal alternative is a clear improvement. Neither condition was satisfied here.

Based on her review of pre-SOX studies, Roberta Romano concluded that "executive loans in a large class of cases served their purpose well, [by] aligning the manager's and shareholders' interest."[58] Accordingly, she contended, the "blanket prohibition of executive loans in SOX" was self-evidently a public policy error."[59]

The provision in the original Senate bill, which was consistent with the conventional federal regulatory approach, required disclosure of executive loans and

57. Id. at 294.
58. Roberta Romano, The Sarbanes-Oxley Act and the Making of Quack Corporate Governance, 114 Yale L.J. 1521, 1539 (2005).
59. Id.

did not prohibit them. Such an approach would have been far less problematic than the final legislative product from the perspective of shareholder welfare. It would have had the effect of facilitating the termination of loans most unlikely to benefit shareholders, by highlighting their presence to investors who could then place those loans' elimination onto a corporate governance agenda (in the many states where they would otherwise not be involved because shareholder approval of loans is not required). Instead, the legislation is a blunderbuss approach that prohibits all loans, whether or not they are useful in facilitating the shareholders' objective of providing a sought-after incentive effect.[60]

Pay Disclosures

Dodd-Frank requires each reporting company's annual proxy statement to contain a clear exposition of the relationship between executive compensation and the issuer's financial performance. It further requires disclosure of "the median of the annual total compensation of all employees of the issuer' except the CEO, the CEO's annual total compensation, and the ratio of the two amounts." This requirement is going to be hugely burdensome:

> [It] means that for every employee, the company would have to calculate his or her salary, bonus, stock awards, option awards, nonequity incentive plan compensation, change in pension value and nonqualified deferred compensation earnings, and all other compensation (e.g., perquisites). This information would undoubtedly be extremely time-consuming to collect and analyze, making it virtually impossible for a company with thousands of employees to comply with this section of the Act.[61]

The Senate Committee cited the Council of Institutional Investors (CII) as having supported this provision.[62] CII's position as a de facto trade association for large, activist investors makes it an important policy entrepreneur. In addition to thus being part of a key interest group's agenda, however, the provision also should be seen as part of the populist backlash against corporations

---

60. Id. at 1539–40.
61. Warren J. Casey & Richard Leu, United States: New Executive Compensation Disclosures Under Dodd-Frank (August 3, 2010), Mondaq.com, http://www.mondaq.com/unitedstates/article.asp?articleid=106962. See also Jean Eaglesham & Francesco Guerrera, Pay Law Sparks "Nightmare" on Wall St, Fin. Times, Aug. 31, 2010, at 1 ("'The rules' complexity means multinationals face a 'logistical nightmare' in calculating the ratio, which has to be based on the median annual total compensation for all employees,' warned Richard Susko, partner at law firm Cleary Gottlieb. 'It's just not do-able for a large company with tens of thousands of employees worldwide.'").
62. S. Rep. No. 111–176, at 135 (2010).

and markets. "The law taps into public anger at the increasing disparity between the faltering incomes of middle America and the largely recession-proof multimillion-dollar remuneration of the typical corporate chief."[63]

Compensation Committees

As the name suggests, the compensation committee reviews and approves (or recommends to the full board) the compensation of senior executives and generally oversees the corporation's compensation policies. Proponents of having a separate compensation committee deal with such matters, rather than the board as a whole, argue that inside directors, even if recused from considering their own compensation, cannot objectively evaluate the compensation of other senior executives in light of the close relationship between one executive's compensation and that of another.

Under NYSE Listed Company Manual § 303A.05, the board of directors of all listed companies must have a compensation committee. The committee must consist solely of independent directors. Only listed companies in which a shareholder or group of shareholders acting together own 50 percent or more of the stock are exempt from this requirement.

The NYSE requires that the compensation committee adopt a written charter setting out the committee's purpose, responsibilities, and powers. At a minimum, the charter must grant the compensation committee power to set performance goals for the CEO to meet, evaluate the CEO's performance in light of those goals, and set the CEO's pay. If the board wishes, the compensation committee may simply recommend a pay figure for the CEO, on which all the independent directors would then act. Notice that, in either case, only independent directors are involved in setting the CEO's salary. The committee must also have power to make recommendations to the board of directors with respect to the pay of other executive officers and any incentive or stock-based compensation plans that are subject to board approval. The power to hire, fire, and compensate compensation consultants must be vested in the compensation committee rather than the CEO.

In order to ensure compensation committee independence, the NYSE definition of independent director includes a somewhat curious provision under which someone will not be deemed independent if he "or an immediate family member is, or has been within the last three years, employed as an executive officer of another company where any of the listed company's present executive officers at the same time serves or served on that company's compensation committee." Suppose, for example, that Jane is a director of

63. Eaglesham & Guerrera, supra note 61.

Ajax Corporation. Jane is also the CFO of Zeus Corporation. Donna is Ajax's CLO (a.k.a. general counsel), a member of Zeus's board of directors, and a member of Zeus's compensation committee. Under the NYSE rule, because Donna is on Zeus's compensation committee, Jane cannot be deemed an independent director of Ajax. Donna can be deemed an independent director of Zeus, however, because the interlock rule runs in only one direction.

Dodd-Frank § 952 contains a number of provisions relating to compensation committees, including a directive that the SEC direct the self-regulatory organizations (SROs) to adopt listing standards requiring that each member of an issuer's compensation committee be independent. Curiously, there is disagreement as to whether Section 952 mandates that SRO listing standards require all listed companies to have an independent compensation committee. The issue has salience because current NASDAQ listing standards permit executive compensation decisions to be made either by a committee comprised solely of independent directors or by a majority of the independent directors. Nothing in § 952 or the legislative history addresses explicitly the status of those standards, thereby creating some uncertainty.

Once again, we see a provision pushed by a powerful policy entrepreneur, in this case the CII, which argued that the bill should "ensure that compensation committees are free of conflicts and receive unbiased advice."[64] Once again, we see another one size fits all model being forced on all public companies. Once again, the mandate lacks support in the empirical evidence. Most empirical studies have rejected the hypothesis that compensation committee independence is positively correlated with firm performance or with improved CEO compensation practices.[65]

Clawbacks

One of the principal political factors driving the passage of Sarbanes-Oxley was the massive wave of corporate earnings restatements in 2000 and 2001. In response to concerns that the original disclosures had been managed by top executives so as to maximize the value of their stock options, Congress included § 304 in Sarbanes-Oxley. Under it, in the event a corporation is obliged to restate its financial statements due to "misconduct," the CEO and CFO must return to the corporation any bonus, incentive, or equity-based compensation they received during the twelve months following the original

---

64. S. Rep. No. 111–176, at 135 (2010).

65. See Iman Anabtawi, Explaining Pay Without Performance: The Tournament Alternative, 54 Emory L.J. 1557, 1582–83 (2005) (reviewing studies).

issuance of the restated financials, along with any profits they realized from the sale of corporate stock during that period.

A key ambiguity in the statute is whether misconduct by persons other than the CEO or CFO could result in the clawback being applied to CEO/CFO compensation. In *SEC v. Jenkins*, a federal district court accepted the SEC's position "that the misconduct of corporate officers, agents or employees acting within the scope of their agency or employment is sufficient misconduct to meet this element of the statute."[66] CSK Auto Corporation had been obliged to restate its financials due to massive fraud by a number of senior officers. Although CEO Maynard Jenkins was not charged with any misconduct, the SEC nevertheless invoked § 304 to claw back Jenkin's pay.

Wachtell Lipton attorneys John Savarese and Wayne Carlin objected that:

> The SEC's decision to depart from its prior reasonable restraint in using Section 304 is a regrettable policy choice. Clearly, the SEC believes fraud occurred at CSK, but apparently can find no basis to assert that the CEO was culpable in it. The SEC has not even pursued any of the lesser charges that would be available against a blameworthy executive in these circumstances, such as a negligence-based administrative case. In these circumstances, it is difficult to discern what conduct by similarly situated CEOs the SEC may think this case will deter or encourage. It also remains to be seen whether a federal agency may constitutionally deprive a person who is not alleged to have violated any law of compensation that was lawfully received, particularly where the statute's intended reach is ambiguous.[67]

The argument in favor of the SEC's position begins by recognizing that, during the 1990s, restating financials became commonplace. Some firms were notorious for taking incredibly aggressive accounting positions. When they were called out for it, they simply restated their financials and claimed the SEC and/or private claim was moot.

As illustrated by other provisions of Sarbanes-Oxley, such as the CEO and CFO certification rules, Congress concluded that too many CEOs and CFOs had simply turned a blind eye to misconduct by subordinates. A clawback rule that essentially imposes strict liability on CEOs and CFOs for subordinate misconduct arguably provides a powerful incentive for CEOs and CFOs to ensure that the company's internal controls work.

---

66. SEC v. Jenkins, 718 F. Supp.2d 1070, 1075 (D. Ariz. 2010).
67. John F. Savarese & Wayne M. Carlin, SEC Pursues Unprecedented Sarbanes-Oxley "Clawback," Harv. L. Sch. Forum on Corp. Gov. & Fin. Reg. (Aug. 1, 2009), http://blogs.law.harvard.edu/corpgov/2009/08/01/sec-pursues-unprecedented-sarbanes-oxley-clawback/.

A related argument is that much corporate financial statement shenanigans during the 1990s appears to have been motivated by efforts to maximize the value of top manager's stock options and other forms of equity and incentive compensation. Or, at least, so Congress concluded. It is precisely those forms of compensation that § 304 targets. The CEO and CFO, one might argue, should not be allowed to benefit from misconduct by subordinates, whether or not the CEO or CFO was aware of the misconduct. Any other rule would perpetuate the incentive to turn a blind eye.

Critics such as Savarese and Carlin argue that strict liability will result in over-deterrence. But over-deterrence of what? What valuable types of conduct are we concerned about overly deterring? If we assume that in this context, under-deterrence would be more costly than over-deterrence, a strict liability like § 304 is preferable to a fault-based rule.

As Savarese and Carlin's argument implies, however, § 304 ignores moral culpability. CEOs and CFOs are not insurers of stockholders, obliged to compensate them for any loss the stockholders may suffer, but that is what strict liability under § 304 makes those officers with respect to misconduct no matter how far down the organization chart it occurs.

However one comes out on applying § 304 in the absence of actual misconduct by the targeted CEO or CFO, the provision is problematic on other grounds. It preempts both state law and the board of director's power over executive compensation. It fails to define the kinds of misconduct that trigger the reimbursement obligation. It will encourage CEOs and CFOs to resist restating flawed financial statements and/or to game the timing of their compensation and stock transactions relative to any such restatements.

Dodd-Frank § 954 extends the clawback regime by adding a new § 10D to the Securities Exchange Act, pursuant to which the SEC is instructed to direct the stock exchanges to require their listed companies to disclose company policies for clawing back incentive-based compensation paid to current or former executive officers in the event of a restatement of the company's financials due to material non-compliance with any federal securities law financial reporting requirement. Issuers failing to adopt such a policy must be delisted.[68] The requisite policy must provide for clawing back any "excess" compensation any such executive officer received during the three-year period prior to the date on which the issuer was obliged to issue the restatement. Excess compensation is defined as the difference between what the executive was paid and what the executive would have received if the financials had been correct.[69]

As with Sarbanes-Oxley § 304, some will argue that § 954 is over-inclusive. It encompasses all executive officers, without regard to their responsibility or

68. S. Rep. No. 111–176, at 135.
69. Id.

lack thereof for the financial statement in question. Some innocent executives therefore will have to forfeit significant amounts of pay. At the same time, however, § 954 is under-inclusive. Executive officers include an issuer's "president, any vice president . . . in charge of a principal business unit, division or function . . ., any other officer who performs a policy making function or any other person who performs similar policy making functions. . . ."[70] As the Senate committee acknowledged, the policy therefore applies only to a "very limited number of employees. . . ."[71] The trouble with this limitation is that "decisions of individuals such as proprietary traders, who may well not be among" an issuer's executive officers nevertheless "can adversely affect, indeed implode, a firm."[72]

Another concern is the high probability of unintended consequences. In response to the Sarbanes-Oxley Act's much narrower clawback provision, "companies increased non-forfeitable, fixed-salary compensation and decreased incentive compensation, thereby providing insurance to managers for increased risk."[73] Because current federal policy seeks to promote pay for performance, mandatory clawbacks undermine that goal. There is a significant risk, moreover, that other unintended consequences will develop in light of the "many ambiguities in the legislative language which will have to be clarified in implementing SEC regulations, e.g. is it retroactive, how to calculate recoverable amount, the dates during which the recovery must be sought."[74]

Say on Pay

Dodd-Frank § 951 creates a new § 14A of the Securities Exchange Act, pursuant to which reporting companies must conduct a shareholder advisory vote on specified executive compensation not less frequently than every three years. At least once every six years, shareholders must vote on how frequently to hold such an advisory vote (i.e., annually, biannually, or triannually). The compensation arrangements subject to the shareholder vote are those set out in Item 402 of Regulation S-K, which includes all compensation paid to the CEO, CFO, and the three other highest paid executive officers. In addition, a shareholder advisory is required of golden parachutes. Both such votes must

---

70. 17 CFR § 240.3b-7.
71. S. Rep. No. 111–176, at 135.
72. Sanjai Bhagat & Roberta Romano, Reforming Executive Compensation: Focusing and Committing to the Long-Term, 26 Yale J. Reg. 359, 366 (2009).
73. Id.
74. Ben W. Heineman, Jr., Making Sense Out of "Clawbacks," Harv. L. Sch. Forum on Corp. Gov. & Fin. Reg. (Aug. 13, 2010), http://blogs.law.harvard.edu/corpgov/2010/08/13/making-sense-out-of-clawbacks/.

be tabulated and disclosed, but neither is binding on the board of directors.[75] The votes shall not be deemed either to effect or affect the fiduciary duties of directors. The SEC is given exemption power and is specifically directed to evaluate the impact on small issuers.

Will Say on Pay Work?

The effectiveness of say on pay is highly contested. The Senate committee report argued that:

> The UK has implemented "say on pay" policy. Professor John Coates in testimony for the Senate Banking Committee stated that the UK's experience has been positive; "different researchers have conducted several investigations of this kind . . . These findings suggest that say-on-pay legislation would have a positive impact on corporate governance in the U.S. While the two legal contexts are not identical, there is no evidence in the existing literature to suggest that the differences would turn what would be a good idea in the UK into a bad one in the U.S."[76]

In contrast, Professor Jeffrey Gordon argues that the U.K. experience with say on pay makes a mandatory vote a "dubious choice."[77] First, because individualized review of compensation schemes at the 10,000-odd U.S. reporting companies will be prohibitively expensive, activist institutional investors will probably insist on a narrow range of compensation programs that will force companies into something close to a one-size-fits-all model. Second, because many institutional investors rely on proxy advisory firms, a very small number of gatekeepers will wield undue influence over compensation. This likely outcome seriously undercuts the case for say on pay. Proponents of say on pay claim it will help make management more accountable, but they ignore the probability that say on pay really will shift power from boards of directors not to shareholders but to advisory firms like RiskMetrics. There is good reason to think that boards are more accountable than those firms. "The most important proxy advisor, RiskMetrics, already faces conflict issues in its dual role of both advising and rating firms on corporate governance that will be greatly magnified when it begins to rate firms on their compensation plans."[78] Ironically, the only constraint on RiskMetrics' conflict is the market—i.e., the

---

75. S. Rep. No. 111–176, at 133 (2010).
76. Id. at 134.
77. Jeffrey N. Gordon, "Say on Pay": Cautionary Notes on the U.K. Experience and the Case for Shareholder Opt-in, 46 Harv. J. Legis. 323, 325 (2009).
78. Id. at 326.

possibility that they will lose credibility and therefore customers—the very force most shareholder power proponents claim does not work when it comes to holding management accountable.

As for the U.K. experience, Gordon's review of the empirical evidence finds that shareholders almost invariably approve the compensation packages put to a vote.[79] He further finds that while there is some evidence that pay for performance sensitivity has increased in the United Kingdom, executive compensation has continued to rise significantly in the United Kingdom. Indeed, the growth rate for long-term incentive plans has been higher than in the United States.

Gordon concludes "that 'say on pay' has some downsides even in the United Kingdom, downsides that would be exacerbated by a simple transplant into the United States."[80] He recommended that any federal rule be limited to an opt-in regime or, if some form of mandatory regime was politically necessary, that it be limited to the very largest firms. Gordon's proposal finds support in a recent behavioral economics laboratory experiment finding that say on pay has a more positive impact on investors when it is voluntarily effected by companies than when it is mandated.[81] As we have seen, however, Congress went in a different direction, despite the considerable uncertainty as to whether say on pay will be effective.

The Departure from Board Centrism

There is no more basic question in corporate governance than "who decides"? Is a particular decision or oversight task to be assigned to the board of directors, management, or shareholders? As we will see in chapter 7, corporate law generally adopts what I have called "director primacy." It assigns decision making to the board of directors or the managers to whom the board has properly delegated authority. Under state law, executive compensation is no exception.

To be sure, the say on pay provision contained in Dodd-Frank is only an advisory vote. Yet, the logic of an advisory vote on pay seems to be the same as that underlying precatory shareholder proposals made pursuant

79. See id. at 341 (explaining that "shareholders invariably approve the Directors Remuneration Report, with perhaps eight turndowns across thousands of votes over a six-year experience"). The same is true of the limited U.S. experience with voluntary say on pay. See id. at 339 ("The number of proposals grew only moderately [in 2008], to seventy, and the level of shareholder support has remained at the same level, approximately forty-two percent.").

80. Id. at 367.

81. Kendall O. Bowlin et al., Say-on-Pay and the Differential Effects of Voluntary Versus Mandatory Regimes on Investor Perceptions and Behavior (August 16, 2010), http://ssrn.com/abstract=1659862.

to Rule 14a-8. Even though shareholder proposals generally are not binding, they nevertheless affect director decisions.[82]

Indeed, the preliminary results from say on pay votes in 2010 and 2011 strongly suggest that say on pay will be turned into a club with which activists will beat boards of directors. In 2010, when several hundred companies voluntarily conducted say on pay votes, two companies at which the vote was negative were subsequently hit with lawsuits alleging waste and breach of fiduciary duty.[83] Given the business judgment rule and the express Congressional statement that say on pay is supposed to be nonbinding, it is difficult to imagine that such suits will have much more than nuisance value. Even so, they may generate negative publicity and withhold vote campaigns against directors. The costs to shareholders of say on pay thus may turn out to be quite significant.

Say on pay is just one small piece of the shareholder activists' agenda, moreover. As we will see in chapter 7, Dodd-Frank accomplished another of those agenda items by authorizing the SEC to go forward with proxy access. Another of the activists' agenda items was recently achieved when states began changing their corporation statutes to allow the use of majority voting in election of directors.[84]

[In sum, there have been] a number of important developments—including increased institutional investing, changes in federal proxy law, the creation of shareholder advisory services, the rise of activist hedge funds, and financial innovations that can magnify activists' voting power—[that] have worked together to significantly shift the balance of power in public firms away from executives and boards and toward activist shareholders. The trend seems likely only to continue as would-be reformers push to increase shareholder power further.[85]

Say on pay thus is part of "the 'disintegrating erosion' of particular exceptions,"[86] to borrow a phrase from Cardozo, by which director primacy is slowly being undermined.

82. See Randall S. Thomas & Kenneth J. Martin, The Effect of Shareholder Proposals on Executive Compensation, 67 U. Cin. L. Rev. 1021, 1065–67 (1999) (finding some support for claim that non-binding shareholder proposals affect compensation outcomes).

83. Schulte Roth & Zabel LLP, "Say on Pay" at 30 Days—Observations from the First Month (Feb. 25, 2011).

84. See J.W. Verret, Pandora's Ballot Box, or a Proxy with Moxie? Majority Voting, Corporate Ballot Access, and the Legend of Martin Lipton Re-Examined, 62 Bus. Law. 1007 (2007) (discussing a 2006 amendment to Delaware's corporate statute authorizing bylaw amendments relating to majority voting for the board of directors).

85. Iman Anabtawi & Lynn Stout, Fiduciary Duties for Activist Shareholders, 60 Stan. L. Rev. 1255, 1261 (2008).

86. Meinhard v. Salmon, 164 N.E. 545, 546 (N.Y. 1928).

As we have seen, regulators and some commentators identified executive compensation schemes that focused bank managers on short-term returns to shareholders as a causal factor in the financial crisis of 2007–2008.[87] As we have also seen, shareholder activists long have complained that these schemes provide pay without performance. This was one of the corporate governance flaws Dodd-Frank was intended to address, most notably via say on pay.

The trouble, of course, is that shareholders and society do not have the same goals when it comes to executive pay. Society wants managers to be more risk averse. Shareholders want them to be less risk averse. If say on pay and other shareholder empowerment provisions of Dodd-Frank succeed, manager and shareholder interests will be further aligned, which will encourage the former to undertake higher risks in the search for higher returns to shareholders.[88] Accordingly, as Christopher Bruner aptly observed, "the shareholder-empowerment position appears self-contradictory, essentially amounting to the claim that we must give shareholders more power because managers left to the themselves have excessively focused on the shareholders' interests."[89]

Say on Pay Quackery

Say on pay is yet another example of quack corporate governance. In Congress, it was strongly supported by institutional investors and their allies, including the CII, "the Consumer Federation of America, AFSCME, and the Investor's Working Group."[90] Even before Dodd-Frank, it had been a long-standing goal of the AFL-CIO.[91] As with other examples of quack corporate governance,

87. Mülbert, supra note 43, at 8.

88. See Carl R. Chen et al., Does Stock Option-Based Executive Compensation Induce Risk-Taking? An Analysis of the Banking Industry, 30 J. Banking & Fin. 915, 943 (2006) (arguing that the structure of executive compensation in the banking industry pre-crisis induced risk taking by managers); Kose John & Yiming Qian, Incentive Features in CEO Compensation in the Banking Industry, FRBNY Econ. Pol'y Rev., Apr., 2003, at 109 (arguing that if executive compensation induces the interests of managers to "closely aligned with equity interests in banks, which are highly leveraged institutions, management will have strong incentives to undertake high-risk investments").

89. Christopher M. Bruner, Corporate Governance in a Time of Crisis 13 (2010), http://ssrn.com/abstract=1617890.

90. S. Rep. No. 111–176, at 134.

91. Doug Halonen, Retirement Policy is Unlikely to be Part of GOP Convention, Pensions & Inv., Sept. 1, 2008, at 3.

say on pay thus is the product of a powerful group of policy entrepreneurs pursuing an agenda unrelated to the financial crisis.

Like other quack corporate governance statutes, say on pay federalizes matters previously left to state corporate law. It does so without strong empirical support. It is inconsistent with the board-centric model that has been the foundation of the U.S. corporate governance system's success.

CHAPTER 5
Internal Controls

That something was wrong at Enron first came to public attention in October 2001, when the firm announced a reduction of $1.2 billion in shareholder equity resulting from transactions with a special purpose entity (SPE) created so as to move substantial amounts of Enron debt off its balance sheet. Enron's roots went back to the 1930 formation of the Northern Natural Gas Company. By the early 1990s, following many mergers and name changes, Enron was a large and seemingly highly successful electricity and natural gas distributor with large investments in power plants, pipelines, and other energy utility infrastructure.

For much of the 1990s, the new financial giant looked like a roaring success. It was widely regarded as one of America's most innovative companies and best employers. In fact, however, there were serious problems behind the façade.

Enron financed its rapid growth and expansion in the 1990s mainly by borrowing. By the late 1990s, Enron was deeply in debt but remained dependent on continued borrowing for expansion and debt service. As the debt mounted, it began to pose a significant threat to Enron's credit rating. In turn, because Enron's energy-trading business was dependent on the company maintaining an investment-grade rating for its debt securities, top Enron management began looking for creative new ways of raising money.

The solution Enron CFO Andrew Fastow hit upon was the use of so-called special purpose entities (SPE), typically limited liability companies or partnerships, which entered into complex transactions with Enron. Although the SPEs technically were independent companies, Enron in fact controlled them and used the money they raised to finance Enron's business ventures.

At the risk of oversimplifying, the basic structure of these deals involved the creation of a limited partnership to which Enron sold stock (or other assets). Using the stock as collateral, the SPE would go to a bank or other lender and borrow money to finance some business venture. Because the SPE initially had no debts and Enron stock was appreciating so rapidly in value, banks would lend to these SPEs on very favorable terms.

The trick was that under arcane accounting rules, as long as someone other than Enron owned at least 3 percent of the SPE's equity, Enron's consolidated financial statements did not have to disclose the SPE's assets and debts. Hence, these SPE investments were "off balance sheet." By thus concentrating debt in these off-balance-sheet SPEs, Enron hoped that both its credit rating and stock price would remain high despite its increasingly precarious financial situation. So long as investors and analysts remained in the dark, the game could go on.

The SPEs were not just an accounting game, however. Despite the obvious conflict of interest inherent in related-party transactions between a corporation and one of its officers or directors, Enron's board routinely waived its ethics rules to allow Fastow's participation in the SPE deals as a part owner of the SPE. According to a subsequent internal investigation, Fastow made over $30 million in profit from these deals. Several other Enron executives also participated in these deals and likewise made millions. In most of these transactions, Enron's internal controls proved inadequate, not least because Enron managers did not even bother to follow the accounting controls the firm had established.

It all started to unravel when investigative journalists and the SEC finally began taking a serious look at the minutiae of Enron's finances. Enron was forced to restate its earnings for the period 1997–2000 to account properly for SPE transactions with two other SPEs. The restatement slashed Enron's earnings, hugely inflated the amount of debt on the balance sheet, and massively cut into shareholder equity. Enron's stock price tumbled from over $90 per share to less than $1. Shareholders and creditors filed numerous lawsuits. Criminal and civil fraud investigations ensued. In December 2001, Enron declared bankruptcy.

In 2004, CFO Fastow entered a guilty plea under which he agreed to testify against former Enron CEO Jeffrey Skilling and chairman Kenneth Lay. Under the deal, Fastow was sentenced to a ten-year prison term. Former Enron executives Michael Kopper and Ben Glisan struck similar deals. In 2006, Lay and Skilling were convicted of numerous counts of securities fraud and conspiracy. Lay passed away in July 2006. In October 2006, Skilling was sentenced to twenty-four years in prison.

Although Enron emerged as the poster child for reform, it was hardly alone. The wave of restated financials in 2001–2002 confirmed that there were basic, widespread deficiencies with the financial disclosures provided by many companies. Congress concluded that there were two basic sets of problems underlying the scandal. First, all of the key players with responsibility for internal controls—management, the outside auditor, and the board of directors and its audit committee—failed in various ways. We will examine the reforms directed at management and the auditors in subsequent chapters. Here we will focus on the role of the audit committee, which emerged from Sarbanes-Oxley as a key player in corporate governance.

> Once a simple board committee with few specific duties, the audit committee is now a key element of corporate governance. . . . The post Sarbanes-Oxley audit committee is more than the supervisor of the issuer's financial functions. . . . Its SOX expanded portfolio makes it a conduit for employee complaints, a hotline for whistleblowers and the investigator of all things gone awry—all with an uncapped budget the company is required to fund. The committee has been transformed into an in-house monitor which at times appears to be virtually a separate entity from the company.[1]

Second, Congress concluded that Enron, WorldCom, and most of the financial world's other scandals resulted from failed internal controls. The problem was not just the people who ran those controls. The processes by which firms recorded, compiled, and documented financial data themselves were flawed. Not surprisingly, those controls received considerable attention from Congress.

THE AUDIT COMMITTEE

The data contained in a corporation's financial statements is the market's best tool for evaluating how well a firm's managers perform. Because management prepares the financial statements, however, how can the market trust those statements to represent fairly and accurately the company's true financial picture? Would managers really tell the truth if it meant losing their jobs?

To ensure that the financial statements are accurate and complete, the SEC requires corporations to have those statements audited by an independent firm of certified public accountants. In order to prevent management and the outside auditor from getting too cozy with one another, it has long been considered good practice for the corporation's board of directors to have an audit committee. As defined by the Sarbanes-Oxley Act, that committee is "established by and amongst the board of directors of an issuer for the purpose of overseeing the accounting and financial reporting processes of the issuer and audits of the financial statements of the issuer."[2]

1. Thomas O. Gorman, Critical Issues in the Sarbanes-Oxley Act 1 (2009).
2. SOX § 2(a)(3).

The Sarbanes-Oxley Act's Mandate

For decades, the NYSE required listed companies to have an audit committee consisting solely of independent directors. The committee had to have at least three members, all of whom were "financially literate." At least one committee member had to have expertise in accounting or financial management.

When Sarbanes-Oxley was under consideration by Congress, a consensus quickly formed in favor of imposing a tougher version of the NYSE requirements on all public corporations. Sarbanes-Oxley § 301 therefore ordered the SEC to adopt rules requiring that the stock exchanges and NASDAQ adopt listing requirements mandating the creation by listed companies of audit committees satisfying the following specifications:

- Committee Responsibilities: The audit committee is responsible for appointing, compensating, and supervising the company's outside auditor. The outside auditor "shall report directly to the audit committee." The committee also must resolve "disagreements between management and the auditor regarding financial reporting."[3]
- Independence: All members of the audit committee must be independent, which § 301 defines as precluding the committee member from being an "affiliated person" of the company and from accepting any "consulting, advisory, or other compensatory fee" from the company except for directors' fees.[4]
- Whistle-Blowers: The audit committee must establish procedures for handling complaints about the way the company conducts its accounting, internal audit controls, and outside audits. The procedure must include a mechanism for "the confidential, anonymous submission by employees . . . of concerns regarding questionable accounting or auditing matters."[5]
- Hiring Advisors: In addition to empowering the audit committee to hire and pay the outside auditor, the company also must empower the committee to hire "independent counsel and other advisors, as it determines necessary to carry out its duties," with the outside advisor's fees paid by the company.[6]

The NYSE and NASDAQ Audit Committee Rules

The Sarbanes-Oxley Act became law while the NYSE and NASDAQ were working up their own reforms to boards, which included planned changes to the

3. 15 U.S.C. § 78j-1(m)(2).
4. Id. § 78j-1(m)(3).
5. Id. § 78j-1(m)(4).
6. Id. § 78j-1(m)(5).

audit committee. Sarbanes-Oxley § 301 and the SEC rules adopted to implement it thus had to be worked into the stock exchanges' plans.

As finally amended post-SOX, NYSE Listed Company Manual § 303A.06 requires that each listed company have an audit committee. Unlike the nominating and compensation committee requirements, even companies with a controlling shareholder must comply with the audit committee rules.

In § 303A.07, the NYSE sets out additional committee requirements:

- The committee must have at least three members. Note that a growing number of firms are appointing as many as five individuals to the audit committee so as to help share the high workload imposed on this committee's members.
- All committee members must be independent, both as defined in Sarbanes-Oxley § 301 and the NYSE Listed Company Manual.
- All committee members must be "financially literate" and at least one member "must have accounting or related financial management expertise."[7] It is left up to the company's board of directors to decide what that means and whether the members qualify.
- The audit committee must have a written charter specifying its duties, role, and powers.
- The committee is charged with oversight of "(1) the integrity of the listed company's financial statements, (2) the listed company's compliance with legal and regulatory requirements, (3) the independent auditor's qualifications and independence, and (4) the performance of the listed company's internal audit function and independent auditors."[8]
- The committee must prepare an annual report on the audit process to be included in the company's annual proxy statement.
- The audit committee must have the power to engage independent counsel and other advisors and to pay such advisors.
- The committee must have the power to set the compensation of the outside auditor.
- At least once a year, the committee must receive a report from the outside auditor on the adequacy of the company's internal controls.
- The committee is to review the company's annual and quarterly disclosure reports, specifically including the MD&A section, as well as the financial statements.
- The committee is to review earnings announcements and other guidance provided analysts.

7. NYSE, Listed Company Manual § 303A.07(a) cmt., http://nysemanual.nyse.com/lcm/.
8. Id. § 303A.07(b).

- The committee must meet periodically in executive session with both the company's internal and outside auditors.
- The committee must review any disagreements between management and the auditors.

The NASDAQ rules are less detailed but substantially similar to the NYSE provisions.

Other Audit Committee Duties

The audit committee is the Sarbanes-Oxley Act's central clearinghouse. The audit committee must approve any non-audit services performed by the company's outside certified public accounting firm. The audit committee supervises the company's whistle-blower policies. The audit committee is required to ensure that the outside auditor can perform its audit unimpeded by management. The audit committee acts as a liaison between management and the outside auditor, especially with respect to any disagreements between them or any other problems that arise during the audit. The audit committee should review the CEO and CFO's certifications with the outside auditor. The audit committee must ensure that every five years the outside auditor rotates both the partner principally responsible for conducting the audit and the partner responsible for reviewing the audit.

SEC Audit Committee Disclosure Rules

The SEC put additional teeth into the exchange's audit committee requirements by mandating that corporate proxy statements include a report from that committee containing a variety of disclosures. The report, for example, must state whether the committee reviewed and discussed the company's audited financial statements with management and the firm's independent auditors. The report also must state whether the audit committee recommended to the board of directors that the audited financial statements be included in the company's annual report on Form 10-K.[9]

Setting an Appropriate Tone at the Top

As a matter of good corporate practice, an audit committee should establish a "tone at the top" that encourages honesty, integrity, and compliance with legal

9. Gorman, supra note 1, at 30.

requirements. In particular, members of an audit committee should not passively rely on management and the outside auditors. While members of the audit committee are not private investigators charged with conducting corporate espionage to detect wrongdoing, they are obliged to make a candid inquiry before accepting the reports they receive from management and outside auditors. As the Delaware Supreme Court observed in *Smith v. Van Gorkom*, the board must "proceed with a critical eye in assessing information" provided by others.[10]

Assessment

As with the other post-SOX federal and stock exchange listing standards governing board composition, the audit committee rules preempt state corporate law. The post-SOX audit committee rules have had other unforeseen consequences. There are important conflicts between § 301's mandate that the audit committee establish and oversee a corporate whistle blowing program and EU directives with respect to data protection, for example. As a result, the French data protection authority struck down whistle blowing systems proposed by two subsidiaries of U.S. corporations subject to both § 301 and French data protection law.[11]

As was true of the other post-SOX federal and stock exchange listing standards governing board composition, the new audit committee rules were imposed despite a lack of compelling empirical justification. Roberta Romano identified and summarized 16 pre-SOX studies of independent audit committees. Four of the studies tried to find a correlation between audit committee independence and firm performance as measured by both accounting and stock market metrics. None found a statistically significant relationship between the two using any metric.[12]

Other studies tried to find a link between audit committee independence and the probability of financial statement misconduct, as measured by such indicia as "abnormal accruals, financial statement restatements and fraud, SEC actions, third-party or contract fraud allegations, and stock market responses to unexpected earnings."[13] Ten of the studies found no such link,

10. Smith v. Van Gorkom, 488 A.2d 858, 872 (Del. 1985).
11. Michael Delikat, Developments Under Sarbanes-Oxley Whistleblower Law, in Internal Investigations 2007: Legal, Ethical & Strategic Issues (June 2007), available on Westlaw at 1609 PLI/Corp 19.
12. Roberta Romano, The Sarbanes-Oxley Act and the Making of Quack Corporate Governance, 114 Yale L.J. 1521, 1530 (2005).
13. Id. at 1531 (footnote omitted).

with one reporting inconsistent results depending on the empirical model being tested.

Studies finding a correlation between audit committee independence and firm performance on some metric must be taken with a grain of salt. It is difficult to draw causality conclusions from these studies. Firms with high-quality disclosure practices opted for an active, fully independent audit committee. Firms that created such a committee may have done so as part of a broader package of accounting and disclosure enhancements. Accordingly, the studies inherently suffer from a serious endogeneity problem.

In so far as post-SOX evidence is available, there appears to be little connection between audit committee independence prompted by the Sarbanes-Oxley law and avoidance of earnings restatements. A study of the relationship between the probability of financial misstatements by a firm and various corporate governance features found no statistically significant correlation between the former and audit committee independence. The study did find a negative correlation between financial expertise on the part of audit committee members and the probability of financial misstatements.[14] That result is hardly surprising. An expert director should do a better job of monitoring corporate performance in his area of expertise than a layperson. All that finding supports is an expertise requirement, however, not the elaborate apparatus erected by the Sarbanes-Oxley Act and the exchange standards.

The additional audit committee responsibilities imposed by that apparatus have been a prime factor in the increased workload of corporate directors and, as a result, the increase in director compensation.[15] On average, the number of times per year an audit committee met rose from five in 2002 to nine in 2005.[16]

Small firms were especially affected because they were less likely to have sufficient independent directors to satisfy the new exchange listing standards. Many of them therefore had to add new independent directors who not only met the heightened standards of independence but also satisfied the new expertise requirements for audit committee membership. In addition, because director compensation does not scale on a one-to-one basis as firm size increases, the increase in director compensation necessary to compensate these new directors for the perceived rise in workload and liability exposure post-SOX also disproportionately affected small firms. A post-SOX empirical study confirms both that director compensation costs rose dramatically after

14. Anup Agrawal & Sahiba Chadha, Corporate Governance and Accounting Scandals, 48 J.L. & Econ. 371, 375 (2005).

15. Judith Burns, Corporate Governance (A Special Report)—Everything you Wanted to Know About Corporate Governance But Didn't Know to Ask, Wall St. J., Oct. 27, 2003, at R6.

16. Jo Lynne Koehn & Stephen C. DelVecchio, Revisiting the Ripple Effects of the Sarbanes-Oxley Act, CPA J. Online, May 2006, http://www.nysscpa.org/printversions/cpaj/2006/506/p32.htm.

Sarbanes-Oxley passed and that those costs disproportionally burdened smaller public corporations.[17]

The world of nonprofit governance provides an interesting insight on the cost-benefit ratio of an independent audit committee. Only two of Sarbanes-Oxley's provisions apply directly to nonprofits: (1) The protections for whistle-blowers and (2) the prohibition of destroying, altering, or falsifying documents so as to prevent their use or discovery in any official proceeding.[18] After Sarbanes-Oxley came into law, however, nonprofits undertook an assessment of whether they should voluntarily comply with Sarbanes-Oxley rules. An Urban Institute study of governance practices at 5,000 nonprofits found varying degrees of Sarbanes-Oxley compliance. Most nonprofits, for example, had an independent outside auditor. Indeed, the practice was almost universal (97 percent) at large nonprofits with annual expenses exceeding $2 million. In contrast, a "separate audit committee was the least commonly adopted practice related to Sarbanes-Oxley issues in all size groups."[19] Even among very large nonprofits, with over $40 million in annual expenses, only 58 percent had an SOX-like independent audit committee. Nonprofits face considerable pressure from key stakeholders, such as outside auditors, major donors, and government regulators, to have effective corporate governance practices. The striking absence of audit committees among nonprofits therefore suggests that the benefits of such a committee do not outweigh the costs.

INTERNAL CONTROLS

Although internal control originated as an accounting concept, it evolved to take on a broader meaning. A 1949 American Institute of Certified Public Accountants (AICPA) committee report defined internal control as "the plan of organization and all of the coordinate methods and measures adopted within a business to safeguard its assets, check the accuracy and reliability of its accounting data, promote operational efficiency, and encourage adherence to prescribed managerial policies."[20] By 1992, the Committee of Sponsoring Organizations of the Treadway Commission (COSO), a group comprised of

17. James S. Linck et al., The Effects and Unintended Consequences of the Sarbanes-Oxley Act, and Its Era, on the Supply and Demand for Directors (2009), http://ssrn.com/abstract=902665.
18. See generally Stephen M. Bainbridge, The Complete Guide to Sarbanes-Oxley 96–108 (2005) (discussing these requirements).
19. Francie Ostrower & Marla J. Bobowick, Urban Institute, Nonprofit Governance and the Sarbanes-Oxley Act 2 (2006), http://www.urban.org/UploadedPDF/311363_nonprofit_governance.pdf.
20. American Institute of Certified Public Accountants Committee on Auditing Procedure, Internal Control—Elements of a Coordinated System and Its Importance to Management and the Independent Public Accountant 5, 6 (1949).

five major accounting professional associations, issued a definition of internal control as "a process, effected by an entity's board of directors, management and other personnel, designed to provide reasonable assurance regarding the achievement of objectives" in the areas of "effectiveness and efficiency of operations, reliability of financial reporting, and compliance with applicable laws and regulations."[21] COSO further opined that internal control consists of five interrelated components: the control environment, risk assessment, control activities, information and communication, and monitoring. All five components must be functioning properly for the internal control to be deemed satisfactory. In turn, those components are further broken down into twenty even more jargon-heavy principles.

In simpler terms, we can loosely divide internal controls into two main categories. First, preventative controls seek to deter misconduct and prevent errors or irregularities that could cause the organization to break the law, issue inaccurate or fraudulent disclosures, or otherwise fail to operate at maximum efficiency. Requiring two signatures for checks over a certain amount is a simple example of such a control. Second, curative controls seek to identify and remediate misconduct and errors that do occur. Auditing expense accounts to identify personal expenditures is a simple example of a control in this category.

The internal control concept began working its way into corporate law through the efforts of Melvin Eisenberg, who saw assigning responsibility for internal controls to the board of directors as a key component in institutionalizing his monitoring model.[22] Eisenberg recognized that the information asymmetry between the board and management impeded the board's ability to effectively monitor the top management team. A properly functioning system of internal controls with the board would help redress that imbalance in two ways. First, it catches and corrects distortions in the information flowing to the board. Second, the corporate personnel charged with effecting internal control become an alternative source of information for the board, which no longer is reliant solely on top management. As we shall see, Eisenberg's views have been highly influential in both state and federal corporate governance law.

21. Committee of Sponsoring Organizations of the Treadway Commission, Internal Control—Integrated Framework 9 (1992).
22. Melvin A. Eisenberg, The Board of Directors and Internal Control, 19 Cardozo L. Rev. 237 (1997).

It is well settled that the duty of care requires directors to pay ongoing attention to the business and affairs of the corporation:

> Directors are under a continuing obligation to keep informed about the activities of the corporation. . . . Directors may not shut their eyes to corporate misconduct and then claim that because they did not see the misconduct, they did not have a duty to look. The sentinel asleep at his post contributes nothing to the enterprise he is charged to protect.[23]

But this leaves open the extent to which the duty of care requires directors to proactively monitor the conduct of corporate subordinates.

The Delaware Supreme Court first took this issue up in *Graham v. Allis-Chalmers Mfg. Co.*[24] In 1937, Allis-Chalmers had entered into two consent decrees with the FTC in connection with alleged antitrust violations. In the 1950s, the firm settled unrelated federal antitrust charges of price fixing by mid-level employees. After the 1950s settlement, a shareholder sued the board of directors for having failed to install a law compliance program to prevent antitrust violations. Because plaintiff's claim was based on an alleged failure to act, the business judgment rule did not apply, and the Supreme Court proceeded to determine whether the directors had satisfied their duty of care.

Plaintiffs argued that the directors knew or were on notice of the 1950s price-fixing violations. The court rejected that argument, however, because there was no credible evidence any of the directors actually knew of the 1950s-era violations until the federal government commenced grand jury proceedings. Plaintiffs then argued that, by virtue of the 1937 consent decrees, the directors were on notice that they had to take steps to prevent future violations and that they had failed to do so. Again, the court rejected that argument. Only a few of the inside directors had actual knowledge of the 1930s consent decrees. Moreover, the few directors who did know of them had reviewed the consent decrees and reasonably concluded that the corporation had done nothing wrong in the 1930s. The company had settled the case simply to avoid litigation. Accordingly, the court held that the directors were not on notice of the possibility of future illegal price fixing. The final theory, and the one on which the case turned, was that the directors were liable for failing to undertake a law compliance program to detect and prevent this type of wrongdoing.

23. Francis v. United Jersey Bank, 432 A.2d 814 (N.J. 1981).
24. 188 A.2d 125 (Del. 1963).

The court also rejected plaintiff's lack-of-oversight claim. The *Graham* court held that directors were entitled to rely on the honesty of their subordinates until something occurred to put them on notice that illegal conduct was taking place. If they were put on notice and then failed to act, or if they recklessly reposed confidence in an obviously untrustworthy employee, liability could follow. Under *Graham*, however, there was no duty to install a law compliance program from the outset, absent such red flags.

Graham is routinely criticized these days. In the 1990s, the Delaware Supreme Court itself described *Graham* as "quite confusing and unhelpful."[25] Yet, there was method behind *Graham*'s supposed madness. Consider the old saying: "every dog gets one bite." This saying was based on the common law principle that a dog's master was only liable for bites if the master knew or had reason to know the dog had a propensity to bite.[26] Such knowledge could be based on either the breed's inherently violent propensities or a prior bite. The economic rationale for such a rule rests on a simple cost-benefit analysis. Keeping an eye on your dog requires costly precautions, such as leashes, fences, and the like. Why require such expenditures if Fido is as gentle as a lamb?

The analogy to *Graham* should be self-evident. Just as a dog owner does not have liability unless the owner knows the dog has a propensity to bite, directors should be liable only if they are on notice that their employees have a propensity for crime. Just as a dog owner is put on such notice by a prior bite, prior criminal violations can put directors on notice. Just as owners have an affirmative duty to control dogs of an inherently vicious breed, directors may not recklessly fail to monitor an obviously untrustworthy employee.

As with the dog bite rule, *Graham* was justified by a straightforward cost-benefit analysis. Law compliance programs are not free. At the very least, a law compliance program requires preparation of a company manual telling employees not to fix prices. It probably also requires training of employees. Beyond that, the firm probably should send lawyers out to do compliance audits from time to time. Programs with real teeth require substantial high-level commitment and review, frequent and meaningful communication to employees, serious monitoring and auditing, and appropriate discipline where violations are discovered. By analogy to the dog bite cases, one reasonably would expect a firm to go through all this only when on notice of a past violation.

Despite the logic of this cost-benefit analysis, recent cases have eviscerated *Graham*. The process began with former Delaware Chancellor William Allen's opinion in *In re Caremark International Inc. Derivative Litigation*,[27] Chancellor Allen

---

25. Cede & Co. v. Technicolor, Inc., 634 A.2d 345, 364 n.31 (Del. 1993).
26. See, e.g., Hyun Na Seo v. Yozgadlian, 726 A.2d 972 (N.J. App. 1999).
27. 698 A.2d 959 (Del. Ch. 1996).

outlined an obligation for directors to take some affirmative law compliance measures. Caremark was a health industry concern that provided a variety of managed care services. Much of Caremark's revenue came from federal government health programs. Under the federal Anti-Referral Payments Law (ARPL), Caremark was prohibited from paying doctors to refer patients to it. Caremark could, however, legally hire doctors under consulting agreements and research grants.

In 1994, the federal government prosecuted Caremark for criminal violations of the ARPL. The government argued that some of Caremark's consulting agreements and research grants with doctors were disguised kickbacks for patient referrals. In 1995, Caremark settled, paying fines and reimbursement of about $250 million. A group of shareholders thereafter filed derivative suits against Caremark directors. Those suits were settled pursuant to an agreement under which the directors paid nothing, Caremark agreed to make some cosmetic changes in the way it ran its business, and the plaintiffs' attorneys collected a fee of $1 million from Caremark. As with all derivative suit settlements, the agreement required judicial approval. Chancellor Allen approved the settlement, although he cut plaintiffs' attorneys fee to a mere $870,000. Because of the procedural posture, the case dealt only indirectly with the real issue of whether Caremark's directors had an obligation to create a working law compliance program. According to extensive dicta in Allen's opinion, however, the duty of care may require such programs.

Allen's analysis begins by distinguishing two scenarios in which directors might be sued with respect to the firm's law compliance. First, where the directors made an ill-advised decision, the business judgment rule will insulate that decision from judicial review "assuming the decision made was the product of a process that was either deliberately considered in good faith or was otherwise rational."

Second, where the board failed to act, courts would review that failure. Famed corporate lawyer and academic Bayless Manning long ago observed that "the business judgment rule [does] not operate at all in respect of fully ninety percent of what directors" actually do.[28] This is so because a discrete exercise of business judgment with respect to a specific decision is an essential precondition to application of the rule, as we saw in *Graham*. Most board activity, however, consists of oversight and supervision that only rarely triggers an actual decision.

Although the *Graham* court was unable to invoke the business judgment rule to insulate Allis-Chalmers' directors from judicial review, its approach to the board's oversight duties created significant obstacles to actually imposing

---

28. Bayless Manning, The Business Judgment Rule and the Director's Duty of Attention: Time for Reality, 39 Bus. Law. 1477, 1494 (1984).

liability on directors for oversight failures. As the monitoring model became pervasive, however, *Graham* began to suffer from the sort of criticisms noted above. As Eisenberg himself put it, "although perhaps correctly decided on its facts, [*Graham*] envisions a passive role for the board that may have been acceptable in 1963, before the evolution of the monitoring model, but is inconsistent with the modern view of the board's monitoring obligation."[29]

Chancellor Allen likewise concluded that *Graham* no longer could be interpreted as meaning that a corporate board has no obligation to create information gathering and monitoring mechanisms designed to ensure corporate law compliance. Instead, the board's monitoring obligation "includes a duty to attempt in good faith to assure that a corporate information and reporting system, which the board concludes is adequate, exists, and that failure to do so under some circumstances may, in theory at least, render a director liable for losses caused by non-compliance with applicable legal standards."[30]

Caremark could have opened the door to expansive directorial liability. Because the board's exercise of its oversight function so often falls outside the business judgment rule, most of what directors actually do would be subject to second-guessing by courts. As a matter of sound policy, it would have been preferable for Allen to reaffirm *Graham*'s replication of the dog bite rule.

Although Allen did not do so, he did take precautions to ensure that *Caremark* did not drastically increase Delaware directors' liability exposure. He held that a board's failure to comply with this obligation—even if negligent— is not sufficient for liability to be imposed. Instead, "only a sustained or systematic failure of the board to exercise oversight—such as an utter failure to attempt to assure a reasonable information and reporting system exists—will establish the lack of good faith that is a necessary condition to liability."[31] As Allen observed, this standard sets the liability bar "quite high."[32] Indeed, earlier in the opinion, he had noted that the claim at issue here is "possibly the most difficult theory in corporation law upon which a plaintiff might hope to win a judgment."[33]

Even though *Caremark* was dicta, the Chancery Court as a whole quickly accepted it as good law. A critical shift in emphasis came in *Guttman v. Huang*, however, in which Vice Chancellor Leo Strine ripped the *Caremark* claim from its original home in the duty of care and reinvented it as a duty of loyalty:

> Although the *Caremark* decision is rightly seen as a prod towards the greater exercise of care by directors in monitoring their corporations' compliance with

---

29. Eisenberg, supra note 22, at 260.
30. *Caremark*, 698 A.2d at 970.
31. Id. at 971.
32. Id.
33. Id. at 967.

legal standards, by its plain and intentional terms, the opinion articulates a standard for liability for failures of oversight that requires a showing that the directors breached their duty of loyalty by failing to attend to their duties in good faith.[34]

This passage "effectively transformed director oversight liability from a duty of care claim into a duty of loyalty claim."[35]

To be sure, *Guttman* did not result in directors facing a higher probability of liability. The business judgment rule, after all, has no more application to cases involving a breach of the duty of care through unconsidered inaction than it does to cases involving breach of the duty of loyalty. So the change mattered little from that perspective.

Granted, by situating the *Caremark* claim within the duty of loyalty, Vice Chancellor Strine precluded the use of § 102(b)(7) exculpatory clauses in these cases. Even so, he probably was correct that his holding effectively replicated "the liability landscape for most corporate directors, who are insulated from monetary damage awards by exculpatory charter provisions."[36] First, Vice Chancellor Strine emphasized that *Caremark* claims are difficult to prove. Second, he premised liability "on a showing that the directors were conscious of the fact that they were not doing their jobs."[37] Mere unconscious inaction seemingly was no longer enough; instead, there must be proof of conscious disregard by the board for its duties. Put another way, "to hold directors liable for a failure in monitoring, the directors have to have acted with a state of mind consistent with a conscious decision to breach their duty of care."[38] Third, Vice Chancellor Strine quoted both Chancellor Allen's admonition that "only a sustained or systematic failure of the board to exercise oversight" would result in liability and Chancellor Allen's acknowledgment that this pegged the liability bar "quite high."[39] Given these high standards, Vice Chancellor Strine concluded, the plaintiffs had "not come close to pleading a *Caremark* claim."[40]

> Their conclusory complaint is empty of the kind of fact pleading that is critical to a *Caremark* claim, such as contentions that the company lacked an audit committee, that the company had an audit committee that met only sporadically

34. Guttman v. Huang, 823 A.2d 492, 506 (Del. Ch. 2003).
35. Peter D. Bordonaro, Comment, Good Faith: Set In Stone?, 82 Tul. L. Rev. 1119, 1126 (2008).
36. *Guttman*, 823 A.2d at 506.
37. Id. at 506.
38. Desimone v. Barrows, 924 A.2d 908, 935 (Del. Ch. 2007).
39. *Guttman*, 823 A.2d at 506.
40. Id.

and devoted patently inadequate time to its work, or that the audit committee had clear notice of serious accounting irregularities and simply chose to ignore them or, even worse, to encourage their continuation.[41]

Although *Caremark* seemed well established by the time *Guttman* was decided, being widely followed both in the Delaware Chancery Court and in other states, the Delaware Supreme Court did not expressly endorse it until *Stone v. Ritter* in 2006.[42] Shareholders of AmSouth Bancorporation brought a derivative suit against the bank's board of directors alleging a *Caremark* claim arising out of an alleged failure by the board to ensure that the bank had an adequate compliance program in place to prevent and detect violations of the federal Bank Secrecy Act.

The Delaware Supreme Court purported to confirm "that *Caremark* articulates the necessary conditions for assessing director oversight liability."[43] In fact, however, what *Stone* really confirmed was *Guttman*'s reinterpretation of *Caremark*. For example, *Stone* held that *Caremark* "draws heavily on the concept of director failure to act in good faith."[44] The Court then quoted with approval *Guttman*'s conflation of good faith and loyalty: "The failure to act in good faith may result in liability because the requirement to act in good faith 'is a subsidiary element[,]' i.e., a condition, 'of the fundamental duty of loyalty.'"[45]

Although there is much to criticize about *Caremark* and its progeny, including *Stone*,[46] the key point for present purposes is that *Stone* confirmed *Guttman*'s emphasis on conscious disregard of the board's duties as being the touchstone of liability in *Caremark* cases:

> We hold that *Caremark* articulates the necessary conditions predicate for director oversight liability: (a) the directors utterly failed to implement any reporting or information system or controls; or (b) having implemented such a system or controls, consciously failed to monitor or oversee its operations thus disabling themselves from being informed of risks or problems requiring their attention. In either case, imposition of liability requires a showing that the directors knew that they were not discharging their fiduciary obligations. Where directors fail to act in the face of a known duty to act, thereby demonstrating a conscious

41. Id. at 506–07.
42. Stone v. Ritter, 911 A.2d 362 (Del. 2006).
43. Id.
44. *Stone*, 911 A.2d at 369.
45. Id. at 369–70 (quoting Guttman v. Huang, 823 A.2d 492, 506 n.34 (Del. Ch. 2003)).
46. See generally Stephen M. Bainbridge et al., The Convergence of Good Faith and Oversight, 55 UCLA L. Rev. 559 (2008).

disregard for their responsibilities, they breach their duty of loyalty by failing to discharge that fiduciary obligation in good faith.[47]

The Supreme Court thereafter quoted *Caremark* for the proposition that "a claim that directors are subject to personal liability for employee failures is 'possibly the most difficult theory in corporation law upon which a plaintiff might hope to win a judgment.'"[48] As had Vice Chancellor Strine in *Guttman*, the Supreme Court further quoted the passages from *Caremark* emphasizing the need for proof of a sustained or systematic failure by the board and the "quite high" bar to liability thereby established.

Caremark and its progeny thus strike a carefully constructed balance between authority and accountability. Here, as elsewhere, the Delaware courts recognize that the power to review is the power to decide. If *Caremark* claims were easy to bring and win, courts routinely would be put in the position of reviewing the effectiveness of corporate internal controls. By making them hard to bring and win, the Delaware courts ensured that the design and operation of internal controls would be left to the wise discretion of the board of directors. Indeed, when properly understood *Caremark* and its progeny even allow the board of directors to make a conscious decision to forego a specific set of internal controls where the board makes an informed decision that the controls' costs outweigh the benefits thereof. The federal government would not be so lenient.

INTERNAL CONTROLS—SARBANES-OXLEY

During the Congressional hearings that led up to Sarbanes-Oxley, much attention was devoted to the internal control failures at Enron, WorldCom, and the like. Congress determined that the state law regime failed adequately to channel board attention to the problem. Accordingly, some of the Sarbanes-Oxley Act's critical provisions were intended to federalize internal control regulation.

Internal Controls of What?

As we have seen, the phrase "internal controls" has a long history and somewhat contested meaning in the accounting profession. Unfortunately, Congress did not do much to clarify the concept. To the contrary, Congress compounded the problem by using the phrase in two different sections of the Sarbanes-Oxley Act, which assign very different meanings to it.

47. *Stone*, 911 A.2d at 370.
48. Id. at 372.

Sarbanes-Oxley § 302 requires a reporting company's CEO and CFO to certify, among other things, that the company has "internal controls to ensure that material information relating to the issuer and its consolidated subsidiaries is made known to such officers by others within those entities." In a June 2003 statement, the SEC explained that internal controls as used in § 302 therefore refers to "disclosure controls and procedures," which the SEC in turn defined "to mean controls and procedures of a company that are designed to ensure that information required to be disclosed by the company in the reports that it files or submits under the Exchange Act is recorded, processed, summarized and reported, within the time periods specified in the Commission's rules and forms." In other words, for purposes of a § 302 certification, the question is whether the company has established appropriate procedures to ensure that the information contained in documents like the 10-K and 10-Q reports is accurate and complete.

In contrast, § 404 refers to "internal control structure and procedures for financial reporting." According to the SEC, the set of internal controls to which § 404 refers is narrower than those dealt with under § 302. Specifically, the SEC defines "internal control" for purposes of § 404 as:

> A process designed by, or under the supervision of, the registrant's principal executive and principal financial officers, or persons performing similar functions, and effected by the registrant's board of directors, management and other personnel, to provide reasonable assurance regarding the reliability of financial reporting and the preparation of financial statements for external purposes in accordance with generally accepted accounting principles and includes those policies and procedures that
>
> - pertain to the maintenance of records that in reasonable detail accurately and fairly reflect the transactions and dispositions of the assets of the registrant;
> - provide reasonable assurance that transactions are recorded as necessary to permit preparation of financial statements in accordance with generally accepted accounting principles, and receipts and expenditures of the registrant are being made only in accordance with authorizations of management and directors of the registrant; and
> - provide reasonable assurance regarding prevention or timely detection of unauthorized acquisition, use or disposition of the registrant's assets that could have a material effect on the financial statements.

In other words, the term *internal controls* as used in § 404 refers to the processes the company uses to ensure that its financial statements comply with GAAP and are free from material misrepresentations and omissions.

As so defined, §§ 302 and 404 do not preempt the field of internal controls. Recall that COSO defined internal controls as relating to the "effectiveness and efficiency of operations, reliability of financial reporting, and compliance with applicable laws and regulations."[49] Even the broader definition of internal control used for purposes of § 302 is limited to the second category. Both §§ 302 and 404 are confined to internal controls related to accounting and disclosure. The state law regime thus remains the controlling law with respect to the first and third COSO categories.

Sarbanes-Oxley § 404

Sarbanes-Oxley § 404(a) ordered the SEC to adopt rules requiring reporting companies to include in their annual reports a statement of management's responsibility for "establishing and maintaining an adequate internal control structure and procedures for financial reporting" and "an assessment, as of the end of the most recent fiscal year of the issuer, of the effectiveness of the internal control structure and procedures of the issuer for financial reporting." Section 404(b) required that the company's independent auditors attest to the effectiveness of the company's internal controls.

Section 404 looks at first like a mere disclosure requirement. It requires inclusion of internal control disclosures in each public corporation's annual report. This disclosure statement must include: (1) a written confirmation by which firm management acknowledges its responsibility for establishing and maintaining a system of internal controls and procedures for financial reporting; (2) an assessment, as of the end of the most recent fiscal year, of the effectiveness of the firm's internal controls; and (3) a written attestation by the firm's outside auditor confirming the adequacy and accuracy of those controls and procedures. It is not the disclosure itself that makes § 404 significant, of course; instead, it is the need to assess and test the company's internal controls in order to be able to make the required disclosures. These costs have two major components. First, there are the internal costs incurred by the corporation in conducting the requisite management assessment. Second, there are the fees the corporation must pay the auditor for carrying out its assessment.

Both the SEC and the Public Company Accounting Oversight Board (PCAOB), which has oversight authority over accounting firms that serve as independent auditors and thus conduct the audit required by § 404(b), emphasize that § 404 requires a top down approach. The § 404 compliance process

49. COSO Report, supra note 21, at 9.

therefore usually starts with formation of a cross-function, multi-disciplinary compliance team consisting of senior professionals. Such a team will typically include representatives from the corporation's internal audit department, the controller's office, information technology, human resources, and key business segments. The team commonly begins with review of those controls that apply company-wide. The compliance team will then evaluate controls that apply to particular business units or functions. Next, the team looks at how particular business units handle significant accounts. Finally, the team evaluates how transactions in those accounts are processed.

Both the SEC and PCAOB insist that companies should devote most attention to those high-risk areas most likely to result in financial reporting problems. Because over 50 percent of financial fraud in the pre-SOX period involved overstating revenues either by prematurely recognizing revenue or by booking fictitious revenue, companies must devote considerable attention to the internal controls they use to monitor revenue recognition. In addition, four other areas have proven especially common sources of financial fraud: (1) stock options and other issuance of equity securities, (2) accounting for reserves, accruals, and contingencies, (3) capitalization of expenses, and (4) inventory levels. All of these are areas where emergent best practice dictates that considerable attention should be devoted during the § 404 assessment process.

Under SEC rules, management cannot claim that its internal controls are effective if one or more material weaknesses exist. In addition, the existence of any material weakness and the steps being taken to correct it must be disclosed in the annual report on Form 10-K. For this purpose, PCAOB Auditing Standard No. 2 defined a material weakness as a "significant deficiency, or combination of significant deficiencies, that results in more than a remote likelihood that a material misstatement of the annual or interim financial statements will not be prevented or detected." In turn, significant deficiency was defined as a problem with the company's internal controls that "adversely affects the company's ability to initiate, authorize, record, process, or report external financial data reliably in accordance with generally accepted accounting principles such that there is more than a remote likelihood that a misstatement of the company's annual or interim financial statements that is more than inconsequential will not be prevented or detected." Internal controls did not have to operate perfectly to be considered effective, so long as the problems did not give rise to "more than a remote likelihood" that the company's financial reporting would be materially and adversely affected.

Significant deficiencies did not have to be disclosed, but as a matter of best practice were to be addressed. If fixing a significant deficiency required a material change to either the disclosure procedures certified per § 302 or to the § 404 internal controls over financial reporting, however, those changes had to be disclosed. In that event, the significant deficiency motivating the change also had to be disclosed.

Recall that, in addition to management's assessment and certification, § 404 also required an assessment and certification of the corporation's internal controls over financial reporting by the firm's independent auditor. As implemented by PCAOB Auditing Standard No. 2, the reporting company's registered outside auditing firm was required to issue two opinions: (1) whether management's assessment of the company's internal controls fairly stated the condition and effectiveness of those controls and (2) whether the auditor believed that the company had established effective internal controls over financial reporting. The former requirement significantly increased the fees auditors charged in connection with § 404 compliance because it resulted in substantial duplication of the work done by management.

If the auditor found material weaknesses in the issuer's internal controls over financial reporting, the auditor could not issue an unqualified opinion. If the auditor identified significant deficiencies, it could still issue an unqualified opinion, so long as those deficiencies were reported to the audit committee. As to its evaluation of management's assessment, an auditor could issue an unqualified opinion even if there were material weaknesses, so long as management's assessment disclosed those weaknesses. The auditor was obliged to issue a disclaimer (i.e., decline to express an opinion) if management failed to carry out its responsibilities under § 404 or limited the scope of the audit.

When Sarbanes-Oxley was adopted, neither Congress nor the SEC appreciated just how costly these compliance processes would prove. The SEC estimated that the average cost of complying with § 404 would be approximately $91,000.[50] In fact, however, a 2005 survey put the direct cost of complying with § 404 in its first year at $7.3 million for large accelerated filers and $1.5 million for accelerated filers.[51] "First-year implementation costs for larger companies were thus eighty times greater than the SEC had estimated, and sixteen times greater than estimated for smaller companies."[52]

These costs include average expenditures of 35,000 staff hours on § 404 compliance alone, which proved to be almost 100 times the SEC's estimate. In addition, firms spent an average of $1.3 million on external consultants and software. Finally, on average, they incurred an extra $1.5 million (a jump of 35 percent) in audit fees.[53]

To be sure, some of these costs were one-time expenses incurred to bring firms' internal controls up to snuff. Yet, many other Sarbanes-Oxley compliance costs recur year after year. For example, the internal control process required by § 404 relies heavily on ongoing documentation. As a result, firms

---

50. Joseph A. Grundfest & Steven E. Bochner, Fixing 404, 105 Mich. L Rev. 1643, 1646 (2007) (footnotes omitted).
51. Id.
52. Id. at 1645–46.
53. Stephen M. Bainbridge, The Complete Guide to Sarbanes-Oxley 4 (2007).

must constantly ensure that they are creating the requisite paper trail. Accordingly, while second year compliance costs dropped, those costs remained many times greater than the SEC's estimate of first-year costs.[54]

Section 404 admittedly had laudatory goals. Faulty internal controls, after all, contributed to many corporate scandals during the dotcom era. Section 404 also has had some beneficial effects. Some of the fall in securities fraud lawsuits mid-decade may have resulted from companies having adopted better internal controls and disclosure procedures in response to § 404, for example. Some companies may have benefited from greater intra-firm transparency.

One must also acknowledge the efforts regulators and Congress have made to alleviate some of the costs associated with § 404 compliance. The SEC's initial response was to delay the date on which § 404 would apply to non-accelerated filers (it has applied to large accelerated filers and accelerated filers since passage). Somewhat later it provided "guidance" on which managers were to rely in complying with § 404 and which would purportedly reduce costs. In so doing, however, the SEC continued to insist that "it is impractical to prescribe a single methodology that meets the needs of every company." As a result, the SEC declined to create safe harbors by which compliant firms are insulated from liability. Indeed, the SEC decided not even to "provide a check-list of steps management should perform in completing its evaluation" of the company's internal controls. Instead, the SEC advised that:

> Management should implement and conduct an evaluation that is sufficient to provide it with a reasonable basis for its annual assessment. Management should use its own experience and informed judgment in designing an evaluation process that aligns with the operations, financial reporting risks and processes of the company. If the evaluation process identifies material weaknesses that exist as of the end of the fiscal year, such weaknesses must be disclosed in management's annual report with a statement that ICFR [i.e., internal controls over financial reporting] is ineffective. If the evaluation identifies no internal control deficiencies that constitute a material weakness, management assesses ICFR as effective.[55]

The SEC's guidance is inherently vague and ambiguous, leaving plenty of room for interpretation and disagreement. Terms like "reasonable" and "material" are standards, which by their very nature fail to offer bright lines between lawful and unlawful conduct. Indeed, the SEC admitted that "there is a range of judgments that an issuer might make as to what is "reasonable" in

---

54. Grundfest & Bochner, supra note 12, at 1646.
55. Management's Report on Internal Control Over Financial Reporting, available at http://www.sec.gov/rules/proposed/2006/33–8762.pdf.

implementing Section 404 and the Commission's rules." As a result, determination of whether a particular firm has complied with its Sarbanes-Oxley obligations is highly fact-specific and contextual. Accordingly, the company and its management cannot be certain that they've fully complied with Section 404 until the SEC or a court, with the benefit and bias of hindsight, decides that they've done so.

Mere guidance, moreover, did not change the incentives of corporate officers and directors. The best way for directors and officers to avoid the new liability risks created by Sarbanes-Oxley was to pump a lot of corporate resources into ensuring compliance with § 404 and the rest of the Sarbanes-Oxley Act. Because it is a corporation's directors and officers who control the purse strings, they get to decide just how much resources the corporation spends on Sarbanes-Oxley compliance. Because the money spent on compliance programs comes out of the corporation's bottom-line, however, the money comes out of the stockholders' pockets. As a result, it was virtually certain that corporations would over invest in Sarbanes-Oxley compliance efforts.

In 2007, the SEC undertook additional measures intended to reduce § 404 compliance costs. Under prior guidance, the auditor had been expected to issue two opinions. One provided the auditor's assessment of the effectiveness of the corporation's internal controls over financial reporting. The other was an evaluation of whether management's assessment fairly stated the conditions of those controls. The SEC now made clear that only the former was actually required.

At the same time, the SEC and PCAOB amended the definitions of material weakness and significant deficiency. As to the former, the new definition replaced the probability trigger language "more than a remote likelihood" with the phrase "reasonable possibility," so as to raise the threshold for evaluating the likelihood of a misstatement. As to the latter, the new definition is "a deficiency, or a combination of deficiencies, in internal control over financial reporting that is less severe than a material weakness, yet important enough to merit attention by those responsible for oversight of a registrant's financial reporting." The change was intended to make clear that the requisite response to a significant deficiency is not disclosure but evaluation by the responsible authorities within the corporation.

In the same year, the PCAOB adopted Auditing Standard No. 5, replacing its previous internal control auditing standard, Auditing Standard No. 2. The revised standard made a number of key changes. It modified the definitions of material weakness and significant deficiency, so as to conform to new SEC definitions. It emphasized that auditors should scale their efforts depending on the size of the company. Auditing Standard No. 5 also tried to reduce duplicative effort by allowing the auditor to rely on the work of internal auditors and other objective and competent company personnel in making its assessment. Critically, while Auditing Standard No. 2 required the auditor to conduct a detailed evaluation of the processes management used in making the latter's assessment, the new standard emphasized that the auditor's focus should not be on management's compliance processes, but on whether or not the company's internal controls over financial reporting are effective. In conjunction with the SEC's guidance requiring only one opinion from the auditor, instead of the two that had become customary under the prior standard, this change also was expected to eliminate much duplication of effort.

The most recent effort to provide § 404 relief came in the 2010 Dodd-Frank Act. Non-accelerated filers have been required to comply with the management assessment provision of § 404(a) for several years, but the SEC had repeatedly delayed implementation with respect to such corporations of the auditor assessment required by § 404(b). Dodd-Frank permanently exempts non-accelerated filers from compliance with § 404(b). The Act further directs the SEC to conduct a study of how to reduce the burden of § 404 compliance on mid-cap issuers (between $75 million and $250 million).

Despite the best of intention and these efforts at remediation, however, there is no doubt that § 404—along with the rest of the Sarbanes-Oxley Act and the broader U.S. regulatory regime—has had and continues to have a deleterious effect on the U.S. capital markets. As the Financial Economists Roundtable observed, there is "little reason to believe that, even [with the adoption of Auditing Standard No. 5], the benefits of § 404 will exceed the costs."[56] Even former Congressman Michael Oxley, for whom the Sarbanes-Oxley Act is named in part, has admitted that both he and Senator Sarbanes "would have written it differently" if they had known at the time that the Sarbanes-Oxley Act would prove so costly.[57]

Repeal of § 404 seems unlikely at this point. Proponents of additional reform, however, point to the various shareholder empowerment provisions in Dodd-Frank and ask why their logic does not extend to § 404. If a shareholder say on pay is informative, would not a shareholder vote on whether the company should be able to opt out of Sarbanes-Oxley § 404 be equally informative? If shareholders ought to have access to the proxy to nominate directors, why not give them access to the proxy to opt out of § 404?

In fact, several prominent bodies have proposed some such reform. The Financial Economists Roundtable, for example, proposed that issuers should be allowed to opt out of § 404.[58] A McKinsey report commissioned by New York City Mayor Michael Bloomberg and Senator Charles Schumer recommended that non-accelerated filers be allowed to opt out of § 404 entirely if

56. Statement of the Financial Economists Roundtable on the International Competitiveness of U.S. Capital Markets, 19 J. Applied Corp. Fin. 54, 57 (2007).
57. Liz Alderman, Spotlight: Michael Oxley, N.Y. Times, Mar. 2, 2007, http://www.nytimes.com/2007/03/02/business/worldbusiness/02iht-wbspot03.4773621.html.
58. Id.

SEC relief efforts did not significantly reduce compliance costs.[59] In addition to providing regulatory relief from a highly burdensome mandate, such a reform would have the wider benefit of providing a precedent for incorporating private ordering into the federal regulatory scheme. Unless and until such reforms are enacted, however, Sarbanes-Oxley § 404 will remain the poster child for quack federal corporate governance regulation.

Sarbanes-Oxley §§ 302 and 906

Part of the SEC's initial reaction to the Enron scandal was an order requiring the CEOs and CFOs of 947 large corporations to file written certifications that their company's latest annual report and any subsequent disclosure documents were free of material misrepresentations or omissions. Congress liked this idea so much that it incorporated it into two separate provisions of Sarbanes-Oxley.

SOX § 302 provides that when a reporting corporation files either an annual or quarterly report both the CEO and CFO must individually certify that he or she has reviewed the report and, to his or her knowledge, the report does not contain any material misrepresentation or omission of material fact. Both officers must also certify that, to their knowledge, the financial statements and other financial information contained in the report fairly present in all material respects the corporation's financial condition and results of operations for the period covered by the report.

This half of § 302 was largely inconsequential. As law professor Lawrence Cunningham observed:

> [T]his sort of certification requirement—that the statements comply with regulations and fairly present results—has always been a requirement of the federal securities laws. Those singled out to make the certifications, CEOs and CFOs, are invariably named as defendants in private securities lawsuits and SEC enforcement actions. . . . The most this provision did was shine attention on the subject, not an incidental effect but far more modest than was widely believed.[60]

At best, he further observed, this half of § 302 simply heightened corporate "executive attention to the stakes" in play when their companies make disclosures.[61]

---

59. McKinsey & Co., Sustaining New York's and the United States' Global Financial Services Leadership 19–20 (2007).
60. Lawrence A. Cunningham, The Sarbanes-Oxley Yawn: Heavy Rhetoric, Light Reform (And It Just Might Work), 35 Conn. L. Rev. 915, 955 (2003).
61. Id. at 942.

It is the second half of § 302 that made a significant change in corporate practice. Specifically, this part of § 302 was designed to give CEOs and CFOs a potent stake in the company's internal controls processes. It thus requires both the CEO and CFO individually to acknowledge in writing that they are responsible for establishing and maintaining the corporation's systems of internal controls and to certify that such internal controls are designed to ensure that material information properly flows from the corporation's business units to the CEO and CFO. They also must certify that they have evaluated the effectiveness of those internal controls within the ninety-day period prior to the filing of the report. To ensure that the certification is not mere boilerplate, the CEO and CFO are required to include in the quarterly or annual report, as the case may be, an assessment of the effectiveness of the company's internal controls.

Section 302 also requires that the CEO and CFO individually certify in writing that they have disclosed to the outside auditors and the audit committee "all significant deficiencies in the design or operation of internal controls which could adversely affect the issuer's ability to record, process, summarize, and report financial data and have identified for the issuer's auditors any material weaknesses in internal controls." They must also certify to having told the auditors and audit committee about "any fraud, whether or not material, that involves management or other employees who have a significant role in the issuer's internal controls." Finally, they must identify any significant changes in internal controls subsequent to the date of their evaluation, including any actions taken to correct any significant deficiencies and material weaknesses in those controls.

As Professor Lawrence Cunningham explains:

> These provisions look to prevent CEOs and CFOs from hiding behind the defense of ignorance. The clear line of provenance points to the Enron scandal, amid which several senior executives testified before Congress that they lacked knowledge of underling financial fraud, contending that they couldn't possibly be aware of all activities, including fraudulent practices, within the massive company.[62]

Now, however, we run into an oddity. As noted above, Congress liked the certification idea so much that they put it into SOX in two different places. In addition to the various certification requirements of § 302, § 906 amended the federal criminal code to add a new provision requiring that each "periodic report" filed with the SEC be accompanied by a written certification from the CEO and CFO that the "periodic report . . . fully complies with" the relevant statutes and that the "information contained in the periodic report fairly

62. Id. at 955–56.

presents, in all material respects, the financial condition and results of operations of the issuer." Someone who makes such a certification "knowing that the periodic report accompanying the statement does not comport with all the requirements set forth in this section shall be fined not more than $1,000,000 or imprisoned not more than 10 years, or both." Someone who "willfully" makes such a certification "knowing that the periodic report accompanying the statement does not comport with all the requirements set forth in this section shall be fined not more than $5,000,000, or imprisoned not more than 20 years, or both."

The § 906 certification requirement does not expressly cross-reference the certification mandated by § 302, which raises many difficult questions. Does a certification made pursuant to the more detailed requirements of § 302 satisfy the obligation under § 906? Does a false § 302 certification expose one to the criminal penalties under § 906? While § 302 clearly applies only to 10-Q and 10-K reports, does § 906 apply not only to them but also to other periodic disclosures (such as Form 8-Ks) that contain financial statements? Can a CEO or CFO qualify his or her certification under § 906 by stating that "to my knowledge" the report complies? Unfortunately, we have very little clear guidance on any of these subjects.

The CEO and CFO need not replicate the internal or external audit as part of the §§ 302 and 906 certification process, but some element of due diligence is necessary. As a matter of best practice, the CEO should receive what might be called "mini-302 certifications" from subordinates providing for their areas of responsibility the affirmations and certifications required by § 302. The certifying officer should meet with the outside auditor to confirm that it has had unrestricted access to conduct its audit and has met with the audit committee. Likewise, the certifying officer should meet with the audit committee to ensure that it has met with the outside auditor and to determine whether the committee knows of any material problems or deficiencies. The CEO and CFO should meet with the disclosure committee and the head of internal audit to ensure that the information necessary to prepare the corporation's disclosure statements is properly flowing within the firm. Finally, because certification covers the MD&A disclosures, the certifying officers should meet with those responsible for drafting the MD&A. Even if the MD&A is drafted internally, it may be appropriate to have outside counsel review the disclosures.

Taken together, §§ 302 and 906 significantly increase the regulatory burden on the CEO and CFO. In turn, because best practice requires the assistance of other key corporate executives, much of the top management team's time will now be devoted to preparing these certifications instead of conducting business. In addition, of course, the heightened liability exposure created by these sections increases the risks to which these executives are subject, for which they will demand compensation. The monetary and opportunity costs associated with compliance thus are not insignificant.

The benefits are far less certain. Economists Utpal Bhattacharya, Peter Groznik, and Bruce Haslem studied the stock price of companies that failed to comply with the SEC's executive certification requirement. They found that those companies experienced no abnormal stock price movements, unusual trading volume, or price volatility. Accordingly, they concluded that requiring CEOs and CFOs to certify the corporation's financial statements was not "value relevant."[63] That the cost-benefit analysis comes out against the certification requirements is further confirmed by a study of Mexican corporations listing on and delisting from U.S. capital markets, which found that the burdens imposed by Sarbanes-Oxley §§ 302 and 906 contributed significantly to delisting decisions.[64] Accordingly, those sections' high costs, limited benefits (if any), and demonstrable negative impact on the competitiveness of U.S. capital markets make it appropriate to add them to the list of quack federal corporate governance regulation.

INTERNAL CONTROLS—RISK MANAGEMENT

A large public corporation these days faces "a myriad of risks . . . ranging from complex financial risk to quality control regarding material manufactured in China."[65] In general, however, the risks corporations face can be broadly categorized as operational, market, and credit. Operational risk encompasses such concerns as "inadequate systems, management failure, faulty controls, fraud, and human error."[66] Related concerns include failure to comply with applicable legal rules, accounting irregularities, bad business models, and strategic planning errors.

Market risk can be broadly defined as changes in firm valuation linked to asset performance. For example, financial risk management views market risk as the expected variance of a portfolio's rate of return. In contrast, the Basel Accords define market risk "as the risks (a) 'in the trading book of debt and equity instruments and related off-balance-sheet contracts and (b) foreign exchange and commodities risks.'"[67] In either case, market risks are identified

63. Utpal Bhattacharya et al., Is CEO Certification of Earnings Numbers Value-Relevant? (June 2008), http://ssrn.com/abstract=332621.

64. Eugenio J. Cardenas, Mexican Corporations Entering and Leaving U.S. Markets: An Impact of the Sarbanes-Oxley Act of 2002?, 23 Conn. J. Int'l L. 281 (2008).

65. Betty Simkins & Steven A. Ramirez, Enterprise-Wide Risk Management and Corporate Governance, 39 Loy. U. Chi. L. J. 571 (2008).

66. Michel Crouhy et al., The Essentials of Risk Management 30–31 (2006).

67. W. Ronald Gard, George Bailey in the Twenty-First Century: Are We Moving to the Postmodern Era in International Financial Regulation with Basel II?, 8 Transactions 161, 183 (2006).

and evaluated by financial models that predict changes in prices, interest rates, liquidity, and foreign exchange rates.

Credit risk is defined as the possibility that a change in the credit quality of a counterparty will affect the firm's value.[68] It thus includes not only the risk of default, but also such risks as the possibility a credit-rating agency might downgrade the counterparty's creditworthiness. The financial crisis revealed that the existing models for measuring and predicting consumer credit risk are poorly developed.

Enterprise risk management is a subset of internal control, falling into mainly into the first COSO category. It is commonly defined as the process by which the board of directors and executives of a corporation define the firm's strategies and objectives so as "to strike an optimal balance between growth and return goals and related risks."[69] It encompasses determining an appetite for risk consistent with the interests of the firm's equity owners and identifying, preparing for, and responding to risks.

Risk management tools include (1) avoiding risk by choosing to refrain from certain business activities, (2) transferring risk to third parties through hedging and insurance, (3) mitigating operational risk through preventive and responsive control measures, and (4) accepting that certain risks are necessary to generate the appropriate level of return. Although primary responsibility for adopting and adapting these tools to the corporation's needs rests with the corporation's top management team, the board of directors is responsible for ensuring that the corporation has established appropriate risk management programs and for overseeing management's implementation of such programs.[70]

The financial crisis of 2008 revealed serious risk management failures on an almost systemic basis throughout the business community. At some firms, the problem was the absence of any system for managing risk. According to a 2002 survey of corporate directors, 43 percent said that their boards had either an ineffective risk management process or no process for identifying and managing risk at all.[71] According to the same survey, 36 percent of directors felt they had an incomplete understanding of the risks faced by their companies.[72]

---

68. Crouhy et al., supra note 66, at 29.
69. Committee of Sponsoring Organizations of the Treadway Commission, Enterprise Risk Management—Integrated Framework: Executive Summary 1 (2004), http://www.coso.org/Publications/ERM/COSO_ERM_ExecutiveSummary.pdf [hereinafter COSO Framework].
70. See American Bar Association Committee on Corporation Laws, Corporate Director's Guidebook 27–28 (5th ed. 2007) (setting out board obligations for risk management and compliance programs) [hereinafter ABA Guidebook].
71. Carolyn Kay Brancato & Christian A. Plath, Corporate Governance Handbook 2005 75 (2005).
72. Id. at 75.

A 2008 Towers Perrin survey of CFOs suggests that risk management remained underdeveloped when the financial crisis hit. Seventy-two percent of the respondents, for example, "expressed concern about their own companies' risk management practices and ability to meet strategic plans."[73] Instructively, 42 percent "foresaw more energized involvement by boards of directors in risk management policies, processes and systems,"[74] which implies that pre-crisis boards were inadequately engaged with risk management. This inference finds support in a 2006 observation that risk management was still "a work in progress at many boards."[75]

Among firms that had undertaken risk management programs prior to the crisis, many used a silo approach in which different types of risk were managed by different teams within the firm using different processes. This sizable group of firms thus failed to adopt an enterprise management approach in which all risk areas are brought into a single, integrated, firm-wide process. Indeed, according to a 2007 survey, only about 10 percent of respondent firms had adopted such a holistic approach to risk management.[76]

The significance of these failures as a causal factor in the financial crisis is highlighted by the Towers Perrin CFO survey. Sixty-two percent of respondents blamed "poor or lax risk management at financial institutions as a major contributor to the current financial mess," a higher figure than either the complexity of financial instruments or speculation (55 percent and 57 percent, respectively).[77] Accordingly, "more than half (55%) of the CFOs' surveyed planned 'to put their risk management practices under a microscope' in an investigation that 'will in many instances reach all levels of the organization, from the board down and from the shop floor up.'"[78]

To be sure, some argue that even effective risk management programs could not have anticipated the financial crisis that struck in 2008. As the argument goes, risks fall into three broad categories: known problems, known unknowns, and unknown unknowns. "There is a view that the financial crisis—while clearly a high-impact; rare-event risk—was unpredictable and possibly unmanageable, an unknown unknown."[79] In fact, however, there were warning signs of an approaching crisis in the housing market, including "easy

73. Towers Perrin, Financial Crisis Intensifies Interest in Risk Management Among CFOs (Sept. 2008), http://www.towersperrin.com/tp/showdctmdoc.jsp?country=global&url=Master_Brand_2/USA/News/Spotlights/2008/Sept/2008_09_30_spotlight_cfo_survey.htm.
74. Id.
75. Crouhy et al., supra note 66, at 85.
76. Simkins & Ramirez, supra note 65, at 584.
77. Towers Perrin, supra note 73.
78. Id.
79. Thomas L. Barton et al., Managing an Unthinkable Event, Fin. Exec., Dec. 1, 2008, at 24.

home-mortgage credit terms combined with rapidly accelerating home prices and reportedly lax credit standards,"[80] which in turn signaled risks for the financial services industry and then the economy as a whole.

Evaluating such extremely low probability but very high magnitude risks is challenging because the outcomes associated with such risks do not follow a normal distribution. Instead, they tend to have long or fat tails.[81] Because risk management focuses on extreme events, requiring one to quantify the probability and magnitude of severe loss events, an uncertainty generating such a fat- or long-tailed distribution poses "a severe problem for risk managers."[82] Indeed, there is considerable evidence that such risks are approached in "a sort of lax, undisciplined way" that results in them being "undermanaged before they first occur and overmanaged afterward."[83] Nonetheless, "it is simply unacceptable to chalk such an event up to "not manageable" and focus on the more predictable, tameable and probably less-severe risks."[84]

Writing off efforts to enhance risk management so as to anticipate future crises is especially unacceptable when one considers the price shareholders paid for management failures in the most recent crisis. In 2008 alone, declining stock prices caused investors to lose $6.9 trillion. Curiously, however, Dodd-Frank did very little to change risk management practices. Instead, risk management remains mainly with the domain of state corporate law.

Caremark and Enterprise Risk Management

State statutory corporate law is silent on risk management. Instead, the relevant body of law is the oversight obligation established by *Caremark* and its progeny. Prior to the crisis of 2008, cases in which plaintiffs brought *Caremark* claims typically involved either law compliance failures or accounting irregularities. In the wake of the crisis, however, plaintiffs' lawyers began fashioning *Caremark* claims around risk management failures. The Delaware

---

80. Id.
81. A fat-tail distribution has a mean and variance similar to the normal distribution but different probability masses at the tails. Linda Allen et al., Understanding Market, Credit, and Operational Risk: The Value at Risk Approach 25 (2004). As such the probability of an extreme outcome is higher in a fat-tailed distribution than the normal distribution. Id. In a long-tail distribution, a small number of high-frequency outcomes is followed by a large set of low-frequency outcomes that gradually tail off asymptotically. Outcomes at the far end of the tail thus have a very low probability of occurrence. Robert Sandy, Statistics for Business and Economics 47 (1989).
82. Allen et al., supra note 81, at 26.
83. Barton et al., supra note 79.
84. Id.

courts first addressed these claims in a shareholder derivative suit brought against Citigroup.

Citigroup is a multinational financial services corporation. In the period prior to the financial crisis, Citigroup's Securities and Banking Unit began marketing collateralized debt obligations (CDOs). This form of derivative security consists of "repackaged pools of lower rated securities that Citigroup created by acquiring asset-backed securities, including residential mortgage backed securities ('RMBSs'), and then selling rights to the cash flows from the securities in classes, or tranches, with different levels of risk and return."[85] In some cases, the CDO's terms included a so-called "liquidity put," which allowed the purchasers to resell the securities to Citigroup at their original cost.

Eventually Citigroup had some $55 billion in exposure to the subprime mortgage market via these CDOs and other investments. As a result, Citigroup faced all three types of enterprise risk. Market risk arose, for example, because changes in interest rates and housing prices could significantly affect the value of CDOs based on mortgage-backed securities. Credit risk arose, for example, because adverse changes in the credit quality of subprime mortgage-backed securities could lead to Citigroup's counterparties exercising their liquidity puts. Operational risk is pervasive in the context of derivative securities, potentially arising from "inadequate systems, management failure, faulty controls, fraud, and human error":[86]

> [In fact,] many of the large losses from derivative trading are the direct consequence of operational failures. Derivative trading is more prone to operational risk than cash transactions are because derivatives, by their nature, are leveraged transactions. The valuation of complex derivatives also creates considerable operational risk. Very tight controls are an absolute necessity if a firm is to avoid large losses.[87]

When the financial crisis hit and the subprime mortgage market collapsed, Citigroup in fact suffered very serious financial losses.

The defendants were current and former directors and officers of Citigroup. Plaintiffs' claims against them included an argument "that the director defendants are personally liable under *Caremark* for failing to "make a good faith attempt to follow the procedures put in place or fail[ing] to assure that adequate and proper corporate information and reporting systems existed that would enable them to be fully informed regarding Citigroup's risk to the subprime

---

85. In re Citigroup Inc. Shareholder Litig., 2009 WL 481906 (Del. Ch. 2009).
86. Crouhy et al., supra note 66, at 30.
87. Id. at 31.

mortgage market."[88] Chancellor William Chandler seemingly was tempted simply to exclude these claims from *Caremark*'s ambit, observing that:

> Although these claims are framed by plaintiffs as *Caremark* claims, plaintiffs' theory essentially amounts to a claim that the director defendants should be personally liable to the Company because they failed to fully recognize the risk posed by subprime securities. When one looks past the lofty allegations of duties of oversight and red flags used to dress up these claims, what is left appears to be plaintiff shareholders attempting to hold the director defendants personally liable for making (or allowing to be made) business decisions that, in hindsight, turned out poorly for the Company. Delaware Courts have faced these types of claims many times and have developed doctrines to deal with them—the fiduciary duty of care and the business judgment rule.[89]

Later in the opinion, the court further observed that: "While it may be tempting to say that directors have the same duties to monitor and oversee business risk, imposing *Caremark*-type duties on directors to monitor business risk is fundamentally different. . . . Oversight duties under Delaware law are not designed to subject directors . . . to personal liability for failure to . . . properly evaluate business risk."[90] On the other hand, the court elsewhere in the opinion stated that it might be possible for plaintiff to state such a claim "under some set of facts."[91]

In fact, risk management and law compliance are not "fundamentally different." First, there are no reasonable grounds in the *Caremark* opinion for limiting the obligations created therein to legal and accounting compliance. Granted, Chancellor Allen made much of the benefits law compliance programs offered corporations under the federal sentencing guidelines. Yet, that was only one of the three justifications Chancellor Allen offered. The necessity for the board to ensure that it is provided with sufficient information to carry out its obligations, which drove Chancellor Allen's other rationales, seems just as relevant to risk management as to legal and accounting compliance. Indeed, such a conclusion is at least implicit in Chancellor Allen's requirement that the board assure itself "that information and reporting systems exist in the organization that are reasonably designed to provide to senior management and to the board itself timely, accurate information sufficient to allow management and the board, each within its scope, to reach informed judgments *concerning*

---

88. *Citigroup*, 2009 WL 481906 at *10.
89. Id.
90. Id. at *16.
91. Id. at *13.

both the corporation's compliance with law and its *business performance*."[92] Chancellor Allen thus obviously intended the *Caremark* duty to extend beyond mere law compliance to include such issues as business risk management.

Second, the risk management role assigned to the board of directors by emergent corporate best practice guides is comparable to the role assigned boards with respect to law compliance and accounting controls. The Corporate Director's Guidebook, for example, conflates risk and compliance oversight into a single topic.[93] In addition, the Guidebook lists "compliance programs" as one of several examples of "typical risk management programs."[94] Likewise, COSO lists "compliance with applicable laws and regulations" as one of four broad categories of enterprise risk management, along with ensuring that the corporation is pursuing appropriate strategic goals, making effective and efficient operational use of resources, and providing reliable disclosures.[95]

Third, the board's role in risk management of the board has been described as one of ensuring that the corporation has put into place an effective risk management program with procedures "for identifying, assessing, and managing all types of risk, i.e., business risk, operational risk, market risk, liquidity risk, and credit risk."[96] The board's role thus includes "making sure that all the appropriate policies, methodologies, and infrastructure are in place."[97] Notice the rather precise parallel to how *Caremark* described the need for the board to ensure that effective reporting structures exist with respect to law compliance.

Finally, risk management failures raise concerns about board-management relations comparable to those raised by law compliance or accounting irregularities. It is probably rare that corporate officers commit accounting fraud or other violations of law solely out of disinterested concern for corporate profit maximization. Instead, most cases probably involve at least a substantial element of self-dealing. "Scott D. Sullivan knowingly continued to lead WorldCom's $11 billion accounting fraud," for example, "in order 'to preserve his $700,000 salary, $10 million bonus and stock options.'"[98]

The success of Sullivan's fraud, in fact, is an excellent example of an operational risk management failure. Even in the absence of actual self-dealing, moreover, management self-interest still may be a contributing factor to risk

92. In re Caremark Intern. Inc. Derivative Litigation, 698 A.2d 959, 970 (Del. Ch. 1996) (emphasis supplied).

93. Corporate Director's Guidebook, supra note 70, at 27.

94. Id.

95. Committee of Sponsoring Organizations of the Treadway Commission, Enterprise Risk Management—Integrated Framework: Executive Summary 3 (2004).

96. Crouhy et al., supra note 66, at 88.

97. Id. at 89.

98. Lisa H. Nicholson, Sarbanes-Oxley's Purported Over-Criminalization Of Corporate Offenders, 2 J. Bus. & Tech. L. 43, 53 (2007).

management failures. In particular, a corporation's failure to adopt effective enterprise risk management may often be attributable to resistance by the CEO and top management. Stock options and related pay-for-performance compensation schemes give management incentives to prefer high volatility.[99] Because boards can use enterprise risk management not only to manage risk, but also as a monitoring device, CEOs therefore may resist implementation or effective operation of risk management programs. In any case, the key point is that enterprise risk management can be understood as a form of agency cost control analogous to monitoring by independent directors or large shareholders, incentive compensation plans, auditing, law compliance programs, and internal controls.

In sum, risk management does not differ in kind from legal compliance or accounting controls. The board of directors appropriately is charged with oversight over them all. *Caremark* claims thus appropriately lie with respect to each. Having said that, however, risk management does differ in degree from law compliance and accounting internal controls. Some of these differences are significant enough to justify being factored into the *Caremark* analysis.

First, risk management is a young discipline. Accordingly, best practice with respect to enterprise risk management is still evolving. In addition, the types of risk management programs that will be effective vary from firm to firm. Devising effective enterprise risk management programs is a particular challenge for the boards of directors of "complex risk-taking organizations such as banks, securities firms, insurance companies, and energy companies," all of which played important roles in the financial crisis, precisely because it is a new board function requiring adaptation of new and evolving risk analytic disciplines.[100]

If, in applying *Caremark* to risk management failures, courts are perceived as imposing liability on boards for failing to adopt some specific model of risk management, the evolutionary market processes by which optimal best practices emerge may be aborted. Accordingly, courts should be extremely leery about rendering opinions perceived as creating a roadmap for approaching risk management.

Second, the most an effective risk management program can do is to prevent risks from materializing and perhaps limit the impact of those that do materialize. In contrast, a law compliance program can not only "significantly reduce the incidence of violations of laws," it also can substantially "reduce or eliminate civil lawsuits, penalties, or prosecution" when violations do occur.[101]

---

99. Kurt A. Desender, The Influence of Board Composition on Enterprise Risk Management Implementation 5 (October 1, 2007), http://ssrn.com/abstract= 1025982.

100. Crouhy et al., supra note 66, at 85.

101. Corporate Director's Guidebook, supra note 80, at 28.

In other words, law compliance programs provide the additional benefit of mitigating or even eliminating sanctions for violations that fall through the program's cracks. The federal sentencing guidelines, for example, authorize courts to significantly reduce the fine to be imposed on convicted corporations if the firm had appropriate and effective law compliance programs in place.[102] A downward adjustment is also available where the corporation discovers and voluntarily discloses a violation.[103] The potential payoff from effective law compliance programs is thus far more immediate and substantial than is the case with respect to risk management.

Finally, and most important, just because a firm has the ability to reduce risk does not mean it should exercise that option. As the firm's residual claimants, shareholders do not get a return on their investment until all other claims on the corporation have been satisfied. All else equal, shareholders therefore prefer high return projects. Because risk and return are directly proportional, however, implementing that preference necessarily entails choosing risky projects.

Even though conventional finance theory assumes shareholders are risk averse, rational shareholders still will have a high tolerance for risky corporate projects. First, the basic corporate law principle of limited liability substantially insulates shareholders from the downside risks of corporate activity. The limited liability principle, of course, holds that shareholders of a corporation may not be held personally liable for debts incurred or torts committed by the firm. Because shareholders thus do not put their personal assets at jeopardy, other than the amount initially invested, they effectively externalize some portion of the business' total risk exposure to creditors.

Accordingly, as Chancellor Allen explained in *Gagliardi v. Trifoods Int'l, Inc.*,[104] shareholders will want managers and directors to take risk:

> Shareholders can diversify the risks of their corporate investments. Thus, it is in their economic interest for the corporation to accept in rank order all positive net present value investment projects available to the corporation, starting with the highest risk adjusted rate of return first. Shareholders don't want (or shouldn't rationally want) directors to be risk averse. Shareholders' investment interests, across the full range of their diversifiable equity investments, will be maximized if corporate directors and managers honestly assess risk and reward and accept for the corporation the highest risk adjusted returns available that are above the firm's cost of capital.[105]

102. U.S. Sentencing Guidelines Manual § 8C2.5(f) (2008).
103. Id. at § 8C2.5(g).
104. 683 A.2d 1049 (Del. Ch. 1996).
105. Id. at 1052.

As the federal Second Circuit explained in *Joy v. North*,[106] this understanding of shareholder risk preferences is an important part of the rationale for the business judgment rule:

> Although the rule has suffered under academic criticism, it is not without rational basis. . . . [B]ecause potential profit often corresponds to the potential risk, it is very much in the interest of shareholders that the law not create incentives for overly cautious corporate decisions. . . . Shareholders can reduce the volatility of risk by diversifying their holdings. In the case of the diversified shareholder, the seemingly more risky alternatives may well be the best choice since great losses in some stocks will over time be offset by even greater gains in others. . . . A rule which penalizes the choice of seemingly riskier alternatives thus may not be in the interest of shareholders generally.[107]

Just as the business judgment rule thus insulates risk taking from judicial review, so *Caremark* should insulate risk management from judicial review.

Risk management necessarily overlaps with risk taking because the former entails making choices about how to select the optimal level of risk to maximize firm value. Recall that there are only four basic ways of managing risk: avoiding it by avoiding risky activities, transferring it through insurance or hedging, mitigating it, and accepting it as unavoidable. All of these overlap with risk taking. Operational risk management, for example, frequently entails making decisions about whether to engage in risky lines of business and, more generally, determining whether specific risks can be justified on a cost-benefit analysis basis. As a result, it is becoming increasingly "difficult to draw a line between corporate governance and risk management."[108]

The fuzzy line between risk taking and risk management is nicely illustrated by how corporations use derivatives. On the one hand, they can be used to hedge risk. On the other hand, they can be used as speculative investments. In many cases, they can be used as both simultaneously.

As Chancellor Chandler correctly recognized in *Citigroup*, *Caremark* claims premised on risk management failures thus uniquely implicate the core concerns animating the business judgment rule in a way typical *Caremark* claims do not. Chancellor Chandler seemingly understood that risk management cannot be easily disentangled from risk taking, because it described plaintiffs' claim as "asking the Court to conclude . . . that the directors failed to see the extent of Citigroup's business risk and therefore made a 'wrong' business

---

106. Joy v. North, 692 F.2d 880, 885 (2d Cir. 1982), cert. denied, 460 U.S. 1051 (1983).

107. Id. at 886.

108. Crouhy et al., supra note 66, at 87.

decision by allowing Citigroup to be exposed to the subprime mortgage market."[109] He declined to do so, explaining that "this kind of judicial second guessing is what the business judgment rule was designed to prevent, and even if a complaint is framed under a *Caremark* theory, this Court will not abandon such bedrock principles of Delaware fiduciary duty law."[110]

Risk Management in Dodd-Frank

Although most of Dodd-Frank's corporate governance provisions applied equally to Main Street and Wall Street, this is not the case with respect to risk management. Instead, Dodd-Frank § 165 mandates creation of board-level risk management committees only for bank holding companies and those non-bank financial services companies supervised by the Federal Reserve.

Likewise, the SEC has refrained from substantive regulation of risk management, which likely is beyond the scope of its regulatory authority in any case. Instead, the Commission amended its proxy disclosure rules in 2009 to require risk management-related disclosures in two contexts. First, if "risks arising from a company's compensation policies and practices for employees are reasonably likely to have a material adverse effect on the company," the proxy statement must discuss those policies and practices.[111] As originally proposed, the rule would have required disclosure of risks that "may have a material effect" on the company. The higher standard included in the rule as adopted is expected to result in fewer disclosures and to confine disclosure mainly to financial services firms.

Second, the proxy statement must include a discussion of how the board of directors administers its risk management oversight. The new rule assumes a board role in risk management, but does not attempt to define substantively what that role ought to be. It seems likely that disclosures will focus on those risks identified in the MD&A section of the corporation's annual report, since those are the ones most likely to have a material impact on the company. The disclosures also likely will focus on such issues as whether the board has a separate risk management committee and how the board interacts with those managers responsible for risk management on an operational basis.

The federal forbearance reflected in these modest developments is rather surprising given the significant role of risk management failures in the crisis. Congress and the SEC reacted to far smaller problems with much more

109. Citigroup, 2009 WL 481906 at *15.
110. Id. at *12.
111. Proxy Disclosure Enhancements, Exchange Act Rel. No. 61,675 (Dec. 16, 2009).

elaborate regulations with far less justification. To be sure, as a policy matter, this reticence is justified by the same factors that justified Chancellor Chandler's caution in *Citigroup*. In particular, given the evolving state of risk management, any federal effort to statutorily mandate specific practices likely would have carved bad ideas into stone.

At the same time, however, the federal reticence on risk management sheds disturbing light on the other ways in which Sarbanes-Oxley and Dodd-Frank regulates corporate governance. Risk management was a new problem. No one had prepackaged solutions to offer. Risk management was not on the agenda of any organized interest group. In particular, the unions, institutional investors, and their academic allies that were so influential on other corporate governance issues were largely indifferent to risk management.

Risk management thus illustrates the core problem with federal bubble laws. They are more about assuaging populist anger than about meaningful reform. Their content thus is driven not by sound public policy prescriptions but by the agenda of corporate governance policy entrepreneurs. Real problems thus go unaddressed while the business community is saddled with new obligations unrelated to the crisis that supposedly motivated them.

CHAPTER 6
The Gatekeepers

Corporate gatekeepers help solve one of corporate governance's most basic agency cost problems. Companies want investors to purchase their securities, but investors may doubt the accuracy and completeness of the disclosures provided by the firm. As a form of bonding the credibility of their disclosures, the company hires various outsiders—such as an outside auditor, underwriters, and legal counsel—to function as reputational intermediaries. Because these outsiders' business depends on their reputation for honesty, probity, and accuracy, they supposedly will not ruin that reputation to aid one client to cheat. In theory, these outsiders thereby function as gatekeepers, policing access to the capital markets.

The gatekeepers failed rather miserably during the dotcom era. Enron was primarily an accounting scandal, little different from the 150-plus other accounting fraud cases that the SEC investigates in most years. Indeed, this was true not just of Enron, but also most of the dotcom era corporate scandals. Management relied upon the substantial flexibility inherent in GAAP to manage earnings and manipulate financial data so that operating results conformed to forecasts. The goal was to keep the firm's stock price high so that the managers could profit from their stock options. Because a standard accounting audit is not a true forensic audit designed to uncover wrongdoing, but rather only a sampling audit that may entirely miss the problem, many managers thought they could get away with cooking the books. The willingness of some accountants to turn a blind eye to questionable practices meant that some managers did get away with doing so, at least for a while.

Auditing firms attracted the attention of Sarbanes-Oxley's drafters because while the frauds at Enron, Global Crossing, and WorldCom differed in many details, they had at least one common element. All three used Arthur Andersen as their outside auditor. Indeed, Arthur Andersen's name figured prominently in many other cases of accounting fraud in the 1990s and early

2000s, including the scandals at Sunbeam, Waste Management, Qwest, and the Baptist Foundation of Arizona.

The government brought both criminal and civil suits against Arthur Andersen and many companies or their shareholders sued Andersen for securities fraud. In 2002, Arthur Andersen was convicted of obstruction of justice charges arising out of destruction of Enron documents. Although the U.S. Supreme Court later overturned the conviction on technical grounds relating to the jury instructions, the verdict sounded Arthur Andersen's death knell. Its sole remaining legacy is the regulatory edifice erected by Sarbanes-Oxley to govern the accounting profession and the auditing process.

Until Sarbanes-Oxley, lawyers would have rejected the idea that they were gatekeepers. The corporate bar long rejected any notion that it owed anything to anyone other than the managers and boards of directors of its clients. The idea that lawyers might have obligations to shareholders, the investing public, or other capital market participants was abhorrent to the bar. Lawyers were advocates, confidents, and advisors, not auditors.

Yet, in almost every financial scandal, lawyers crop up as facilitators of or even participants in client misconduct. In litigation arising out of the 1980s savings and loan crisis, Judge Stanley Sporkin famously asked:

> Where were these professionals, a number of whom are now asserting their rights under the Fifth Amendment, when these clearly improper transactions were being consummated? Why didn't any of them speak up or disassociate themselves from the transactions? Where also were the outside accountants and attorneys when these transactions were effectuated? What is difficult to understand is that with all the professional talent involved (both accounting and legal), why at least one professional would not have blown the whistle to stop the overreaching that took place in this case.[1]

A decade or so later, the same questions were asked of lawyers who worked for firms like Enron.

There is little doubt that lawyers played an important role in the scandals. Sometimes their negligence allowed management misconduct to go undetected. Sometimes lawyers even acted as facilitators and enablers of management impropriety. According to Enron's internal investigation, for example, there "was an absence of forceful and effective oversight [of the company's disclosures] by . . . in-house counsel, and objective and critical professional advice by outside counsel at Vinson & Elkins,"[2] along with senior management

---

1. Lincoln Sav. & Loan Ass'n v. Wall, 743 F. Supp. 901, 920 (D.D.C. 1990).
2. William C. Powers, Jr., et al., Report of Investigation by the Special Investigative Committee of the Board of Directors of Enron Corp. 17 (Feb. 1, 2002).

and the auditors. The report expressly criticized Vinson & Elkins, which the investigators argued "should have brought a stronger, more objective and more critical voice to the disclosure process."[3]

An internal investigation at WorldCom likewise faulted, among others, the firm's lawyers as part of a pervasive "breakdown in the . . . the company's corporate-governance structure."[4] An internal investigation criticized World-Com's general counsel because his legal department was not properly structured "to maximize its effectiveness as a control structure upon which the Board could depend."[5]

It was against this background that, in the floor debate over Sarbanes-Oxley, Senator John Edwards (D-NC) argued that when "executives and/ or accountants are breaking the law, you can be sure that part of the problem is that the lawyers who are there and involved are not doing their jobs."[6] Edwards further argued that after "all the . . . corporate misconduct we have seen, it is . . . clear that corporate lawyers should not be left to regulate themselves no more than accountants should be left to regulate themselves."[7] Accordingly, just as the Sarbanes-Oxley Act federalized regulation of the accounting profession, so too did Sarbanes-Oxley bring the corporate lawyer–client relationship into the federal sphere.

THE AUDITORS

The Sarbanes-Oxley Act made many changes in the issuer-auditor relationship. It emphasized that the auditor works for the audit committee of the board, not management. Section 303 banned agents of the issuer from seeking to coerce the auditor into giving a favorable opinion. Sarbanes-Oxley § 203 requires registered public accounting firms to rotate (1) the partner having primary responsibility for the audit and (2) the partner responsible for reviewing the audit every five years. The audit committee must ensure that the requisite rotation actually takes place. Herein, however, we focus on two issues that proved especially problematic: namely, oversight of the accounting profession and the restrictions on non-audit services.

3. Id. at 26.

4. Rebecca Blumenstein & Susan Pulliam, WorldCom Fraud was Widespread, Wall St. J., June 10, 2003, at A3.

5. Rebecca Blumenstein & Jesse Drucker, MCI's Treasurer, Counsel to Resign After Disclosure, Wall St J., June 11, 2003, at A3, A12.

6. 148 Cong. Rec. S6551 (2002).

7. Id. at S6552.

Prior to Sarbanes-Oxley, the accounting profession was largely self-regulating. The key actors—FASB and the AICPA—were private-sector entities subject to minimal SEC oversight. FASB set accounting standards, while the AICPA provided guidance and contributed to the development of generally accepted principles and standards.

The Sarbanes-Oxley Act dramatically shook up that cozy little world. Section 101 established the Public Company Accounting Oversight Board (PCAOB) as a nonprofit corporation to "oversee the audit of public companies that are subject to the securities laws." Among the PCAOB's many duties, the most important for our purposes are:

1. Develop a system for registration of public accounting firms that prepare audit reports for reporting companies. Per Sarbanes-Oxley § 102, only registered accounting firms can audit the books of reporting companies. In order to register, an accounting firm must make extensive disclosures about its clients, fees, and practices, as well as consent to cooperate in any PCAOB investigation.
2. Establish standards governing auditing, quality control, ethics, independence, and other matters relating to the preparation of audit reports for reporting companies.
3. Conduct regular inspections of registered public accounting firms to ensure that the firms are complying with PCAOB and SEC rules. Large accounting firms (with more than 100 reporting company clients) get inspected annually, while smaller ones are inspected every three years. If the PCAOB finds any violations, it reports them to the SEC and any relevant state accountant licensing board. Even if the PCAOB finds no violations, it still must send a written report to the SEC and the relevant state agencies.
4. Conduct investigations and disciplinary proceedings of misconduct by registered public accounting firms and any individuals associated with such firms. The PCAOB can impose a wide range of sanctions on violators, up to and including permanent revocation of the right to conduct audits of reporting companies.

The Free Enterprise Fund, an activist think tank, brought suit to challenge the PCAOB's constitutionality.[8] The Fund argued that the Sarbanes-Oxley Act vests the PCAOB with extensive governmental functions and powers,

---

8. In the interest of full disclosure, I note that I signed amicus briefs supporting the Fund's position. I did so pro bono.

including a quasi-law enforcement investigatory power and a quasi-judicial power to impose substantial fines for violations of its rules. Accordingly, the Fund contended, the PCAOB violated a number of constitutional provisions, most notably the Appointments Clause.

The Appointments Clause of Article II, section 2 of the Constitution provides that:

> [The President] shall have Power, by and with the Advice and Consent of the Senate, to make Treaties, provided two thirds of the Senators present concur; and he shall nominate, and by and with the Advice and Consent of the Senate, shall appoint Ambassadors, other public Ministers and Consuls, Judges of the supreme Court, and all other Officers of the United States, whose Appointments are not herein otherwise provided for, and which shall be established by Law: but the Congress may by Law vest the Appointment of such inferior Officers, as they think proper, in the President alone, in the Courts of Law, or in the Heads of Departments.

Because the SEC rather than the President appoints the PCAOB's members, the statute presented three key constitutional questions. First, were the members of the PCAOB "Officers of the United States" and thus subject to the Appointments Clause? Second, if so, were the members of the PCAOB "inferior Officers" whose appointment Congress "may by Law vest" in one of the specified alternative mechanisms other than the advice and consent process? Third, if so, did the SEC Commissioners collectively qualify as a Head of Department for this purpose?

There was surprisingly little guidance on these questions, but there nevertheless was a strong argument in favor of the Fund's position. Although putatively private, the PCAOB in fact is a regulatory agency in all but name. It has an enormously broad Congressional mandate to create and enforce rules for the accounting profession and the auditing process. It can fine accounting firms up to $2 million and individual accountants up to $100,000 for violations.

While it thus wields extensive quasi-governmental powers, the PCAOB is almost immune from direct Congressional or Presidential oversight. The board is funded by a general power to tax all public companies. Compared to other regulatory agencies, which are limited in their reach by the amount of money appropriated to them by Congress, the PCAOB's independent power to tax as needed means there is very little Congressional or Presidential control on the power of the PCAOB.

The lack of de facto institutional control via the budgetary process is compounded by the formal lack of control created by the statutory structure. The President can neither appoint nor remove PCAOB members. Instead, it is the SEC acting collectively that appoints those members. Likewise, the President has no removal power. Only the SEC can remove board members, and only if they can be shown to have willfully violated federal laws.

All of this seemed highly problematic under the relevant precedents. In *Edmond v. United States*, for example, the Court wrote:

> By vesting the President with the exclusive power to select the principal (noninferior) officers of the United States, the Appointments Clause prevents congressional encroachment upon the Executive and Judicial Branches. . . . This disposition was also designed to assure a higher quality of appointments: The Framers anticipated that the President would be less vulnerable to interest-group pressure and personal favoritism than would a collective body. . . . The President's power to select principal officers of the United States was not left unguarded, however, as Article II further requires the "Advice and Consent of the Senate." This serves both to curb Executive abuses of the appointment power . . . and "to promote a judicious choice of [persons] for filling the offices of the union. . . ." By requiring the joint participation of the President and the Senate, the Appointments Clause was designed to ensure public accountability for both the making of a bad appointment and the rejection of a good one.[9]

Instead, as we have just seen, the PCAOB seems to have been designed to avoid public accountability.

In *Edmond*, the court also held that:

> Generally speaking, the term "inferior officer" connotes a relationship with some higher ranking officer or officers below the President: Whether one is an "inferior" officer depends on whether he has a superior. It is not enough that other officers may be identified who formally maintain a higher rank, or possess responsibilities of a greater magnitude. If that were the intention, the Constitution might have used the phrase "lesser officer." Rather, in the context of a Clause designed to preserve political accountability relative to important Government assignments, we think it evident that "inferior officers" are officers whose work is directed and supervised at some level by others who were appointed by Presidential nomination with the advice and consent of the Senate.[10]

Because the members of the PCAOB are not subject to such oversight except to the very limited extent they are overseen by the SEC, it would seem that the members of the PCAOB are not inferior officers.

9. Edmond v. United States, 520 U.S. 651, 659–60 (1997).
10. Id. at 662–63.

Likewise, the Fund could draw support from *Freytag v. CIR*, in which the Court opined that:

> The Framers understood . . . that by limiting the appointment power, they could ensure that those who wielded it were accountable to political force and the will of the people. . . . The Appointments Clause prevents Congress from distributing power too widely by limiting the actors in whom Congress may vest the power to appoint. The Clause reflects our Framers' conclusion that widely distributed appointment power subverts democratic government. Given the inexorable presence of the administrative state, a holding that every organ in the executive Branch is a department would multiply the number of actors eligible to appoint.[11]

Holding that the SEC is a Department empowered to appoint the PCAOB would threaten precisely the democratic values the Founders intended the Appointments Clause to protect.

The Fund thus had a very strong case that the provisions of Sarbanes-Oxley creating the PCAOB are unconstitutional. Because Congress in its rush to adopt Sarbanes-Oxley failed to include a clear severability provision, moreover, the Fund might well have been able to persuade a reviewing court that the entire Sarbanes-Oxley law had to be thrown out.

The Supreme Court dismissed all of these arguments almost out of hand, expressing "no hesitation in concluding that under *Edmond* the Board members are inferior officers whose appointment Congress may permissibly vest in a 'Hea[d] of Departmen[t].'"[12] Next, the majority held that the SEC is a Department and that the five commissioners acting collectively constitute a Head of said Department. "Because the Commission is a freestanding component of the Executive Branch, not subordinate to or contained within any other such component, it constitutes a 'Departmen[t]' for the purposes of the Appointments Clause."[13] The trouble, of course, is that the SEC really is part of the so-called Fourth Branch; i.e., the independent agencies. The President's powers to remove members of the SEC are far more limited than his powers to remove, say, a Cabinet Secretary. The independent agencies are, in Scalia's apt phrase, a "headless fourth branch."[14]

With the constitutionality of the PCAOB—and thus of the Sarbanes-Oxley Act itself—assured by Supreme Court fiat, attention can turn to how effective the board has been in regulating the accounting profession. In chapter 5,

11. Freytag v. CIR, 501 U.S. 868, 884–885 (1991).
12. Free Enterprise Fund v. Public Co. Accounting Oversight Bd., 130 S.Ct. 3138, 3162 (2010).
13. Id. at 3163.
14. Freytag v. Commissioner, 501 U.S. 868, 921 (1991) (Scalia, J., concurring).

we saw that the PCAOB has struggled at great length with making § 404 compliance less burdensome and more informative. As we will see in the Conclusion, despite those struggles, the PCAOB has failed to ameliorate § 404 costs sufficiently to make U.S. capital markets globally competitive.

The PCAOB also has failed in making audit firm quality more transparent. Recall that the PCAOB is charged with making regular inspections of registered public accounting firms and with investigating misconduct by such firms. A study by Clive Lennox and Jeffrey Pittman, however, found that less is now known about audit firm quality than was the case under the pre-SOX regime. PCAOB inspection reports disclose an auditor's engagement weaknesses but not its quality control problems. The report also fails to provide an overall assessment of the auditor's quality. As a result, the study found no evidence that corporations "view PCAOB reports as being informative about differences in audit firm quality."[15] In contrast, the pre-SOX peer review system provided precisely such information.

A more recent study by a team of economists found that the PCAOB's inspection reports for large auditors consist mainly of anecdotal evidence of deficiencies. The lack of any statistical context makes it difficult for consumers of the PCAOB reports to determine the quality of auditing firms.[16]

The PCAOB's short history precludes drawing any firm conclusions. On the evidence to date, however, it seems fair to doubt whether the board has lived up to the hopes Congress placed in it.

Limits on Non-Audit Services

A key concern motivating the Sarbanes-Oxley Act's drafters was the conflict of interest inherent when accounting firms sell other services to the corporations whose books they audit. Title II of the act therefore limited the extent to which accountants may provide consulting services to their audit clients. Some non-audit services were banned outright. The outside auditor, for example, may not provide bookkeeping or related services, design or implement financial information systems, provide fairness opinions in connection with corporate transactions, conduct internal audits on an outsourced basis, provide humans relations services, or act as an investment banker or legal expert. In addition, the PCAOB is authorized to ban other non-audit services as it deems fit.

15. Clive Lennox & Jeffrey Pittman, Auditing the Auditors: Evidence on the Recent Reforms to the External Monitoring of Audit Firms 4 (Oct. 2008).

16. James Wainberg et al., An Investigation into PCAOB Reporting Deficiencies (Feb. 2010).

Contrary to conventional wisdom, however, the Sarbanes-Oxley Act did not completely ban all such services. Provided the client's audit committee approves the retention in advance, in fact, the auditor may perform any non-audit services not banned by the Sarbanes-Oxley Act or the PCAOB. For example, a corporation's outside auditor can also prepare its corporate tax returns.

The SEC requires disclosure of any "fees paid to the independent accountant for (1) audit services, (2) audit-related services, (3) tax services, and (4) other services" in the annual report on Form 10-K. The SEC has also cautioned companies that there are "some circumstances where providing certain tax services to an audit client would impair the independence of an accountant, such as representing an audit client in tax court or other situations involving public advocacy." The SEC did create an exception for de minimis non-audit services, pursuant to which a registered accounting firm still is independent even if it provides non-approved, non-audit services. The aggregate compensation for all such services may constitute no more than 5 percent of the total fees paid the auditor by the client during the relevant fiscal year. Once the company recognizes that it is compensating its auditor for non-audit services without prior approval by the audit committee, the management promptly must bring the oversight to the audit committee's attention and have the services approved by the committee.

Was all of this necessary? Yale law professor Roberta Romano compiled the results of numerous studies of auditor performance and concluded that the "overwhelming majority" "suggest that the Sarbanes-Oxley Act's prohibition of the purchase of non-audit services from an auditor is an exercise in legislating away a non-problem."[17] Most of the studies found that there was no connection between provision of non-audit services and the quality of the audit. Several even found that auditors who provided non-audit services performed higher quality audits, presumably because providing such services gives the auditor more and better information about the company.

Conversely, there are several reasons to think that the prohibition on non-audit services has had very high costs. First, consolidations and the demise of Arthur Andersen have shrunk the Big Eight to the Big Four. Only they have the resources, expertise, and global reach to effectively audit large public corporations. If such a corporation gets non-audit services from three of the Big Four, it is effectively locked into the fourth as its auditor. The rule thus reduced competition. By promoting quasi-permanent relationships between the auditor and the client, moreover, it may contribute to precisely the sort of problems the Sarbanes-Oxley Act sought to avoid.

17. Roberta Romano, The Sarbanes-Oxley Act and the Making of Quack Corporate Governance, 114 Yale L.J. 1521, 1535–36 (2005).

Second, providing non-audit services permitted auditor and client to take advantage of economies of scale and scope. The knowledge gained in providing non-audit services could permit the auditor to perform the audit more efficiently. The expertise and knowledge gained in conducting audits improves the quality of the auditor's non-audit services. Because accounting firms were willing to discount services when clients purchased both audit and non-audit services from the same company, the ban on non-audit services raised costs by forcing issuers to hire two accounting firms. This is another example of how the Sarbanes-Oxley Act raised the cost of being public. Because accounting costs are a disproportionately large budget item for smaller firms, it also is another example of how the Sarbanes-Oxley Act especially hurts such firms.

THE LAWYERS

The nature of the legal market gives lawyers—both in-house and outside counsel—strong incentives to overlook management wrongdoing. As to the former, even if the board of directors formally appoints the in-house general counsel, his tenure normally depends mainly on his relationship with the CEO. As for outside legal counsel, because clients hire attorneys or firms and not the reverse, attorneys must please their clients in order to retain their business, and to attract the business of future clients. This pressure is especially strong given the large number of capable firms and attorneys available for hire; law firms are something akin to a fungible good. Consequently, despite an attorney's overarching legal obligations to report misconduct, he might be inclined to intentionally or subconsciously "overlook" marginal conduct. As to both types of attorney, moreover, although their ultimate duty is owed to the corporation itself, their daily responsibilities involve dealing with management and they thus often develop a de facto loyalty to management that trumps their de jure duties. As Senator Edwards explained in the floor debate over the Sarbanes-Oxley:

> We have seen corporate lawyers sometimes forget who their client is. What happens is their day-to-day conduct is with the CEO or the chief financial officer because those are the individuals responsible for hiring them. So as a result, that is with whom they have a relationship. When they go to lunch with their client, the corporation, they are usually going to lunch with the CEO or the chief financial officer. When they get phone calls, they are usually returning calls to the CEO or the chief financial officer.[18]

18. 148 Cong. Rec. S6551–52 (2002).

The attorney-management relationship is problematic on two grounds. First, as we know, there is a persistent information asymmetry between the board and management. Managers inherently have better direct access to firm information than outside board members who devote but a small portion of their time and effort to the firm. In addition to being more deeply embedded in intra-firm information flows, insiders have many informal contacts with one another and key corporate stakeholders, which provides them with even better access to information vis-à-vis outsiders. Finally, by virtue of their position with the firm, insiders typically are better able to put data in their broader context, seeing the relationships and connections any particular datum has to the firm as a whole.

The post-SOX emphasis on having a board whose majority consists not just of outsiders but of outsiders so insulated from management as to satisfy the demanding definition of independence has made management's information advantages even more acute. Addressing the board-management information asymmetry thus becomes even more imperative in their wake. The post-reform board simply must have better access to unbiased and independent information.

Both the general counsel and outside lawyers necessarily have access to a wide range of information, including but hardly limited to information relating to law compliance by the organization. Because the management-attorney relationship tends to become the focus of the attorney's relationship with the firm, however, lawyers have strong incentives to help management control the flow of information to the board of directors.

Worse yet, attorneys may be tempted to turn a blind eye to managerial misconduct or even to facilitate such misconduct. As we saw at the beginning of this chapter, attorneys in the dotcom era committed both misfeasances and malfeasances on behalf of the managerial "clients." Dependent on management for work, counsel all too often were reluctant to prevent management misconduct, let alone to pursue it aggressively, such as by reporting it to the board of directors.

Sarbanes-Oxley § 307

When the Senate took up the bill that became the Sarbanes-Oxley Act, Senator Edwards proposed a floor amendment, subsequently enacted as § 307 of the Act, requiring the SEC to:

> [I]issue rules . . . setting forth minimum standards of professional conduct for attorneys appearing and practicing before the Commission in any way in the representation of issuers, including a rule—(1) requiring an attorney to report evidence of a material violation of securities law or breach of fiduciary

duty or similar violation by the company or any agent thereof, to the chief legal counsel or the chief executive officer of the company (or the equivalent thereof); and (2) if the counsel or officer does not appropriately respond to the evidence . . . requiring the attorney to report the evidence to the audit committee of the board of directors of the issuer or to another committee of the board of directors comprised solely of directors not employed . . . by the issuer, or to the board of directors.

Edwards explained that the bill gave lawyers a very "simple" obligation: "You report the violation. If the violation isn't addressed properly, then you go to the board."[19] Note the emphasis on reporting to the board. Section 307 clearly is directed at enhancing the role of the board vis-à-vis that of management.

SEC Implementation

In response to § 307, the SEC in January 2003 promulgated attorney conduct regulations.[20] At the heart of these so-called "Part 205" regulations is a version of the up-the-ladder reporting requirement envisioned by Senator Edwards. In promulgating the Part 205 regulations, the SEC postponed action with regard to mandatory noisy withdrawals. The original proposal obligated an attorney whose internal complaints did not receive an adequate mitigating response by the issuer to resign from the corporation and to file a notification with the SEC explaining the basis for such resignation. This noisy withdrawal rule met with substantial criticism from the bar. As adopted, Part 205 permits, but does not require, an attorney to disclose confidential client information to the SEC under specified conditions, most notably where necessary to prevent "injury to the financial interest or property of the issuer or investors."[21]

Unlike the much-debated noisy withdrawal issue, an up-the-ladder reporting requirement does not require the lawyer to violate client confidences. The ABA Model Rules make clear that an attorney's client is the corporate entity, rather than an individual employee or group of employees.[22] Consequently, discussing client information with anyone authorized to make decisions within the organization is not a breach of confidence. The Part 205 Regulations make this point explicit: "By communicating such information [i.e., about

19. 148 Cong. Rec. S6552 (2002).
20. Implementation of Standards of Professional Conduct for Attorneys, Securities Act Release No. 8185 (Jan. 29, 2003), available at http://www.sec.gov/rules/final/33–8185.htm.
21. 17 C.F.R. § 205.3(d)(2).
22. See Model Rules of Prof'l Conduct R. 1.13(a).

securities violations] to the issuer's officers or directors, an attorney does not reveal client confidences or secrets. . . ."[23]

Preliminary Matters: Jurisdiction and Preemption

The initial jurisdictional question is whether a lawyer is "appearing and practicing before the Commission in the representation of an issuer."[24] Only lawyers doing so are subject to the SEC's ethics standards. Unfortunately, the definition of "appearing and practicing" is sweeping but quite vague. As a result, many non-securities lawyers may be surprised to find that their conduct is covered by the Part 205 regulations.

In particular, the applicable rule provides, in pertinent part, that:

> Appearing and practicing before the Commission: (1) Means: . . . Providing advice in respect of the United States securities laws or the Commission's rules or regulations thereunder regarding any document that the attorney has notice will be filed with or submitted to, or incorporated into any document that will be filed with or submitted to, the Commission, including the provision of such advice in the context of preparing, or participating in the preparation of, any such document. . . .[25]

To be sure, the adopting release states "an attorney's preparation of a document (such as a contract) which he or she never intended or had notice would be submitted to the Commission, or incorporated into a document submitted to the Commission, but which subsequently is submitted to the Commission as an exhibit to or in connection with a filing, does not constitute 'appearing and practicing' before the Commission."[26] Yet, many non-securities lawyers may know that their documents will be so filed and thus will find themselves "appearing and practicing" before the Commission.

The Part 205 regulations facially preempt state rules of professional conduct.[27] As a result, where there is conflict between a state's rules and part 205, the latter prevails, unless the state imposes a more stringent obligation upon its attorneys that is consistent with Part 205. Attorneys who comply with the Regulation's procedures in good faith will be immune from liability for violating state ethics rules that conflict. Because it will not always be self-evident whether counsel is "appearing and practicing" before the SEC, the organized

23. 17 C.F.R. § 205.3(b)(1).
24. 17 C.F.R. § 205.2.
25. 17 C.F.R. § 205.2(a)(1)(iii).
26. Securities Act Release No. 8185, supra note 20.
27. 17 C.F.R. §§ 205.6(b)–(c).

bar thus likely will be compelled to square its rules with those promulgated by the SEC.

The Issuer as Client

As originally proposed, Part 205.3 provided that an attorney "shall act in the best interest of the issuer and its shareholders."[28] As finally adopted, however, the relevant rule provides only that: "An attorney appearing and practicing before the Commission in the representation of an issuer owes his or her professional and ethical duties to the issuer as an organization."[29] The Part 205 Regulations, however, do emphasize that the attorney "represents the issuer as an entity rather than the officers."[30]

Up-the-Ladder Reporting

Former ABA Model Rule 1.13 acknowledged the potential need for an attorney to report on suspected wrongdoing within the organization, but it also limited the ability of an attorney to do so effectively. The language of the Rule was discretionary rather than prescriptive, allowing an attorney to use his judgment about whether or not to proceed with reporting evidence of misconduct to the board of directors or even to high-level corporate officers. In contrast, Part 205 uses the prescriptive word "shall" to describe an attorney's duty. In pertinent part, the rule provides:

> If an attorney, appearing and practicing before the Commission in the representation of an issuer, becomes aware of evidence of a material violation by the issuer or by any officer, director, employee, or agent of the issuer, the attorney shall report such evidence to the issuer's chief legal officer (or the equivalent thereof) or to both the issuer's chief legal officer and its chief executive officer (or the equivalents thereof) forthwith.[31]

As a result, an attorney will not have the luxury of using his own judgment about whether or not to report wrongdoing once the statutory level of evidence is triggered. As Senator Edwards anticipated, counsel must report up within the chain of command.

---

28. Securities Act Release No. 8185, supra note 20.
29. 17 C.F.R. § 205.3(a).
30. Securities Act Release No. 8185, supra note 20.
31. 17 C.F.R. § 205.3(b)(1).

The initial obligation of a lawyer who "becomes aware of evidence of a material violation by the issuer or by any officer, director, employee, or agent of the issuer" is to report such evidence to the issuer's chief legal or executive officer.[32] Subject to a slew of exceptions and alternatives, unless the lawyer "reasonably believes that [that officer] has provided an appropriate response within a reasonable time, the attorney shall report the evidence of a material violation to" the audit committee of the board of directors.[33]

Assessment

The nature of the market for legal services gives management a set of carrots by which to align the interests of corporate counsel with those of management. Sarbanes-Oxley did not attempt to change that set of incentives. Instead, Sarbanes-Oxley § 307 gave the SEC a set of sticks in hopes of enlisting corporate counsel in the prevention of fraud and related corporate scandals. In doing so, § 307 is part of the statute's goal of empowering boards of directors.

The goal is laudable.[34] In the statutory corporate-governance model, the board of directors "possesses [the corporation's property], and act[s] in every way as if they owned it."[35] Managerialism is a corruption of this statutory model, albeit one that has been inescapable ever since corporations got large enough to require full-time professional managers. By enlisting legal counsel as aides of the board, Sarbanes-Oxley sought properly to help shift the de facto balance of power between boards and managements toward the de jure model of director primacy. But will it work?

Relying on Self-Policing by Lawyers

The SEC made clear, in adopting the final rules, that it had abandoned an initial effort to "exclude the subjective element" from the concept of "reasonable belief."[36] An attorney who receives what he "reasonably believes is an appropriate and timely response" from management, for example, "need do nothing more."[37] As a result, the decision to report up the ladder is largely in the hands of the lawyer.

---

32. Id.
33. 17 C.F.R. § 205.3(b)(3).
34. Whether the valid goal of strengthening the board of directors vis-à-vis management should have been pursued at the federal level is another question.
35. Manson v. Curtis, 119 N.E. 559, 562 (N.Y. 1918).
36. Securities Act Release No. 8185, supra note 20.
37. See 17 C.F.R. § 205.3(b)(8).

A related problem, having the same effect, is that several key provisions are expressly permissive rather than mandatory. For example, § 205.3(b) contemplates that reporting to the board be a "last resort" rather than mandating that all evidence of wrongdoing be automatically disclosed to the board. Under Part 205, an attorney should only go up the ladder where management has failed to properly address or remedy the situation. In practice, this approach means that only a fraction of reports will ever make it beyond the CEO/CLO stage.

To be sure, § 205.3(b)(4) allows attorneys to bypass management and go directly to the board to report misconduct if it would be futile to report to the CEO or CLO. The problem here may be best illustrated by example. Suppose attorney Anne suspects wrongdoing by the CEO. Knowing full-well that reporting the CEO's wrongdoing to the CEO and/or the CLO would be pointless, but considering that the "futility provision" is only discretionary, Anne may choose to talk to the CEO and CLO rather than go over their heads to the board for fear of alienating those individuals. If there is any risk that Anne is mistaken about the wrongdoing, going over the heads of the CEO and CLO will permanently poison her relationship with them. If Anne opts to first speak to the CEO or CLO, and they give Anne her statutorily mandated assurance that the problem is being investigated and reasonably resolved, Anne has fulfilled her duties. Yet, the CEO and CLO may be allowed to continue their misconduct.

Much the same problem is presented by the purportedly objective standard requiring a lawyer to report "evidence" of misconduct. After an attorney reports evidence of a material violation to management,[38] the manager shall "cause such inquiry into the evidence of a material violation as he or she reasonably believes is appropriate to determine whether the material violation described in the report has occurred . . ."[39] The discretionary standard by which lawyers are to determine whether there is evidence a violation has occurred— namely, whether a "prudent attorney" would think it was "reasonably likely" that a material violation had occurred[40]—allows for professional concerns and other conflicts of interest to skew the lawyer's assessment, minimizing the chances that the potential violation would be reported to management, let alone to the board. Because of the two-tiered reporting system in which disclosure to the board is contemplated only after management inaction, the corporate managers may often look at evidence presented by a concerned attorney, "reasonably" determine that in fact no violation has occurred

---

38. The standard is (confusingly) defined as "credible evidence, based upon which it would be unreasonable, under the circumstances, for a prudent and competent attorney not to conclude that it is reasonably likely that a material violation has occurred, is ongoing, or is about to occur." 17 C.F.R. § 205.2(e).
39. 17 C.F.R. § 205.3(b)(2).
40. 17 C.F.R. § 205.2(e).

(notwithstanding ever-present conflicts of interest), and dismiss the whole matter without any knowledge by the board. The attorney would have complied with his statutory obligation to report up-the-ladder, yet the board's monitoring function would have been eviscerated.

The Lawyer Who Cried Wolf

If Sarbanes-Oxley § 307 in fact changes attorney incentives, itself a highly debatable point, attorneys may begin to act in unnecessarily risk-averse ways, which will pervert the traditional lawyer-client relationship. A particular source of concern is the possibility that risk-averse lawyers may invoke the reporting up-the-ladder option too often. To be sure, as we saw in the preceding section, the reliance on self-policing may lead to under-reporting. Given the uncertainty about the scope of the rules and the potentially severe sanctions for guessing wrong, it seems equally plausible—and equally problematic—that lawyers may err in the other direction. First, invoking the up-the-ladder reporting right to report evidence about possible wrongdoing allows attorneys to cover themselves. When lawyers routinely use reporting up-the-ladder as a CYA mechanism, however, their conduct changes the signaling effect of disclosure. In other words, if reporting up-the-ladder occurs more frequently, it will become a routine procedure that does not necessarily indicate real doubt by the attorney about the propriety of the managers' actions. Indeed, so as to preserve their relationship with management, lawyers may try to take the sting out of disclosing possible misconduct within an organization by de-stigmatizing the practice. Once reporting up-the-ladder loses its sting, however, the impact of the disclosure is lessened. In such an environment, senior management and the board will not take accusations as seriously as they should.

Structural Concerns in the Market for Legal Services

The roles played by prominent Texas law firm Vinson & Elkins as Enron's principal outside counsel can be separated into three distinct categories: First, the aggressive structuring of the controversial special purpose entity transactions used in Enron's accounting scam. Second, drafting Enron's disclosure documents. Third, conducting an internal investigation of a whistle-blower's allegations.[41] The latter category is a rare undertaking and differs significantly

---

41. See generally Jill E. Fisch & Kenneth M. Rosen, Is There a Role for Lawyers in Preventing Future Enrons?, 48 Vill. L. Rev. 1097 (2003).

from the far more common transactional work now governed by Sarbanes-Oxley and its progeny. Yet, Sarbanes-Oxley § 307 and the Part 205 Regulations seem better designed to deal with the third context than with either of the first two. It is only in the third context, for example, that lawyers deliberately set out to look for evidence of wrongdoing.

In the more common transactional settings, § 307 issues may arise in one of three main ways. First, counsel may be aware of aggressive or risky conduct by management, but is unaware of fraud or other illegality. As we shall see, this is likely to be the most common situation in which questions of reporting up-the-ladder arise. In these cases, as we shall also see, however, the lawyer is unlikely to report up-the-ladder. Second, counsel may have actively participated in—or at least facilitated—actual fraud. In these cases, the lawyer also is unlikely to report up-the-ladder, albeit for the different reason that he now has something to hide. Third, counsel may have grounds for suspicion—but no direct evidence—of fraud or other illegality.

Only in the latter scenario does the up-the-ladder reporting requirement come into play, but it likely is rare. Corporate managers are highly unlikely to seek legal assistance with outright fraud, as opposed to conduct that merely pushes the edge of the envelope. In the post-Sarbanes-Oxley § 307 environment, managers are even more likely to conceal any hint of impropriety from counsel. In addition, lawyers will very rarely perceive their own situation to fall within the third scenario. As former Delaware Chancellor Allen aptly noted, albeit in a rather different context, "human nature may incline even one acting in subjective good faith to rationalize as right that which is merely personally beneficial."[42] It typically is personally beneficial for lawyers to refrain from antagonizing the corporate managers who hire and fire them. The claim is not that lawyers are pervasively co-opted or immoral. The claim is only that lawyers have both economic incentives and cognitive biases that systematically incline them to stay on the good side of the corporation's managers. Hence, absent the proverbial smoking gun, we can expect lawyers to turn a blind eye to indicia of misconduct by those managers. Section 307 does too little to change those incentives.

Management Will Bypass the Lawyers

Managers who intentionally commit fraud or breaches of fiduciary duty rarely consult their legal counsel. Instead, counsel will be consulted by a manager who is pursuing an aggressive course of conduct or one who has inadvertently

42. City Capital Associates Ltd Partnership v. Interco Inc., 551 A.2d 787, 796 (Del. Ch. 1988).

strayed over the line into illegality. Vinson & Elkins, for example, most likely "knew of aggressive and risky transactions and reporting decisions [by Enron's management] but did not have actual knowledge of illegal conduct."[43] It is therefore noteworthy that § 307 does not require counsel to report evidence of uninformed, excessively aggressive, or unethical conduct to the board but only evidence of fraud and breaches of fiduciary duty. Even though Sarbanes-Oxley § 307 and its progeny have many ambiguities and uncertainties, it seems unlikely that most legal counsel would regard those provisions as mandating up-the-ladder reporting of aggressive management. Nor does it seem likely that most boards of directors would welcome such reporting. At the very least, legal counsel who frequently complain to the board that management is pushing the edge of the envelope risk developing a "boy who cried wolf" reputation. Because much (probably most) of the board's monitoring function involves preventing (or at least supervising) overly aggressive management, § 307 thus fails to address the basic information asymmetry between management and the board.

As many commentators complained during the regulatory process, the Part 205 Regulations nevertheless still may have a chilling effect on attorney-client communication.[44] Even corporate managers not engaged in actual misconduct will not welcome the investigation that an attorney's reporting up would engender, especially where there is a possibility that counsel will go over their heads. Managers therefore may withhold information from counsel, so as to withhold it from the board, especially when the managers are knowingly pursuing an aggressive course of conduct. Indeed, in many of the recent corporate scandals, the misconduct was committed by a small group of senior managers who took considerable pains to conceal their actions from outside advisors such as legal counsel.[45] Many commentators complained that § 307 will diminish the quality of the attorney's representation of the client because counsel will lack unfettered access to information.[46] More pertinent for our purposes, however, the likelihood that an attorney will encounter evidence of misconduct also is reduced.[47]

43. Fisch & Rosen, supra note 41, at 1115.
44. See Securities Act Release No. 8185, supra note 20 (summarizing commentators' views).
45. See, e.g., Mark Maremont, Rite Aid Case Gives First View of Wave of Fraud on Trial, Wall St J., June 10, 2003, at A1 (describing the "great lengths" to which defendants went in order to "cover their tracks").
46. See Securities Act Release No. 8185, supra note 20 (summarizing commentators' views).
47. If counsel cannot be bypassed, management may seek to intimidate them. The Enron abuses long went undetected, in part, because Enron management "either overruled or intimidated" subordinates. Steven L. Schwarz, Enron and the Use and Abuse of Special Purpose Entities in Corporate Structures, 70 U. Cin. L. Rev. 1309, 1317 (2002). In-house counsel may be particularly vulnerable to such pressures.

Counsel therefore is most likely to come across evidence of misconduct when conducting an affirmative investigation, such as when performing due diligence in connection with the issuance of securities. Yet, it may be doubted that the due diligence will often turn up direct evidence of misconduct. In the first place, even a full-fledged accounting audit is not a true forensic audit designed to uncover wrongdoing, but rather only a sampling audit that may entirely miss the problem.[48] In the second place, due diligence is time-consuming. It is therefore expensive. It therefore tends to be done by young associates. As a result, much client misconduct will go undetected by outside counsel because the lawyers with the most direct exposure to the raw data frequently lack experience. In the third place, due diligence is currently limited to issuances of securities. Routine disclosures and other matters constituting "appearing and practicing" before the SEC traditionally have not triggered a due diligence investigation.

Will Lawyers Know It When They See It?

As we have seen, the dotcom era frauds typically involved cooking the books so as to raise—or at least support—the firm's stock price so that the managers could profit from their stock options. The problem is that generally accepted accounting principles (GAAP) provide substantial flexibility, which permits the phenomenon of earnings management by which corporate managers manipulate financial data so that operating results conform with forecasts. Even trained corporate lawyers often lack the mathematical skills and accounting knowledge to tell the difference between earnings management allowed by GAAP and illegal financial chicanery. In Enron itself, for example, "Enron and its accountants were (in many cases) making exquisitely fine judgment calls."[49] Few lawyers likely have the expertise necessary to second-guess such judgments. As Professor Lawrence Cunningham observed, "an important lesson from Enron is the danger that prevailing professional cultures create a crack between law and accounting that resolute fraud artists exploit."[50]

48. Larry E. Ribstein, Market vs. Regulatory Responses to Corporate Fraud: A Critique of the Sarbanes-Oxley Act of 2002, 28 J. Corp. L. 1, 31 (2002).
49. Schwarz, supra note 47, at 1313.
50. Lawrence A. Cunningham, Sharing Accounting's Burden: Business Lawyers in Enron's Dark Shadows, 57 Bus. Law. 1421, 1422 (2002). In the selective disclosure context, the SEC acknowledges that: "In many cases, an issuer's chief financial officer or investor relations officer may have a keener awareness than company counsel of the significance of information to investors." Exchange Act Release No. 46,898 (Nov. 25, 2002). In my view, the qualifiers "many" and "may" were unnecessary.

The SEC was quite reticent in exercising its authority under § 307. Consistent with the spirit of Sarbanes-Oxley the SEC might have been even more aggressive in pressing lawyers to communicate with the board of directors. The SEC might have required, for example, that the audit committee and/or the board meet periodically with the general counsel outside the presence of other managers and inside directors.

The SEC might have required the counsel to report possible violations to the board even if the chief legal or executive officer undertook a reasonable response to the violation. After all, it is the board of directors that has a responsibility to assure that "appropriate information and reporting systems are established by management" and that "appropriate information will come to its attention in a timely manner as a matter of ordinary operations."[51]

A more radical way of promoting the anti-managerial intent inherent in Sarbanes-Oxley § 307 would be an enhanced due diligence obligation, which would effectively transform securities lawyers into auditors. A legal audit of the firm in connection with major transactions and/or the preparation of significant disclosure documents would increase the likelihood that counsel would become aware of evidence of client misconduct, which could then be reported up-the-ladder. Indeed, Sarbanes-Oxley has already moved in this direction by imposing a new obligation for the chief executive officer and chief and financial officer to certify disclosure documents.[52] Given the amount of client misconduct that went undetected by accounting audits and legal due diligence, however, it may be doubted whether the benefits of such a radical solution would outweigh the costs.

To be sure, these ideas push the edge of the envelope insofar as the SEC's regulatory authority is concerned. Although § 307 only explicitly mandated an up-the-ladder reporting requirement, the statutory reference to "minimum standards of professional conduct" sweeps far more broadly and could easily encompass additional, more extensive obligations. The SEC thus doubtless has wider authority than it has chosen to exercise to date.

The Case against § 307

There is a very real risk that the new post-SOX legal ethics rules will make the lawyer-client relationship more adversarial and less productive. Such a deterioration in the lawyer-client relationship would be most unfortunate.

51. In re Caremark International Inc. Derivative Litigation, 698 A.2d 959, 969–70 (Del. Ch. 1996).
52. Sarbanes-Oxley § 302.

Corporate lawyers are one of basic categories of advisors who play a critical role in virtually all corporate transactions. But why?

The reason people hire litigators is obvious—either they are being sued or they want to sue somebody else. Unauthorized practice of law statutes and bar admission rules give lawyers a near-total monopoly on litigation.

The rationale for hiring transactional lawyers, by contrast, is less obvious. Much of the work of transactional lawyers entails giving advice that could be given by other professionals. Accordingly, it seems fair to ask: why does anybody hire transactional lawyers?

Two competing hypotheses suggest themselves. The first might be termed the "Pie-Division Role." In this version of the transactional lawyer story, lawyers strive to capture value—maximizing their client's gains from the deal. Although there are doubtless pie-division situations in transactional practice, this explanation of the lawyer's role is flawed. Pie division assumes a zero-sum game in which any gains for one side come from the other side's share. Assume two sophisticated clients with multiple advisors, including competent counsel. Is there any reason to think that one side's lawyer will be able to extract significant gains from the other? No. A homely example may be helpful: You and a friend go out to eat. You decide to share a pizza, so you need to agree on its division. Would you hire somebody to negotiate a division of the pizza? Especially if they were going to take one of your slices as their fee?

The second hypothesis might be termed the "Pie-Expansion Role." In this version of the story, people hire transactional lawyers because they add value to the deal. This conception of the lawyer's role rejects the zero-sum game mentality. Instead, it claims that the lawyer makes everybody better off by increasing the size of the pie.

For the most part, lawyers increase the size of the pie by reducing transaction costs. One way of lowering transaction costs is through regulatory arbitrage. The law frequently provides multiple ways of effecting a given transaction, all of which will have various advantages and disadvantages. By selecting the most advantageous structure for a given transaction, and ensuring that courts and regulators will respect that choice, the transactional lawyer reduces the cost of complying with the law and allows the parties to keep more of their gains.

An example may be helpful. Acme Corporation wants to acquire Ajax, Inc., using stock as the form of consideration to be paid Ajax shareholders. Acme is concerned about the availability of appraisal rights to shareholders of the two corporations. Presumably Acme doesn't care about the legal niceties of doing the deal—Acme just wants to buy Ajax at the lowest possible cost and, by hypothesis, with the minimal possible cash flow. In other words, the client cares about the economic substance of the deal, not the legal form it takes. As Acme's transactional lawyer, you know that corporate law often elevates form over substance—and that the law provides multiple ways of acquiring another company. A solution thus suggests itself: Delaware law only permits shareholders to exercise appraisal rights in connection with mergers. Appraisal rights are not allowed in connection with an acquisition structured as a sale of assets. Hence, while there is no substantive economic difference between an asset sale and a merger, there is a significant legal difference. By selecting one form over another, the transactional lawyer ensures that the deal is done at the lowest possible cost.

Parties would experience some transaction costs even in the absence of regulation, however. Reducing those non-regulatory costs is another function of the transactional lawyer. Information asymmetries are a good example. A corporation selling securities to an investor has considerably greater information about the firm than does the prospective buyer. The wise potential investor knows about this information asymmetry and, as a result, takes precautions. Worse yet, what if the seller lies? Or shades the truth? Or is itself uninformed? The wise investor also knows there is a risk of opportunistic withholding or manipulation of asymmetrically held information. One response is investigation—due diligence—by the buyer. Another response is for the seller to provide disclosures including representations and warranties. In either case, by finding ways for the seller to convey credibly information to the investor, the transactional lawyer helps eliminate the information asymmetry between them. In turn, a variety of other transaction costs will fall. There is less uncertainty, less opportunity for strategic behavior, and less need to take costly precautions.

Opponents of § 307 argue that much of the benefits that thus flow from a collegial working environment between counsel and management will be lost as that relationship becomes more distant or even more adversarial in the face of the reporting up obligation. Much else in § 307 also is worthy of criticism. There are serious and legitimate issues of federalism raised by Congress's intrusion into legal ethics, an area long governed by states. Likewise, legislative intrusion into a regulatory area traditionally within the purview of courts raises legitimate separation of powers concerns

Summation

At the end of the day, § 307—warts and all—was necessary to break the organized bar's resistance to legal ethics reforms intended to reduce the managerialist bias of the rules of professional conduct. Corporate counsel work for the board, not management. Only by threatening lawyers who fail to report up-the-ladder with discipline could the balance of power be shifted in favor of directors relative to managers.

In practice, firms should still be able to ensure that the client gets the full benefit of transactional lawyering services by developing a best practice approach to dealing with possible material violations. In consultation with the audit committee, the general counsel and principal outside counsel should develop a written policy for identifying and reporting violations. The board members, CEO, and CFO should be briefed on their legal obligations with respect to reports, but also encouraged to view a report as a potential win-win situation rather than a zero-sum or adversarial game. Up-the-ladder reporting can give the firm an opportunity to cut off potential violations before they mature into a legal or public relations nightmare, but only if counsel and managers are willing to trust one another.

CHAPTER 7
Shareholder Empowerment

The last two decades saw repeated efforts by corporate governance activists to extend the shareholder franchise and otherwise empower shareholders to take on a more expansive governance role. Even before the 2007–2008 financial crisis, they had scored some important successes. SEC reforms of the proxy rules in 1992 facilitated communication among shareholders.[1] More recently, in 2003, the major stock exchanges implemented new listing standards expanding the number of corporate compensation plans that must be approved by shareholders.[2] The DGCL and the MBCA both were amended in 2006 to allow corporations to require a majority vote—rather than the traditional plurality—to elect directors.[3]

The financial crisis of 2008, the election of Barack Obama as President of the United States, the expansion of Democratic majorities in both houses of Congress, and the installation of a Democratic majority at the SEC gave such efforts renewed impetus. Echoing the claims of key political supporters, such as unions and state and local government pension plans, Washington Democrats blamed the financial crisis in large part on corporate governance failures.[4] Accordingly, their response included a hefty dose of new shareholder entitlements.

---

1. See Stephen Choi, Proxy Issue Proposals: Impact of the 1992 SEC Proxy Reforms, 16 J.L. Econ. & Org. 233, 266 (2000); Norma M. Sharara & Anne E. Hoke-Witherspoon, The Evolution of the 1992 Shareholder Communication Proxy Rules and Their Impact on Corporate Governance, 49 Bus. Law 327 (1993).

2. See, e.g., NYSE, Listed Company Manual § 3.12.

3. Del. Code Ann., tit. 8, § 141(b), 216; Mod. Bus. Corp. Act. § 10.22.

4. See Transcript, The Federalist Society—Corporations Practice Group: Panel on the SEC and the Financial Services Crisis of 2008, 28 Review of Banking & Financial Law 237, 238 (2008) (remarks of Stephen M. Bainbridge) ("We have heard many calls for financial services reform, a so-called 'new New Deal.'").

The Department of Treasury's implementation rules for the Troubled Assets Relief Program (TARP), for example, contained a so-called "say on pay" provision requiring TARP recipient institutions to hold an annual non-binding shareholder vote on executive compensation. Senator Charles Schumer's (D-NY) proposed Shareholder Bill of Rights Act would have added "a new Section 14A to the Securities Exchange Act of 1934 requiring each proxy state-ment covered by it to provide for a non-binding shareholder vote on executive compensation as disclosed in the proxy statement," as well as requiring share-holder approval of golden parachutes in certain acquisition transactions.[5] As we saw in chapter 4, say on pay in fact made it into Dodd-Frank.

The financial crisis also gave final impetus to the corporate governance activist community's long-standing goal of proxy access. As Dodd-Frank was working its way through Congress, the SEC was engaged in a rule-making pro-ceeding evaluating a proposal to allow certain shareholders to nominate can-didates for the board of directors and to have those candidates included in the company's proxy materials.[6] To avert a widely expected challenge to the SEC's authority to adopt such a rule, the authors of Dodd-Frank included a provi-sion expressly authorizing the SEC to do so.

SHAREHOLDER RIGHTS IN STATE LAW

In contrast to the new federal regime of shareholder empowerment, state cor-porate law has traditionally limited shareholder voting rights. Under the Delaware code, for example, shareholder voting rights are essentially limited to the election of directors and approval of charter or bylaw amendments, mergers, sales of substantially all of the corporation's assets, and voluntary dissolution. As a formal matter, except for electing directors and amending the bylaws, board approval is required before shareholder action is possible.[7] In practice, of course, even the election of directors (absent a proxy contest) is predetermined by the existing board nominating the next year's board.

Until recently, state corporate law's direct restrictions on shareholder power were for the most part supported by federal rules that indirectly prevent shareholders from exercising significant influence over corporate decision making. Three sets of federal statutes are especially noteworthy: (1) disclosure requirements pertaining to large holders; (2) shareholder voting

---

5. Joseph E. Bachelder III, TARP, "Say on Pay" and Other Legislative Developments, The Harvard Law School Forum on Corporate Governance and Financial Regulation (July 4, 2009), http://tinyurl.com/lvb7xo.

6. Stephen M. Bainbridge, Rising Threat of Dysfunctional Boards, Agenda, May 25, 2009, at 3.

7. Del. Code Ann., tit. 8, §§ 109, 211 (2000).

and communication rules; and (3) insider trading and short swing profits rules.[8] These laws affect shareholders in two respects. First, they discourage the formation of large stock blocks. Second, they discourage communication and coordination among shareholders.

To the extent shareholders exercise any control over the corporation, they do so only through control of the board of directors. Accordingly, it is the shareholders' ability to affect the election of directors that determines the degree of influence they will hold over the corporation. The proxy regulatory regime discourages large shareholders from seeking to replace incumbent directors with their own nominees.[9] Despite the SEC's 1992 reforms, the proxy rules also still impede the ability of shareholders to communicate with one another.[10]

Securities Exchange Act § 13(d) and the SEC rules thereunder require extensive disclosures from any person or group acting together that acquires beneficial ownership of more than 5 percent of the outstanding shares of any class of equity stock in a given issuer.[11] The disclosures required by § 13(d) impinge substantially on investor privacy raise the risk of liability for failing to provide adequate disclosures, and thus discourage investors from holding blocks greater than 4.9 percent of a company's stock.[12]

Large block formation may also be discouraged by state corporate law rules governing minority shareholder protections. Under Delaware law, a controlling shareholder has fiduciary obligations to the minority.[13] A controlling shareholder that uses its power to force the corporation to enter into contracts with the shareholder or its affiliates on unfair terms can be held liable for the resulting injury to the corporation.[14] A controlling shareholder that uses its influence to effect a freeze-out merger in which the minority shareholders are bought out at an unfairly low price likewise faces liability.[15]

Success in a proxy contest is directly correlated with the size of the insurgent's share holdings. By both discouraging the formation of groups of insurgents and the acquisition of large blocks by individual activists, these

---

8. See Stephen M. Bainbridge, The Politics of Corporate Governance, 18 Harv. J. L. & Pub. Pol'y 671, 712–13 (1995) (noting insider trading concerns raised by shareholder activism).

9. See Stephen M. Bainbridge, Redirecting State Takeover Laws at Proxy Contests, 1992 Wis. L. Rev. 1071, 1075–84 (describing incentives against proxy contests).

10. See Stephen Choi, Proxy Issue Proposals: Impact of the 1992 SEC Proxy Reforms, 16 J. L. Econ. & Org. 233 (2000) (explaining that liberalization of the proxy rules has not significantly affected shareholder communication practices).

11. 15 U.S.C. § 78m (2001).

12. Bernard S. Black, Shareholder Activism and Corporate Governance in the United States, in The New Palgrave Dictionary of Economics and the Law 459, 461 (1998).

13. See, e.g., Zahn v. Transamerica Corp., 162 F.2d 36 (3d Cir. 1947).

14. See, e.g., Sinclair Oil Corp. v. Levien, 280 A.2d 717 (Del. 1971).

15. See, e.g., Weinberger v. UOP, Inc., 457 A.2d 701 (Del. 1983).

laws have the (presumably unintended) consequence of indirectly insulating incumbent directors from proxy challenges. They thus serve to help perpetuate the separation of ownership and control that is built into the core DNA of state corporate law.

This chapter contends that state corporate law gets it right. The board-centric system of U.S. corporate governance has served investors and society well. This record of success occurred not in spite of the separation of ownership and control, but because of that separation. The federal shareholder empowerment mandates of recent years thus chip away at the very foundation of corporate governance.

BYLAW AMENDMENT VIA SHAREHOLDER PROPOSAL

Under state law, the board of directors controls the issuer's proxy statement. Shareholders have no right to include proposals or other materials in the proxy statement or to have them appear on the proxy card. If shareholders wish to have their fellow shareholders vote on some matter, the shareholders' only practicable state law option is conducting a proxy contest in favor of whatever proposal they wish to put forward.

In 1942, the SEC adopted the predecessor to modern Rule 14a-8, which requires issuers to include in the corporation's proxy statements proposals made by shareholders meeting certain specified criteria. In the decades following, the shareholder proposal became a principal tool of activist shareholders. The chief advantage of the shareholder proposal rule, from the perspective of the proponent, is that it is cheap. The proponent need not pay any of the printing and mailing costs, all of which must be paid by the corporation, or otherwise comply with the expensive panoply of regulatory requirements applicable to a proxy solicitation.

Under the current federal rule, a qualifying shareholder may put forward a proposal and accompanying supporting statement that does not exceed 500 words in length for inclusion in the issuer's proxy statement. In order to qualify, the shareholder-proponent must have owned at least 1 percent or $2,000 (whichever is less) of the issuer's voting securities for at least one year prior to the date on which the proposal is submitted. The proponent may only submit one proposal per corporation per year. There is no limit to the number of companies to which a proponent can submit proposals in a given year, however. As long as the proponent meets the eligibility requirements for each firm, an activist thus may press the same proposal at multiple firms.

Until recently, mainly social activists used shareholder proposals. Before the end of apartheid in South Africa, for example, many proposals favored divestment from South Africa. Although social activists still commonly use the rule to advance their causes, corporate governance activists have also seized upon it in recent years as vehicle of shareholder empowerment. Proposals relating to such issues as executive compensation, majority voting for directors, requiring an independent board chairman, shareholder access to the issuer's proxy solicitation materials, the right of shareholders to call a special meeting, and repeal of classified boards and other takeover defenses, have become increasingly common.

Using Proposals to Amend the Bylaws

Most shareholder proposals are phrased as requests or recommendations directed to the board. The use of precatory language follows from Rule 14a-8(i)(1), which provides that a shareholder proposal must be a proper subject of action for security holders under the law of the state of incorporation. This proviso comes into play most often with respect to the foundational state corporate law principle that corporate powers generally are exercised by or under the authority of the board.[16] Because state corporate law thereby commits most powers of initiation to the board of directors, the shareholders may not initiate corporate actions. Instead, shareholder voting rights typically are reactive. With few exceptions, shareholders may only approve or disapprove of corporate actions placed before them for a vote. The SEC's explanatory note to Rule 14a-8(i)(1) defers to state law in this regard by explaining that mandatory proposals purporting to direct the board to take some action may be improper. The note goes on, however, to explain the SEC's belief that such a shareholder proposal often will be proper if phrased as a request or recommendation to the board.

In recent years, shareholder activists have seized on bylaw amendments as a way of bypassing Rule 14a-8(i)(1). Under state law, the incorporators or the initial directors adopt the corporation's initial bylaws at the corporation's organizational meeting. At early common law, only shareholders had the power thereafter to amend the bylaws. Most states eventually adopted statutes allowing shareholders to delegate the power to amend the bylaws to the board of directors. DGCL § 109(a) typifies this approach. It provides that only shareholders have the power to amend bylaws, unless the articles of incorporation expressly confer that power on the board of directors. An article provision authorizing the board to amend the bylaws, moreover, does not divest the shareholders of their residual power to amend the bylaws. Instead, bylaw amendments remain one of the very few issues as to which shareholders possess the power to initiate corporate action without prior board approval.

16. See, e.g., DGCL § 141(a).

Because shareholders retain the unilateral power to amend the bylaws, a proposal mandating a particular amendment often will be a proper subject of shareholder action under state law. Not all bylaw proposals pass muster, however. DGCL § 109(b) imposes an important limitation on the otherwise sweeping scope of permissible bylaws:

> The bylaws may contain any provision, *not inconsistent with law or with the certificate of incorporation*, relating to the business of the corporation, the conduct of its affairs, and its rights or powers or the rights or powers of its stockholders, directors, officers or employees.

In a variety of settings, Delaware courts therefore have reviewed bylaws to determine whether they have a permissible purpose.[17]

For present purposes, the critical issue is whether shareholder-adopted bylaws may limit the board of directors' discretionary power to manage the corporation. Unfortunately, there is an odd circularity in the Delaware code with respect to this issue. On the one hand, DGCL § 141(a) provides that "[t]he business and affairs of every corporation organized under this chapter shall be managed by or under the direction of a board of directors." A bylaw that restricts the board's managerial authority thus seems to run afoul of DGCL § 109(b)'s prohibition of bylaws that are "inconsistent with law." On the other hand, DGCL § 141(a) also provides that the board's management powers are plenary "except as may be otherwise provided in this chapter." Does an otherwise valid bylaw adopted pursuant to § 109 but that limits board management discretion squeeze through that loophole?

In *Teamsters v. Fleming Companies*,[18] the Oklahoma Supreme Court upheld a bylaw limiting the board of directors' power to adopt a poison pill (a type of corporate takeover defense). The bylaw provided:

> The Corporation *shall* not adopt or maintain a poison pill, shareholder rights plan, rights agreement or any other form of "poison pill" which is designed to or has the effect of making acquisition of large holdings of the Corporation's shares of stock more difficult or expensive . . . unless such plan is first approved by a majority shareholder vote. The Company *shall* redeem any such rights now in effect.

The board argued that shareholders could not adopt a bylaw imposing such mandatory limitations on the board's discretion. The court rejected that argument.

---

17. See generally Allen v. Prime Computer, Inc., 540 A.2d 417 (Del. 1988) (holding that court may review reasonableness of a bylaw).

18. International Broth. of Teamsters General Fund v. Fleming Companies, Inc., 975 P.2d 907 (Okla. 1999).

Absent a contrary provision in the articles of incorporation, shareholders of Oklahoma corporations therefore may use the bylaws to limit the board's managerial discretion.

Although the relevant Oklahoma and Delaware statutes are quite similar, it long seemed likely that Delaware courts would reach a different result than did the court in *Fleming*. In *General DataComm Industries, Inc. v. State of Wisconsin Investment Board*,[19] for example, Vice Chancellor Strine observed:

> [W]hile stockholders have unquestioned power to adopt bylaws covering a broad range of subjects, it is also well established in corporate law that stockholders may not directly manage the business and affairs of the corporation, at least without specific authorization either by statute or in the certificate or articles of incorporation. There is an obvious zone of conflict between these precepts: in at least some respects, attempts by stockholders to adopt bylaws limiting or influencing director authority inevitably offend the notion of management by the board of directors.[20]

Strine cautioned, however, that the conflict remained unresolved.

The Delaware Supreme Court finally addressed this hole in its case law in *CA, Inc. v. AFSCME Employees Pension Plan*.[21] The AFSCME pension plan used Rule 14a-8 to propose an amendment to CA's bylaws pursuant to which a shareholder who successfully conducted a short slate proxy contest would be entitled to reimbursement of its reasonable expenses.[22] CA objected to inclusion of the proposal in the proxy statement and asked the SEC for a no-action letter supporting exclusion.

Before answering CA's request, the SEC invoked a newly adopted Delaware constitutional provision allowing the SEC to certify questions of law to the Delaware Supreme Court. The SEC asked the court to answer two questions. (1) Was the pension plan's proposal a proper subject for shareholder action under Delaware law? (2) Would the proposal, if adopted, cause CA to violate any Delaware law? The second question comes into play because Rule 14a-8(i)(2) permits an issuer to omit any proposal that would cause it to violate, inter alia, state laws to which it is subject.

---

19. 731 A.2d 818 (Del. Ch. 1999).
20. Id. at 821 n.2.
21. 953 A.2d 227 (Del. 2008).
22. In a short slate contest, the activist shareholder puts forward fewer nominees than the number of director seats to be filled. If successful, a short slate gives the activist access to the board with less risk of incurring the liabilities associated with being deemed a controlling shareholder than would be the case if all of the newly elected directors had been nominated by the activist.

In holding that the proposal was a proper subject of shareholder action, the court recognized the recursive loop between DGCL § 109 and § 141(a). The Supreme Court nevertheless declined to "articulate with doctrinal exactitude a bright line" that would divide those bylaws that shareholders may permissibly adopt from those that go too far in infringing upon the directors' right to manage the corporation.[23] Instead, the court contented itself with noting that "well-established Delaware law" differentiated between bylaws that seek to "mandate how the board should decide specific substantive business decisions" from those that "define the process and procedures by which those decisions are made."[24] The former are improper, while the latter are generally proper. The bylaw at issue here related to the process for electing directors, which the court further noted is "a subject in which shareholders of Delaware corporations have a legitimate and protected interest."[25] Accordingly, the AFSCME pension plan's proposal was a proper subject for stockholder action.

Turning to the SEC's second question, the Supreme Court held that the proposal could cause CA to violate Delaware law in some cases. As phrased, the proposal would require the board to reimburse a successful short slate proxy contestant even if doing so might cause the board to breach its fiduciary duties. As examples of such cases, the Court pointed to a proxy contest undertaken for "personal or petty concerns, or to promote interests that do not further, or are adverse to, those of the corporation."[26] In order not to violate the board's fiduciary duties under Delaware law, the proposed bylaw therefore would have to include a so-called "fiduciary out" pursuant to which the directors retain "full power to exercise their fiduciary duty to decide whether or not it would be appropriate, in a specific case, to award reimbursement at all."[27]

In assessing the extent to which CA will allow shareholder activists to effect significant governance change via Rule 14a-8 proposals to amend the bylaws, it is critical to note that the court's opinion early recognized that no "broad management power is statutorily allocated to the shareholders."[28] To the contrary, "it is well-established that stockholders of a corporation subject to the DGCL may not directly manage the business and affairs of the corporation, at least without specific authorization in either the statute or the certificate of incorporation."[29] A second critical factor is that the proposal related to the shareholder's right to elect directors. Delaware courts regard the shareholder

---

23. Id. at 234.
24. Id. at 234–35.
25. Id. at 235.
26. Id. at 240.
27. Id.
28. Id. at 232.
29. Id.

franchise as "the ideological underpinning upon which the legitimacy of directorial power rests."[30] They therefore "have long exercised a most sensitive and protective regard for the free and effective exercise of voting rights."[31] Proposals relating to less well-protected procedures therefore may not receive the same sort of deference.

Bylaws and Director Primacy

In order to evaluate this emergent body of law, we must begin with the basic precepts of the contractarian theory of the corporation, which will be developed at greater length below. In brief, shareholders do not own the corporation. Instead, they are merely one of many corporate constituencies bound together by a complex web of explicit and implicit contracts. Consequently, the normative claims associated with ownership and private property are inapt in the corporate context.

In this model, the directors are not agents of the shareholders subject to the control of the shareholders. To be sure, shareholders elect the board and exercise certain other control rights through the franchise. Even so, those rights are quite limited. Accordingly, the board of directors functions as a sort of Platonic guardian—a sui generis body that serves as the nexus for the various contracts making up the corporation. The board's powers flow from that set of contracts in its totality and not just from shareholders. The board's exercise of its discretionary authority therefore may not be unilaterally limited by any corporate constituency, including the shareholders.

This model is consistent with the spirit of Delaware corporate law. As the Delaware Supreme Court opined:

> One of the most basic tenets of Delaware corporate law is that the board of directors has the ultimate responsibility for managing the business and affairs of a corporation. Section 141(a) requires that any limitation on the board's authority be set out in the certificate of incorporation.[32]

Note that, read literally, this dictum precludes the result reached in *Fleming* and *CA*.

The board's primacy has a compelling economic justification. The separation of ownership and control mandated by corporate law is a highly efficient solution to the decision-making problems faced by large corporations. Recall that

30. Blasius Indus., Inc. v. Atlas Corp., 564 A.2d 651, 659 (Del. Ch. 1988).
31. Id. at 660 n.2.
32. Quickturn Design Systems, Inc. v. Shapiro, 721 A.2d 1281, 1291 (Del. 1998).

because collective decision making is impracticable in such firms, they are characterized by authority-based decision-making structures in which a central agency (the board) is empowered to make decisions binding on the firm as a whole.

To be sure, this separation of "ownership" and control results in agency costs. Those costs, however, are the inevitable consequence of vesting discretion in someone other than the residual claimant. We could substantially reduce, if not eliminate, agency costs by eliminating discretion; that we do not do so confirms that discretion has substantial virtues. Given those virtues, one ought not lightly interfere with management or the board's decision-making authority in the name of accountability.

This line of argument explains much of corporate law. It is the principle behind such diverse doctrines as the business judgment rule, the limits on shareholder derivative litigation, the limits on shareholder voting rights, and the board's power to resist unsolicited corporate takeovers. Here it justifies strong skepticism as to the validity of shareholder-adopted bylaws that restrict management discretion. Indeed, absent an express statutory command to the contrary, courts should invalidate such bylaws.[33]

All of these problems would go away if state corporation codes treated bylaws the same way as articles of incorporation or, for that matter, virtually every other corporate action. The shareholder power to initiate bylaw amendments without prior board action is unique. It is also a historical anachronism unthinkingly codified from old common law principles lacking either rhyme or reason. There simply is no good reason to treat bylaws differently than articles of incorporation.

A Note on Social Proposals

Rule 14a-8(i)(5) provides that a proposal relating to operations accounting for less than 5 percent of the firm's assets, earnings, or sales, and that is not otherwise significantly related to the firm's business, may be omitted from the proxy statement. The principal problem here is deciding whether a proposal falling short of the various 5 percent thresholds is "otherwise significantly related to the firm's business." The classic case is *Lovenheim v. Iroquois Brands, Ltd.*[34] The defendant imported various foodstuffs into the United States,

---

33. A useful analogy may be drawn to shareholder agreements that restrict board discretion. At one point, such agreements were per se invalid. See, e.g., McQuade v. Stoneham, 189 N.E. 234 (N.Y. 1934). The modern trend is to allow such agreements, but only in close corporations. See, e.g., MBCA § 7.32; Galler v. Galler, 203 N.E.2d 577 (Ill. 1964).

34. 618 F. Supp. 554 (D.D.C. 1985).

including pâté de foie gras from France. Lovenheim suspected that Iroquois Brands' French suppliers force-fed their geese, which produces larger livers, and which Lovenheim believed was a form of animal cruelty. Lovenheim proposed that Iroquois Brands form a committee to investigate the methods used by the firm's suppliers in producing pâté and report its findings to the shareholders.

Iroquois Brands' pâté operations clearly did not satisfy Rule 14a-8(i)(5)'s 5 percent threshold tests. Pâté sales constituted a mere $79,000 per year, on which Iroquois Brands lost money, relative to annual revenues of $141 million and profits of $6 million. The result therefore turned on whether the pâté operations were "otherwise significantly related" to its business. Iroquois Brands contended that the phrase related to economic significance. Lovenheim contended that noneconomic tests of a proposal's significance were appropriate.

The court agreed with Lovenheim, holding that while the proposal related "to a matter of little economic significance,"[35] the term "otherwise significantly related" is not limited to economic significance. Rather, matters of ethical and social significance also can be considered.

As evidence that Lovenheim's proposal possessed "ethical or social" significance, the court observed that humane treatment of animals was one of the foundations of Western civilization, citing various old and new statutes, ranging from the Seven Laws of Noah to the Massachusetts Bay Colony's animal protection statute of 1641, to modern federal and state humane laws. Additional support came from the fact that "leading organizations in the field of animal care" supported measures aimed at eliminating force-feeding.

Similar issues arise under Rule 14a-8(i)(7), which allows the issuer to exclude proposals relating to so-called "ordinary business matters." The question here is whether a proposal is an ordinary matter for the board or an extraordinary matter on which shareholder input is appropriate. The answer hinges on whether the proposal involves significant policy questions. As for deciding whether a policy question is significant, most courts assume that *Lovenheim*-style ethical or social significance qualifies.

The SEC's policy on enforcing Rule 14a-8(i)(7) with respect to shareholder proposals concerned mainly with social—rather than economic—issues has fluctuated over the years. The SEC long handled such proposals on a case-by-case basis. In 1992, however, it departed from that practice and adopted a bright-line position that for the first time effectively excluded an entire category of social issue proposals. Cracker Barrel Old Country Stores attempted to exclude a shareholder proposal calling on the board of directors to include sexual orientation in its anti-discrimination policy. In a no-action letter issued by the SEC's Division of Corporation Finance, the Commission took the

35. Id. at 559.

position that all employment-related shareholder proposals raising social policy issues could be excluded under the "ordinary business" exclusion.

Subsequent litigation developed two issues. First, if a shareholder-proponent sued a company whose management relied on *Cracker Barrel* to justify excluding an employment-related proposal from the proxy statement, should the reviewing court defer to the SEC's position? In *Amalgamated Clothing and Textile Workers Union v. Wal-Mart Stores, Inc.*,[36] a federal district court held that deference was not required and, moreover, that proposals relating to a company's affirmative action policies were not per se excludible as ordinary business under Rule 14a-8(i)(7).

Second, was the SEC's *Cracker Barrel* position valid? In other words, could the SEC properly apply the *Cracker Barrel* interpretation in internal agency processes, such as when issuing a no-action letter? In *New York City Employees' Retirement System v. SEC*, the district court ruled that the SEC's *Cracker Barrel* position was itself invalid because the SEC had failed to comply with federal administrative procedures in promulgating the position. The Second Circuit reversed, thereby allowing the SEC to apply *Cracker Barrel* internally, but in doing so concurred with the trial court's view that *Cracker Barrel* was not binding on courts.[37]

In 1998, the SEC adopted amendments to Rule 14a-8 that, among other things, reversed its *Cracker Barrel* position.[38] In promulgating this change, the SEC emphasized that employment discrimination was a consistent topic of public debate, thereby highlighting the ongoing importance of *Lovenheim*-style social and ethical considerations. Indeed, the SEC explicitly noted its belief that the Rule 14a-8(i)(7) exception did not justify excluding proposals that raise significant social policy issues.

Reversal of the *Cracker Barrel* position returned the SEC to its prior case-by-case approach. Specific management decisions relating to employment, such as hiring, promotion, and termination of employees, as well as other business decisions, such as product lines and quality, remain excludable. The SEC does not want shareholders to "micro-manage" the company. Proposals broadly relating to such matters but focusing on significant social policy issues, such as affirmative action and other employment discrimination matters, however, generally are not excludable.

We thus were returned to the frustratingly ambiguous task of deciding whether a particular proposal is "significant." On this issue, the federal district court decision in *Austin v. Consolidated Edison Company of New York, Inc.*[39] is

36. 821 F. Supp. 877 (S.D.N.Y. 1993).
37. N.Y. City Employees' Retirement Sys. v. SEC, 45 F.3d 7 (2d Cir. 1995).
38. Amendments To Rules On Shareholder Proposals, Exchange Act Release No. 40018 (May 21, 1998).
39. 788 F. Supp. 192 (S.D.N.Y. 1992).

both instructive and troubling. The plaintiffs put forward a proposal that the issuer provide more generous pension benefits to its employees. The court authorized the issuer to exclude the proposal as impinging on an ordinary business matter. Acknowledging that shareholder proposals relating to senior executive compensation were not excludable, the court observed that the issue of "enhanced pension rights" for workers "has not yet captured public attention and concern as has the issue of senior executive compensation." Apparently, the significance of a proposal therefore turns on whether its subject matter has become a routine story for CNBC or CNN.

It is troubling that federal bureaucrats and judges are required to determine whether a politically charged proposal has enough ethical or social significance to justify its inclusion in the proxy statement. The issue is particularly troubling because many proposals have less to do with a company's economic performance than with providing a soapbox for the proponent's pet political cause. In *Lovenheim*, for example, the plaintiff knew that his proposal had little economic significance to the company. Instead, he wanted to make a political statement about animal cruelty.

Likewise, the result in *Austin*—exclusion—doubtless was correct. The proposal was put forward by shareholders who were also officials of a union that represented company employees.[40] The proposal mandated a specific change in company pension policy; namely, to allow employees to retire with full benefits after 30 years of service regardless of age. This was precisely the sort of (self-interested) micro-management that even the SEC agrees ought not be allowed. Yet, we need a better test.

Instead of the *Lovenheim/Austin* approach, courts should ask whether a reasonable shareholder of this issuer would regard the proposal as having material economic importance for the value of his shares. This standard is based on the well-established securities law principle of materiality. It is intended to exclude proposals made primarily for the purpose of promoting general social and political causes, while requiring inclusion of proposals a reasonable investor would believe are relevant to the value of his investment. Such a test seems desirable so as to ensure that an adopted proposal redounds to the benefit of all shareholders, not just those who share the political and social views of the proponent. Absent such a standard, the shareholder proposal rule becomes nothing less than a species of private eminent domain by which the federal government allows a small minority to appropriate someone else's property—the company is a legal person, after all, and it is the

40. The issuer argued these facts entitled it to exclude the proposal as under Rule 14a-8(i)(4). Under that provision, an issuer may exclude proposals designed to redress a private grievance or further a private interest of the proponent not shared with the shareholders at large. The court declined to reach that issue.

company's proxy statement at issue—for use as a soapbox to disseminate their views. Because the shareholders hold the residual claim, and all corporate expenditures thus come out of their pocket, it is not entirely clear why other shareholders should have to subsidize speech by a small minority.

MAJORITY VOTING

In most cases, state corporate law contemplates that shareholder action requires the affirmative votes of a majority of the shareholders present at a meeting at which there is a quorum.[41] When it comes to electing directors, however, state law until recently merely required a plurality shareholder vote. Delaware General Corporation Law § 216(3) formerly provided, for example, that "Directors shall be elected by a plurality of the votes of the shares present in person or represented by proxy at the meeting and entitled to vote on the election of directors." The comments to MBCA § 7.28(a), which also used a plurality standard, defined that term to mean "that the individuals with the largest number of votes are elected as directors up to the maximum number of directors to be chosen at the election."

The federal proxy rules accommodated state law by providing, in former SEC Rule 14a-4(b), that the issuer must give shareholders three options on the proxy card with respect to electing directors. A shareholder could vote for all of the nominees for director, withhold support for all of them, or withhold support from specified directors by striking out their names.

The net effect of these rules was that the corporate electoral system did not provide for a straight up or down vote for directors. Instead, one either granted authority to the proxy agent to vote for the specified candidates or one withheld authority for the agent to do so. Absent a contested election, because only a plurality vote was required, so long as the holder of at least a single share granted authority for his share to be cast in favor of the nominees, the slate of directors nominated by the incumbent board therefore would be elected even if every other shareholder withheld authority for their shares to be voted.

The origins of the plurality rule are somewhat obscure. It presumably arose to deal with situations in which there are more nominees than vacant director positions, which is most commonly the case in contested elections. In a close

---

41. The precise requirements vary from state to state. MBCA § 7.25(c) provides that "action on a matter . . . is approved if the votes cast . . . favoring the action exceed the votes cast opposing the action." In contrast, DGCL § 216 states that "the affirmative vote of the majority of shares present in person or represented by proxy at the meeting and entitled to vote on the subject matter shall be the act of the stockholders." In effect, Delaware treats abstentions as no votes, while the MBCA ignores them.

race, abstentions and spoiled ballots might mean that fewer nominees than the number of vacancies would receive a majority of the votes cast. In the worst case, which is made more likely by the use of slate voting, the election might fail completely as no directors would receive a majority. Plurality voting avoided that risk and the adverse consequences that might follow.

Over time, withholding authority to vote for some or all of the nominees put forward by the incumbent board became a common protest tactic by shareholder activists. In the 2004 shareholder revolt at the Walt Disney Company, for example, shareholder activists opposed the election of CEO Michael Eisner and certain other candidates. Under the then-existing plurality standard, Eisner would have been reelected even if holders of a majority of the shares had withheld authority for their shares to be voted for him. In the event, holders of 43 percent of Disney shares withheld such authority. Although Eisner was reelected, the high vote was seen as a powerful protest. Shortly thereafter, he initiated a succession process.

State Law Developments

The Disney episode triggered considerable interest in changing the traditional plurality standard so as to transform the process from a mere opportunity to send a protest signal into a real election. In 2006, Delaware responded to considerable pressure from activists and others by amending the statutory provisions on director election to accommodate various forms of majority voting.

A number of Delaware corporations had responded to post-Disney pressure from shareholder activists by voluntarily adopting so-called Pfizer policies—named after the first prominent corporation to adopt one—pursuant to which directors who receive a majority of withhold "votes" are required to submit their resignation to the board. Section 141(b) of the Delaware General Corporation Law was amended to accommodate such bylaws. It does so by providing that: "A resignation [of a director] is effective when the resignation is delivered unless the resignation specifies a later effective date or an effective date determined upon the happening of an event or events. A resignation which is conditioned upon the director failing to receive a specified vote for reelection as a director may provide that it is irrevocable."

The trouble with these so-called Pfizer or plurality-plus policies, at least from the perspective of shareholder activists, is that the board retains authority to turn down the resignation of a director who fails to get the requisite majority vote. In *City of Westland Police & Fire Retirement System v. Axcelis Technologies, Inc.*,[42] the Delaware Supreme Court confirmed that the board has

42. 1 A.3d 281 (Del. 2010).

substantial discretion to do just that. Axcelis Technologies had a seven-member board staggered into three classes. In 2008, all three of the incumbent directors up for reelection failed to receive a majority of the votes cast. Pursuant to the company's plurality-plus policy, all three submitted their resignations. The board rejected all three resignations. A shareholder initiated a § 220 request to inspect the relevant books and records of the company preparatory to filing a derivative suit challenging the board's decision. In order to prevent shareholders from conducting fishing expeditions, Delaware courts will grant such inspection requests only where there is a credible basis from which to infer that some wrongdoing may have occurred. In acknowledging that § 220 requests sometimes can be meritorious in this context, the Court observed that "the question arises whether the directors, as fiduciaries, made a disinterested, informed business judgment that the best interests of the corporation require the continued service of these directors, or whether the Board had some different, ulterior motivation."[43] It thus seems fair to infer that the business judgment rule will be the standard by which courts evaluate board decisions under such policies.

Activists also objected to the Pfizer-style approach because it typically was effected by changing board of directors corporate governance policies rather than by amending the bylaws or articles. As such, continuation of the policy was subject to the discretion of the directors.

Shareholder activists therefore began using Rule 14a-8 to put forward bylaw amendments mandating true majority voting. A bylaw voluntarily adopted by Intel received wide activist support as a model for bylaw amendments at other issuers. Under it, a director who fails to receive a majority of the votes cast is not elected. In the case of an incumbent director who fails to receive a majority vote in favor of his reelection, there is the complication that, under DGCL § 141(b), a director's term continues until his successor is elected. The Intel (a.k.a. majority-plus) model requires resignation of such a director.

Shareholder activists preferred a bylaw approach to one based on the articles of incorporation because of the latter's board approval requirement. In most states, however, a shareholder-adopted bylaw would be vulnerable to subsequent board amendment or even repeal. Recall that DGCL § 109(a) provides that the articles of incorporation may confer the power to amend the bylaws on the board of directors, but that such a provision does not divest the shareholders of their residual power to amend the bylaws.

The resulting concurrent power of both shareholders and boards to amend the bylaws raises the prospect of cycling amendments and counter-amendments. Suppose the shareholders adopt a majority vote bylaw. The board

43. Id. at 291.

then repeals the new bylaw provision using its concurrent power to amend the bylaws. The MBCA allows the shareholders to forestall such an event. MBCA § 10.20(b)(2) authorizes the board to adopt, amend, and repeal bylaws unless "the shareholders in amending, repealing, or adopting a bylaw expressly provide that the board of directors may not amend, repeal, or reinstate that bylaw." In the absence of such a restriction, however, the board apparently retains its power to amend or even repeal the bylaw. If the board does so, the shareholders' remedies presumably are limited to readopting the term limit amendment, this time incorporating the necessary restriction, and/or electing a more compliant board.

Delaware § 109 lacks any comparable grant of power to the shareholders. Worse yet, because the board only has power to adopt or amend bylaws if that power is granted to it in the articles of incorporation, a bylaw prohibiting board amendment arguably would be inconsistent with the articles and, therefore, invalid.

In *American Int'l Rent a Car, Inc. v. Cross*,[44] the Delaware Chancery Court suggested that, as part of a bylaw amendment, the shareholders "could remove from the Board the power to further amend the provision in question." Dicta in several other Delaware precedents, however, was to the contrary. In *General DataComm Industries, Inc. v. State of Wisconsin Investment Board*,[45] for example, Vice Chancellor Strine noted the "significant legal uncertainty" as to "whether, in the absence of an explicitly controlling statute, a stockholder-adopted bylaw can be made immune from repeal or modification by the board of directors." In *Centaur Partners, IV v. National Intergroup, Inc.*,[46] the Delaware Supreme Court addressed a shareholder-proposed bylaw limiting the number of directors. As proposed, the bylaw contained a provision prohibiting the board from amending or repealing it. Noting that the corporation's articles gave the board authority to fix the number of directors through adoption of bylaws, the Supreme Court opined that the proposed bylaw "would be a nullity if adopted." Consequently, it seemed doubtful that restrictions on the board's power over the bylaws would pass muster in Delaware or other states likewise lacking a MBCA-style provision.

In response to activist shareholder pressure, however, Delaware amended § 216 by adding the following sentence: "A bylaw amendment adopted by stockholders which specifies the votes that shall be necessary for the election of directors shall not be further amended or repealed by the board of directors." It is curious that the legislature did not adopt a more explicit validation of bylaw provisions requiring that a director receive a majority vote in order to

44. 1984 WL 8204 (Del. Ch. 1984).
45. 731 A.2d 818, 821 n.1 (Del. Ch. 1999).
46. 582 A.2d 923, 929 (Del. 1990).

be elected. Section 216, however, clearly seems to imply their validity and, if so, ensures that such bylaws could not be undercut by subsequent unilateral board action.

Congress Punts

An early Senate version of the legislation that became the Dodd-Frank Act included a majority-voting mandate. Under it, public corporations would have been required to accept the resignation of any director who receives less than a majority vote in an uncontested election, unless the board unanimously declined to accept the resignation. In the face of the state developments and the reality that majority voting is now the norm, however, Congress opted to omit any version of majority voting.

Assessment

Critics of majority-voting schemes contend that failed elections can have a destabilizing effect on the corporation. Selecting and vetting a director candidate is a long and expensive process, which has become even more complicated by the new stock exchange listing standards defining director independence. Suppose, for example, that the shareholders voted out the only qualified financial expert sitting on the audit committee. The corporation immediately would be in violation of its obligations under those standards.

Critics also complain that qualified individuals will be deterred from service. The enhanced liability and increased workload imposed by Sarbanes-Oxley and related regulatory and legal developments has made it much harder for firms to recruit qualified outside directors. The risk of being singled out by shareholders for a no vote presumably will make board service even less attractive, especially in light of the concern board members demonstrate for their reputations.

Finally, critics claim that, at least as it is being implemented so far, majority voting is "little more than smoke and mirrors."[47] William Sjostrom and Young Sang Kim conducted an event study of firms adopting some form of majority vote bylaw. They found no statistically significant market reaction to the adoption.[48] The implication is that the campaign for majority voting has created little shareholder value.

47. William K. Sjostrom Jr. & Young Sang Kim, Majority Voting for the Election of Directors, 40 Conn. L. Rev. 459 (2007).
48. Id.

Proxy contests are enormously expensive. Any serious contest requires the services of lawyers, accountants, financial advisers, printers, and proxy solicitors. None of these folks come cheap. Even incidental costs, such as mailing expenses, mount up very quickly when one must communicate (usually several times) with the thousands of shareholders in the typical public corporation. As it is always more pleasant to spend someone else's money than it is to spend one's own, both incumbents and insurgents will want the corporation to pay their expenses.

In theory, incumbent directors do not have unbridled access to the corporate treasury. In practice, however, incumbents rarely pay their own expenses. Under state law, the board of directors may use corporate funds to pay for expenses incurred in opposing the insurgent, provided the amounts are reasonable and the contest involves policy questions rather than just a "purely personal power struggle."[49] Only the most poorly advised of incumbents find it difficult to meet this standard. The board merely needs have its lawyers parse the insurgent's proxy materials for policy questions on which they differ. Such a search is bound to be successful: if the insurgent agrees with all of management's policies, why is it trying to oust them?

In contrast, insurgents initially must bear their own costs. Insurgents have no right to reimbursement out of corporate funds. Rather, an insurgent will be reimbursed only if an appropriate resolution is approved by a majority of both the board of directors and the shareholders.[50] If the incumbents prevail, of course, they are unlikely to look kindly on an insurgent's request for reimbursement of expenses. In effect, the insurgent must win to have any hope of getting reimbursed.

As noted above, the Delaware Supreme Court in *CA, Inc. v. AFSCME Employees Pension Plan*,[51] partially validated a shareholder-proposed amendment to CA's bylaws pursuant to which a shareholder who successfully conducted a short slate proxy contest would be entitled to reimbursement of its reasonable expenses. Although the basic concept of such a bylaw passed muster with the court, it held that such a bylaw could not divest the board of directors of its power—indeed, its fiduciary duty—to refuse reimbursement where doing so might injure the corporation.

In response to *CA*, the Delaware legislature adopted new DGCL § 113. The new statute expressly authorizes proxy expense reimbursement bylaws.

---

49. E.g., Rosenfeld v. Fairchild Engine & Airplane Corp., 128 N.E.2d 291 (1955), reh'g denied, 130 N.E.2d 610 (1955).

50. E.g., Steinberg v. Adams, 90 F. Supp. 604 (S.D.N.Y. 1950); Grodetsky v. McCrory Corp., 267 N.Y.S.2d 356 (Sup. Ct. 1966).

51. 953 A.2d 227 (Del. 2008).

The bylaw must be adopted prior to the record date of the meeting at which the insurgent solicited proxies, thereby preventing an insurgent from seeking to simultaneously elect directors and amend the bylaws. Section 113 also permits the bylaw to impose a number of conditions on reimbursement. The bylaw may condition reimbursement on the insurgent seeking to elect a short slate rather than to replace the entire board. The amount to be reimbursed can be determined based on the proportion of votes received by the insurgent's candidate(s). The list of conditions is non-exclusive.

Although § 113 mostly codifies the *CA* decision, the statute does not expressly require a fiduciary out. Whether courts will follow the *CA* decision and continue to require that a bylaw include a fiduciary out in order to be valid remains uncertain. A precedent for doing so is provided by the Delaware Supreme Court's treatment of Delaware's force-the-vote statute. In *Smith v. Van Gorkom*,[52] the Delaware Supreme Court held that directors could not submit a merger to shareholders without making a recommendation that it be approved. The Delaware legislature later overturned that result by adopting DGCL § 251(c), which provides: "The terms of the agreement may require that the agreement be submitted to the stockholders whether or not the board of directors determines at any time subsequent to declaring its advisability that the agreement is no longer advisable and recommends that the stockholders reject it." In *Omnicare, Inc. v. NCS Healthcare, Inc.*,[53] the court held that § 251 did not trump the fiduciary duties of directors. "Taking action that is otherwise legally possible, however, does not ipso facto comport with the fiduciary responsibilities of directors in all circumstances. . . . Section 251 provisions . . . are "presumptively valid in the abstract." Such provisions in a merger agreement may not, however, "validly define or limit the directors" fiduciary duties under Delaware law or prevent the [NCS] directors from carrying out their fiduciary duties under Delaware law."[54] If so, however, what is the point of § 251? In any case, *Omnicare* thus stands as a clear precedent for a judicial mandate that § 113 bylaws include a fiduciary out despite the statute's silence on the point.

PROXY ACCESS

Board of director elections usually look a lot like elections in the former Soviet Union—there is only one slate of candidates and the authorities know how each voter voted. Absent the very unusual case of a proxy contest, in which a

---

52. 488 A.2d 858 (Del.1985).
53. 818 A.2d 914 (Del.2003).
54. Id. at 937–38.

dissenting shareholder puts forward an alternative slate of director candidates, the slate nominated by the outgoing board of directors will be reelected by default. Corporate reformers long have complained that boards simply rubberstamped the CEOs choices.

Recent years have seen two important developments in this area. First, there has been increased use of nominating committees of the board of directors. Second, Dodd-Frank authorized a so-called "proxy access" system under which shareholders are entitled to nominate candidates for election to the board.

Nominating Committees

NYSE Listed Company Manual § 303A.04 requires that listed companies set up "a nominating/corporate governance committee composed entirely of independent directors." The committee must have a written charter specifying how it will go about identifying and selecting candidates for board membership. The committee should have sole power to select headhunters and negotiate their fees. NASDAQ gives companies an alternative. Under Marketplace Rule 4350(c), new directors must be nominated either by a majority of the independent directors or a nominating committee comprised solely of independent directors. Both the NYSE and NASDAQ exempt companies in which a shareholder or group of shareholders acting together control 50 percent or more of the voting power of the company's stock from the nominating committee requirement.

In addition to nominating director candidates, many companies assign responsibility for selecting new CEOs to the nominating committee. In cooperation with the compensation committee, the nominating committee may take the lead in negotiating the terms of a newly appointed CEO's employment agreement. Finally, the nominating committee may be tasked with setting director compensation, although many firms assign that job to the compensation committee.

Note that the NYSE listing requirement includes "corporate governance" as part of the nominating committee's job. This aspect of the committee's duties remains relatively poorly defined. In general, however, the intent seems to be that the nominating committee should serve as the board of directors' principal point of contact with shareholders. As a practical matter, one common task given this committee is assigning directors to other board committees (typically subject to approval by the entire board).

In theory, having a separate committee of independent directors who are in charge of the nomination process should weaken the CEO's grip on power. There is some evidence to support this theory. Business school professors James Westphal and Edward Zajac demonstrated that as board power increases relative to the CEO—measured by such factors as the percentage of insiders and whether the CEO also served as chairman—newly appointed directors become more demographically similar to the board.[55] In other words, instead of replicating the CEO and staffing the board with his cronies, independent directors controlling the nomination process tend to replicate themselves.

Proxy Access

In 2003, the SEC proposed a dramatic shake-up in the process by which corporate directors are elected. Under both state and federal law, the director nomination machinery is under the control of the incumbent board of directors. When it is time to elect directors, the incumbent board nominates a slate, which it puts forward on the company's proxy statement. There is no mechanism for a shareholder to put a nominee on the ballot. Instead, a shareholder who wishes to nominate directors is obliged to incur the considerable expense of conducting a proxy contest to elect a slate in opposition to that put forward by the incumbents.

If adopted, proposed Rule 14a-11 would have permitted shareholders, upon the occurrence of certain specified events and subject to various restrictions,[56] to have their nominees placed on the company's proxy statement and ballot. A shareholder-nominated director thus could be elected to the board in a fashion quite similar to the way shareholder-sponsored proposals are now put to a shareholder vote.

As proposed back in 2003, draft Rule 14a-11 then contemplated a two-step process stretching over two election cycles. Under the rule, a shareholder could place his or her nominee on the corporation's proxy card and statement if one of two triggering events occurs. First, a Rule 14a-8 proposal to authorize shareholder nominations had been approved by the holders of a majority of the outstanding shares at a meeting of the shareholders. Second, shareholders representing at least 35 percent of the votes withheld authority on their proxy cards for their shares to be voted in favor of any director nominated by the incumbent board of directors. In either case, at the next annual meeting of the shareholders, shareholder nominees would be included in the company's proxy statement and ballot.

---

55. James D. Westphal & Edward J. Zajac, Who Shall Govern? CEO/Board Power, Demographic Similarity, and New Director Selection, 40 Admin. Sci. Q. 60 (1995).

56. For a detailed description and critique of the proposal, see Stephen M. Bainbridge, A Comment on the SEC's Shareholder Access Proposal, Engage, April 2004, at 18.

The SEC failed to act on the proposal, neither adopting nor withdrawing it. In lieu of SEC action, some activist investors began putting forward Rule 14a-8 proposals to amend the bylaws to permit shareholder access to the company proxy. In response, corporate boards argued that such proposals could be excluded under Rule 14a-8(i)(8), which permits the issue to exclude a proposal that "relates to an election for membership on the company's board of directors or analogous governing body."

When the SEC agreed that proxy access bylaw proposals could be excluded under Rule 14a-8(i)(8), the American Federation of State, County, & Municipal Employees' pension plan (AFSCME) indirectly challenged that decision by seeking an injunction requiring American Insurance Group (AIG) to include an AFSCME proxy access proposal in AIG's proxy statement. The Second Circuit held that AIG could not exclude the proposal.[57] The pertinent legal question should have been whether Rule 14a-8(i)(8) allows firms to exclude all proposals concerning corporate elections or only proposals relating to a particular seat in a particular election. The court did not reach that issue, however, instead basing its opinion on a quirk of administrative law.

In 1976, the SEC had issued a statement asserting that "the election exclusion is limited to shareholder proposals used to oppose solicitations dealing with an identified board seat in an upcoming election" and rejecting "the somewhat broader interpretation that the election exclusion applies to shareholder proposals that would institute procedures making such election contests more likely."[58] Around 1990, the SEC reversed its position to take the latter view, "although at first in an ad hoc and inconsistent manner."[59] The SEC did so informally through issuing no-action letters in response to issuer requests to exclude such proposals. Only in an amicus brief in the AFSCME litigation did the SEC formally announce the new policy.

The court acknowledged that there might be good policy reasons for the SEC's shift in position. It also recognized that the SEC is entitled to change its mind. Where the rule is ambiguous, as was the case with the 14a-8(i)(8) exclusion, however, the SEC may not change its interpretation without giving reasons. Instead, it has a "duty to explain its departure from prior norms."[60] Accordingly, the court held that it would defer to the 1976 statement as the authoritative agency pronouncement.

In the wake of the *AIG* decision, the SEC began a rule-making process to determine whether Rule 14a-8(i)(8) should be amended to permit or deny shareholder access to the corporate ballot. On November 28, 2007, the SEC

---

57. AFSCME v. AIG, Inc., 462 F.3d 121 (2d Cir. 2006).
58. Id. at 128.
59. Id. at 123.
60. Id. at 129.

announced an amendment to Rule 14a-8(i)(8), pursuant to which the Rule would now read:

> (i) Question 9: If I have complied with the procedural requirements, on what other bases may a company rely to exclude my proposal? . . .
>
> (8) Relates to election: If the proposal relates to a nomination or an election for membership on the company's board of directors or analogous governing body or a procedure for such nomination or election.

The amendment thus reversed the 1976 statement and effectively overturned the substantive result of the *AIG* case. At the same time, however, the SEC announced its intention to continue studying the issue.

The 2008 election of President Barack Obama shifted control of the SEC from Republican to Democratic hands. The new Democratic SEC Chairman, Mary Shapiro, promptly announced that the Commission would revisit the proxy access question. In response, a coalition of business interests announced their intent to challenge the SEC's authority. In their view, proxy access fell on the substantive side of the line the *Business Roundtable* decision (see chapter 1.C) had drawn between state and federal law.

Proponents of proxy access therefore persuaded Congress to include a provision in Dodd-Frank affirming that the SEC has authority to adopt proxy access rules.[61] Section 971 did not require that the SEC do so.[62] On the other hand, if the SEC chose to do so, § 971 expressed Congress's intent that the SEC "should have wide latitude in setting the terms of such proxy access."[63] In particular, § 971 expressly authorizes the SEC to exempt "an issuer or class of issuers" from any proxy access rule and specifically requires the SEC to "take into account, among other considerations, whether" proxy access "disproportionately burdens small issuers."[64]

As already noted, proxy access is a long-standing goal of shareholder activists, especially among the institutional investor community. Not surprisingly, § 971 therefore found support from policy entrepreneurs such as the CII, AFSCME, CalPERS, and the Investor's Working Group.[65] As former SEC Commissioner Paul Atkins observed, "[u]nions and special-interest groups successfully lobbied Congress to include [§ 971] in the recent Dodd-Frank Act."[66]

---

61. Dodd-Frank § 971.
62. S. Rep. No. 111–176, at 146 (2010) (discussing proxy access provision then numbered § 972).
63. Id.
64. Dodd-Frank § 971(c).
65. S. Rep. No. 111–176, at 147 (2010).
66. Paul Atkins, The SEC's Sop to Unions, Wall St. J., Aug. 27, 2010, at A15.

The special interests he identified are "politically powerful trade-union activists, self-nominated shareholder-rights advocates, [and] trial lawyers."[67]

Section 971 probably was unnecessary. As noted, an SEC rule-making proceeding on proxy access was well-advanced long before Dodd-Frank was adopted, so a shove from Congress was superfluous. As to the question of SEC authority, although *Business Roundtable* had held that the SEC lacks authority to regulate the substance of shareholder voting rights, the opponents of proxy access likely erred in claiming proxy access fell on the substantive side of the line. To the contrary, proxy access almost certainly fell within the disclosure and process sphere over which the SEC has unquestioned authority.[68] By adopting § 971, however, Congress did preempt an expected challenge to any forthcoming SEC regulation.

In any case, the ink was hardly dry on Dodd-Frank when the SEC announced final adoption of new Rule 14a-11.[69] The rule will require companies to include in their proxy materials, alongside the nominees of the incumbent board, the nominees of shareholders who own at least 3 percent of the company's shares and have done so continuously for at least the prior three years.[70] A shareholder may only put forward a short slate consisting of at least one nominee or up to 25 percent of the company's board of directors, whichever is greater.[71] Oddly, this entitlement applies even to minority shareholders of a corporation that has a controlling shareholder with sufficient voting power to elect the entire board. Application of the rule to small companies will be deferred for three years, while the SEC studies its impact.[72]

As was the case with the 2003 proposal, in order for an individual to be eligible to be nominated under Rule 14a-11, that individual must satisfy the applicable stock exchange listing standard definition of independence from the company. The 2003 proposal also contemplated that the nominee must satisfy a number of independence criteria (e.g., no family or employment relationships) vis-à-vis the nominating shareholder or group. The SEC at that

---

67. Id.

68. See Stephen M. Bainbridge, The Scope of the SEC's Authority Over Shareholder Voting Rights, Engage, June 2007, at 25 (analyzing relevant case law and legislative history).

69. Facilitating Shareholder Director Nominations, Exchange Act Rel. No. 62,764 (Aug. 25, 2010).

70. Id. at 108. This was a considerable change from the 2003 proposal, which would have allowed holders of a mere 1% of the issuer's shares to make such nominations. See Jill E. Fisch, The Destructive Ambiguity of Federal Proxy Access 13 (Feb. 23, 2011) ("For the largest companies, this change was a substantial increase from the 1% threshold originally proposed."), http://papers.ssrn.com/sol3/papers.cfm?abstract_id=1769061. On the other hand, the rule allows groups of shareholders to aggregate their holdings for purposes of meeting the 3% threshold. Id. at 14.

71. Exchange Act Rel. No. 62,764, supra note 69, at 26.

72. Id. at 70–71.

time clearly was concerned that the proposal would be used to put forward special-interest directors who would not broadly represent the shareholders as a whole but rather only the narrow interests of those who nominated them. In contrast, as adopted, Rule 14a-11 contains no such requirement. Accordingly, there is a very real risk shareholder-nominated directors will perceive themselves as representatives of their electoral constituency rather than all shareholders.[73]

Insurgents, however, may not use the rule to bypass a proxy contest for control. Shareholders whose disclosed intent is to seek control of the company may not use the rule to nominate directors. Likewise, shareholders whose disclosed intent is to elect more directors than the number authorized by the rule may not use the rule to nominate directors. They will have to run a traditional proxy contest.

Multiple shareholders can put forward nominees. In such a case, priority goes to the nominee(s) of the shareholders holding the largest proportion of the issuer's equity securities.

Concurrently, the SEC amended Rule 14a-8(i)(8). As amended, the new rule states that a proposal may be excluded if it:

> (i) Would disqualify a nominee who is standing for election; (ii) Would remove a director from office before his or her term expired; (iii) Questions the competence, business judgment, or character of one or more nominees or directors; (iv) Seeks to include a specific individual in the company's proxy materials for election to the board of directors; or (v) Otherwise could affect the outcome of the upcoming election of directors.

In adopting these amendments, the SEC explained that proxy access bylaws no longer were automatically excludable. To the contrary, bylaws that expand proxy access rights to a broader group of shareholders or create alternative proxy access rights are expressly authorized. A shareholder proposal to eliminate or restrict proxy access rights, however, is impermissible. It is an odd sort of shareholder democracy that treats shareholders as adults for purposes of expanding proxy access but paternalistically blocks them from restricting it.

---

73. A nominating shareholder must file a Schedule 14N providing notice of its intention to nominate a candidate under the rule. The disclosure statement must include information about the relationship, if any, between the nominating shareholder and the nominee. 17 C.F.R. § 240.14n-101. Disclosure will at least allow other shareholders to consider possible conflicts of interest.

The SEC offers two explanations for adopting proxy access. First, because shareholders who appear in person at an annual stockholders' meeting would have the power to nominate a director, the rule simply ensures that shareholders can exercise that right via the proxy system. In other words, the SEC claims, the rule simply effectuates existing state law rights. In fact, however, the SEC's argument is false. On the one hand, in some respects the rule is more restrictive of shareholder rights than is the state law it supposedly effectuates. On the other hand, however, the rule creates new federal entitlements that do not exist under state law.

As to the former, the proxy system as a whole was already more restrictive than what may be done by a shareholder in person. Rule 14a-11 simply continues that pattern. Under state law, for example, any shareholder could make a nomination at the annual meeting, not just those meeting Rule 14a-11's criteria on issues like the ownership threshold.[74]

As to the latter, Rule 14a-11 disallows restrictions on the shareholder nominating power that are likely permissible under state law.[75] In *Harrah's Entertainment, Inc. v. JCC Holding Co.*,[76] Vice Chancellor Leo Strine addressed the extent to which Delaware law permits restrictions on that power:

> Because of the obvious importance of the nomination right in our system of corporate governance, Delaware courts have been reluctant to approve measures that impede the ability of stockholders to nominate candidates. Put simply, Delaware law recognizes that the "right of shareholders to participate in the voting process includes the right to nominate an opposing slate." And, "the unadorned right to cast a ballot in a contest for [corporate] office . . . is meaningless without the right to participate in selecting the contestants. As the nominating process circumscribes the range of choice to be made, it is a fundamental and outcome-determinative step in the election of officeholders. To allow for voting while maintaining a closed selection process thus renders the former an empty exercise."[77]

Vice Chancellor Strine went on to explain, however, that a corporation may in fact opt out of the default voting—and nominating—rules of state law, provided it does so clearly and unambiguously:

> When a corporate charter is alleged to contain a restriction on the fundamental electoral rights of stockholders under default provisions of law—such as the

74. Fisch, supra note 70, at 19.
75. Id.
76. 802 A.2d 294 (Del.Ch. 2002).
77. Id. at 310–11 (citations omitted).

right of a majority of the shares to elect new directors or enact a charter amendment—it has been said that the restriction must be "clear and unambiguous" to be enforceable.[78]

Consequently, the SEC's claim that the shareholder power to nominate and elect directors is imposed by state law and "cannot be bargained away" is likely erroneous.

The extent to which Rule 14a-11 thereby displaces state corporate law with new federal entitlements was a key point in SEC Commissioner Troy Paredes' dissent from adoption of the rule. He explained that "Rule 14a-11's immutability conflicts with state law. Rule 14a-11 is not limited to facilitating the ability of shareholders to exercise their state law rights, but instead confers upon shareholders a new substantive federal right that in many respects runs counter to what state corporate law otherwise provides."[79] On both sides of the equation, Rule 14a-11 thus is hardly a means of facilitating shareholders' state law rights.

The SEC's second justification is that proxy access will promote director accountability.[80] In fact, however, because the effect of proxy access will be to increase the number of short slates, albeit to an uncertain extent, its impact on corporate governance likely will be analogous to that of cumulative voting. Both result in divided boards representing differing constituencies. Experience with cumulative voting suggests that adversarial relations between the majority block and the minority of shareholder nominees commonly dominate such divided boards.

The likely effects of proxy access therefore will not be better governance. It is more likely to be an increase in interpersonal conflict (as opposed to the more useful cognitive conflict). There probably will be a reduction in the trust-based relationships that are the foundation of effective board decision making.[81] There may also be an increase in the use by the majority of pre-meeting caucuses and a reduction in information flows to the board as a whole. Not surprisingly, early research suggests that proxy access reduces shareholder wealth.[82]

78. Id. at 310.

79. Troy Paredes, Comm'r, Sec. & Exch. Comm'n, Statement at Open Meeting to Adopt the Final Rule Regarding Facilitating Shareholder Director Nominations ("Proxy Access") (Aug. 25, 2010), http://www.sec.gov/news/speech/2010/spch082510tap.htm.

80. Fisch, supra note 70, at 18.

81. Cf. Stephen M. Bainbridge, Why a Board? Group Decision Making in Corporate Governance, 55 Vand. L. Rev. 1, 35–38 (2002) (discussing how trust and cooperation norms affect horizontal monitoring within the board).

82. Ali C. Akyol et al., Shareholders in the Boardroom: Wealth Effects of the SEC's Rule to Facilitate Director Nominations (Dec. 2009).

In his dissent, Commissioner Paredes pointed to additional pre-Rule 14a-11 studies undercutting the SEC's position:

> The mixed empirical results do not support the Commission's decision to impose a one-size-fits-all minimum right of access. Some studies have shown that certain means of enhancing corporate accountability, such as de-staggering boards, may increase firm value, but these studies do not test the impact of proxy access specifically. Accordingly, what the Commission properly can infer from these data is limited and, in any event, other studies show competing results. Recent economic work examining proxy access specifically is of particular interest in that the findings suggest that the costs of proxy access may outweigh the potential benefits, although the results are not uniform. The net effect of proxy access—be it for better or for worse—would seem to vary based on a company's particular characteristics and circumstances.
>
> To my mind, the adopting release's treatment of the economic studies is not evenhanded. The release goes to some length in questioning studies that call the benefits of proxy access into doubt—critiquing the authors' methodologies, noting that the studies' results are open to interpretation, and cautioning against drawing "sharp inferences" from the data. By way of contrast, the release too readily embraces and extrapolates from the studies it characterizes as supporting the rulemaking, as if these studies were on point and above critique when in fact they are not.[83]

In sum, proxy access is bad public policy, unsupported by the empirical evidence, and the pet project of a powerful interest group. In other words, quack corporate governance.

The SEC's Setback

In July 2011, as this book went to press, the U.S. Court of Appeals for the District of Columbia struck down Rule 14a-11 in a lawsuit brought by the Business Roundtable and the U.S. Chamber of Commerce. Even though the SEC clearly had authority to adopt the rule, the court found that the SEC had:

> [A]cted arbitrarily and capriciously for having failed once again—as it did most recently in American Equity Investment Life Insurance Company v. SEC, 613 F.3d 166, 167–68 (D.C. Cir. 2010), and before that in Chamber of Commerce, 412 F.3d at 136—adequately to assess the economic effects of a new rule. Here the Commission inconsistently and opportunistically framed the costs and

83. Id.

benefits of the rule; failed adequately to quantify the certain costs or to explain why those costs could not be quantified; neglected to support its predictive judgments; contradicted itself; and failed to respond to substantial problems raised by commenters.

The court agreed with those who argue that, if proxy access were validly adopted, a board often will have not just the right—but the duty—to oppose shareholder nominees:

> [T]he American Bar Association Committee on Federal Regulation of Securities commented: "If the [shareholder] nominee is determined [by the board] not to be as appropriate a candidate as those to be nominated by the board's independent nominating committee . . ., then the board will be compelled by its fiduciary duty to make an appropriate effort to oppose the nominee, as boards now do in traditional proxy contests."

The court also decisively rejected the SEC's claim—which parroted the claims of shareholder power advocates—that shareholder activism is beneficial for corporate performance:

> The petitioners also maintain, and we agree, the Commission relied upon insufficient empirical data when it concluded that Rule 14a-11 will improve board performance and increase shareholder value by facilitating the election of dissident shareholder nominees. . . . The Commission acknowledged the numerous studies submitted by commenters that reached the opposite result. . . . One commenter, for example, submitted an empirical study showing that "when dissident directors win board seats, those firms underperform peers by 19 to 40% over the two years following the proxy contest." Elaine Buckberg, NERA Econ. Consulting, & Jonathan Macey, Yale Law School, Report on Effects of Proposed SEC Rule 14a-11 on Efficiency, Competitiveness and Capital Formation 9 (2009), available at www.nera.com/upload/Buckberg_Macey_Report_FINAL.pdf. The Commission completely discounted those studies "because of questions raised by subsequent studies, limitations acknowledged by the studies' authors, or [its] own concerns about the studies' methodology or scope."
>
> The Commission instead relied exclusively and heavily upon two relatively unpersuasive studies, one concerning the effect of "hybrid boards" (which include some dissident directors) and the other concerning the effect of proxy contests in general, upon shareholder value. Id. at 56,762 & n.921 (citing Chris Cernich et al., IRRC Inst. for Corporate Responsibility, Effectiveness of Hybrid Boards (May 2009), available at www.irrcinstitute.org/pdf/IRRC_05_09_EffectiveHybridBoar ds.pdf, and J. Harold Mulherin & Annette B. Poulsen, Proxy Contests & Corporate Change: Implications for Shareholder Wealth, 47 J. Fin. Econ. 279 (1998)). Indeed, the Commission "recognize[d] the limitations of the

Cernich (2009) study," and noted "its long-term findings on shareholder value creation are difficult to interpret." Id. at 56,760/3 n.911. In view of the admittedly (and at best) "mixed" empirical evidence, id. at 56,761/1, we think the Commission has not sufficiently supported its conclusion that increasing the potential for election of directors nominated by shareholders will result in improved board and company performance and shareholder value. . . .

Third, the Court agreed with those who argue that certain institutional investors—most notably union pension funds and state and local government pension funds—would use proxy access as leverage to extract private gains at the expense of other:

> Notwithstanding the ownership and holding requirements, there is good reason to believe institutional investors with special interests will be able to use the rule and, as more than one commenter noted, "public and union pension funds" are the institutional investors "most likely to make use of proxy access." . . . Nonetheless, the Commission failed to respond to comments arguing that investors with a special interest, such as unions and state and local governments whose interests in jobs may well be greater than their interest in share value, can be expected to pursue self-interested objectives rather than the goal of maximizing shareholder value, and will likely cause companies to incur costs even when their nominee is unlikely to be elected.

Note how this passage vindicates the arguments made by SEC Commissioners Paredes and Casey on that issue.

The D.C. Circuit opinion is a big win for those who believe in the board-centric model of corporate governance and the dominance of state law in regulating corporate governance. But it is not the end of the story. As this book went to print, it was unclear what next steps—if any—the SEC would take. Obviously, the SEC could appeal. The SEC could also go back to the rule-making process and try again. Neither would be surprising. Proxy access is a major goal of union pension funds and therefore has strong support from Democrats in Congress and the Democratic members of the Commission.

In addition, there is a private ordering solution. Shareholders who want proxy access can put forward proposals under Rule 14a-8 to amend the issuer's bylaws so as to permit shareholder nominees to be included on the proxy card.

ASSESSING SHAREHOLDER EMPOWERMENT

As we have seen, separation of ownership and control is a fundamental building block of state corporate law. Although the SEC and Congress occasionally invoked the rhetoric of shareholder democracy, until recently federal law did little to truly empower shareholders. To the contrary, federal law indirectly supplemented the separation of ownership and control by discouraging formation of large blocks or cohesive investor groups. Dodd-Frank and related developments, however, decisively brought the federal government down on the side of shareholder activists. Assessed individually, each of these purported reforms proved to be of dubious merit. This section takes a broader perspective, evaluating the entire shareholder empowerment project within the context of foundational corporate governance theory.[84]

The Ownership Misnomer

Any evaluation of shareholder rights must begin by identifying the nature of those rights, which necessitates a preliminary inquiry into the nature of the corporation. The law treats the corporation as a person, with virtually all of the rights and powers of a natural person, but this is obviously a fiction. Centuries ago, Edward, First Baron Thurlow and Lord Chancellor of England, asked: "Did you ever expect a corporation to have a conscience, when it has no soul to be damned, and no body to be kicked?"

Many people view the corporation as a quasi-public creature of the state, exercising powers delegated by the state. In this view, incorporation is a privilege granted by the state, in return for which the corporation may be required to pursue the public interest. This so-called concession theory of the corporation may have made sense in the eighteenth and early nineteenth centuries, when the legislature had to pass a separate charter for each new corporation and most corporations served public purposes such as building and operating roads, mills, canals, and the like. In today's legal environment, however, in which general incorporation statutes permit formation of a corporation simply by filing articles of incorporation with some state official and paying filing fees and franchise taxes, and in which virtually all corporations are formed to pursue private profit, the concession theory is widely discredited.

The principal alternative to concession theory characterizes the corporation as a species of private property. In this view, the corporation is a thing capable of being owned. Specifically, many observers regard the shareholders

---

84. Readers of my earlier book, The New Corporate Governance in Theory and Practice, will find the argument herein familiar. See Stephen M. Bainbridge, The New Corporate Governance in Theory and Practice 23–76, 201–236 (2008) (discussing the board-centric model of corporate governance and making the case against shareholder empowerment). Because the case for board- rather than shareholder-centric corporate governance rests on the director primacy model espoused in that earlier work, it seems appropriate to briefly recapitulate it for the benefit of new readers. Those familiar with my prior work on director primacy may wish to skip ahead to the next section.

as the owners of the corporation.[85] Law professor Melvin Eisenberg, for example, argues that shareholders possess most of the incidents of ownership, such as "the rights to possess, use, and manage, and the rights to income and to capital."[86] In fact, however, what shareholders own is stock, which represents only a proportionate claim on the corporation's net assets in the event of liquidation, the right to a pro rata share of such dividends as may be declared by the board of directors from time to time, and limited electoral rights. Corporate shareholders have no right to use or possess corporate property, whether acting individually or collectively.[87] Shareholders have no right to direct the business affairs of the corporation. Instead, management rights are assigned by statute solely to the board of directors and those officers to whom the board properly delegates such authority. Indeed, to the extent that possessory and control rights are the indicia of a property right, in light of the statutory regime discussed above, the board of directors is a better candidate for identification as the corporation's owner than are the shareholders.[88]

A common problem with all these theories is that treating the corporation as some type of real entity is a form of reification, which is the fallacy of treating an abstraction as if it were a real thing. Admittedly, reification is semantically useful. It permits us to utilize a form of shorthand. It is easier to say General Motors did so and so than to attempt describing the complex process that actually occurred. Reification, however, can be dangerous. When we describe the corporation as a legal entity or as a thing capable of being owned, we ignore the reality that a corporation consists not only of a collection of assets but also of the relationships between the people who have various stakes in the enterprise.

Indeed, because those assets only have value when they are put to use by people, the corporation is properly understood as a set of relationships among people. Many corporate law and governance specialists therefore speak of the corporation as a nexus of contracts. These so-called "contractarians" view the firm not as an entity, but as an aggregate of various stakeholders acting together to produce goods or services. Employees provide labor. Creditors provide debt capital. Shareholders initially provide equity capital and subsequently bear the risk of losses and monitor the performance of management.

85. I omit herein discussion of theories under which non-shareholder stakeholders are thought to have ownership-like rights with respect to the corporation.

86. Melvin A. Eisenberg, The Conception That the Corporation Is a Nexus of Contracts, and the Dual Nature of the Firm, 24 J. Corp. L. 819, 825 (1999).

87. Cf. W. Clay Jackson Enters. v. Greyhound Leasing & Fin. Corp., 463 F. Supp. 666, 670 (D.P.R. 1979) (holding that "even a sole shareholder has no independent right which is violated by trespass upon or conversion of the corporation's property").

88. See Manson v. Curtis, 119 N.E. 559, 562 (N.Y. 1918) (explaining that "the directors in the performance of their duty possess [the corporation's property], and act in every way as if they owned it").

Management coordinates the activities of all the firm's stakeholders. From a contractarian perspective, the corporation thus is not a thing, but rather a nexus or web of explicit and implicit contracts establishing rights and obligations among the various inputs making up the firm.[89]

The concept of ownership thus is inconsistent with the very nature of the corporation. Ownership implies a thing capable of being owned. In the case of the corporation, however, there simply is no entity or thing capable of being owned. Shareholders are just one of many constituencies that contract with the corporation, which itself is a legal fiction. Granted, because the shareholders hold the residual claim on the corporation's assets, their contract with the corporation has certain ownership-like rights, including the right to vote and the fiduciary obligations of directors and officers. Even so, shareholders have only those rights specified by their contract, as that contract is embodied in state corporate law and the firm's organic documents.

This remains true even if a single shareholder (or cohesive group) owns a majority of the corporation's voting stock. To be sure, ownership of such a control block gives shareholders substantial de facto control by virtue of their ability to elect and remove directors, yet this still does not confer, as a matter of law, either possessory or management rights on such shareholders. Indeed, an effort by such a shareholder to exercise such rights might well constitute a breach of fiduciary duty by the controlling shareholder. In appropriate instances of such misconduct by a controlling shareholder, the board may well have a fiduciary duty to the minority to take steps to dilute the majority shareholder's control (as by issuing more stock).[90] That rule would make no sense if majority-voting control equaled ownership.

Why Separate Ownership of the Residual Claim and Control?

The next logical step in our inquiry is to ask why the shareholders' contract denies them meaningful control rights. In common parlance, this is referred to as the separation of ownership and control. As just discussed, it is more

89. To be clear, I am using the term "contract" here to mean something different than the way it is used either in law or common parlance. Instead of limiting the term to those relationships that constitute legal contracts, I use it herein to refer to any process by which property rights to assets are created, modified, or transferred. The relationship between shareholders and creditors of a corporation is contractual in this sense, for example, even though there is no single document we could identify as a legally binding contract through which they are in privity.

90. See, e.g., Delaware Chancellor Allen's opinion in Mendell v. Carroll, 651 A.2d 297, 306 (Del. Ch. 1994), in which he suggested that the board of directors could "deploy corporate power against the majority stockholders" to prevent "a threatened serious breach of fiduciary duty by the controlling stock."

accurate to speak of the separation of ownership of the residual claim and control, because shareholders own not the corporation itself but rather a security whose main right is the claim to whatever assets are left over after the claims of all other stakeholders are satisfied. For semantic convenience, however, we will use the conventional phrasing as a shorthand reference.

At the outset, it is important to recognize that U.S. corporate governance has been board- rather than shareholder-centric from the earliest days. "Banks, and the other public-issue corporations of the [pre-Civil War] period, contained the essential elements of big corporations today: a tripartite internal government structure, a share market that dispersed shareholdings and divided ownership and control, and tendencies to centralize management in full-time administrators and to diminish participation of outside directors in management."[91] Because there never was a time in which unity of control and ownership was a central feature of U.S. corporations, we may take as a starting point the proposition that the separation of ownership and control is not a flaw in the corporation's design but rather an essential characteristic thereof. Accordingly, our inquiry can focus on the question of what survival value the separation of ownership and control confers on the corporate form.

Separating ownership and control was essential because the corporate form requires a central decision-making body vested with the power of fiat. This claim derives from Ronald Coase's insight that firms emerge when it is efficient to substitute entrepreneurial fiat for the price mechanisms of the market.[92] By creating a central decision maker—a nexus—with the power of fiat, the firm thus substitutes ex post governance for ex ante contract.

The inquiry now shifts from Coase to the work of Kenneth Arrow. The latter described governance arrangements as falling out on a spectrum between "consensus" and "authority."[93] Authority-based decision-making structures are characterized by the existence of a central office empowered to make decisions binding on the firm as a whole. Such structures typically are adopted when the organization's constituencies have different interests and access to information. The public corporation satisfies both of those conditions and adds to them an array of collective action problems that also can be mitigated by relying on authority rather than consensus.

Overcoming the collective action problems presented when one is dealing with many thousands of shareholders would be difficult and costly, of course, if not impossible. Just as cities get too big to be run by New England–style town meetings, so do corporations. Even if the sheer mechanical difficulties of

91. Walter Werner, Corporation Law in Search of its Future, 81 Colum. L. Rev. 1611, 1637 (1981).
92. Ronald Coase, The Nature of the Firm, 4 Economica (n.s.) 386 (1937).
93. Kenneth J. Arrow, The Limits of Organization 63–79 (1974).

achieving consensus amongst thousands of decision makers could be overcome, however, shareholders lack both the information and the incentives necessary to make sound decisions on either operational or policy questions. Although neoclassical economics assumes that shareholders come to the corporation with wealth maximization as their goal, and most presumably do so, once uncertainty is introduced it would be surprising if shareholder opinions did not differ on which course will maximize share value. More prosaically, shareholder investment time horizons are likely to vary from short-term speculation to long-term buy-and-hold strategies, which in turn is likely to result in disagreements about corporate strategy. Even more prosaically, shareholders in different tax brackets are likely to disagree about such matters as dividend policy, as are shareholders who disagree about the merits of allowing management to invest the firm's free cash flow in new projects.

As to Arrow's information condition, shareholders lack incentives to gather the information necessary to actively participate in decision making. A rational shareholder will expend the effort necessary to make informed decisions only if the expected benefits of doing so outweigh its costs. Given the length and complexity of corporate disclosure documents, the opportunity cost entailed in making informed decisions is both high and apparent. In contrast, the expected benefits of becoming informed are quite low, as most shareholders' holdings are too small to have significant effect on the vote's outcome. Corporate shareholders thus are rationally apathetic. Instead of exercising their voting rights, disgruntled shareholders typically adopt the so-called Wall Street Rule—it's easier to switch than fight—and sell out.

Under these conditions, it is "cheaper and more efficient to transmit all the pieces of information to a central place" and to have the central office "make the collective choice and transmit it rather than retransmit all the information on which the decision is based."[94] Accordingly, shareholders will prefer to irrevocably delegate decision-making authority to some smaller group; namely, the board of directors.

The Principal-Agent Problem

As we saw in connection with the SEC's justification for proxy access, proponents of shareholder empowerment claim it is a necessary constraint on the principal-agent problem created by the separation of ownership and control. One can concede the existence of such a principal-agent problem, however, without conceding that shareholder empowerment is an appropriate response. First, corporate managers operate within a pervasive web of accountability

94. Arrow, supra note 93, at 68–69.

mechanisms that substitute for monitoring by residual claimants. The capital and product markets, the internal and external employment markets, and the market for corporate control all constrain shirking by firm agents. Second, agency costs are the inescapable result of placing ultimate decision-making authority in the hands of someone other than the residual claimant. We could substantially reduce agency costs by eliminating discretion. That we do not do so implies that discretion has substantial virtues.

In order to develop a complete theory of the corporation, neither the necessity for a central agency with power to wield discretionary authority nor the necessity to ensure that that power is used responsibly can be ignored.[95] Unfortunately, however, these concerns ultimately are in opposition. Because the power to hold to account differs only in degree and not in kind from the power to decide, one cannot have more of one without also having less of the other:

> [Accountability mechanisms] must be capable of correcting errors but should not be such as to destroy the genuine values of authority. Clearly, a sufficiently strict and continuous organ of [accountability] can easily amount to a denial of authority. If every decision of A is to be reviewed by B, then all we have really is a shift in the locus of authority from A to B and hence no solution to the original problem.[96]

Hence, directors cannot be held accountable without undermining their discretionary authority.

The predictive power of this insight is demonstrated in the host of legal doctrines and governance structures that resolve the tension between authority and accountability in the favor of the former. Consider, for example, the justification courts have offered for business judgment rule:

> To encourage freedom of action on the part of directors, or to put it another way, to discourage interference with the exercise of their free and independent judgment, there has grown up what is known as the "business judgment rule." "Questions of policy of management, expediency of contracts or action, adequacy of consideration, lawful appropriation of corporate funds to advance corporate interests, are left solely to their honest and unselfish decision, for their powers therein are without limitation and free from restraint, and the exercise of them for the common and general interests of the corporation

---

95. Michael P. Dooley, Two Models of Corporate Governance, 47 Bus. Law. 461, 471 (1992).

96. Arrow, supra note 93, at 78.

may not be questioned, although the results show that what they did was unwise or inexpedient."[97]

In a passage from its leading *Van Gorkom* decision that has received less attention than it deserves, the Delaware Supreme Court likewise explained that:

> Under Delaware law, the business judgment rule is the offspring of the fundamental principle, codified in [DGCL] § 141(a), that the business and affairs of a Delaware corporation are managed by or under its board of directors. . . . The business judgment rule exists to protect and promote the full and free exercise of the managerial power granted to Delaware directors.[98]

In other words, like much of corporate law, the business judgment rule exists to protect director primacy by allowing authority to trump accountability absent bad faith or self-dealing.

Balancing Authority and Accountability

The principal argument against shareholder empowerment follows ineluctably from this line of analysis. The corporate form succeeded because it provides a hierarchical decision-making structure well suited to the problem of operating a large business enterprise with numerous employees, managers, shareholders, creditors, and other inputs. In such a complex firm, someone must be in charge: "Under conditions of widely dispersed information and the need for speed in decisions, authoritative control at the tactical level is essential for success."[99]

The American Bar Association's Committee on Corporate Laws, which has drafting responsibility for the widely adopted Model Business Corporation Act, recently affirmed that "the deployment of diverse investors' capital by centralized management maximizes corporate America's ability to contribute to long-term wealth creation."[100] As the Committee explained, the "board centric" model gives shareholders "the regular opportunity to elect the members of the board, but during the directors' terms, the board has the power,

---

97. Bayer v. Beran, 49 N.Y.S.2d 2 (1944) (citations omitted).
98. Smith v. Van Gorkom, 488 A.2d 858 (Del. 1985).
99. Id. at 69.
100. Committee on Corporate Laws of the American Bar Association Section of Business Law, Report on the Roles of Boards of Directors and Shareholders of Publicly Owned Corporations 4 (2010), http://www.abanet.org/media/nosearch/task_force_report.pdf.

informed by each director's decisions in the exercise of his or her fiduciary duties, to direct and oversee the pursuit of the board's vision of what is best for the corporation."[101] Accordingly, although the drafters acknowledged the political need to offer some concessions to shareholder activism, they also reaffirmed the Act's basic commitment to vesting "the power to direct and oversee the management of the corporation in the board of directors, rather than in the shareholders."[102]

As justification for its board-centric approach, the Committee argued that:

> If corporations were directly managed by shareholders, and the actions of management were the subject of frequent shareholder review and decision making, the ability to rely on management teams would be diluted and the time and attention of managers could, in many cases, be diverted from activities designed to pursue sustainable economic benefit for the corporation. For example, valuable board time might have to be diverted to address referenda items propounded by particular shareholders who may have interests that diverge from those of other shareholders or interests other than sustainable economic benefit. In addition, since shareholders generally do not owe fiduciary duties to each other or the corporation, such power would not be accompanied by corresponding accountability.[103]

In sum, given the significant virtues of discretion, one ought not lightly interfere with management or the board's decision-making authority in the name of accountability. Indeed, the claim should be put even more strongly: Preservation of managerial discretion should always be default presumption. Because the separation of ownership and control mandated by U.S. corporate law has precisely that effect, by constraining shareholders both from reviewing most board decisions and from substituting their judgment for that of the board, that separation has a strong efficiency justification.

The Rise of Institutional Investors

Does the foregoing analysis change when we take into account the rise of institutional investors? Since the early 1990s, various governance activists and academics have argued that institutional investor corporate governance activism is becoming an important constraint on the principal-agent problem.

101. Id.
102. Id.
103. Id.

The Theory

Institutional investors, they argue, approach corporate governance quite differently than individual investors. Because institutions typically own larger blocks than individuals, and have an incentive to develop specialized expertise in making and monitoring investments, the former should play a far more active role in corporate governance than retail investors. The institutions' greater access to firm information, coupled with their concentrated voting power, should enable them to more actively monitor the firm's performance and to make changes in the board's composition when performance lagged. As a result, concentrated ownership in the hands of institutional investors might lead to a reduction in shirking and, hence, a reduction in agency costs.

In Practice

In the 1990s, it seemed plausible that the story might eventually play out. Institutional investors increasingly dominated U.S. equity securities markets. They also began to play a somewhat more active role in corporate governance than they had in earlier periods: taking their voting rights more seriously and using the proxy system to defend their interests. They began voting against takeover defenses proposed by management and in favor of shareholder proposals recommending removal of existing defenses. Many institutions also no longer routinely voted to reelect incumbent directors. Less visibly, institutions influenced business policy and board composition through negotiations with management. While there seemed little doubt that institutional investor activism could have effects at the margins, however, the question remained whether the impact would be more than merely marginal.

By the end of the 1990s, the answer seemed to be no. A comprehensive survey found relatively little evidence that shareholder activism mattered.[104] Even the most active institutional investors spent only trifling amounts on corporate governance activism. Institutions devoted little effort to monitoring management; to the contrary, they typically disclaimed the ability or desire to decide company-specific policy questions. They rarely conducted proxy solicitations or put forward shareholder proposals. They did not seek to elect

104. Bernard S. Black, Shareholder Activism and Corporate Governance in the United States, in The New Palgrave Dictionary of Economics and the Law 459 (1998). Due to a resurgence of direct individual investment in the stock market, motivated at least in part by the day trading phenomenon and technology stock bubble, the trend toward institutional domination stagnated. Large blocks held by a single investor remained rare. Few U.S. corporations had any institutional shareholders who owned more than 5–10 percent of their stock.

representatives to boards of directors. They rarely coordinated their activities. Most importantly, empirical studies of U.S. institutional investor activism found "no strong evidence of a correlation between firm performance and percentage of shares owned by institutions."[105]

Today, institutional investor activism remains rare. It is principally the province of union and state and local public employee pension funds. An important study by Stephen Choi and Jill Fisch published in 2008 found that much public pension fund activism, moreover, takes the form of securities fraud litigation rather than corporate governance activities.[106] With some notable exceptions, most funds do not engage in such core governance activities as nominating directors or making shareholder proposals. Choi and Fisch conclude that their "findings offer reasons to be skeptical of the so-called promise of institutional activism."[107]

Even Institutions Are Rationally Apathetic

Cost-benefit analysis suggests that activism is not a game worth playing for most institutional investors. On the cost side of the equation, monitoring expenses loom especially large. Because it is impossible to predict ex ante which corporations would benefit from activist attention, activist institutions must constantly monitor all of their portfolio firms. Because corporate disclosures rarely give one a full picture of the corporation's prospects, moreover, an activist cannot simply be content perusing disclosure documents for signs of trouble. Instead, costly direct monitoring mechanisms must be established. With many institutional investors holding portfolios of shares in hundreds or even thousands of corporations, the aggregate cost of such mechanisms would be very substantial. The high churn rate at many funds further compounds the problem as the makeup of the portfolio rapidly changes, requiring constant creation of new monitoring mechanisms to deal with new holdings.

Monitoring costs are just the price of entry for activist institutions, however. Once they identify a problem firm, steps must be taken to address the problem. In some cases, it may suffice for the activist institution to propose some change in the rules of the game, but less tractable problems will necessitate more extreme remedial measures, such as removal of the incumbent board of directors.

---

105. Id. at 462.
106. Stephen J. Choi & Jill E. Fisch, On Beyond CalPERS: Survey Evidence on the Developing Role of Public Pension Funds in Corporate Governance, 61 Vand. L. Rev. 315 (2008).
107. Id. at 318.

In public corporations with dispersed ownership of the sort under debate here, such measures necessarily require the support of other shareholders, which makes a shareholder insurrection against inefficient but entrenched managers a costly and difficult undertaking. Putting together a winning coalition will require, among other things, ready mechanisms for communicating with other investors. Unfortunately, SEC rules on proxy solicitations, stock ownership disclosure, and controlling shareholder liabilities have long impeded communication and collective action. Even though the 1992 SEC rule amendments somewhat lowered the barriers to collective action, important impediments remain.

Putting a precise dollar amount on the costs to an institutional investor—or group thereof—of waging an activist campaign obviously is difficult. It will depend on such factors as the form the activism takes, the size of the target, the extent to which target management resists, and so on. One effort to estimate the costs incurred by an activist who goes so far as to conduct a proxy contest, however, found that the average campaign cost $10.5 million, which represented 12 percent of the mean activist stake.[108] The cost of an activist campaign thus was significant both in absolute terms and, in particular, relative to the activist's mean return on its investment.

Turning to the benefits side of the equation, the returns to activism likely are low. Because many companies must be monitored, and because careful monitoring of an individual firm is expensive, institutional activism is likely to focus on crisis management. In many crises, however, institutional activism is unlikely to be availing. In some cases, intervention will come too late. In others, the problem may prove intractable, as where technological changes undercut the firm's competitive position.

Even where gains might arise from activism, only a portion of the gains would accrue to the activist institutions. Suppose that the troubled company has 110 outstanding shares, currently trading at $10 per share, of which the potential activist institution owns ten. The institution correctly believes that the firm's shares would rise in value to $20 if the firm's problems were solved. If the institution is able to effect a change in corporate policy, its ten shares will produce a $100 paper gain when the stock price rises to reflect the company's new value. All the other shareholders, however, will also automatically receive a pro rata share of the gains.[109] As a result, the activist institution confers a gratuitous $1,000 benefit on the other shareholders.

---

108. Nickolay M. Gantchev, The Costs of Shareholder Activism: Evidence from a Sequential Decision Model 4 (April 2010).

109. One could plausibly expect institutions to surmount this problem by seeking private benefits, which makes investor activism even less appealing. See infra text accompanying notes 115–19.

Put another way, the gains resulting from institutional activism are a species of public goods. They are costly to produce, but because other shareholders cannot be excluded from taking a pro rata share, they are subject to non-rivalrous consumption. As with any other public good, the temptation arises for shareholders to free ride on the efforts of those who produce the good.

Granted, if stock continues to concentrate in the hands of large institutional investors, there will be marginal increases in the gains to be had from activism and a marginal decrease in its costs.[110] A substantial increase in activism seems unlikely to result, however. Most institutional investors compete to attract either the savings of small investors or the patronage of large sponsors, such as corporate pension plans. In this competition, the winners generally are those with the best relative performance rates, which makes institutions highly cost-conscious.[111] The problem is exacerbated by the performance metrics applied to many asset managers. Investment managers commonly are assessed on the basis of short-term—mostly quarterly—returns as compared to the returns earned by other managers.[112] This makes fund managers even more cost-conscious than otherwise would be the case.

Given that activism will only rarely produce gains, and that when such gains occur they will be dispensed upon both the active and the passive, it makes little sense for cost-conscious money managers to incur the expense entailed in shareholder activism. Instead, they will remain passive in hopes of free riding on someone else's activism. As in other free-riding situations, because everyone is subject to and likely to yield to this temptation, the probability is that the good in question—here shareholder activism—will be under produced.

This is especially true of the ever-growing number of passively managed index funds. Index funds tend to be especially cost-conscious, because they compete almost exclusively on keeping fees low and tracking their index as closely as possible. Investing resources in governance activism makes no sense for such funds given their business model.

Even if activism made sense from a cost-benefit perspective, corporate managers are well positioned to buy off most institutional investors that attempt to act as monitors. Bank trust departments are an important class of institutional investors, but are unlikely to emerge as activists because their parent banks often have or anticipate commercial lending relationships with the firms they will purportedly monitor. Similarly, insurers "as purveyors

110. Edward Rock, The Logic and Uncertain Significance of Institutional Investor Activism, 79 Geo. L.J. 445, 460–63 (1991).

111. Id. at 473–74.

112. Simon C. Y. Wong, Why Stewardship is Proving Elusive for Institutional Investors, Butterworth J. Int'l Bank. & Fin. L., July/Aug. 2010, at 406, 406–07.

of insurance products, pension plans, and other financial services to corporations, have reason to mute their corporate governance activities and be bought off."[113]

Mutual fund families whose business includes managing private pension funds for corporations are subject to the same concern. A 2010 study examined the relationship between how mutual funds voted on shareholder proposals relating to executive compensation and pension-management business relationships between the funds' families and the targeted firms. The authors concluded that such ties influence fund managers to vote with corporate managers rather than shareholder activists at both client and non-client portfolio companies.[114] Voting with management at non-client firms presumably is motivated by a desire to attract new business and send signals of loyalty to existing clients.

With many categories of institutional investors thus eliminated as potential activists, we are left mainly with union and state and local pension funds, which in fact generally have been the most active institutions with respect to corporate governance issues.[115] Unfortunately for the proponents of institutional investor activism, however, these are precisely the institutions most likely to use their position to self-deal or to otherwise reap private benefits not shared with other investors. With respect to union and public pension fund sponsorship of Rule 14a-8 proposals, for example, Roberta Romano observes that:

> It is quite probable that private benefits accrue to some investors from sponsoring at least some shareholder proposals. The disparity in identity of sponsors— the predominance of public and union funds, which, in contrast to private sector funds, are not in competition for investor dollars—is strongly suggestive of their presence. Examples of potential benefits which would be disproportionately of interest to proposal sponsors are progress on labor rights desired by union fund managers and enhanced political reputations for public pension fund managers, as well as advancements in personal employment. . . . Because such career concerns—enhancement of political reputations or subsequent employment opportunities—do not provide a commensurate benefit to private fund managers, we do not find them engaging in investor activism.[116]

113. Mark J. Roe, Strong Managers, Weak Owners: The Political Roots of American Corporate Finance 62 (1994).

114. Rasha Ashraf et al., Do Pension-Related Business Ties Influence Mutual Fund Proxy Voting? Evidence from Shareholder Proposals on Executive Compensation (November 23, 2010), http://ssrn.com/abstract=1351966.

115. See Randall S. Thomas & Kenneth J. Martin, Should Labor Be Allowed to Make Shareholder Proposals?, 73 Wash. L. Rev. 41, 51–52 (1998).

116. Roberta Romano, Less Is More: Making Shareholder Activism A Valued Mechanism Of Corporate Governance, 18 Yale J. Reg. 174, 231–32 (2001). None of

There have been several troubling incidents of the sort to which Romano refers. In 2004, for example, CalPERS organized a proxy campaign to remove Steven Burd, Safeway's CEO and chairman of the board. At that time, Safeway was in the middle of acrimonious collective bargaining negotiations with the United Food and Commercial Workers Union. It turned out that CalPERS had acted at the behest of Sean Harrigan, Executive Director of the United Food and Commercial Workers Union, who was then also serving as president of CalPERS board.[117] Nor is this an isolated example. Union pension funds tried to remove directors or top managers, or otherwise affect corporate policy, at over 200 corporations in 2004 alone.[118] Union pension funds reportedly have also tried shareholder proposals to obtain employee benefits they could not get through bargaining.[119]

Public employee pension funds are vulnerable to being used as a vehicle for advancing political/social goals unrelated to shareholder interests generally. Mid-decade activism by CalPERS, for example, reportedly was "fueled partly by the political ambitions of Phil Angelides, California's state treasurer and a CalPERS board member," who planned on running for governor of California in 2006.[120] In other words, Angelides allegedly used the retirement savings of California's public employees to further his own political ends.

To be sure, like any other agency cost, the risk that management will be willing to pay private benefits to an institutional investor is a necessary consequence of vesting discretionary authority in the board and the officers. It does not compel the conclusion that we ought to limit the board's power. It does suggest, however, that we ought not to give investors even greater leverage to extract such benefits by further empowering them.

Rearranging the Deck Chairs

The analysis to this point suggests that the costs of institutional investor activism likely outweigh any benefits such activism may confer with respect to redressing the principal-agent problem. Even if one assumes that the

---

this is to deny, of course, that union and state and local pension funds also often have interests that converge with those of investors generally. See Stewart J. Schwab & Randall S. Thomas, Realigning Corporate Governance: Shareholder Activism by Labor Unions, 96 Mich. L. Rev. 1020, 1079–80 (1998).

117. Iman Anabtawi & Lynn Stout, Fiduciary Duties for Activist Shareholders, 60 Stan. L. Rev. 1255, 1258–60 (2008).

118. Stephen M. Bainbridge, Flanigan on Union Pension Fund Activism, available at http://www.professorbainbridge.com/2004/04/flanigan_on_uni.html.

119. Id.

120. Stephen M. Bainbridge, Pension Funds Play Politics, Tech Central Station, April 21, 2004, available at http://www.techcentralstation.com/042104G.html.

cost-benefit analysis comes out the other way around, however, institutional investor activism does not solve the principal-agent problem but rather merely relocates its locus.

The vast majority of large institutional investors manage the pooled savings of small individual investors. From a governance perspective, there is little to distinguish such institutions from corporations. The holders of investment company shares, for example, have no more control over the election of company trustees than do retail investors over the election of corporate directors. Accordingly, fund shareholders exhibit the same rational apathy as corporate shareholders. Kathryn McGrath, a former SEC mutual fund regulator, observes: "A lot of [fund] shareholders take ye olde proxy and throw it in the trash."[121] The proxy system thus costs fund "shareholders money for rights they don't seem interested in exercising."[122] Indeed, Ms. McGrath concedes that she herself often tosses a proxy for a personal investment onto a "to-do pile," where "I don't get around to reading it, or when I do, the deadline has passed."[123] Nor do the holders of such shares have any greater access to information about their holdings, or ability to monitor those who manage their holdings, than do corporate shareholders. Although an individual investor can always abide by the Wall Street Rule with respect to corporate stock, moreover, he cannot do so with respect to such investments as an involuntary, contributory pension plan.

For beneficiaries of union and state and local government employee pension funds, the problem is particularly pronounced. As we have seen, those who manage such funds may often put their personal or political agendas ahead of the interests of the fund's beneficiaries. Accordingly, it is not particularly surprising that pension funds subject to direct political control tend to have poor financial results.[124]

What about Hedge Funds and Private Equity Firms?

Shareholder activism by hedge and private equity funds differs in a number of respects from that of other institutional investors. Activist pension funds are typically reactive, intervening where they perceive (or claim to perceive) that a portfolio company is underperforming. In contrast, hedge fund activism typically is proactive, identifying a firm whose performance could be improved

---

121. Karen Blumenthal, Fidelity Sets Vote on Scope of Investments, Wall St. J., Dec. 8, 1994, at C1, C18.

122. Id.

123. Id.

124. Roberta Romano, Public Pension Fund Activism in Corporate Governance Reconsidered, 93 Colum. L. Rev. 795, 825 (1993).

and then investing in it.[125] As a result, both the forms and goals of hedge fund activism differ from those of other institutions, as does the extent of their activism.

A 2007 study by Robin Greenwood confirmed hedge fund's growing impact:

[B]etween 1994 and 2006, the number of public firms targeted for poor performance by hedge funds grew more than 10-fold.

More importantly, hedge funds may be up to the task of monitoring management—a number of recent academic papers have found that hedge funds generate returns of over 5 percent on announcement of their involvement, suggesting that investors believe these funds will increase the value of the firms they target.[126]

But do these funds generate value by effecting governance or operational change? Greenwood argues that hedge fund managers generally are poorly suited to making operational business decisions and, with their short-term focus, are unlikely "to devote time and energy to a task delivering long-term value. After all, there are no guarantees that the effort will pay off, or that other shareholders would recognize the increase in value by paying a higher price per share."

Instead, hedge funds profit mainly through transactions in corporate control, rather than corporate governance activism. Private equity funds like KKR long have been active acquirers. In the 1980s, for example, KKR was the famously prevailing barbarian at the gate in the fight over RJR Nabisco.[127] More recently, however, private equity acquisitions have simply exploded. The dollar value of announced private equity deals went from less than $50 billion in the first quarter of 2003 to $400 billion in the second quarter of 2007.[128] A mid-2007 credit crunch put the brakes on private equity deals, but long-term fundamentals continue to favor an active role for private equity in the market for corporate control.

A hedge fund typically seeks not to acquire the target company, of course, but rather to put the target into play so that the fund can profit on its stake when someone else buys the target. If the target is successfully put into play, the stock price runs up, attracting arbitragers and other short-term speculators

125. Marcel Kahan & Edward B. Rock, Hedge Funds in Corporate Governance and Corporate Control, 155 U. Pa. L. Rev. 1021, 1069 (2007).
126. Robin Greenwood, The Hedge Fund as Activist, HBR Working Knowledge, Aug. 22, 2007.
127. Bryan Burrough & John Helyar, Barbarians at the Gate: The Fall of RJR Nabisco (1990).
128. Grace Wong, Buyout Firms: Pain Today, Gain Tomorrow, CNNMoney.com. Sept. 27, 2007.

who then put intense pressure on management to cut a deal. In some cases, hedge funds holding shares in the target also may actively intervene in a pending deal by refusing to support the deal or threatening litigation unless the price and/or other important terms are improved.[129] If the deal goes through, the successful bidder typically pays a premium of 30–50 percent, sometimes even higher, over the pre-bid market price of the target's stock. The hedge fund that started the ball rolling thus will sell its shares can then sell its shares at a substantial premium.

Conversely, where a hedge fund holds shares in a potential acquirer, it may seek to prevent the deal from happening at all. Studies of acquiring company stock performance report results ranging from no statistically significant stock price effect to statistically significant losses.[130] By some estimates, bidders overpay in as many as half of all takeovers. Being aware of this risk, private equity holders have sometimes tried to block the acquirer from going forward.[131]

Greenwood argues that a preference for control rather than governance activism makes sense because "hedge funds are better at identifying undervalued companies, locating potential acquirers for them, and removing opposition to a takeover."[132] His study of over 1000 cases of hedge fund activism confirmed that claim, finding that "targets of investor activism earn high returns only for the subset of events in which the activist successfully persuades the target to merge or get acquired."[133]

Another study of hedge fund engagements likewise found that:

> The financial yield . . . is disappointing. The hedge funds prove better at extracting target concessions and getting into boardrooms than at yielding long-term, market-beating financial gain. On the one hand, activist intervention led to something tangible in 88 percent of the cases, whether an asset sale, a stepped up cash payout, a board seat, or a legislative concession. On the other hand, only a minority of the targets' stock prices beat market indices over the period of engagement, with financial underperformance being particularly notable in cases where the hedge fund entered the target boardroom.[134]

129. See, e.g., Marcel Kahan & Edward B. Rock, Hedge Funds in Corporate Governance and Corporate Control, 155 U. Penn. L. Rev. 1021, 1037–39 (2007) (citing examples).

130. See, e.g., Julian Franks et al., The Postmerger Share-Price Performance of Acquiring Firms, 29 J. Fin. Econ. 81 (1991).

131. Kahan & Rock, supra note 129, at 1034–37 (citing examples).

132. Greenwood, supra note 126.

133. Id.

134. William W. Bratton, Hedge Funds and Governance Targets: Long-term Results 2 (Institute for Law and Economics Res. Paper No. 10–17, Sept. 2010).

As a result, neither hedge nor private equity funds seem plausible candidates for being the ultimate solution to the principal-agent problem inherent in the public corporate form. Instead, they merely offer an alternative form—i.e., the private company.

Because the net gains to investors from corporate takeovers are positive, even considering the probability that the acquirer will lose money, one can plausibly argue that hedge fund and private equity activism is beneficial to all investors. In several high-profile cases, however, activist hedge funds have used financial innovations to pursue private gains at the expense of other shareholders. In 2005, for example, a hedge fund launched a proxy campaign to elect three candidates to the board of Exar Corporation. The hedge fund had boxed 96 percent of the shares it owned—i.e., had taken offsetting short positions on those shares—and "was thus almost completely indifferent to how the company performed since a 'boxed' position is capable of generating no further profit or loss."[135] Another well-known case involved Perry Capital's innovative investments in King Pharmaceuticals and Mylan Laboratories. The hedge fund was a large shareholder in both Mylan and King. Mylan proposed an acquisition of King at a price many industry observers thought excessively high. Perry nevertheless supported the acquisition. As it turned out, Perry had used derivatives to hedge away its economic interest in Mylan. As a result, the only way Perry could make money on the deal was through its investment in King stock. Accordingly, Perry would prefer that Mylan overpay for King, even though that obviously would be detrimental to Mylan's other shareholders.[136] Scholars have identified several other examples of such private rent-seeking by hedge funds and other activist investors.[137] As is the case with union and state and local government pension funds, there thus is a risk that further shareholder empowerment will simply encourage additional rent-seeking by hedge funds.

Overall Assessment

If the separation of ownership and control is a problem in search of a solution, encouraging institutional investors to take an active corporate governance role simply moves the problem back a step: it does not solve it. Yet, it is not at all clear that the separation of ownership and control is a pathology requiring treatment. To the contrary, our system of corporate governance

---

135. Thomas W. Briggs, Corporate Governance and the New Hedge Fund Activism: An Empirical Analysis, 32 J. Corp. L. 681, 702 (2007).

136. Anabtawi & Stout, supra note 117, at 1287–88 (describing transaction).

137. See, e.g., Anabtawi & Stout, supra note 117, at 1285–92; Briggs, supra note 135, at 695–701.

long functioned effectively despite the dearth of shareholder activism. As the Wall Street Journal explained in 2003:

> The economy and stock market have performed better in recent years than any other on earth. "How can we have done marvelously if the system is fundamentally flawed?" [economist Bengt] Holmstrom asks. If the bulk of American executives were stealing from shareholders and financial markets were rigged, they reason, then capital would flow to the wrong places and productivity wouldn't be surging.[138]

Economists Holmstrom and Kaplan likewise concluded that:

> Despite the alleged flaws in its governance system, the U.S. economy has performed very well, both on an absolute basis and particularly relative to other countries. U.S. productivity gains in the past decade have been exceptional, and the U.S. stock market has consistently outperformed other world indices over the last two decades, including the period since the scandals broke. In other words, the broad evidence is not consistent with a failed U.S. system. If anything, it suggests a system that is well above average.[139]

As discussed below, the subsequent housing bubble and credit crisis does not invalidate that conclusion.

Conversely, while there is considerable evidence for the proposition that activist shareholders can profit through private rent-seeking, there is little evidence that activism has benefits for investors as a class. Navigant Consulting recently undertook a review of the most basic form of shareholder activism—Rule 14a-8 proposals—and found no evidence that it resulted in either short- or long-term increases in market value.[140] This was true of both social and governance proposals.

This result is not surprising, of course. First, "the high costs and low success rate of activism suggest that its net gains are substantially lower than" many proponents of shareholder activism claim.[141] Second, if activism increases the target firm's stock price, all of its shareholders can free ride on the activist's efforts. It makes no sense for an activist to expend substantial resources when the bulk of the gains from doing so will be captured by others.

---

138. David Wessel, "The American Way" is a Work in Progress, Wall St. J., Nov. 13, 2003, at A2.

139. Bengt R. Holmstrom & Steven N. Kaplan, The State of U.S. Corporate Governance: What's Right and What's Wrong?, 15 J. App. Corp. Fin. 8 (2003).

140. Joao Dos Santos & Chen Song, Analysis of the Wealth Effects of Shareholder Proposals (U.S. Chamber of Comm. Res. Paper, July 2008).

141. Gantchev, supra note 108, at 23.

Instead, we would expect activists to pursue an agenda of private rent-seeking rather than altruistic public service.

The importance of private rents to a successful activist campaign is illustrated by the effort to get investors to withhold authority for their shares to be voted to elect directors at Disney's 2004 annual shareholder meeting. Instructively, the campaign had a central organizing figure—Roy Disney— with a private motivation for doing so.[142] Disney management later persuaded Roy Disney to drop his various lawsuits against the board and sign a five-year standstill agreement pursuant to which he would not run an insurgent slate of directors in return for being named a Director Emeritus and consultant to the company, which nicely illustrates how a company can buy off the requisite central coordinator when that party has a private agenda.[143] In contrast, when CalPERS, struck out on its own in 2004, withholding its shares from being voted to elect directors at no less than 2700 companies, including Coca-Cola director and legendary investor Warren Buffet, the project went no where.[144]

Does the financial crisis require us to rethink the merits of shareholder empowerment, as President Obama, the Washington Democrats, and the corporate governance activist community insist? No. On the one hand, to the extent corporate governance contributed to the financial crisis, it did so because shareholders are already too strong, not because they were too weak. Professor Lawrence Mitchell explains that:

> Managers thrive by increasing their portfolios' value. That is a hard thing to do and it takes time. So for years fund managers have increased their pay by putting pressure on corporate managers to increase short-term stock prices at the expense of long-term business health. Doing business that way puts jobs and sustainable industry at risk, now and in the future.
>
> For example, managers responded to the pressure by using their retained earnings to engage in large stock buybacks. In the three years leading up to September 2007, companies in the S&P 500 used more money to buy back stock than to invest in production. With retained earnings gone, all that was left to finance production was debt. When the credit markets collapsed, these corporations could not borrow, and thus could not produce. Are boards and managers to blame? Sure. But so are the big shareholders who have been pushing

142. Even then, a plurality of the shares was voted to reelect the incumbent board. Disney: Restoring Magic, Econ., July 16, 2005, available at 2005 WLNR 11134752.

143. Roy Disney, Gold Agree to Drop Suits, Corp. Gov. Rep. (BNA), August 1, 2005, at 86.

144. See Dale Kasler, Governor's Plan Could Erode CalPERS Clout, Sac. Bee, Feb. 28, 2005, available on Westlaw at 2/28/05 SACRAMENTOBEE A1.

management for this kind of behavior for years. They are more the problem than the solution. Enhancing their voting rights will only make things worse.[145]

Mitchell continues:

> The proposals [to enhance those rights] are fighting the last war. Inattentive boards of non-financial companies may have been a big factor in the corporate scandals at the start of the century. But it is hyperbolic to suggest, as the Schumer bill does, that this had anything significant to do with the current recession. The Schumer bill and the SEC proposal only exacerbate the problem by chaining boards to the ball of stock prices—which helped to cause those scandals in the first place.[146]

Mitchell therefore asks:

> Do we really want speculators telling corporate boards how to manage their businesses? Those who say "yes" want to increase short-term management pressure and thus share prices, regardless of the corporate mutilation this induces. They do not seem to care that their profits come at the expense of future generations' economic well-being. But if our goal is to give expert managers the time necessary to create long-term, sustainable, and innovative businesses, the answer is a clear "no."[147]

On the other hand, having contributed to creating the structural flaws that created the crisis, activist investors essentially set out the crisis itself. Brian Cheffins found, for example, that except for "a few hedge funds" institutional shareholders "were largely mute as share prices fell."[148] Even in the U.K., where shareholders already possess more governance powers than do shareholders of U.S. firms, big institutional investors simply stood by as the crisis unfolded.[149] In contrast, directors of troubled firms commonly played an active role in responding to the crisis, as evidenced by their orchestration of CEO turnover at a rate far exceeding the norm in public companies.[150]

In sum, the separation of ownership and control did not cause the financial crisis of 2008. Efforts to reduce the degree to which ownership and control are

---

145. Lawrence Mitchell, Protect Industry From Predatory Speculators, Fin. Times, July 8, 2009.
146. Id.
147. Id.
148. Brian R. Cheffins, Did Corporate Governance, "Fail" During the 2008 Stock Market Meltdown? The Case of the S&P 500, 65 Bus. Law. 1, 3 (2009).
149. Brian R. Cheffins, The Stewardship Code's Achilles' Heel, 73 Modern L. Rev. 1004, 1005–06 (2010).
150. Cheffins, supra note 148, at 39–40.

separated by empowering shareholders will not help prevent future crises. To the contrary, such efforts undermine the system of corporate governance that served us well for a very long time and that, if protected from the reformists' zeal, can continue to do so when the current crisis abates.

IF INVESTORS VALUED GOVERNANCE PARTICIPATION RIGHTS, THE MARKET WOULD PROVIDE THEM

Delaware state corporate law prohibited nothing Dodd-Frank mandates. Anyone seeking to take a company public could have conferred Dodd-Frank style rights on shareholders in the corporation's organic documents. Accordingly, if it is true that the "mechanism by which stocks are valued ensures that the price reflects the terms of governance and operation,"[151] which seems to be the case, there is a logical negative inference to be drawn from the race to the top account:

> Although agency costs are high, many managerial teams are scrupulously dedicated to investors' interests. . . . By increasing the value of the firm, they would do themselves a favor (most managers' compensation is linked to the stock market, and they own stock too). Nonexistence of securities said to be beneficial to investors is telling.[152]

By the same token, if investors valued the rights Dodd-Frank confers upon them, we would expect to have observed entrepreneurs taking a company public to offer such rights either through appropriate provisions in the firm's organic documents or by lobbying the Delaware legislature to provide such rights off the rack in the corporation code. Because we observe neither, we may conclude investors do not value these rights.

A NOTE ON PROXY ADVISORY FIRMS

In arguing that institutional investors have incentives to be rationally apathetic, we emphasized the costs entailed in monitoring and responding to problems at portfolio companies. These costs could be reduced if activist investors could make use of economies of scale by developing standardized voting procedures on recurring issues and standard responses to common types of

---

151. Frank H. Easterbrook & Daniel R. Fischel, The Economic Structure of Corporate Law 18 (1991).
152. Id. at 205.

managerial derelictions. We in fact observed just such a response very early in the evolution of institutional investor activism as many institutions adopted standard voting practices on issues such as takeover defenses.

Significant savings, however, would require collective action. Only by clubbing together in monitoring their portfolio companies, could institutions truly achieve economies of scale. As long as they were obliged to act individually, the size and high rate of turnover of their portfolios made achieving real economies of scale impractical.

The emergence of Institutional Shareholder Services (ISS) offered a solution to these problems. ISS was founded in 1985 to provide proxy advisory services to institutional investors.[153] The premise was that institutions could outsource to ISS the tasks of monitoring corporate governance at portfolio firms and making decisions about how to vote their shares.

ISS got a major boost in 1988 when the Department of Labor announced that ERISA pension plan fiduciaries had a fiduciary duty to make informed decisions about how they voted shares of portfolio companies. In response, pension plans began to rely on ISS for analysis of issues upon which a shareholder vote would be required and advice as to the best voting decision. A similar 2003 SEC ruling that mutual funds and other investment company advisors must adopt policies designed to ensure that shares of portfolio companies are voted in the best interests of their clients added a whole new class of institutions that outsourced their proxy decision making to ISS.

Today, ISS services some 1700 institutional investor clients, which collectively manage some $25 trillion in equity securities. The goal of reducing the expenses of activism through economies of scale thus seems well within reach.

ISS has proven highly successful at influencing shareholder voting. By some estimates, an ISS recommendation can effect a swing of 15 to 20 percent in a proxy vote.[154] Although competitors have entered the market for proxy advisory services, ISS remains the most powerful player in that market. Only one other advisory service, Glass, Lewis & Co., has a measurable effect on the outcome of shareholder votes and its impact remains minor compared to that of ISS.[155]

The shareholder empowerment provisions of Dodd-Frank are widely expected to further enhance ISS's influence, especially with respect to executive

153. ISS was acquired by RiskMetrics Group in 2006. For purposes of semantic consistency, however, I shall refer to it as ISS throughout.

154. David Larker & Bryan Tayan, RiskMetrics: The Uninvited Guest at the Equity Table 2 (Stanford Grad. Sch. Bus. Closer Look series CGRP-01, May 17, 2010), http://ssrn.com/abstract=1677630.

155. Stephen Choi. et al., The Power of Proxy Advisors: Myth or Reality?, 59 Emory L.J. 869 (2010). On the other hand, this study also argues that "popular accounts substantially overstate the influence of ISS" and that "the impact of an ISS recommendation is reduced greatly once company- and firm-specific factors important to investors are taken into consideration." Id.

compensation. Institutional investors will look to ISS for guidance on both the say when on pay and say on pay votes. The biggest effect of Dodd-Frank on proxy advisory services, however, is likely to come indirectly via NYSE Rule 452.

The NYSE rule deals with voting of shares held in brokerage accounts. The typical retail investor account is set up with the broker as the legal owner of the shares and the investor as the beneficial owner thereof. Under state law, the brokers therefore are the ones who vote the shares. Under federal law, brokers are obliged to request voting instructions from their client. Many retail investors, however, fail to provide instructions. In such cases, Rule 452 permits the broker to vote the shares in its discretion with respect to routine matters. As to non-routine matters, however, a broker without instructions must abstain.

In the past, brokers routinely voted as management recommended. As a result, management often had a substantial base of support on many issues. A 2009 amendment to Rule 452 significantly altered the environment, however, by changing the treatment of an uncontested director election from a routine to a non-routine matter. As a result, the number of retail investor-owned shares voted in director elections has fallen, increasing the proportion of institutional investor votes as a percentage of those being cast, and thereby enhancing the effect of an ISS recommendation.

Dodd-Frank § 957 will have a similar effect in a potentially wide range of issues. At a minimum, § 957 requires that votes on executive compensation be deemed non-routine. The proportion of votes coming from institutional investors therefore will rise with respect to both say on pay and say when on pay decisions. Because § 957 directs the SEC to undertake a rule-making proceeding to determine whether there are "other significant matters" that should be deemed non-routine, which proceeding is expected to be completed by late 2012, ISS's influence likely will continue to grow. Indeed, it seems fair to say that Dodd-Frank does more to empower ISS than it does shareholders.

Despite its success (or, perhaps, because of it), ISS has been controversial. Some critics argue that ISS is too rigid and mechanical in its advice. Martin Lipton complains, for example, that ISS routinely recommends against reelection of a board's nominating committee if those members allow the firm's CEO to provide recommendations or advice:

> It would be a totally dysfunctional process if input and advice from the CEO were prohibited until after the committee meets and makes its decisions. There is nothing in the NYSE rule or "best practices" that warrants restricting the CEO from voicing advice or opinion until after the committee has acted.[156]

156. Martin Lipton, ISS Goes with Form over Substance, Harv. L. Sch. Forum Corp. Gov. & Fin. Reg. (Mar. 17, 2011), http://blogs.law.harvard.edu/corpgov/2011/03/17/iss-goes-with-form-over-substance/.

A related example of excessive rigidity on these issues came in 2004, when ISS urged its clients to oppose reelecting Warren Buffett as a director of Coca-Cola because Buffett did not satisfy ISS's strict definition of director independence. Shortly thereafter, CalPERS announced that it would oppose Buffett's reelection on the same grounds. Critics of the ISS and CalPERS positions pointed out that Warren Buffett is probably the most respected investor of all time, with a long record of integrity. At the time in question, Buffet's Berkshire Hathaway Company owned almost 10 percent of Coca-Cola's stock, which meant that his personal financial interests were closely aligned with those of other shareholders (albeit not perfectly). Buffett qualified as an independent director under the NYSE's listing standards. As I argued at the time, if "Buffett doesn't qualify as independent under the ISS and CalPERS standards, the problem is with the standards not Mr. Buffett."[157]

Critics link this sort of check-the-box mentality back to the very reason for outfits like ISS to exist; namely, the cost associated with making informed voting decisions about numerous issues posed on the proxy statements of the thousands of publicly traded companies. The globalization of institutional investor holdings has compounded the problem by forcing ISS to stretch its resources to include many foreign issuers. In 2009, for example, ISS had to prepare voting recommendations with respect to more than 37,000 issuers around the world. The constantly growing number of voting recommendations that must be made, most of which are concentrated into the three- to four-month annual meeting season, reportedly forces even ISS to automate decision making to the fullest possible extent and, accordingly, to rely on one-size-fits-all standards instead of giving careful consideration to the specific needs and circumstances of each individual firm.

Finally, there is the question of accountability. Although both the SEC and the Department of Labor are considering regulation of the proxy advisory business, as of this writing they remain essentially unregulated. Ironically, market forces are the only thing holding ISS accountable; i.e., the same forces most shareholder power proponents claim do not work when it comes to holding management accountable.

Taken together, these concerns raise serious issues as to whether shareholder activism is an appropriate solution to the principal-agent problems of corporate governance. The view that institutional investor activists will carefully scrutinize portfolio companies to reach informed voting decisions is exposed as a fiction. Instead, shareholder activism depends on the whims of a

157. Stephen M. Bainbridge, Directors Cut?, ProfessorBainbridge.com (Apr. 29, 2004), http://www.professorbainbridge.com/professorbainbridgecom/2004/04/directors-cut.html.

single proxy advisor who offers limited transparency and is largely unaccountable, essentially unregulated, and poorly informed.[158]

A NOTE ON THE GOVERNMENT AS SHAREHOLDER

The various corporate bailouts of 2008 and 2009 resulted in the federal government becoming a shareholder in almost 700 of the nation's banks, as well as major businesses such as AIG, Fannie Mae, Freddie Mac, Chrysler, and GM. In many of these cases, the government's stake and the rules to which that stake were subjected turned the government into a de facto controlling shareholder.

To be sure, when President Obama was asked: "what kind of shareholder are you going to be," he responded that "our first role should be shareholders that are looking to get out." Even so, the precedent set is a troubling one.

Experience in countries where government ownership of financial institutions is more common confirms that governments often use their ownership stakes to advance political agendas that may be contrary to the interests of the enterprise and/or its other shareholders. Law professor J.W. Verret has collected a number of examples in which the Obama administration and Congress likewise exercised their influence over government-controlled corporations for political purposes.[159] When GM tried to cancel a contract with a Montana source of palladium in favor of a cheaper foreign source, Congressional pressure forced GM to continue using the Montana source.[160] When GM tried to close many dealerships, Congressional pressure forced GM to reinstate them.[161] In other instances, Verret shows that the "government gives preferential regulatory treatment to the entities it controls."[162]

The key problem is that by virtue of a combination of traditional sovereign immunity principles and various exemptions and waivers contained in the governing legislation, the federal government is essentially immune from the fiduciary obligations of controlling shareholders. Likewise, the government is effectively immune from stock exchange listing standards intended to prevent

158. See Choi & Fisch, supra note 106, at 318 (explaining that the trend of pension funds delegating decisions to ISS "raises a substantial concern that the effectiveness of institutional activism will be limited by fund agency problems, including the economic incentives of those exercising delegated governance powers").

159. J.W. Verret, The Bailout Through a Public Choice Lens: Government-Controlled Corporations as a Mechanism for Rent Transfer, 40 Seton Hall L. Rev. 1521 (2010).

160. Id. at 1524.

161. Id.

162. Id.

rent-seeking by controlling shareholders. This lack of accountability poses significant risks for other shareholders. Congress would do well to revisit this issue to impose limits on the federal government's powers in this area before the next economic crisis triggers calls for another round of government investment in private companies.

Conclusion

For almost a century, Delaware has had little difficulty facing off competitors who challenged its position as chief provider of corporate governance law. In the wake of the financial crises of the last decade, however, Delaware now faces a real threat. Unlike the horizontal state-to-state competition of earlier periods, this threat emanates from above. The sweeping constitutional powers of the federal government over commerce, coupled with Washington's power under the Supremacy Clause to preempt state law, means that Delaware can no longer prevail simply by offering a product of superior quality. As our case studies of the rules that merged from Sarbanes-Oxley and Dodd-Frank demonstrated, the federal government can—and all too often does—preempt state corporate law with new federal mandates even if they are so bad as to qualify for the sobriquet quack corporate governance.

THE GLOBAL IMPACT OF FEDERALIZING CORPORATE GOVERNANCE

We saw in chapter 1 that there is a long-running debate over whether states compete in providing corporate governance regulations and, if so, whether that competition produces a race to the top or a race to the bottom. Wherever one comes out on that debate, the case studies of federal corporate governance regulation confirm that the new form of vertical competition between the states and Washington is no improvement.

It is only when one steps back from individual case studies and evaluates the systemic impact of the new federal rules, however, that the true scope of the problem becomes clear. To be sure, it is still too soon to draw firm conclusions about Dodd-Frank, although the preliminary case-by-case evidence is discouraging. The evidence from Sarbanes-Oxley, however, is quite conclusive.

Given the magnitude of the crises that bracketed the decade, U.S. capital markets inevitably suffered throughout much of the decade. In the wake of the dotcom bubble's bursting as the decade opened, the secondary equity trading markets suffered the first three-year consecutive stock market decline since the 1930s. In turn, the financial crisis at the end of the decade triggered an extended bear market that ran from October 2007 to March 2009.

The primary equity markets also suffered for much of the decade. A decline in primary market transactions like IPOs was to be expected given the adverse economic climate, of course. The data, however, reveal a far more troubling trend. U.S. capital markets steadily became less competitive globally throughout the decade.

The U.S. share of the global IPO market declined, for example, as foreign firms no longer treated the American stock markets as their first choice for raising capital. Likewise, foreign companies long present in the United States delisted from U.S. stock markets, while U.S. firms went dark or private at an unusually high rate. At around the same time, the Eurobond market surpassed the U.S. bond markets in the global share of debt issuances.

The growing concern surrounding these developments prompted three major studies, each of which reached broadly similar conclusions and offered comparable policy prescriptions: the Bloomberg-Schumer Report,[1] the Paulson Committee Interim Report,[2] and the Chamber Report.[3] Taken together, and evaluated in light of subsequent developments, the evidence they gathered confirms that the U.S. capital markets became less competitive vis-à-vis other markets in the last decade.

In the 1990s, the number of foreign issuers listed on the NYSE roughly quadrupled, with NASDAQ experiencing similar growth, while London and the other major European exchanges were losing market share. Since 2000, however, the situation appears to have reversed. Using global IPOs as an indicator of the relative competitiveness of capital markets, for example, there

---

1. Michael R. Bloomberg & Charles E. Schumer, Sustaining New York's and the U.S.' Global Financial Services Leadership (2007) [hereinafter the Bloomberg-Schumer Report].

2. Comm. on Capital Mkts. Reg., Interim Report of the Committee on Capital Markets Regulation (2006). The Committee on Capital markets regulation—or, as it is better known—the Paulson Committee subsequently issued a follow up report identifying thirteen competitive measures that the Committee tracks on a quarterly basis. Comm. on Capital Mkts. Regulation, The Competitive Position of the U.S. Public Equity Market (2007) [hereinafter the Paulson Committee Report].

3. U.S. Chamber of Comm., Capital Markets, Corporate Governance, and the Future of the U.S. Economy (2006) [hereinafter the Chamber Report].

was a dramatic decline in the U.S. market share from 48 percent to 8 percent between 2000 and 2006.[4]

Although the Paulson Committee reported slight improvement in 2008 and 2009, by the first quarter of 2010 the Committee was again reporting continued "deterioration in the competitiveness of U.S. public equity markets."[5] As a result, by nearly all measures, the U.S. equity capital market today remains "much less competitive than it was historically."[6]

There are many factors contributing to this decline. It is generally agreed, for example, that the growing maturity and liquidity of European and Asian markets is a very important factor. All three studies, however, concluded that the regulatory burden imposed by Sarbanes-Oxley was a major contributing factor. According to the Paulson Commission, for example, "one important factor contributing to this trend is the growth of U.S. regulatory compliance costs and liability risks compared with other developed and respected market centers."[7]

The same decline occurred in the bond markets and for the same reason. A study of foreign firms' decisions to issue bonds in the United States before and after Sarbanes-Oxley was adopted found that foreign firms were less likely to do so in the latter period. The authors argue their results are consistent with a significant shift in the costs (upward) and benefits (downward) associated with a U.S. debt offering post-SOX.[8]

Regulatory Compliance Costs

Issuers seeking access to the U.S. capital markets face a daunting array of complex and costly regulatory requirements. In contrast to the U.K., where the Financial Services Authority is the sole regulator, U.S. capital-market participants are slotted into multiple regulatory silos, each with one or more government regulatory agencies. Dealing with multiple bodies of regulation and multiple regulators inevitably adds complexity, redundancy, and cost to

---

4. Luigi Zingales, Is the U.S. Capital Market Losing its Competitive Edge 2 (ECGI Fin. Working Paper 192/2007). Global IPOs are those in which the issuer sells shares outside of its domestic market.

5. Press Release, Comm. on Capital Mkts. Reg., Q1 2010 Sees Fresh Deterioration in Competitiveness of U.S. Public Equity Markets, Reversing Mild Improvements (June 2, 2010).

6. Press Release, Comm. on Capital Mkts. Reg., Third Quarter 2009 Demonstrates First Signs of Mild Improvement in Competitiveness of U.S. Public Equity Markets, Reversing Mild Improvements (Dec. 1, 2009).

7. Paulson Committee Report, supra note 2, at x.

8. Yu Gao, The Sarbanes-Oxley Act and the Choice of Bond Market by Foreign Firms (March 22, 2011), http://ssrn.com/abstract=1792963.

transactions. Accordingly, as the Chamber concluded, "this patchwork structure is not keeping up with the extraordinary growth and internationalization of our markets."[9]

In the U.K., the FSA has adopted a so-called principles-based approach to regulation, in contrast to the rules-based approach of U.S. securities regulation. This distinction plays out in three key dimensions.[10] First, rules generally are detailed and complex, while principles are broad and abstract. Second, rules are defined ex ante with little scope for ex post discretion, while principles are set out broadly ex ante and are developed ex post for application in a highly contextual way. Third, principles entrust a substantial amount of discretion to regulators to make decisions on a case-by-case basis, while rules do not do so.

Proponents of principles-based regulatory schemes argue that they allow firms to adapt their individual compliance procedures to their own unique business needs and practices. In contrast, rules-based systems assume one size fits all. In addition, principles-based regulatory schemes are less adversarial and litigious than rules-based ones because regulators in the former tend to focus on guidance rather than litigation. The Bloomberg-Schumer Report argued that these differences put U.S. capital markets at a significant disadvantage:

> Without the benefit of accepted principles to guide them, U.S. regulators default to imposing regulations required by various legislative mandates, many of which date back several decades. These mandates are not subject to major reviews or revisions and therefore tend to fall behind day-to-day practice. This failure to keep pace with the times has made it hard for business leaders to understand how the missions of different regulators relate to their business, and this in turn means that regulators have come to be viewed as unpredictable in their actions toward business. The cost of compliance has also risen dramatically over the last several years. Securities firms reported on average almost one regulatory inquiry per trading day, and large firms experienced more than three times that level. The cost of compliance estimated in a Securities Industry Association report had reached $25 billion in the securities industry alone in 2005 (up from $13 billion in 2002). This increase is equivalent to almost 5 percent of the industry's annual net revenues. Although there are benefits from an increase in compliance-related expenditures, the report found that "a substantial portion of these increased costs were avoidable, reflecting, among other things: duplication of

9. Chamber Report, supra note 3, at 5.

10. See generally Lawrence A. Cunningham, A Prescription to Retire the Rhetoric of 'Principles-Based Systems' in Corporate Law, Securities Regulation, and Accounting, 60 Vand. L. Rev. 1411 (2007), which nevertheless criticizes the principles versus rules dichotomy as imprecise and inexact.

examinations, regulations and supervisory actions; inconsistencies/lack of harmonization in rules and regulations; ambiguity; and delays in obtaining clear guidance."[11]

The problem is not simply the rules-based nature of the U.S. system, but also the sheer volume of regulations with which issuers must comply:

> A recent study by the Federal Financial Institutions Examination Council, the coordinating group of U.S. banking and thrift regulators, revealed that more than 800 different regulations have been imposed on banks and other deposit-gathering institutions since 1989. Regulations to implement the legislative requirements of the Sarbanes-Oxley Act of 2002 (Sarbanes-Oxley) are a good example. They are universally viewed by CEOs and other executives surveyed as being too expensive for the benefits of good governance they confer. Consequently, Sarbanes-Oxley is viewed both domestically and internationally as stifling innovation. "The Sarbanes-Oxley Act and the litigious environment are creating a more risk-averse culture in the United States," one former senior investment banker stated. "We are simply pushing people to do more business overseas rather than addressing the real issues head on."[12]

The Sarbanes-Oxley Debacle

Over the last decade, the Sarbanes-Oxley Act has emerged as the poster child for burdensome compliance costs. As our case studies of its various provisions demonstrate, its reputation is well deserved. In addition to the direct provision-by-provision compliance costs recounted in those case studies, firms incurred a number of indirect costs. Director workload increased, for example, forcing firms to increase director compensation. Audit committees have been especially affected; on average meeting more than twice as often post Sarbanes-Oxley as they did pre-SOX. Director liability exposure also increased due to the harsh criminal and civil sanctions associated with violations of § 404 and other Sarbanes-Oxley requirements. As a result, not only did director compensation rise, but D&O insurance premiums more than doubled post-SOX.

These costs are disproportionately borne by smaller public firms. Director compensation at small firms increased from $5.91 paid to non-employee directors on every $1,000 in sales in the pre-SOX period to $9.76 on every $1,000 in sales in the post-SOX period.[13] In contrast, large firms incurred

---

11. Bloomberg-Schumer Report, supra note 1, at 83.
12. Id.
13. Stephen M. Bainbridge, The Complete Guide to Sarbanes-Oxley 5 (2007).

13 cents in director cash compensation per $1,000 in sales in the pre-SOX period, which increased only to 15 cents in the post-SOX period.[14] Likewise, companies with annual sales less than $250 million incurred $1.56 million in external resource costs to comply with § 404.[15] In contrast, firms with annual sales of $1–2 billion incurred an average of $2.4 million in such costs.[16] Accordingly, while Sarbanes-Oxley compliance costs do scale, they do so only to a rather limited extent. At many smaller firms, the disproportionately heavy additional costs imposed by § 404 are a significant percentage of their annual revenues. For those firms operating on thin margins, Sarbanes-Oxley compliance costs can actually make the difference between profitability and losing money.

Both the recurring nature and disproportionate impact of these costs is confirmed by a recent study of the impact Sarbanes-Oxley had on the operating profitability of a sample of 1,428 firms. Average cash flows declined by 1.3 percent post-SOX. Costs ranged from $6 million for small firms to $39 million for large firms. These costs were not limited to one-time first-year implementation expenses. Instead, substantial costs and reduced profits recurred throughout the four-year study period. In the aggregate, the sample firms lost about $75 billion over that period.[17]

These costs have substantially distorted corporate financing decisions. On the one hand, Sarbanes-Oxley discouraged privately held corporations from going public. Start-up companies opted for "financing from private-equity firms," rather than using an IPO to raise money from the capital markets. Because "going public is an important venture capital exit strategy, partially closing the exit could impede start-up financing, and therefore make it harder to get ideas off the ground."[18] In addition to the decline in domestic IPOs, there was a decrease in new foreign listings on U.S. secondary markets.[19] The net effect was the declining market share of U.S. markets in such transactions as global IPOs. "Martin Graham, director of the London Stock Exchange's (LSE's) market services, said that Sarbanes-Oxley has "undoubtedly assisted

14. Id.
15. Id.
16. Id.
17. Anwer S. Ahmed et al., How Costly is the Sarbanes Oxley Act? Evidence on the Effects of the Act on Corporate Profitability (Sept. 2009), available at http://ssrn.com/abstract=1480395.
18. Bainbridge, supra note 13, at 6 (quoting Larry Ribstein). The undesirability of becoming subject to the Sarbanes-Oxley regime is further confirmed by evidence of a trend for start ups to follow an exit strategy of selling to private rather than public companies. Ehud Kamar et al., Going-Private Decisions and the Sarbanes-Oxley Act of 2002: A Cross-Country Analysis (Rand Working Paper No. WR-300-2-EMKF, 2008).
19. See Joseph D. Piotroski & Suraj Srinivasan, Regulation and Bonding: The Sarbanes-Oxley Act and the Flow of International Listings, 46 J. Acct. Res. 383 (2008).

our efforts" and emphasized the LSE's ability to draw new listings from foreign companies."[20]

Conversely, there has been a trend toward public companies exiting the public capital markets. A Foley & Lardner survey, for example, found that after Sarbanes-Oxley some 21 percent of responding publicly held corporations were considering going private.[21] A study by William Carney of 114 companies going private in 2004 found that 44 specifically cited Sarbanes-Oxley compliance costs as one of the reasons they were doing so.[22] Several other studies likewise report that the increased costs associated with Sarbanes-Oxley are one reason for an increase in the number of public corporations deciding to go private, for example.[23]

In light of this evidence, it is hardly surprising that all of the major reports on capital market competitiveness viewed Sarbanes-Oxley and, especially, § 404 as a significant drag on the competitiveness of those markets. The Bloomberg-Schumer Report cited the "concerns of small companies and non-US issuers regarding the Section 404 compliance costs involved in a U.S. listing."[24] The Paulson Committee noted that § 404 compliance "costs can be especially significant for smaller companies and foreign companies contemplating entry into the U.S. market."[25] The Chamber of Commerce argued that:

> European, Chinese, and Indian companies that do not list their shares on U.S. markets are not required to comply with Section 404. They can save that money—this year and for every year hereafter—and direct it toward R&D, customer discounts, or a host of other uses that serve to improve their long-term competitiveness and make it that much harder for U.S. companies to compete.[26]

20. Chamber Report, supra note 3, at 7.
21. Bainbridge, supra note 13, at 6.
22. William J. Carney, The Costs of Being Public After Sarbanes-Oxley: The Irony of 'Going Private,' 55 Emory L.J. 141 (2006).
23. See, e.g., Stanley B. Block, The Latest Movement To Going Private: An Empirical Study, J. Applied Fin., Spring/Summer 2004, at 36; Ellen Engel et al., The Sarbanes-Oxley Act and Firms' Going-Private Decisions, 44 J. Acct. & Econ. 116 (2007); Christian Leuz et al., Why Do Firms Go Dark? Causes and Economic Consequences of Voluntary SEC Deregistrations, 45 J. Acct. & Econ. 181 (2008).
24. Bloomberg-Schumer Report, supra note 1, at 20.
25. Paulson Committee Report, supra note 2, at 5. The Committee downgraded the importance of § 404 relative to the other concerns it identified, which Romano suggests may have been the result of political calculations about the feasibility of obtaining legislative approval for the Committee's various recommendations and the Committee's focus on the problems faced by the stock markets rather than those of small companies. Roberta Romano, Does the Sarbanes-Oxley Act Have a Future?, 26 Yale J. on Reg. 229, 246 (2009).
26. Chamber Report, supra note 3, at 14.

Roberta Romano's detailed review of the empirical studies confirms the official commissions' critique. Romano concludes her review of the evidence:

> Sarbanes-Oxley . . . adversely affected U.S. exchanges through the loss of small-firm listings. The contraction in investing opportunities has, no doubt, adversely affected U.S. investors as well, as they would have to bear currency risk and the other transaction costs of investing abroad rather than domestically in order to invest in such firms. In sum, a fair reading of the empirical literature investigating U.S. capital-market competitiveness post-SOX indicates, at a minimum, that the statute has negatively impacted the stock exchanges' competitiveness due to losses of small-firm listings. Those are also the firms that have been shown to encounter the greatest proportionate operating cost increase due to Sarbanes-Oxley, in the literature documenting the changing cost of being a public company post-enactment.[27]

Egregious as it was, the failure of Congress and the SEC to accurately forecast the impact of § 404 in particular and Sarbanes-Oxley in general was not especially surprising in retrospect. As Roberta Romano observed:

> Simply put, the corporate governance provisions were not a focus of careful deliberation by Congress. Sarbanes-Oxley was emergency legislation, enacted under conditions of limited legislative debate, during a media frenzy involving several high-profile corporate fraud and insolvency cases. These occurred in conjunction with an economic downturn, what appeared to be a free-falling stock market, and a looming election campaign in which corporate scandals would be an issue. The healthy ventilation of issues that occurs in the usual give-and-take negotiations over competing policy positions, which works to improve the quality of decision making, did not occur in the case of Sarbanes-Oxley.[28]

It's hardly surprising that legislation crafted in such a haphazard fashion turned out to be far more costly than anyone expected.

CAN ANYTHING BE DONE?

There are three major reasons why federal intervention in corporate governance tends to be ill-conceived. First, federal bubble laws tend to be enacted in

27. Roberta Romano, Does the Sarbanes-Oxley Act Have a Future?, 26 Yale J. on Reg. 229, 255 (2009).
28. Roberta Romano, The Sarbanes-Oxley Act and the Making of Quack Corporate Governance, 114 Yale L.J. 1521, 1528 (2005).

a climate of political pressure that does not facilitate careful analysis of costs and benefits. Second, federal bubble laws tend to be driven by populist anti-corporate emotions. Finally, the content of federal bubble laws is often derived from prepackaged proposals advocated by policy entrepreneurs skeptical of corporations and markets.

The problem is compounded because the supremacy of federal law and the uniform opposition of Congress and the SEC to private ordering eliminates opportunities for experimentation with alternative solutions to the many difficult regulatory problems that arise in corporate law. As Justice Brandeis pointed out many years ago, "It is one of the happy incidents of the federal system that a single courageous State may, if its citizens choose, serve as a laboratory; and try novel social and economic experiments without risk to the rest of country."[29] So long as state legislation is limited to regulation of firms incorporated within the state, as it generally is, there is no risk of conflicting rules applying to the same corporation. Experimentation thus does not result in confusion, but instead may lead to more efficient corporate law rules.

In contrast, the uniformity imposed by federal law precludes experimentation with differing modes of regulation. As such, there will be no opportunity for new and better regulatory ideas to be developed—no "laboratory" of federalism. Likewise, the persistent refusal to accommodate private ordering eliminates solutions from emerging from competition in the market. Instead, the federalization of corporate governance has resulted in rules that were wrong from the outset or may quickly become obsolete, but are effectively carved into stone with little prospect for change.

In sum, the federal role in corporate governance appears to be a case of what Robert Higgs identified as the ratchet effect.[30] Higgs demonstrated that wars and other major crises typically trigger a dramatic growth in the size of government, accompanied by higher taxes, greater regulation, and loss of civil liberties. Once the crisis ends, government may shrink somewhat in size and power, but rarely back to pre-crisis levels. Just as a ratchet wrench works only in one direction, the size and scope of government tends to move in only one direction—upward—because the interest groups that favored the changes now have an incentive to preserve the new status quo, as do the bureaucrats who gained new powers and prestige. Hence, each crisis has the effect of ratcheting up the long-term size and scope of government.

29. New State Ice Co. v. Liebmann, 285 U.S. 262, 311 (1932) (Brandeis, J., dissenting).

30. See Robert Higgs, Crisis and Leviathan: Critical Episodes in the Growth of American Government 150-56 (1987) (describing the 'ratchet effect' by which Congress increases not only the scale but also the scope of the federal government on a permanent basis).

We now observe the same pattern in corporate governance. As we have seen, the federal government rarely intrudes in this sphere except when there is a crisis. At that point, policy entrepreneurs favoring federalization of corporate governance spring into action, hijacking the legislative response to the crisis to advance their agenda. Although there may be some subsequent retreat, such as Dodd-Frank's § 404 relief for small reporting companies, the overall trend has been for each major financial crisis of the last century to result in an expansion of the federal role.

The take-home lesson thus is that the states—especially Delaware and the drafters of the MBCA—must do a better job of playing defense. The game must be played in Delaware not Washington. The interest groups that dominate Delaware politics must anticipate possible instances of federal intervention and proactively preempt them through new legislation or case law whenever possible. In addition, they must develop sufficient strength in Washington to successfully lobby against federal intervention. To be sure, the political dynamics described in Part I may render such a defensive strategy unavailing in times of crisis. If Delaware sits out future crises as it did in 2008, however, there will be no resistance to the steady federalization of corporate governance.

IN CLOSING

Like their predecessors in Sarbanes-Oxley, the six key corporate governance provisions of Dodd-Frank satisfy the key criteria of quack corporate governance. A powerful interest-group coalition centered on activist institutional investors hijacked the legislative process so as to achieve long-standing policy goals essentially unrelated to the causes or consequences of the financial crisis that began back in 2007. Without exception, the proposals lack strong empirical or theoretical justification. To the contrary, there are theoretical and empirical reasons to believe that each will be at best bootless and most will be affirmatively bad public policy. Finally, each erodes the system of competitive federalism that is the unique genius of American corporate law by displacing state regulation with federal law. Unfortunately, this has become a recurring pattern whenever the federal government is moved to action by a new economic crisis. The federalization of corporate governance thus continues to creep ahead.

Postscript to the Paperback Edition

This book offered three basic claims: (1) the federal government normally intervenes in corporate governance only in response to a serious financial crisis; (2) when the federal government does intervene, the results are almost always flawed in very substantial ways; and (3) federal intervention operates like a ratchet, always increasing but never being pared back. In the years since this book was first published, nothing has happened to alter those conclusions. To the extent the federal government has acted in the corporate governance space, it has done so only through rulemaking proceedings—such as the SEC's adoption of the pay ratio disclosure rules—that were mandated by Dodd-Frank. The scope of the rules created by SOX and Dodd-Frank, moreover, remains as expansive—and as flawed—as ever.

Having said that, however, there have been developments in two specific areas covered by this book that warrant updating: executive compensation and shareholder activism. In both, the flaws identified in this book in the regimes mandated by SOX and Dodd-Frank proved especially problematic.

EXECUTIVE COMPENSATION

Executive pay critics saw the financial crisis as a once-in-a-lifetime opportunity to impose federal limits on what they saw as excessive compensation. As my UCLA School of Law colleagues Steven Bank and George Georgiev have demonstrated, however, "the main result has been a thicker executive compensation rulebook, more complex pay structures, and a heavy compliance burden that is only set to increase as a result of major recent SEC initiatives."[1]

---

1. Steven A. Bank & George S. Georgiev, Paying High for Low Performance, 100 Minn. L. Rev. Headnotes __ (forthcoming 2016).

CEO pay has continued to increase and there is no strong evidence of a greater link between pay and performance.[2] Put simply, the regime described in Chapter 4 has failed to achieve its intended purposes while burdening companies with higher costs and investors with information they neither need nor want.

The much-ballyhooed say on pay rule, for example, has done little to justify the costs companies and investors incur. In the first four shareholder annual meeting cycles in which the rule was in effect, the average shareholder vote in favor of the company's compensation scheme was over 90% and shareholder disapproved plans at only about 2% of companies holding a vote.[3] To be sure, there is some evidence that say on pay caused some companies to change the mix of executive compensation, but net pay in all forms at those companies nevertheless increased.[4]

As Chapter 4 explained, Dodd-Frank required the SEC to pay disclosure rules in two areas. Section 953(a) of the Act required "a clear description...the relationship between executive compensation actually paid and the financial performance of the issuer, taking into account any change in the value of the shares of stock and dividends of the issuer and any distributions." It took the SEC the better part of five years to propose such a rule. The rule the SEC finally proposed in April 2015, moreover, is seriously flawed. It requires a rigid, one-size-fits-all comparison of compensation actually paid to the CEO and certain other senior executives to the company's total stock return (TSR) and a comparison of the latter figure to the average (TSR) of selected peer companies. In dissenting from the rulemaking, SEC Commissioner Daniel Gallagher observed that "the stock-based TSR can be prone to emphasizing short-term corporate goals over long-term ones."[5] In addition, the peer group selection process likely will be the subject of substantial gaming by companies so as to produce the most favorable result. Finally, the mandated metrics can be distorted by one-time events that render the disclosures meaningless.[6] Put simply, "both the 'pay' and 'performance' in 'pay-versus-performance' are simply too complex as concepts to fit comfortably within the table required by the SEC's proposed disclosure rule."[7]

The SEC was even more dilatory in implementing Dodd-Frank § 953(b)'s requirement that companies disclose the median annual total compensation

2. Jill E. Fisch, The Mess at Morgan: Risk, Incentives and Shareholder Empowerment, 83 U. Cin. L. Rev. 651, 671 (2015).
3. Id.
4. Bank & Georgiev, supra note 1.
5. SEC Proposes Pay-Versus-Performance, Security-Based Swaps Rules, 34 No. 6 Banking & Fin. Services Pol'y Rep. 28 (2015).
6. Bank & Georgiev, supra note 1.
7. Id.

of all corporate employees other than the CEO, the annual total compensation of the CEO, and the ratio of the two (thereby sparing readers the need to reach for the calculator app on their smartphones). As finally proposed in August 2015, the rule attempted to offer companies some relief from the potentially burdensome requirements of gathering the requisite data. Corporations will be permitted to select their own methodology for identifying the median employee and that employee's compensation. Corporations only need to undertake the median employee determination once every three years. Although beneficial for individual companies, it is noteworthy that these concessions undermine the whole point of the rule by making comparisons across companies and across time more difficult.

Of particular relevance for large multinational corporations, the SEC specifically authorized the use of statistical sampling rather than requiring a census of the entire employee population. Such multinationals will also benefit from provisions allowing, in addition, companies to exclude data about non-U.S. employees located in countries in which data privacy regulations preclude them from complying with the rule and creating a de minimis exemption for non-U.S. employees. Even so, as commentator Marc Hodak observed, there are many unanswered questions about the rule:

> How, exactly, will this "simple benchmark" help investors do those things? What number, or range, for this ratio tells an investor that a company is treating its average workers well or poorly, or that a company is paying its CEO reasonably? What economic or financial standards can be created using this or other data to enable investors to figure these things out?[8]

As such, it's hard to argue with Hodak's view that "the SEC is simply being used in an experiment in social engineering."[9] It's equally hard to argue with his conclusion that the experiment will fail, as have so many before. Among other things, "the rule could be gamed in particularly damaging ways. For example, companies can make their pay ratio look better by cutting the lowest-paid workers from the payroll via outsourcing, without making any changes to CEO pay."[10]

---

8. Marc Hodak, Welcome the CEO Pay Ratio, HodakValue.com (August 6, 2015), available at http://hodakvalue.com/blog/welcome-the-ceo-pay-ratio/.
9. Id.
10. Bank & Georgiev, supra note 1.

Compensation Committees

Dodd-Frank § 952 effectively codified the existing SRO compensation committee requirements, while also requiring the SEC to adopt a new rule tightening the standard for determining the independence of committee members. In June 2012, the SEC promulgated Rule 10C-1 to implement that requirement.

> Rule 10C-1 requires, among other things, each exchange to adopt rules providing that each member of the compensation committee of a listed issuer must be a member of the board of directors of the issuer, and must otherwise be independent. In determining the independence standards for members of compensation committees of listed issuers, Rule 10C-1 requires the exchanges to consider relevant factors, including, but not limited to: (a) the source of compensation of the director, including any consulting, advisory or other compensatory fee paid by the issuer to the director...; and (b) whether the director is affiliated with the issuer, a subsidiary of the issuer or an affiliate of a subsidiary of the issuer....

> In addition, Rule 10C-1 requires the listing rules of exchanges to mandate that compensation committees be given the authority to retain or obtain the advice of a compensation adviser, and have direct responsibility for the appointment, compensation and oversight of the work of any compensation adviser they retain. The exchange rules must also provide that each listed issuer provide for appropriate funding for the payment of reasonable compensation, as determined by the compensation committee, to any compensation adviser retained by the compensation committee. Finally, among other things, Rule 10C-1 requires each exchange to provide in its rules that the compensation committee of each listed issuer may select a compensation consultant, legal counsel or other adviser to the compensation committee only after taking into consideration six factors specified in Rule 10C-1, as well as any other factors identified by the relevant exchange in its listing standards.[11]

11. Self-Regulatory Organizations; New York Stock Exch. LLC; Notice of Filing of Amendment No. 3, & Order Granting Accelerated Approval for Proposed Rule Change, As Modified by Amendment Nos. 1 & 3, to Amend the Listing Rules for Comp. Committees to Comply with Sec. Exch. Act Rule 10c-1 & Make Other Related Changes, Release No. 68639 (Jan. 11, 2013).

In January 2013, the SEC approved changes to the NYSE and NASDAQ's corporate governance listing standards effected to bring those standards into compliance with Rule 10C-1.[12]

Clawbacks

In July 2015, the SEC tardily proposed a rule to implement Dodd-Frank § 954's de facto requirement that companies adopt policies allowing them to claw back incentive-based compensation from current or past executive officers in the event of a restatement of the company's financials due to material non-compliance with the federal securities laws. Like § 954 itself, the proposed rule is overbroad:

> It covers payments not just to the CEO and CFO, but to a large class of executives, including the principal accounting officer, any vice-president in charge of a principal business unit, division or function, and any other person who "performs a policy-making function for the company." Moreover, the rule covers compensation paid over a three-year period to both current and former executives. And, once triggered by a restatement, clawbacks are automatic for all covered payments to all covered executives, regardless of whether fraud occurred or who was at fault.[13]

In Chapter 4 of this book, I predicted that § 954 likely would have a number of unintended consequences, as companies and managers attempt to tweak their pay so as to minimize the risk of having it clawed back.

Bank and Georgiev predict the rule will only exacerbate the problem:

> The best case scenario is that the requirements will lead executives to spend large amounts of money ensuring technical compliance with the complex accounting rules.

> More concerning, the rule may actually motivate executives to push for changes in their compensation or in the operation of the company. One easy way to game the rules would be to restructure pay packages, so they contain more fixed salary and less incentive compensation. Even if fixed salary turns out to be unattractive for tax reasons or because the company wants to retain some form of incentives to motivate employees, executives could avoid clawbacks if their incentive pay is determined by the board based on a general assessment of performance,

12. Id.
13. Bank & Georgiev, supra note 1.

or if it is tied to metrics not found in the company's financial statements, such as opening a specified number of stores, obtaining regulatory approvals, or completing a merger, divestiture, restructuring, or financing transaction. These performance metrics may be less clearly connected to the financial performance of the company or its stock than current incentive pay.[14]

In short, the SEC took a quack corporate governance prescription and made it quackier.

SHAREHOLDER ACTIVISM

Chapter 7 argued that shareholder empowerment threatened to undermine the core policy foundation on which our system of corporate governance rests. Corporate governance in the United States is premised on director primacy; i.e., on control of the corporation by the board of directors and its subordinate managers rather than by the shareholders.

In the years since the first edition of this book was published, however, shareholder activism has continued to grow by leaps and bounds. This is especially true of activist hedge funds. Both the number of such funds and the amounts they have available to invest in target companies have grown dramatically. As a result, some companies now find themselves the targets of multiple activist fund managers, often with conflicting agendas for corporate action.

Interventions by activist hedge funds can be loosely divided into five broad categories:

1. Addressing general target undervaluation to maximize shareholder value.
2. Promoting corporate governance changes (e.g., rescinding takeover defenses, ousting one or more top managers), board composition, and executive compensation.
3. Changing the target corporation's capital structure (e.g., demanding an equity issuance, restructuring of debt, or a recapitalization).
4. Addressing change of control transactions, such as:
    a. encouraging the target to sell itself;
    b. opposing a sale of the target (e.g., where price is perceived as too low);
    c. opposing an acquisition by the activist's targeted corporation.
5. Encouraging changes in the target's business strategy.

14. Id.

As a policy matter, it is the fifth category that is most troubling:

> Do we really want speculators telling corporate boards how to manage their businesses? Those who say "yes" want to increase short-term management pressure and thus share prices, regardless of the corporate mutilation this induces. They do not seem to care that their profits come at the expense of future generations' economic well-being. But if our goal is to give expert managers the time necessary to create long-term, sustainable, and innovative businesses, the answer is a clear "no."[15]

This argument is supported by empirical studies finding that it is difficult to establish a causal relationship between improved firm performance, if any, and business strategy changes effected at companies targeted by shareholder activists.[16]

The lack of such a relationship is not surprising, of course. After all, do we really think a hedge fund manager is systematically going to make better decisions on issues such as the size of widgets a company should make than are the company's incumbent managers and directors? Of course, a hedge fund is more likely to intervene at a higher level of generality, such as by calling for the company to enter into or leave certain lines of business, demanding specific expense cuts, opposing specific asset acquisitions, and the like, but the argument still has traction. Because the hedge fund manager inevitably has less information than the incumbents and likely less relevant expertise (being a financier rather than an operational executive), that manager's decisions on those sorts of issues are likely to be less sound than those of the incumbents. It was not a hedge fund manager who invented the iPhone, after all, but it was a hedge fund manager who ran TWA into the ground.

In the near term, however, rolling back the regulatory and legislative gains made by shareholder activists and their academic proponents likely will not be politically viable. Given the evidence that some shareholder interventions can have beneficial effects by enhancing managerial and directorial accountability,

---

15. Lawrence Mitchell, Protect Industry from Predatory Speculators, Fin. Times, July 8, 2009.

16. Stuart Gillian & Laura Starks, The Evolution of Shareholder Activism in the United States, 19 J. App. Corp. Fin. 55, 69 (2007). Mitchell's argument also finds support in Brian Cheffins's finding that, except for "a few hedge funds," institutional shareholders "were largely mute as share prices fell." Brian R. Cheffins, Did Corporate Governance "Fail" During the 2008 Stock Market Meltdown? The Case of the S&P 500, 65 Bus. Law 1, 3 (2009). Even in the U.K., where shareholders already possess more governance powers than do shareholders of U.S. firms, big institutional investors simply stood by as the crisis unfolded. Strikingly, however, directors of troubled firms commonly played an active role in responding to the crisis, as evidenced by their orchestration of CEO turnover at a rate far exceeding the norm in public companies. Id. at 30.

moreover, doing so may be unadvisable even if it is possible. Unfortunately, proponents of shareholder activism are not satisfied with the gains they have already made. Indeed, there seems to be no limit to their ambitions. The states and federal government therefore should begin looking for a limiting principle to be imposed from above.

A mechanism for roughly sorting those interventions in this category that should be encouraged from those that should be discouraged is suggested by the Delaware Supreme Court's decision in *CA, Inc. v. AFSCME Employees Pension Plan*.[17] AFSCME invoked SEC Rule 14a-8 to propose an amendment to CA's bylaws pursuant to which a shareholder who successfully conducted a short slate proxy contest would be entitled to reimbursement of its reasonable expenses. CA objected to inclusion in the proxy statement of the proposal and asked the SEC for a no-action letter supporting exclusion.

Before answering CA's request, the SEC invoked Delaware's new constitutional provision allowing the SEC to certify questions of law to the Delaware Supreme Court. The SEC certified two questions: (1) Was AFSCME's proposal a proper subject for shareholder action under Delaware law and (2) would the proposal, if adopted, cause CA to violate any Delaware law?

In answering the first of those questions, the court declined to draw a sharp line between permissible and impermissible bylaws. The court did, however, emphasize the broad statutory grant of managerial power to the board of directors and the absence of any such power on the part of shareholders:

> 8 Del. C. § 141(a) ... pertinently provides that: "The business and affairs of every corporation organized under this chapter shall be managed by or under the direction of a board of directors, except as may be otherwise provided in this chapter or in its certificate of incorporation."

> No such broad management power is statutorily allocated to the shareholders. Indeed, it is well-established that stockholders of a corporation subject to the DGCL may not directly manage the business and affairs of the corporation, at least without specific authorization in either the statute or the certificate of incorporation.[18]

On the other hand, the court recognized that it is equally well established "that a proper function of bylaws is not to mandate how the board should decide specific substantive business decisions, but rather, to define the process and procedures by which those decisions are made."[19]

17. 953 A.2d 227 (Del. 2008).
18. Id. at 233.
19. Id. at 234-35.

This distinction between substance (disallowed) and process (allowed) captures an appropriate balance between authority and accountability. If shareholder interventions directed at substantive decisions can be discouraged, the board's decision-making authority is respected. Indeed, if it is the case—as seems likely—that private rent seeking most often will take the form of substantive interventions, discouraging that category of interventions provides a useful prophylactic solution to the rent-seeking problem. Conversely, process and procedural interventions do not deprive the board of its authority but rather can be used to ensure that that authority is used accountably.

This approach raises two questions. First, how do you tell the difference between substance and process? In *CA*, the Delaware Supreme Court declined to provide specific guidance on that issue. A plausible (albeit rough) cut at the problem, however, would focus on shareholders' existing rights under state law. Shareholder interventions directed at issues on which they are statutorily entitled to a vote—election of directors, removal of directors, approving mergers or other changes of control, amending the bylaws, and so on—would be presumptively permissible. So would interventions making use of existing shareholder rights to communicate with the board, to bring direct and derivative litigation, or to acquire additional shares and/or control of the company. Shareholder interventions designed to provide procedures for effecting such interventions—such as bylaw amendments relating to nomination of directors—likewise would be permissible. If shareholders are not entitled to a vote (or other form of governance action) with respect to a given issue under state corporate law, however, that issue presumptively would be deemed substantive and thus impermissible.

Second, assuming some version of that solution is workable, how would it be effectuated? Here we must take into account the various tactics activists have adopted. According to Brav et al. (2008, 1743), they fall into seven broad categories:

1. The hedge fund intends to communicate with the board/management on a regular basis with the goal of enhancing shareholder value.
2. The hedge fund seeks board representation without a proxy contest or confrontation with the existing management/board.
3. The hedge fund makes formal shareholder proposals, or publicly criticizes the company and demands change.
4. The hedge fund threatens to wage a proxy fight in order to gain board representation, or to sue the company for breach of fiduciary duty, etc.
5. The hedge fund launches a proxy contest in order to replace the board.
6. The hedge fund sues the company.

7. The hedge fund intends to take control of the company, for example, with a takeover bid.[20]

Space does not permit a comprehensive examination of how all of these various tactics might be regulated, but note that almost all entail using the federal proxy rules. Accordingly, it is on those rules that regulatory attention should first focus.

An appropriate starting point would be the shareholder proposal rule, which figures in about a third of shareholder interventions.[21] Under current law, companies may not opt out of Rule 14a-8. If the law were changed to permit companies to adopt provisions in their articles of incorporation— either in the initial pre-IPO articles or by charter amendment thereafter— that would both provide a check on shareholder interventions and, if widely adopted, provide evidence that investors prefer such provisions.

A less sweeping opt-out provision would allow corporations to opt out of the current exemption in Rule 14a-8(i)(1) for proposals that are not proper as a matter of state corporate law. Under present law, a corporation must include in its proxy statement a shareholder proposal that is not a proper subject of a shareholder action under the law of the state of incorporation provided that the proposal is framed as a recommendation. Allowing companies to exclude such proposals even if phrased in precatory terms would provide a rough first cut at effecting the proposed substance/procedure distinction.

In order to effect that distinction, the exemption under Rule 14a-8(i)(7) for proposals relating to ordinary business expenses needs to expanded and revitalized. Under current law, the ordinary business exclusion is essentially toothless. The SEC requires companies to include proposals relating to stock option repricing, sale of genetically modified foods and tobacco products by their manufacturers, disclosure of political activities and support to political entities and candidates, executive compensation, and environmental issues. Obviously, however, these sorts of ordinary business decisions are core board prerogatives. Because deference to board authority remains the default presumption, this exemption therefore needs to be expanded and revitalized.

Activist shareholders who make use of Rule 14a-8 should be required to provide greater disclosures with respect to their motivations, goals, economic interests, and holdings of the issuer's securities (including derivative positions), so that their fellow shareholders can assess whether the activist's goals are consistent with the interests of all shareholders. Toward the same end, the eligibility threshold for using Rule 14a-8 should be increased to require that

20. Alon Brav, Alon, Wei Jiang, Frank Partnoy, & Randall Thomas. Hedge Fund Activism, Corporate Governance, and Firm Performance, 63 J. Fin. 1729, 1743 (2008).
21. Id. at 1742.

the proponent has held a net long position of 1 percent of the issuer's voting stock for at least two years. In addition to decreasing the risk that the activist would be pursuing private rent seeking, by discouraging proposals from activists using an empty voting strategy, such a change will ensure that activists are long-term investors rather than short-term speculators.

The proxy rules also should be amended to prevent hedge funds from compensating those members of an issuer's board of directors that were nominated by the fund. The recent trend toward such payments raises serious conflicts of interest, as the hedge fund's nominees likely will be loyal to the fund rather than the issuer. In particular, such directors have financial incentives to acquiesce in—or even assist—private rent seeking by their fund sponsor.

Ex ante rules such as these tweaks to the proxy rules are unlikely to be a complete solution. Prophylactic rules, after all, are inevitably both under- and over-inclusive. The complexity of the problem likely will require some mechanism for case-by-case analysis of specific shareholder interventions, especially those allegedly involving rent seeking by the activist. As a set of muddy defaults providing flexible standards that are "context-specific in application," fiduciary duties are well suited to effecting just such analyses.[22]

Anabtawi and Stout (2008, 1261-62) have proposed extending the existing fiduciary duties of controlling shareholders "to activist minorities who succeed in influencing management with respect to a single transaction or business decision [and should apply more generally] in any factual situation where a shareholder reaps a unique personal economic benefit to the detriment or exclusion of other shareholders."[23] Their proposal is particularly well suited to preventing private rent seeking because they argue that those duties "would be triggered whenever a particular shareholder—whether or not it is technically a shareholder capable of controlling the board's decisions as to all matters—in fact manages to successfully influence the company's actions with regard to a particular issue in which that shareholder has a material, personal economic interest."[24]

CONCLUSION

It may be that changes such as those described above will be politically impossible. As the first edition of this text demonstrated, federal interven-

---

22. William B. Chandler III & Leo E. Strine, Jr., The New Federalism of the American Corporate Governance System: Preliminary Reflections of Two Residents of One Small State, 152 U. Penn. L. Rev. 953 (2003).

23. Iman Anabtawi & Lynn Stout, Fiduciary Duties for Activist Shareholders, 60 Stan. L. Rev. 1255, 1261-62 (2008).

24. Id. at 1301.

tions in corporate governance tend to have a ratchet effect that moves toward ever greater federal control and ever greater degrees of shareholder empowerment. Yet, if the system of corporate governance created by state law is worth preserving, as I believe to be the case, the states and the business community will have to unite in seeking to undo the quack corporate governance the federal responses to the financial crises left us with.

INDEX

federal intervention, staving off, 270
franchise taxes, 24
horizontal competition, 21–25
informed decision making by
    directors, 97
interest groups in, 36–37
monitoring management role of
    board, 46
as most popular state for
    incorporations, 16, 261
price-fixing violations, 149–52
proxy expense reimbursement,
    221–22
pseudo-foreign corporations, 22n3
reincorporation in, effect on stock
    price, 24
standards-setting by, 96
takeover statute, 25
vertical competition, 27–39
Demsetz, Harold, 48, 73
Deposit insurance, 11
Derivatives, 175
Director independence, 17–18, 77–107
agency costs and, 88–90
bias of outside directors, 89–90
CEO/chairman duality, 104–7
CEO/chairman duality and, 14, 15,
    104–7
duty of directors to be informed,
    96–99
financial crisis related to, 103–4
incentivizing of independents,
    92–102
    compensation practices, 92–95
    evidence of independence,
        100–101
    new metrics, 99–100
    reputational concerns, 95–97
    uniform approach to, 101–2
insider representation, benefits
    of, 103
interlocks and decision making,
    86–88
negatives of, 102–3
pre-crises empirical evidence, 90–92
ratio of inside to outside directors, 78
reasons for, 86–92
in Sarbanes-Oxley Act, 81–86
    shortcomings of, 102
SOX and stock exchange listing
    standards, 81–86

board committees, 86
    importance of, 81–82
    majority independent board,
        83–84
    pre-SOX listing standards, 82–83
    state law, 79–81
Director role. *See* Board of directors
Disclosures
accounting standards and, 99
audit committee and SEC rules, 144
of executive compensation, 14,
    127–28
internal control disclosures in annual
    reports, 157
therapeutic disclosure requirement of
    SEC, 34
Disney, Roy, 253
Disney case (2006). *See* Walt Disney
    Company
Dodd-Frank Act of 2010
section 165, 176
section 951, 14, 132
section 952, 14, 129
section 953, 14, 36
section 954, 14, 131–32
section 971, 14, 226–27
section 972, 14
section 973, 36, 104, 105, 107
section 989G, 15
clawback regime, 131–32
disclosure requirements, 35, 127–28
enactment of, 1, 9–15
executive compensation, 122–37
internal controls, 162
majority voting provision dropped
    from, 220
monitoring functions of board, 60
non-accelerated filers from
    compliance with § 404(b), 162
proxy access, 14, 15, 135, 176
risk management, 176–77
Dotcom crash, 3, 5, 59, 118–19, 160, 198
Douglas, William O., 30, 50
Due diligence, 199
Dutch tulip bulb mania (1630s), 5
Duty of loyalty, 152–54

Ebbers, Bernard, 125
Edmond v. United States (1997), 184, 185
Edward, First Baron Thurlow, 234
Edwards, John, 181, 188, 189–90, 192

Mortgage-backed securities (MBSs), 119, 170
Mulbert, Peter O., 120
Mulherin, J. Harold, 232
Murphy, Kevin J., 117
Mutual funds, 246, 256
Mylan Laboratories, 251

Nader, Ralph, 43, 51–52, 80
NASDAQ
  audit committee rules, 142–44
  foreign issuers listed on, 262
  listing standards, 31, 81, 84, 129, 142
  nominating committee rules, 223
National Association of Corporate Directors, 66, 93
Navigant Consulting, 252
New York City Employees' Retirement Sys. v. SEC (1995), 214
New York Stock Exchange (NYSE)
  audit committee rules, 59, 86, 142–44
  committees of board of directors, requirements for, 86
  compensation committee rules, 128
  foreign issuers listed on, 262
  listing standards, 31, 58–59, 81–86, 142
  nominating committee rules, 223
  proxy advisory services, 257
  report on corporate governance (2010), 10, 17
Nominating committees
  NYSE requirements, 86
  proxy access, 223–24
Non-accelerated filers, exemption from compliance with § 404(b), 162
Non-audit services of auditors, 186–88
Nonprofit governance, 147
North Dakota Publicly Traded Corporations Act (2007), 25–28
NYSE. *See* New York Stock Exchange

Obama, Barack
  on bank bailouts, 123
  on corporate governance reform, 253
  on executive compensation, 109
  on government as shareholder in bailouts, 259
  on proxy access question, 226

Oklahoma corporation with bylaw on poison pill, 208–9
O'Mahoney, Joseph C., 30
Omnicare, Inc. v. NCS Healthcare, Inc. (2003), 222
Organization for Economic Cooperation and Development (OECD), 9
Outside directors, 49
Ovitz, Michael, 121–22
Ownership misnomer for shareholders' interest, 234–36
Oxley, Michael, 162

Paredes, Troy, 230, 231, 233
Part 205 regulations, 190–92, 194, 196
Paulson Committee Report, 262, 263, 267
Pay without performance, 112
PCAOB. *See* Public Company Accounting Oversight Board
Penn Central, 51, 52
Performance-based compensation, 114–15, 118, 132, 173. *See also* Stock options
Perks, executive, 117
Pfizer policies, 217–18
Pitt, Harvey, 8
Pittman, Jeffrey, 186
Plurality rule for board election, 216–17
Poison pill, 208–9
Policy entrepreneurs and bubbles, role of, 36–39
Posner, Richard, 120
Poulsen, Annette B., 232
Preemption
  of state corporation laws, 261
  of state rules of professional conduct, 191–92
Pre-SOX listing standards, 82–83
Price-fixing violations, 149
Principal-agent problem, 2, 3, 238–40, 247–48, 251
Principles-based approach of regulatory scheme, 264
Private equity firms, 248–51
Private Securities Litigation Reform Act of 1995 (PSLRA), 7
Production teams, 73n98
Proxy access, 204, 222–33
  Dodd-Frank on, 14, 15, 135, 176
  nominating committees, 223–24